URBAN RUNOFF QUALITY–

Impact and Quality Enhancement Technology

Proceedings of an Engineering Foundation Conference

New England College
Henniker, New Hampshire
June 23-27, 1986

Organized by the
Urban Water Resources Research Council of the
Technical Council on Research of the
American Society of Civil Engineers

Co-sponsored by the
U.S. National Science Foundation
American Public Works Association
U.S. Environmental Protection Agency

Funded by the
U.S. Environmental Protection Agency

Conference Committee
Ben Urbonas, Chairman
Thomas O. Barnwell, Jr.
D. Earl Jones
Larry A. Roesner
L. Scott Tucker

Edited by Ben Urbonas and Larry A. Roesner

Published by the
American Society of Civil Engineers
345 East 47th Street
New York, New York 10017-2398

ABSTRACT

This book contains the papers presented at the Engineering Foundation Conference, "Urban Runoff Quality," held June 22-27, 1986 in Henniker, New Hampshire. Topics covered include data needs and collection technology, pollution sources and potential impacts on receiving waters, institutional issues, effectiveness of best management practices, detention, retention, and wetlands. A workshop on research and future activities needs is summarized. Three supplemental papers on urban runoff quality not presented at the conference are also included.

Library of Congress Cataloging-in-Publication Data

Urban runoff Quality.

Incudes index.
    1. Urban runoff—Congresses. 2. Water quality management—Congresses. 3. Environmental impact analysis—Congresses. I. Urbonas, Ben. II. Roesner, Larry A. III. American Society of Civil Engineers. Urban Water Resources Research Council. IV. National Science Foundation (U.S.) V. American Public Works Association. VI. United States. Environmental Protection Agency. VII. Engineering Foundation Conference on Urban Runoff Quality (1986 : New England College)
TD657.U76 1986   363.7'394   86-26541
ISBN 0-87262-577-X

FOREWORD

The Urban Water Resources Research Council of the American Society of Civil Engineers has for more than 20 years strongly promoted the transfer of urban runoff technology among researchers, practitioners and administrators. The primary vehicle used by the Council for the transfer are Engineering Foundation Conferences, International Symposia, and technical sessions at professional meetings. In each case a proceedings or series of papers has been published.

This Engineering Foundation Conference on Urban Runoff Quality is one of a series of more than ten organized by the Council on the subject of urban stormwater management. This conference builds in particular upon the 1974 Engineering Foundation Conference on Urban Runoff Quantity and Quality held in Rindge, New Hampshire.

All papers presented at this conference were by invitation. Papers were reviewed prior to acceptance for publication by the appropriate session chairman, and by the editors of this proceedings. Each paper was presented by the author and subjected to open forum discussion and review by conference participants. This proceeding contains all papers presented at the conference. The papers are grouped by session, with a session summary paper prepared by the session chairman included as the last paper in each group. Supplemental papers are also included at the end of the proceedings. All papers are eligible for discussion in the appropriate ASCE Journal and all papers are eligible for ASCE awards.

The conference organizing committee expresses its thanks to the Engineering Foundation for providing administrative support in organizing this conference. Thanks also goes to EFC support staff headed by Dr. Robert Seaman at New England College, whose day to day management of the conference facilities provided a comfortable working conference atmosphere. The committee also expresses its gratitude to Mr. Patrick Tobin and to Dennis Athayde for arranging funding support by the U.S. Environmental Protection Agency for this conference.

CONTENTS

CONFERENCE OVERVIEW

Ben Urbonas[1]
Larry Roesner, Ph. D.[2]

INTRODUCTION

An Engineering Foundation Conference organized by the ASCE Urban Water Resources Research Council was held at New England College in Henniker, New Hampshire, June 22-27, 1986. It was co-sponsored by the U.S. Environmental Protection Agency, and Water Resources Institute of the American Public Works Association. Nine scheduled sessions and several ad hoc sessions were held in which a total of 31 formal papers were presented and discussed. At one of the ad hoc sessions, Ms. Kathy O'Connell of EPA Headquarters discussed at length the promulgation of the NPDES regulations for separate storm sewers.

The organizing activities for this conference began in the Fall of 1984 as a continuation of the Council's long standing tradition of organizing technology transfer conferences on this topic (see References 1 through 9). It was the goal of the Urban Water Resources Council to bring together researchers, practicing engineers and local, state and federal agencies to discuss their current knowledge about and experience with the quality aspects of urban stormwater runoff. The Council observed that this topic was receiving considerable attention at the Federal level, yet all the indications were that the implementation of any stormwater quality management program would have to take place at the local government level. As a result, the Council decided this conference needed to bridge the gap between the various levels of government, the professionals that have been active in implementing urban runoff quality controls and the researchers and technology developers in this field.

The following pages attempt to provide a general overview of topics presented and discussed. Obviously, the richness of detail contained in the papers of these proceedings can not be adequately described in a summary paper. The reader needs to read and study papers of interest to him or her to fully appreciate the contribution of the individual authors. We wanted to draw upon some of the best expertise in this field. The quality the papers in these proceedings clearly shows that this goal was achieved.

[1] Chief, Master Planning Program, Urban Drainage and Flood Control District, 2780 West 26th Avenue, Suite 156B, Denver, CO 80211 and Conference Chairman.

[2] Regional Director of Water Resources, Camp Dresser and McKee, Inc., Maitland, FL and Chairman, Urban Water Resources Council of ASCE.

OPENING SESSION

At the opening session, three papers on recent developments and activities were presented. We learned from Marsalek that the European community's main concern with stormwater quality is the control of combined sewer overflows. They are also beginning to show interest in and concern over the impacts of runoff quality and its control technology.

Meanwhile in U.S.A., Jennings described how the United States Geological Survey is attempting to make statistical sense out of the massive data base collected during the National Urban Runoff Pollution Program. The USGS is also involved in research of detention ponds used for pollutant removal. It is hoped that this ongoing effort by USGS will lead to reliable design guidelines for the engineer.

It was clear from Huber's presentation that we now have several good stormwater management computer models. It is important, according to Huber, to select the right model for the task at hand. Although models can be used to simulate runoff quantity fairly accurately, the same cannot be said about modeling of water quality. Huber stressed that modeling of water quality requires a good data base for calibration and verification before the modeling results can be considered reliable.

DATA COLLECTION

If there was one consistent theme expressed by the papers presented by Ellis, Herricks, Davies and Sonnen, it was the need for data that helps us identify the impacts on the environment of various constituents in urban stormwater. For years we have seen discrepancies between what has been reported in the laboratory and what is being observed in the field. Heavy metal concentrations sometimes observed in stormwater runoff should kill fish in the streams if we are to believe laboratory results. However, field experience often shows that not to be the case.

Here we have a set of papers that not only describe the complexities involved in trying to link field observations with laboratory results, but also sheds light on why there may be a misunderstanding between bioenvironmental scientists and water resources engineers. At least for metals, it appears that both groups have been using the same words, but the meaning of these words was not the same for each group. While the bioenvironmental scientist was performing experiments in the laboratory using metals concentrations of the ionic forms, which are fully available as toxicants, the engineers have been reporting field data that also include forms of these same metals that are not in toxicologically available form.

The argument concerning metals data is an indicator that we have yet much to learn about urban runoff and its impacts on receiving waters. This was further confirmed by the two sessions that followed. It is clear that we need to pay much more attention, when collecting data, to the purpose for which data is being collected. There appears to be a crying need for not only clarification of data collection goals, but also for the standardization of the sampling and analytical methods to be used in urban stormwater quality data collection.

POLLUTION SOURCES AND POTENTIAL IMPACTS

Terstriep, Driver and Mancini were asked to explore sources of pollutants and the potential impacts of these pollutants on the environment, which they did superbly. Driver described ongoing USGS analysis of the NURP data and their attempts to relate observed constituents in stormwater to meteorology, rainfall and land use of the tributary watershed.

Terstriep, on the other hand, described his findings using the EPA data that was not collected by USGS. He finally concluded that we need to learn much more about the fundamental processes of "...sources, transport, and fate of urban pollutants." He also brought to our attention that his evaluation of the priority pollutants data indicates no widespread problems in urban stormwater. There may be however, a need for concern over the long term of what is being found in the sediments.

A very challenging paper in this session was presented by Mancini. He very clearly describes how urban stormwater runoff may differ from wastewater treatment plant effluent in its impacts on the receiving waters. Mancini conceptually wove together the temporal and spatial effects to argue that dry weather stream standards should not be applied towards regulating stormwater quality. His argument becomes very strong when combined with the information of other presenters, especially by Davies, Ellis, Herricks, and Jenkins.

IMPACT ON RECEIVING WATERS

Here we had papers by Jenkins, Odum, Bastian and Jones discussing the impacts on receiving waters. One is persuaded by these four speakers that the topic of impacts on the receiving waters provides the greatest challenges yet to be faced by researchers and investigators. While Odum and Jones discuss in detail these challenges and the things we know and don't know, Bastian talks about the direction the regulatory requirements may take. He warns us that the lawmakers and the lawyers prefer "risk-based" regulations to those that rely on Best Management Practices. In other words "treatment" of urban stormwater, according to Bastian, may be the requirement of the future.

Drawing on estuary studies, Odum points out that there is little to be found in literature concerning specific effects of urban runoff on estuaries. He states that further research on long term effects is required, but cautions that such research may be difficult because urban stormwater runoff effects may be "...inexorably and synergistically associated with the effects of dredging, chemical spills, point source contaminants and other serious alterations."

On the cutting edge of technology is a methodology being developed by Jenkins and his colleagues that should help identify the biological effects of contaminants. The technology described by Jenkins will permit in situ assessment of toxicological stress on aquatic biota and may even replace the currently available, but expensive and time consuming, bio-assay testing. If we were to select the topic that was most widely discussed throughout the remainder of the conference, Jenkins' presentation would be definitely at the top.

Jones wound up the session with a excellent overview on impacts of urban stormwater on receiving waters. Despite the fact that over $100 million dollars has been spent to characterize stormwater runoff quality, we still are at a loss when trying to quantity the impacts on receiving waters.

INSTITUTIONAL ISSUES

D. E. Jones and Urbonas pointed out in the opening session that "...we are unable to separate consideration of scientific and institutional issues and questions." This session explored many of these issues by looking at what is being done in the United States where stormwater quality problems have been identified and at what is being discussed at the federal level.

Livingston described how Florida's urban stormwater regulation evolved since it was first proposed in 1980 and since its promulgation in 1982. Since then, Florida has become very aggressive in controlling runoff quality. To them, control of runoff quality is needed to protect the states' limited water resources. As an adjunct to Livingston's presentation, Zeno and Palmer presented a local government's example of how the City of Orlando is implementing the State's program. Zeno and Palmer described how Orlando is retrofitting older areas of the city with water quality enhancement facilities and is attempting to restore the water quality of many of its lakes.

About as far as one can go from Florida in the contiguous USA, Bellevue, Washington is also aggressively pursuing urban stormwater quality management. Bissonnette described how Bellevue is accomplishing that goal through the creation of a stormwater utility. Their main thrust at this time is source control and local government accountability. Bellevue may be the first in USA to receive a National Pollution Elimination System permit for stormwater.

Athayde outlined the U. S. Environmental Protection Agency's perspective of urban nonpoint sources. According to Athayde, EPA has traditionally viewed urban runoff as a local matter. Although the agency is in the process of promulgating NPDES permit requirements for urban stormwater runoff, it plans no Federal program, outside enforcement, to implement it.

Tucker wrapped up this session with an excellent summary of the issues discussed. He concludes that, "...local and state governments, will, and do solve pollution problems attributed to urban stormwater runoff if they perceive it as a high priority concern." Tucker further concluded that stormwater management has to be addressed at the local government level.

EFFECTIVENESS OF BEST MANAGEMENT PRACTICES

Shaver presented an excellent survey of experience with Maryland's relatively new stormwater infiltration program. Although he believes that infiltration can be made to work, the program's "Implementation has not gone as well as expected to date." Shaver attributes the problems due to lack of understanding by the implementers regarding design and installation and due to improper maintenance. He specifically singled out inadequate erosion control as a particularly serious source of infiltration bed plugging. He further cautioned that we should also build a maintenance infrastructure if our stormwater quality control programs are to continue to function.

Soil erosion processes and erosion control technology were presented by Byron Lord. It is clear that soil erosion accounts for many of the problems associated with urban runoff. It is also clear from Lord's presentation that we have a good understanding of soil erosion control technology. The only thing that is needed is commitment at the local, state and federal agency level to apply it whenever the land surfaces are disturbed by man.

Pitt summarized a voluntary nonpoint pollution control program in Wisconsin. To encourage participation, the state will contribute 50 to 70 percent of the implementation cost. The program includes rural and urban stormwater runoff controls, even though most plans to date were prepared for rural areas.

Stormwater retention, vegetated swales, street and catch basin cleaning, parking lot infiltration and erosion control efficiencies and design considerations were discussed by Wanielista. He relates various retention volumes to pollutant trap efficiencies and provides design example for a site in Florida.

RETENTION, DETENTION, WETLANDS AND OTHER TREATMENT

These forms of runoff quality controls are an emerging technology and there is great interest in how to use these techniques in the most cost effective manner. This session expands and updates previous work sponsored by the Urban Water Resources Research Council (7), (8), (9) which resulted in excellent state-of-the-art papers and recommendations for the design of stormwater quality enhancement facilities. We will attempt to summarize here the four excellent presentations at this conference.

Grizzard described recent research investigation of urban stormwater quality for a 34.4 acre watershed in Maryland. The work included stormwater quality monitoring, tube settler tests, correlation of various pollutants to TSS particle surface areas, and comparison of laboratory results with the field data at a extended detention pond.

Wanielista presented a paper on behalf of Yousef about the effectiveness of retention basins. As in Grizzard's presentation, the results presented were backed up by field data. Findings are presented for surface waters, heavy metal accumulations in sediments, and impacts on groundwater.

To help planners, designers and policy makers Hartigan discussed the advantages and cost effectiveness of regional stormwater management facilities. He showed not only cost advantages, but went on to describe design, land planning, effectiveness and maintenance advantages of regional facilities as compared with piecemeal on-site facilities.

Wiegand presented information on the costs of various stormwater quality enhancement facilities such as ponds, porous pavement, infiltration basins and infiltration trenches. The cost information is based on an extensive data base of construction costs in the Washington, D.C. area. This cost information comprises one of the best organized sets of cost data ever assembled for urban stormwater quality facilities. Wiegand used this information to compare the cost effectiveness of treatment and determined also that regionalization of detention is more cost effective than many small on-site detention ponds.

Randall presented a discussion of all the papers presented in this session on behalf of Driscoll. After analyzing all the papers he further recommended that a concerted effort be made to compile all the past and ongoing study data into a single data base for examination. To do this he suggests that we standardize the nomenclature, testing procedures, cost data and cost effectiveness comparisons, that we initiate studies to determine long term fate of pollutants, and that we encourage presentation of systems that have not performed well. The last item should help us learn from each other's failures.

WORKSHOPS ON RESEARCH AND FUTURE ACTIVITIES NEEDS

The last evening session of the conference was set aside for workshops on research needs and future activities needs. The workshops were organized by Thomas Barnwell, Jr. and D. Earl Jones. Everyone attending the conference was assigned to a work group to explore the topics discussed at this conference and to present recommendations on research and future activities needs. Each group prepared a report for the next mornings session. These conference proceedings contain the work group reports and a summary of key recommendations prepared by Barnwell and Jones.

From our perspective, the reports and the summation paper are extremely valuable for identifying what we have yet to learn about urban stormwater, its impacts, control technology and the institutional issues that have to be dealt with whenever deciding to implement control programs. It is clear from reading all of these reports that accessibility to authoritative information is sorely lacking. The establishment of a national center for the collection and distribution of data, publications, studies, ordinances, state regulations, computer models and state-of-the-art technology was recommended by many of the work groups.

Clearly, there is a strong demand for technology transfer concerning this topic beyond specialty conferences. This attitude is symptomatic of an emerging scientific or engineering field, where the practitioners feel that there is still much to learn. The true experts in the field, and we had our share of them at this conference, realize that we have yet to learn much more, especially if we are to develop truly effective programs to deal with urban stormwater quality. We urge every reader to study the work group reports in order to gain insight into what we are talking about.

CLOSING REMARKS - WHAT DID WE ACCOMPLISH?

As we said at the outset, the goal of convening a forum of practitioners, researchers and administrators from various levels of government was met. This auspicious group of individuals, many of who are the leading experts in the field had an opportunity for a week to exchange ideas on the topic of urban stormwater quality. The results of this exchange are reported in these proceedings and will also be seen as these ideas begin to influence the practices in this field. From that alone we can pat each other on the back and say that we had a good conference. Unfortunately, we still sense that the complete understanding of urban runoff water quality issues is still confined to a very few.

It is estimated that between the federal, state and local governments we already spent over $100 million on urban stormwater quality studies. Yet at this conference we still heard that we do not know nearly enough. Despite this feeling, the presentations and discussions resulted in a tremendous step forward. We saw for the first time the involvement at an engineering level of bioenvironmental scientists. We are beginning to understand each others terminology and progress and, as a result, have learned that future advances will require much greater cooperation with non-engineering disciplines. We also had an opportunity to examine the differences between receiving water quality criteria for continuous discharges and urban runoff. Much more work is needed on this, however these proceedings can act as a foundation for work that needs to be done.

We have also learned that traditional laboratory experimental techniques may fall short at telling us what the real impacts of urban runoff are on aquatic biota. For one, the laboratory setting itself may strain the biota being investigates. In addition, the sinergistic, antiganistic, and pulse dosing conditions found in the receiving waters cannot be duplicated in the laboratory. It is clear that we need changes in how we develop information if we are to make meaningful progress. We need short term and long term field research, and need it badly to answer the many questions we have raised about real impacts on the environment.

In the area of non-structural and structural controls we see an emergence of field data based assessments of performance and cost. We no longer have to rely on theory alone, but now have supporting empirical performance data for many types of controls. We still have much to learn before we can feel confident in the performance of our designs, but we are getting there.

WHERE DO WE NEED TO GO FROM HERE?

Clearly, a national information center, as suggested at this conference would be a major step forward. The establishment of this center could be funded by the federal government. After it is established, federal funding could then be tapered off with the idea that this national center will become self supporting. It could then be funded by membership fees and through fees for information transfer. As an alternative, it could be a group within EPA established specifically as a Technology Transfer Center for stormwater runoff quality.

We need to develop and then implement education and training programs to prepare practitioners and administrators entering this field. Urban stormwater quality management need to be introduced in engineering curricula at both the undergraduate and graduate level if we are ever going to adequately train professionals for this field. Continuing education programs and workshops are also needed to supplement formal university degree programs.

The profession, with or without outside funding, needs to develop design criteria and guidelines for the design of runoff quality control facilities. We now have sufficient knowledge to begin the development of these documents to assist designers. Although the actual performance can only be approximated, there is a body of knowledge of what works the best and what practices should be avoided. We suggest that emphasis be placed on facilities to reduce nutrients. Field evidence suggests that facilities designed to remove nutrients, especially phosphorus, will be very efficient in removing most other pollutants.

It is time to begin quantifying the effects of urban runoff on receiving waters. This does not mean simple comparisons between urban runoff chemistry and water quality standards, but rather in-situ assessment of impacts on aquatic habitat and fisheries. It is necessary to develop standard research techniques that reflect the effect of pollutants on receiving waters with respect to concentrations, frequency and duration, form and species of pollutants, and the synergistic and antagonistic effects of pollutants. This is very much a research area, but the research must be performed in a representative laboratory. The attendees suggested an urban experiment like the Hubbard Brook experimental watershed where urban pollutant sources, transport and transformations, control technologies, and receiving water impacts could be studied. Study of urban runoff should not end with the National Urban Runoff Program. Rather the questions raised by NURP should be answered.

Any new regulatory program needs a rational basis, namely the understanding of the benefits it achieves and of the costs for its implementation. In the area of urban stormwater quality this basis needs to include information on aquatic habitat, biosurveys of water bodies with and without urban runoff, public health effects, and the costs and benefits of stormwater quality controls. So far we have only laboratory studies to guide regulatory decisions. Although laboratory studies are needed to provide very basic information, they can never reproduce field behavior.

In view of the above, and the fact that society is moving toward requiring stormwater quality controls, it is necessary that we move ahead immediately with the following activities.

1. Develop a design manual for urban runoff controls. To this end we recommend that the Engineering Foundation convene a

conference on "Design Criteria for Urban Runoff Quality Control" in 1988 to compile the design data that is being and will be déveloped over the next two years.

2. The federal government should:

   a. establish Technology Transfer Center that serves as focal point for collection and dissemination of data, studies and regulations pertaining to urban runoff quality.

   b. fund a "Hubbard Book" type of study to determine the impacts of urban runoff on fisheries and aquatic habitat.

3. Universities, and institutions offering continuing education courses, need to introduce runoff quality effects and control technology into their urban hydrology and water quality courses.

REFERENCES

1. ASCE Urban Water Resources Research Council, Water and Metropolitan Man, Report on the Second Conference on Urban Water Research, Andover, New Hampshire, ASCE 1969.

2. ASCE Urban Water Resources Research Council, Urban Resources Management, Report on the Third Conference on Urban Water Research, Deerfield, Mass. ASCE, 1970.

3. Whipple Jr., William, et al, Urban Runoff Quantity and Quality, Proceedings of Research Conference, Ringde, New Hampshire, ASCE, 1974.

4. Alley, William M., Guide For Collection, Analysis, and Use of Urban Stormwater Data, A Conference Report, Easton, Maryland, ASCE, 1976.

5. ASCE Urban Water Resources Research Council, Urban Runoff Quality - Measurement and Analysis, Fall Convention Preprint No. 3091, San Francisco, California, ASCE, 1977.

6. Whipple Jr., William, et al, Water Problems of Urbanizing Areas, Proceedings of the Research Conference, Henniker, New Hampshire, ASCE, 1978.

7. DeGroot, William, et al, Stormwater Detention Facilities, Proceedings of the Engineering Foundation Conference, Henniker, New Hampshire, ASCE, 1982.

8. ASCE Task Committee on the Design of Outlet Control Structures, Stormwater Detention Outlet Control Structures, Committee Report, ASCE, 1985.

9. Torno, Harry C., Jirri Marsalek, Michael Desbordes, et al, Urban Runoff Pollution, Proceedings of the 1985 NATO Advanced Research Workshop, Montpellier, France, NATO ASI Series, Series G: Ecological Sciences, Vol. 10, Springer-Verlag, 1986.

Conference on Urban Runoff Quality-Objectives

D. Earl Jones, F. ASCE[1]
and
Ben Urbonas, M. ASCE[2]

One of the long standing goals of the American Society of Civil Engineers Urban Water Resources Research Council's is to facilitate technology transfer among scientists, practitioners and public works administrators. Often this task requires transformation of scientific data and findings into practical terms that can be used to improve engineering and institutional practices. To accomplish this, the Council has always tried to focus on topics that are timely and could benefit the largest number of users.

The agenda for this conference on urban runoff quality was structured to expedite technology transfer through the expression, consolidation and evaluation of opinions, facts, experience and past research on the topic of urban runoff quality. The conference brings together the leaders in the field and provides an opportunity for researchers, practitioners and administrators to explore urban runoff quality, its impacts on receiving waters and impacts mitigation technologies.

The participants are reminded that we must never lose sight of the fact that good science and technology must operate within the human social, political and economic systems. By their natures, these systems ultimately will determine how successfully the various technologies may be applied, if at all.

We have come a long way since the Council's major study which identified urban non-point source pollution as a potentially significant contributor of pollutants to the nation's receiving waters. This resulted in the easing of pressures for a multi-billion dollar program to separate combined sewer effluents. Today, twenty years later, we need to re-examine thoughtfully what should be appropriate responses to current pressures to "do something" to control urban stormwater runoff quality. Fortunately, the conference is co-sponsored by the U.S. Environmental Protection Agency and by the Water Resources Institute of the American Public Works Association. Where EPA is responsible for the national implementation of the Clean Water Act, the members of APWA are often the implementers or "troops in the trenches"

[1]Chief Engineer, U.S. Department of Housing and Urban Development and Member of Conference Organizing Committee.

[2]Chief, Master Planning Program of Urban Drainage and Flood Control District, Denver, CO and Conference Chairman.

that must design, build, operate and maintain facilities needed to get the job done.

A one-week conference can properly address only a limited range of water quality issues. As a result, the conference focus is upon basic scientific and institutional issues affecting impacts of urban runoff quality on receiving waters and on institutional complexities affecting realization of water quality improvements. Each speaker has been asked to emphasize practical applications of scientific knowledge and practical solutions of water quality and institutional issues.

It is hoped that a gathering of leading minds in this field also will identify where knowledge is lacking and where further actions are needed. Realizing that implementation of programs presents institutional challenges that can equal or exceed the scientific or technical ones, the conference treats institutional issues as inseparable from scientific and technical issues.

A major stumbling block in implementing urban runoff water quality controls is the high cost of controlling widespread, non-centralized, randomly occurring source of pollutants that vary in both location and concentration over time. There also exists a lack of universal agreement about what is meant by "improved water quality" and "impacts on receiving waters", and about whether we should consider actual, probable, or possible pollutants.

Clearly, different interests perceive differing water quality objectives. Purveyors of domestic water seek supplies that require minimum pre-distribution treatment, essentially "pure" water. Ecologists and environmentalists seek waters with sufficient "pollutants" to support viable aquatic life communities. The general public is conditioned to seek "fishable, swimmable waters", which actually is a statement of two different sets of somewhat incompatible water quality objectives. Irrigators seek essentially mineral-free waters but often must use them in excess to flush away natural soil mineral concentrations that inhibit agricultural productivity.

Public officials responsible for maintenance and individual homeowners, farmers, commercial and industrial establishments make extensive use of herbicides, fertilizers, insecticides and de-icers. When faced with the issue of limiting such uses, each resist water quality constraints that would inhibit their freedom to use such products.

The construction industry is rankled by requirements for erosion and sedimentation controls and with some justification when similar controls are not placed upon agricultural interests that can be greater sediment generators. Agricultural chemical users seek zero constraints upon their actions. Even the Federal government "looks the other way" rather than restricting overgrazing and resulting soil loss on Federal lands. Conflicting and unquantified water quality objectives are legion.

If it is essential to quantify water quality objectives in some logical manner, it is equally essential to specify the conditions under

which those objectives should , or might be, realistically attained.
What is critical? Is it low-flow during drought or dry season, or is
it the short-term peak flow, or average flow and load conditions? How
about the number of days per year? Are specific seasonal conditions,
including odor and mosquito breeding of importance? Is concentration
measured in milligrams per liter or the load measured in tons/year the
critical factor, or is each important?

How may we best compromise inherently conflicting objectives?
Unfortunately, there is a dearth of guidance for selection of logical
water quality objectives and a frightening tendency to specify
"uniform" water quality standards for administrative expediency,
regardless of whether or how well such standards may fit different
situations. What can the sciences contribute to a sensible
objectives-setting process? Shouldn't the sciences bring some order
into such processes?

The scientific community recognizes a need to re-examine and
expand water quality measurement technology. Commonly used tests
measure only a few basic things; at least 1,500 recognized potential
pollutants are generally not measured and typically can be measured
only with complex procedures and at great cost. Water quality tests
required by statutes and ordinances generally are limited in scope and
made at infrequent intervals, possibly only once in many years. There
are no recognized tests for potentially harmful viral organisms and
even bacteriological testing is usually limited to observing
concentrations of a single bacillus and assuming that its presence is
indicative of other bacterial contamination.

What is a meaningful sampling and measurement technology for
metals, ammonia, toxicants? How can water quality measurement
technology and practices be improved? What goals are viewed as
essential? Is there any unused information that should be put into
practice immediately? Can better tests be developed and standardized?
We sincerely hope that this conference will examine these and other
"measurement" technology questions.

Professionally, we must blend scientific knowledge with a diverse
array of practical realities. Uncertainty resulting from Natural
variations should be considered realistically as we evolve requirement
and strategies. We should recognize that the Missouri River was
nicknamed the "Big Muddy" before tillage and grazing affected it. We
should also recognize that removal of sediment loads and reduction in
flood frequency can adversely affect erosion, agriculture, fisheries
and other natural regimes, as has occurred on the River Nile. It makes
little sense to prescribe maximum suspended solids content when Nature
itself will frequently exceed the regulatory maximum, and it makes even
less sense to spend money in a futile attempt to reverse Natural
processes. Perhaps the sciences and professions should begin to
emphasize these fundamentals to the public -- and even to seemingly
cloistered and sometimes idealistic practitioners.

Basic scientific information about good and bad impacts on
receiving waters is largely unavailable in forms useable by most
professional practitioners. Few inventories of local aquatic life

forms are available. Even less information is available to identify total food chains and their critical nodes that are essential for healthy aquatic life. Is water temperature as critical as water mineralogy? Where can reliable limnologic information be easily obtained for a specific situation? Under what conditions should primary credibility be placed upon laboratory testing, as contrasted with aquatic life inventories? Where is this information available? What is its importance? Who can provide it? And last, but probably most important, what are the actual impacts on the existing or designated receiving water uses such as aquatic, domestic water supply, etc?

Can we answer at this time whether the problems will increase or decrease with time? We saw some of this with bio-amplification of mercury in the food chain and the reduction of lead in runoff as use of leaded gasoline decreased. Again, clearly, the challenge is on the scientific and professional communities to develop answers to these questions. There also is a challenge to academia, policymakers (especially research support policy) and legislators to support development of such knowledge, before various costly "corrective" programs are mandated. When we are not sure of all dimensions of problems, how can we properly solve them and how can we justify expending resources to support new programs?

We also need to ask ourselves what "benefits" derive from the control of urban runoff quality? Will water quality and/or the potential uses of the receiving waters improve, marginally improve or not improve? As an example, will habitat availability control aquatic life viability? If so, water quality improvements may have little actual impact on aquatic life. Can we quantify benefits in economic and social terms to the public? Should not the public know what it gets for its tax dollars, regardless of whether they come from Federal, State or Local government sources? Should not industry be enabled to understand the benefits (and their costs) that will result from englightened regulations?

Regardless of what we might recommend as scientists and professionals, won't government decisions be based upon what the public considers acceptable and economically worthwhile? Economic and social quantifications of benefits must provide the foundation for public education, which should be prerequisite for public actions. Shouldn't we, as professionals, explore ways in which to improve the public education process? Should we become more involved in public forums? How?

The sciences and professions can identify problems and their possible solutions, but actual control of non-point source pollutants can only be accomplished by public actions. Officials responsible for focusing public actions often have more regulatory authority than they are willing to implement, and often will take action only reluctantly and when faced with near-epidemic conditions. These officials generally do the best they can and are dedicated, but they pragmatically recognize that they must not displease local influentials. If they do so, their jobs are on the line. Are there weaknesses in our institutional arrangements that should be corrected?

What corrective alternatives are promising. Can we suggest practical improvements? What new strategies might help stimulate realization of urban water quality enhancements?

As you have probably gathered by now, we are unable to separate consideration of scientific and institutional issues and questions. We have only touched upon a few of the myriad scientific and institutional subjects worthy of examination to provide some indication of their diversity.

The challenge to each of you as a conference participant is to share your knowledge and experiences to help identify the most important questions and issues upon which our limited resources should be focused. In the process, we hope to identify new information that may be introduced, rapidly and beneficially, into routine practice.

We trust that everyone will take away from the Conference an enhanced appreciation of the multi-dimensional and multi-disciplinary nature of urban water quality challenges, and how to better address them. We know that we each will benefit from meeting and exchanging views with others and trust that the social opportunities will lead to many mutually supportive relationships.

We are delighted that all of you could attend and trust that this will be a great week for you. We also hope that the conference proceedings will disseminate to all interested professionals the information that all of you will share with each other at this Conference.

Report on NATO Workshop on Urban Runoff Quality

Jiri Marsalek*

Major presentations and discussions from the 1985 NATO advanced research workshop on urban runoff quality are summarized. The topics discussed include the characterization of urban runoff quality, impacts of
runoff discharges on receiving water quality, and future research.

Introduction

In August 1985, a research workshop on urban runoff pollution was
held under the sponsorship of NATO and several other agencies in Montpellier, France. The workshop was attended by more than 40 invited experts from 15 countries. The main objectives of the workshop were to
prepare the state of the art papers on various aspects of urban runoff
quality, facilitate the exchange of information and encourage cooperation among the participants, and recommend directions for future research.

When planning the workshop program, the session topics were selected
to cover all principal aspects of urban runoff pollution. Each session
started with a state of the art paper followed by supplementary papers
and discussions. The same order was followed in the workshop proceedings. The paper that follows attempts to summarize the workshop proceedings. Recognizing that a short summary can hardly do justice to the
proceedings which contain almost 900 pages, the main purpose of this
summary paper is to highlight the important topics discussed at the
workshop and to induce the reader to examine the complete proceedings.

Characterization of Urban Runoff Quality

Numerous studies of urban runoff composition proved that runoff may
carry fairly high concentrations of a variety of pollutants. In spite
of this fact, it has been rather difficult to evaluate urban runoff as
a source of pollution, because such an evaluation inherently depends on
the type of pollutant, loadings carried by runoff in relation to those
from other sources, and the receiving waters. By synthesis of results
from many studies, the understanding of urban runoff pollution has been
advanced as summarized below.

The main pollutional aspects of urban runoff are generally associated with runoff pollution by solids, substances exerting oxygen demand,
toxic substances, bacteria, and nutrients(Ellis, 1986).

* Research Scientist, National Water Research Institute, 867 Lakeshore
  Road, Burlington, Ontario L7R 4A6, Canada

Stormwater runoff and overflows carry large quantities of both inorganic and organic solids in either particulate or colloidal form. From the environmental point of view, the suspended solids fraction is particularly important because of induced turbidity, pollutant adsorption, substrate smothering and benthal accumulation(Ellis, 1986).

Organic and other oxidizable materials carried by runoff may exert substantial oxygen demands on receiving waters. Such demands cannot be measured by the biochemical oxygen demand(BOD) parameter, because its capability to measure oxygen demand is inhibited by toxicity of urban runoff and inability to detect substantial delayed oxygen demands resulting from benthal deposition in receiving waters.

The toxic substances found in stormwater runoff include heavy metals, hydrocarbons and some chlorinated organics. Heavy metal levels in runoff typically exceed the safe threshold limits for freshwater biota (Ellis, 1986). Among the organic priority pollutants, polyaromatic hydrocarbons occur in greatest quantities(Marsalek, 1986).

Stormwater runoff and particularly combined sewer overflows are contaminated by bacteria, viruses and pathogens. With sediment-water bacterial ratios of 45:1, these microorganisms accumulate in both dry weather pipe deposits as well as in benthal receiving waters and may affect public health and recreational water use(Ellis, 1986).

Phosphorus and nitrogen loadings in stormwater and overflows may accelerate eutrophication problems in quiescent reaches of urban water bodies and exert subtoxic effects on aquatic organisms. The annual nutrient loadings in runoff are significantly lower than those in treatment plant effluents(Waller, 1986). Furthermore, benthal sediments act as efficient sinks of both phosphorus and nitrogen(Ellis, 1986).

Salts used for highway ice control contribute sodium and chloride to receiving waters. The effects of increased salinity include the establishment of density gradients that prevent mixing and lead to stagnation of bottom layers, pH increases and shifts in ecological communities(Waller and Hart, 1986).

Ellis(1986) concluded that although the characterization of urban runoff quality with its inherent variability and transient nature is a difficult task, it is desirable to undertake this task in areas with high runoff and pollutant concentrations such as parking lots, roof and road surfaces, catchbasins, and areas with sewers with dry weather deposits. Some selected data on composition of stormwater, overflows and treated effluents are shown in Fig.1.

Recognizing the pollutional aspects of urban runoff, it is often required to study runoff quantity and quality by field investigations, computer modelling, or combinations of both approaches as described in next two sections.

Field Studies of Urban Runoff Quality

The composition of urban runoff is frequently determined by field

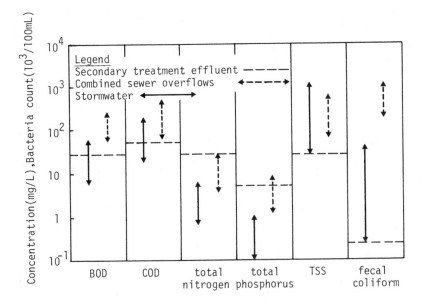

Fig.1. Composition of Stormwater, Combined Sewer Overflows and Secondary Treatment Effluents(Hvitved-Jacobsen, 1986)

studies which may be classified as planning studies, studies for calibration/verification of models, and research studies of pollutant sources and pathways(Malmqvist, 1986). The characteristics of individual types of studies vary widely depending on study objectives(Geiger, 1986).

Planning studies typically deal with the effects of urban runoff on receiving waters and are done at various levels. The list of parameters studied at the national level is fairly short and includes such common parameters as total suspended solids, chemical oxygen demand,total nitrogen and phosphorus, and selected heavy metals. This list is often expanded, at a municipal level, by adding indicator bacteria and additional parameters reflecting local sources(Malmqvist, 1986).

Field studies done in support of model calibration and verification have special characteristics which follow from the structure of the model applied. One of the main difficulties with urban runoff quality models is the evaluation of the pollutant accumulation rates.

Field investigations for research purposes focus on physical and chemical processes that control the composition of urban runoff. These studies require full control of experimental conditions which is generally possible only in small experimental plots. Difficulties with transposition of results from these micro scale areas to large urban catchments are selfevident.

Data acquisition systems are very important in field studies. Technological advances in instrumentation were documented by a data acquisition system which was used in one of the runoff studies conducted under the National Urban Runoff Program(Terstriep, 1986). In this centra-
lly-controlled system, the central microcomputer communicates with end
of the line devices by leased phone lines.

Besides instrumentation, many other aspects of experimental design
have to be considered in the planning of field studies of runoff quality. One of such considerations is the selection of the sampling interval for various quality parameters. Such a problem can be solved using
the available statistical techniques as shown by van de Ven(1986).

In spite of technological advances in the sensing, recording and
transmission of field data, there is an indication that the commonly
perceived good accuracies of runoff flow measurements may not be achie-
vable in the field. Flow measurement errors for a concrete sewer installed in the laboratory were as high as ±50% for flows calculated from
measured depths, ±25% for a Venturi flume, and less than ±25% for an
electromagnetic flowmeter(Malmqvist, 1986). Similar magnitudes of error
would apply to water quality data.

High costs and general limitations of field studies of urban runoff
quality prompted the development of computer models for simulation of
runoff quality. Such developments are described in next section.

Modelling of Urban Runoff Quality

During the last 15 years, many urban runoff quality models have been
developed using both physically-based and statistically-based approaches. Historically, the first operational models were physically based
and the statistically-based models followed.

Urban runoff quality models were reviewed by Huber(1986) who noted
that there are six fully operational runoff quality models(see Table 1).
The criteria for operational character include the availability of the
user's manual and documentation, continued support by an agency, and
the use by others than just the model builder. Much of the current de-
velopmental work concentrates on developing "new and improved" versions
of these six existing models(Huber, 1986).

Among the approaches to runoff quality prediction, the consideration
of pollutant buildup, removal and washoff is the most common. Many new
developments have been produced in the formulation of such processes.
Recently investigated sources include atmospheric fallout, vegetation
and leaf litter, land surface erosion, spills, pavement wear, automobile emissions and decay, and anti-skid and deicing compounds(James and
Boregowda, 1986). Removals include street sweeping, wind erosion, ex-
traneous water flows and others. It was noted, however, that without
sufficient data to support these new developments, all models eventually return to largely empirical formulations which can be supported by
the existing end of pipe data(Huber, 1986).

All the operational models are capable of simulating accurately hydrographs and pollutographs, if adequate calibration data are available. None of these models may be assumed to accurately predict magnitudes of pollutant concentrations and loadings without calibration data, although even in that case, these models are still useful for comparative studies and estimation of relative effects(Huber, 1986).

Table 1. Six Operational Urban Runoff Quality Models(Huber, 1986)

Model	Sponsoring Agency	Simulation Type*	Number of Pollutants	Year Originated
DR3M-QUAL	U.S. Geological Survey	C, DE	4	1982
FHWA	Federal Highway Administration	DE	13	1981
HSPF	Environmental Protection Agency	C, DE	10	1976
QQS	Environmental Protection Agency	C, DE	2	1976
STORM	Hydrologic Engineering Center	C	6	1974
SWMM	Environmental Protection Agency	C, DE	10	1971

*C = continuous simulation; DE = discrete event simulation

Another approach to runoff quality modelling is by using statistically-based empirical models. Such models are developed from statistical analysis of experimental data which have to meet certain criteria established before the start of data collection(Hemain, 1986).

Statistically-based models are very powerful in identifying the explanatory variables which have the greatest influence on runoff quality. It was noted that although statistical analyses of runoff data sometimes do not detect any significant influence of the antecedent dry period on runoff quality, this period is one of the most important parameters in conventional physically-based models(Hemain, 1986).

Although statistical models offer an alternative to physically-based models, their use is somewhat restricted because of rigorous requirements on supporting data and the limited validity of results which cannot be extrapolated or transferred. Statistically-based models are best applicable to operation of combined sewer systems with real-time controls and to certain planning studies.

The usefulness of statistically-based modelling was demonstrated by two case studies. The first one dealt with the prediction of oxygen depletion in stagnant waters receiving combined sewer overflows(van der Heijden et al., 1986). The second study dealt with statistical analyses of runoff quality data collected under the French national urban runoff

program. A two-step accumulation/transport model worked well for suspended solids and an one-step model produced the best results for BOD
and COD(Servat, 1986).

Runoff Pollution Impact on Receiving Waters

    The nature of pollutants and variations of their load in urban run-
off cause both short-term and long-term impacts on receiving waters.
The short-term impacts may then produce immediate as well as delayed effects. Intermittent runoff discharges lead to increased pollutant levels which accelerate certain processes adversely affecting water quality. Rare runoff events with exceptional pollutant loads may even cause critical effects in receiving waters. Beside the input of pollutants
to receiving waters, runoff discharges may lead to scouring and resuspension of sediment in receiving waters and further deterioration of
water quality. The nature and time scales of urban runoff impacts on
receiving water quality are illustrated in Fig.2. The discussion of characteristic impacts follows.

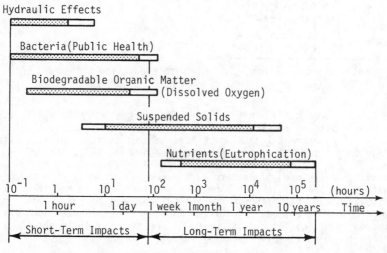

Fig.2. Time Scales of Urban Runoff Pollution Impacts on
Receiving Waters(after Hvitved-Jacobsen, 1986)

    Combined sewer overflows and stormwater runoff exert oxygen demands
which may lead to oxygen depletion mostly by degradation of discharged
organic matter and sediment scoured in the vicinity of outfalls. Scouring and resuspension bring large amounts of easily biodegradable organics and reduced species from deeper anoxic layers to the surface and
these materials then exert oxygen demand. Another effect of runoff on
dissolved oxygen levels is through disruption of diurnal variations in
dissolved oxygen levels in urban rivers. During wet weather, the peaks

of diurnal dissolved oxygen cycles are depressed, almost to the trough
levels, by increased turbidity and reduced sunlight penetration(Hvitved
-Jacobsen, 1986).

Bacterial contamination of stormwater and overflows may adversely
affect public water supply, recreation and aesthetics, fishing, shell
fishing, and agricultural and irrigation water supply. Generally, sewage overflows are particularly strong sources of bacterial contamination, although storm runoff may be also contaminated by leakage from
sanitary sewers and septic tanks, and by some other sources. The bacteriological contamination of receiving waters by stormwater and overflows is of short duration, because bacteria start to die off shortly
after the cessation of discharges. Bacteria adsorbed on sediments may
survive longer because of abundance of nutrients and protection from
sunlight(Hvitved-Jacobsen, 1986).

Overflows and stormwater discharges also convey nutrients which contribute to eutrophication of certain types of receiving waters. This
problem is particularly important in the case of combined sewer overflows discharging into lakes, estuaries and the enclosed coastal zone.
The influx of nutrients leads to their accumulation in receiving waters, often in bottom sediments, and to a long-term impact. Therefore,
long-term nutrient loadings rather than instantaneous concentrations
are of interest. For eutrophication of receiving waters, phosphorus
contributions, particularly in overflows, are much more important than
contributions of nitrogen. This follows from the facts that receiving
waters are typically phosphorus-limited and that urban loadings of phosphorus, in relation to rural loadings, are relatively higher than those of nitrogen(Hvitved-Jacobsen, 1986).

Concerns about the impacts of toxic pollutants on receiving waters
are fairly recent. Consequently, such impacts are poorly understood and
need to be further studied. Furthermore, many point sources of toxic
pollutants, such as industrial discharges or leachates from toxic dumps,
have not been properly controlled as yet and this lowers the relative
importance of urban runoff as a source of toxics. Once the point sources have been controlled, the relative importance of toxic loadings in
stormwater runoff and combined sewer overflows will increase.

Ferrara(1986) reported that a general methodology for assessing the
impact of toxics in urban runoff on receiving waters was available. Following the characterization of toxic substances in runoff, their distribution in receiving waters can be modelled with the existing models
predicting concentration distributions. Such results can then be compared with water quality criteria which were developed for many toxic
substances by assessing their impacts on human health. The understanding of toxic impacts on human health will require further improvements.

A methodology for assessing the impact of combined sewer overflows
on river water quality was reported by Villeneuve and Lavallee(1986).
Sediments immediately downstream of outfalls were 10-50 times more contaminated than those upstream of outfalls and instream pollutant concentrations downstream of outfalls increased during wet weather 2-7 times above the dry-weather levels. The recovery period was 48 hours for

most parameters.

Modelling of Water Quality in Receiving Waters

Ultimate decisions in water management projects generally follow from considerations of receiving water quality. For this purpose, particularly when comparing various intervention measures, it is desirable to model water quality in receiving waters. Medina(1986) recommended a hierarchical approach to instream water quality analysis characterized by the four levels described below.

Level I - preliminary screening. This level of analysis comprises the collection of existing data, inventories of pollutant sources, routine computations of means and extremes of water quality parameters, and estimates of their impacts.

Level II - statistically-based frequency analysis. At this level, pollutant cumulative frequency distributions are derived from historical data and used to identify potential water quality impacts.

Level III - intermediate, physically-based frequency analysis. At this level, steady-state deterministic continuous simulation is used to derive cumulative frequency distributions for causes and effects addressed in water quality considerations. Historical data on system response to combinations of waste inputs and various levels of control are included.

Level IV - advanced, physically based frequency and duration analysis. Deterministic, continuous simulation of receiving water quality transients is used to derive frequencies and durations of water quality standards. Such data are then used to assess biological damage.

Various approaches to the modelling of receiving water quality were demonstrated in several papers describing case studies. A practical methodology fpr selection of water quality models was proposed by Roesner et al.(1986). This methodology consists of ten steps ultimately leading to the model selection. The model selection should be further guided by extensive modelling experience and the available model selection summary reports.

The impacts of urban runoff discharges on eutrophication of small urban lakes were modelled by Jacobsen and Nyholm(1986). In their model, an early cycle of phytoplankton growth and nutrient transformation was considered for a lake receiving steady-state nutrient inputs form external sources. Without calibration, the agreement between observed and simulated data was only fair. It was felt, however, that even the non-calibrated model could be successfully used for comparison of control alternatives.

Applications of several models for evaluations of urban drainage impacts in several Ontario watersheds were described by Weatherbe(1986). His studies indicated a general utility of continuous simulation in spite of relatively high resource requirements. Different parameters presented unique problems in simulation. Continuously monitored water quality parameters were more amenable to continuous simulation than discretely-sampled parameters. For bacterial parameters, probabilistic models might be more suitable, because of a large random component in observed bacterial data. A hierarchical approach in which steady-state modelling preceded continuous simulation was found very effective.

Mulkey et al.(1986) reported on experience with the modelling of transport and fate of selected toxic substances. For specific condi - tions and   constant loads of toxics, steady-state models produced acceptable estimates of instream concentrations. For pulse loads, non-steady state models were required. Contaminant transfers between sediment and the water column could be neglected only for high dissolved contaminant concentrations.

Runoff Quality Management

During the last 20 years, numerous diverse methods for controlling pollution from urban stormwater discharges and combined sewer overflows have been developed, demonstrated and documented in guides and manuals(Field, 1986). Only selected, more important methods were highlighted in the workshop session on runoff quality management.

Runoff management alternatives are sometimes classified according to location where controls are implemented. Typical approaches include controls at the source by land management, in the collection system, or offline by storage and treatment. Land management comprises nonstructural, semi-structural and structural measures designed to reduce urban runoff and pollutant flux before they enter drainage. The typical control measures recommended for this purpose include land use and drainage planning utilizing natural drainage, the use of facilities required for flood and erosion control for pollution control, porous pavement, surface sanitation, and chemical use control(Field, 1986).

Collection system controls deal with management alternatives for stormwater interception and transport. The recently studied methods include improved design and maintenance of sewers and catchbasins, elimination of cross-connections, in-sewer and in-channel storage, and real-time control which is primarily applicable to combined sewer systems.

Real-time control may be applied in operation of combined sewer systems in order to reduce the impact of overflows on the environment. At present, there are about 50 real-time control systems operating in Europe and North America and these systems proved to be effective in abating combined sewer overflows(Schilling, 1986). Typical systems comprise rain gauges and water level sensors, pumps, inflatable dams or other regulators, telephone line telemetry, and a distributed digital control system with on-site microprocessors and dual central microcomputers. Experience with various hardware components of typical real-time control systems was presented by Delattre et al.(1986).

Operational concepts employed in the existing real-time control systems can be classified as simple local control schemes. Very few systems employ advanced automatic system controls(Schilling, 1986). Operational algorithms were discussed in some detail by Patry(1986) who

reported that although it is possible to define operational control algorithms, it is difficult to demonstrate the advantages of real-time
controls in comparison to other schemes. Furthermore, the mathematical
formulation of a predictive overflow control strategy is adversely affected by   uncertainties in water quality and quantity forecasts and
the lack of real-time water quality data.

Schilling(1986) concluded that there is hardly any need for more research on real-time controls and that further progress can be achieved
only by making municipal engineers aware of the benefits and potential
of these control systems.

High volume and large variations in quantity and quality of stormwater make storage an important control alternative. Practical experience indicates that storage should be always considered in system planning, because it allows for the maximum utilization of the existing dry-
weather and other treatment plant facilities at the lowest costs of pollutant removal(Stahre, 1986). Relatively high capital costs of storage
facilities are dramatically reduced in a new in-receiving water flow
balance system which was recently developed(Field, 1986). Such a system
contains stormwater in plastic curtain compartments installed in the
receiving water body. After cessation of overflow, the contents of these compartments are pumped back to the treatment plant.

In all storage facilities, some treatment of stormwater by sedimentation takes place. Depending on flow conditions, such a treatment may
not be very effective and special treatment facilities or equipment may
be needed to increase pollutant removal. Intense flows and unpredictable shock-loading effects reduce the adaptability of conventional wastewater treatment processes, such as biological treatment, to runoff
treatment. Physical/chemical treatment was found   much more suitable for such purposes. The treatment processes of which suitability for
runoff treatment was fully demonstrated and documented include fine
mesh screening, sedimentation, disinfection, swirl degritting, fine
mesh screening/high rate infiltration, and fine mesh screening/dissol-
ved air flotation(Field, 1986).

Some of the above treatment processes were further discussed in additional presentations. Lygren and Damhaug(1986) discussed the use of
a swirl concentrator for removal of suspended solids from runoff and
snowmelt. Characteristics of suspended solids were found to be critical
for the magnitude of removal rates. Dartus and Alquier(1986) presented
a conceptual probabilistic model for degritting chambers. The model incorporates descriptions of two phases of chamber operation - a quick-
response phase with particle deposition and a slow-response phase with
resuspension of earlier deposited sediment.

Procedures for design of stormwater detention ponds for phosphorus
removal were developed by extensive analysis of the information available in the literature(Urbonas and Ruzzo, 1986). It was concluded that
properly designed ponds can effectively improve runoff quality and remove significant amounts of phosphorus. Wet ponds seem to be more suitable for this purpose than dry ponds. Phosphorus removals as high as
50% can be achieved if settling in the pond is followed by filtration

or infiltration of stormwater. A standardized outlet design for a wet
pond serving for stormwater quality control is shown in Fig.3.

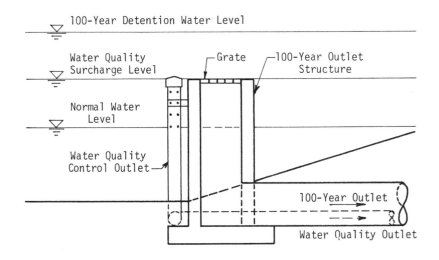

Fig.3. Standardized Water Quality Control Outlet for
Wet Ponds (after Urbonas and Ruzzo, 1986)

Among various off-line control alternatives, the integrated systems
incorporating flow control and treatment are the most promising(Field,
1986; Stahre, 1986). Such systems include storage/treatment by settling
and feedback to municipal works, dual use wet-weather flow/dry-weather
flow facilities and, finally, control/treatment/reuse. In the last system, treatment is incorporated in the storage facility, so that the effluent is suitable for subpotable industrial and irrigational water
supplies.

Future Research Needs

During the workshop, a survey of perceived future research needs was
conducted and the survey results were further discussed in the closing
session. The top eight research needs which were identified by the
highest percentage of participants are listed below. For the complete
listing, reference is made to the workshop proceedings(Torno, 1986).

1. The understanding of the processes and mechanisms, including the
related mathematical models, of pollutant accumulation and transport in
runoff.

2. The effects of metals and other toxic pollutants on aquatic biota,
including the means to monitor these effects.

3. The impacts of urban runoff pollution on receiving waters, including the impairment of beneficial uses and modelling of these impacts.

4. Better understanding of the processes of sedimentation and scour of solid particles in sewers.

5. The development of standards for sampling, analysis and data reporting for urban runoff pollutants.

6. The performance of stormwater and combined sewer overflow treatment devices.

7. The economic and institutional impacts of pollution control programs.

8. The development of stormwater and combined sewer overflow discharge criteria based on receiving water impacts.

Closure

The understanding of sources, pathways and controls of urban runoff pollutants has been further advanced by continuing research in many countries. To meet new challenges, recent studies focused on fundamental processes controlling runoff quality and on the modelling of such processes. The scope of runoff quality considerations has been considerably expanded by including both conventional as well as priority pollutants and the impacts of pollutant discharges on receiving waters. Such expanded considerations will require further research on pollutant accumulation and transport in urban runoff, effects of runoff pollutants on receiving waters, the modelling of such effects, performance of control measures, and the development of runoff discharge criteria on the basis of receiving water impacts.

References

Dartus, D., and Alquier, M., "A Conceptual Model Optimizing the Maintenance of Grit Chambers in Combined Sewers," Proceedings of the NATO Workshop on Urban Runoff Pollution, Springer-Verlag, Heidelberg, FRG, 1986, pp.725-738(in press).

Delattre, J.M., Bachoc, A., and Jacquet, G., "Performance of Hardware Components for Real-Time Management of Sewer Systems," Proceedings of the NATO Workshop on Urban Runoff Pollution, Springer-Verlag, Heidelberg, FRG, 1986, pp.819-842(in press).

Ellis, J.B., "Pollutional Aspects of Urban Runoff," Proceedings of the NATO Workshop on Urban Runoff Pollution, Springer-Verlag, Heidelberg, FRG, 1986, pp.1-38(in press).

Ferrara, R., "Toxic Pollutants: Impact and Fate in Receiving Waters," Proceedings of the NATO Workshop on Urban Runoff Pollution, Springer-Verlag, Heidelberg, FRG, 1986, pp.423-462(in press).

Field, R., "Urban Stormwater Runoff Quality Management: Low-Structurally Intensive Measures and Treatment," Proceedings of the NATO Workshop on Urban Runoff Pollution, Springer-Verlag, Heidelberg, FRG, 1986, pp.677-700(in press).

Geiger, W., "Use of Field Data in Urban Drainage Planning," Proceedings of the NATO Workshop on Urban Runoff Pollution, Springer-Verlag, Heidelberg, FRG, 1986, pp.103-126(in press).

Hemain, J.-C., "Statistically Based Modelling of Urban Runoff Quality: State of the Art," Proceedings of the NATO Workshop on Urban Runoff Pollution, Springer-Verlag, Heidelberg, FRG, 1986, pp.277-304(in press).

Huber, W., "Deterministic Modelling of Urban Runoff Quality," Proceedings of the NATO Workshop on Urban Runoff Pollution, Springer-Verlag, Heidelberg, FRG, 1986, pp.167-242(in press).

Hvitved-Jacobsen, T., "Conventional Pollutant Impacts on Receiving Waters," Proceedings of the NATO Worskhop on Urban Runoff Pollution, Springer-Verlag, Heidelberg, FRG, 1986, pp.345-378(in press).

Jacobsen, B.N., and Nyholm, N., "Eutrophication Modelling of Small Urban Lakes," Proceedings of the NATO Workshop on Urban Runoff Pollution, Springer-Verlag, Heidelberg, FRG, 1986, pp.587-620(in press).

James, W., and Boregowda, S., "Continuous Mass-Balance of Build-Up Processes," Proceedings of the NATO Workshop on Urban Runoff Pollution, Springer-Verlag, Heidelberg, FRG, 1986, pp.243-272(in press).

Lygren, E., and Damhaug, T., "The Swirl Concentrator as an Urban Runoff Treatment Device," Proceedings of the NATO Workshop on Urban Runoff Pollution, Springer-Verlag, Heidelberg, FRG, 1986, pp.713-724 (in press).

Malmqvist, P.-A., "Field Studies of Urban Runoff Quality," Proceedings of the NATO Workshop on Urban Runoff Pollution, Springer-Verlag, Heidelberg, FRG, 1986, pp.89-102(in press).

Marsalek, J., "Toxic Contaminants in Urban Runoff: A Case Study," Proceedings of the NATO Workshop on Urban Runoff Pollution, Springer-Verlag, Heidelberg, FRG, 1986, pp.39-58(in press).

Medina, M.A., "State-of-the-Art, Physically-Based and Statistically-Based Water Quality Modelling," Proceedings of the NATO Workshop on Urban Runoff Pollution, Springer-Verlag, Heidelberg, FRG, 1986, pp.499-586(in press).

Mulkey, L.A., Ambrose, R.B., and Barnwell, T.O., "Aquatic Fate and Transport Modeling Techniques for Predicting Environmental Exposure to Organic Pesticides and Other Toxicants - A Comparative Study," Proceedings of the NATO Workshop on Urban Runoff Pollution, Springer-Verlag, Heidelberg, FRG, 1986, pp.463-498(in press).

Patry, G.G., "Operational Algorithms for Application in Real-Time Control of Combined Sewer Systems," Proceedings of the NATO Workshop on Urban Runoff Pollution, Springer-Verlag, Heidelberg, FRG, 1986, pp.843-868(in press).

Roesner, L.A., Walton, R., and Hartigan, J.P., " Realistic Water Quality Modeling," Proceedings of the NATO Workshop on Urban Runoff Pollution, Springer-Verlag, Heidelberg, FRG, 1986, pp.621-648(in press).

Schilling, W., "Urban Runoff Quality Management by Real-Time Control," Proceedings of the NATO Workshop on Urban Runoff Pollution,

Springer-Verlag, Heidelberg, FRG, 1986, pp.765-818(in press).

Servat, E., "TSS, BOD$_5$ and COD Accumulation and Transport Over Urban Catchment Surfaces: A Modelling Approach," Proceedings of the NATO Workshop on Urban Runoff Pollution, Springer-Verlag, Heidelberg, FRG, 1986, pp.325-342(in press).

Stahre, P., "Structural Measures for Runoff Quality Management," Proceedings of the NATO Workshop on Urban Runoff Pollution, Springer-Verlag, Heidelberg, FRG, 1986, pp.701-712(in press).

Terstriep, M., "Design of Data Collection Systems," Proceedings of the NATO Workshop on Urban Runoff Pollution, Springer-Verlag, Heidelberg, FRG, 1986, pp.127-148(in press).

Torno, H.C., "Future Research Needs," Proceedings of the NATO Workshop on Urban Runoff Pollution, Springer-Verlag, Heidelberg, FRG, 1986, pp.873-879(in press).

Urbonas, B., and Ruzzo, W.P., " Standardization of Detention Pond Design for Phosphorus Removal," Proceedings of the NATO Workshop on Urban Runoff Pollution, Springer-Verlag, Heidelberg, FRG, 1986, pp.739-760(in press).

van der Heijden, R.T.J.M., Lijklema, L., and Alderink, R.H., "A Statistical Methodology for the Assessment of Water Quality Effects of Storm Water Discharges," Proceedings of the NATO Workshop on Urban Runoff Pollution, Springer-Verlag, Heidelberg, FRG, 1986, pp.305-324(in press).

van de Ven, F.H.M., "Data Evaluation in Field Studies of Urban Runoff Quality: Aspects of Assessing the Measurement Interval," Proceedings of the NATO Workshop on Urban Runoff Pollution, Springer-Verlag, Heidelberg, FRG, 1986, 147-162(in press).

Villeneuve, J.-P., and Lavallee, P., "Measured CSO Contribution to River Quality Deterioration and Methodologic Approach for Negative Influence Evaluation," Proceedings of the NATO Workshop on Urban Runoff Pollution, Springer-Verlag, Heidelberg, FRG, 1986, pp.379-418(in press).

Waller, D., and Hart, W.C., "Solids, Nutrients and Chlorides in Urban Runoff,"Proceedings of the NATO Workshop on Urban Runoff Pollution, Springer-Verlag, Heidelberg, FRG, 1986, pp.59-86(in press).

Weatherbe, D.G., "Continuous Simulation Models to Evaluate Urban Drainage Impacts in Ontario," Proceedings of the NATO Workshop on Urban Runoff Pollution, Springer-Verlag, Heidelberg, FRG, 1986, pp.649-674 , (in press).

Urban Stormwater-Quality Investigations by the USGS

Marshall E. Jennings, M.ASCE*
Timothy L. Miller**

Abstract

U.S. Geological Survey (USGS) urban stormwater investigations, in
cooperation with local and Federal agencies, have produced significant
national data bases of information and enhanced understanding of urban
hydrologic processes. Studies in progress include statistical regionalization of urban stormwater quality, the effects of stormwater
detention on water quality, ways of improving instrumentation for
urban hydrology studies, and an evaluation and update of urban gaging
networks. Studies performed by USGS since 1968, including 12 studies
that were in the Environmental Protection Agency Nationwide Urban
Runoff Program, are being summarized in a USGS report.

Introduction

The U.S. Geological Survey (USGS) has been involved in urban
hydrology investigations since at least the late 1940's. Beginning in
the late 1960's with the passage of the Flood Control Act of 1964,
national coordination of USGS studies began. Early emphasis was on
flooding problems in urban areas but this was broadened to address
storm drainage design, water supply, urban lakes, watershed modeling,
stormwater quality, and improved instrumentation for gaging urban
catchments. These urban hydrology topics continue to be water
resource issues in USGS investigations. During the period 1979-83, in
cooperation with the U.S. Environmental Protection Agency (EPA) in the
Nationwide Urban Runoff Program (NURP), a significant national focus
was placed on urban stormwater quality. The NURP studies participated
in by USGS are now completed. The NURP and similar studies, carried
out in USGS field offices at more than 22 metropolitan areas, resulted
in the publication of numerous project and data reports. In addition,
all data have been compiled into a national urban stormwater data
base.

This paper highlights ongoing urban hydrology efforts of the USGS
including compilation of national urban stormwater data bases, instrumentation for collecting urban runoff data, a national study to

*Hydrologist and National Coordinator of Urban Hydrology Studies, U.S.
Geological Survey, NSTL, Mississippi 39529.

**Hydrologist, U.S. Geological Survey, 847 NE 19th Avenue, Suite 300,
Portland, Oregon 97232.

29

characterize urban stormwater quality, and new project studies in
stormwater detention and urban gaging networks. The findings of the
NURP and similar studies, as well as all USGS urban runoff investigations since about 1968, are being compiled for publication by the
second author. These findings, in condensed form, will be a part of
the oral presentation of this paper. Included, however, are major
findings of one USGS-EPA study in Bellevue, Washington.

USGS Urban Stormwater Data Bases

   In 1969, the Urban Hydrology Research Council of the American
Society of Civil Engineers (ASCE) prepared a report (ASCE, 1969)
citing the need for urban water data to be collected by USGS. The
report recommended central objectives, direction, and scope of a
national urban water information program. While not all of the objectives of the recommended program have been met, many have. In 1981,
during the preparation of a national study and data compilation of
flood characteristics of urban watersheds (Sauer and others, 1983), it
was revealed that at least three years of runoff data from almost 600
urbanized sites were available nationwide.

   Of specific interest to participants at this conference, a national
urban-stormwater data base, including water quality, has been compiled
for 22 metropolitan areas throughout the United States (Driver and
others, 1985). The data base contains information on more than 700
storms for about 100 urban gaging stations. Data, with water quality,
for five or more storms are available for about two-thirds of the
watersheds. The entire data base is available on magnetic tape;
selected sites are also available on PC diskette. Copies of the above
report are being made available to conference participants. In addition to simultaneous rainfall, runoff, and runoff-quality data, atmospheric deposition data is also available for 31 watersheds.

   It is believed that the USGS urban stormwater data bases will be of
substantial benefit to continuing urban hydrology research as well as
practice-oriented studies. Those persons interested in special studies using the data bases may contact the first author for assistance.

Instrumentation

   Instrumentation for urban stormwater gaging is being constantly
refined by the USGS. Most new data are being collected by micro-
processor based data loggers. While conventional, open-channel
streamgaging is the typical method of data collection, many studies
require stormsewer flow measurement and recording systems. A recent
report (Kilpatrick and others, 1985) discusses these gaging methods.
Increasing use of special flumes, stage measurement by pressure trans-
ducers, unsteady-flow dye-dilution measurement technique, and automatic water-quality sampling is occurring within USGS field offices.
Data-reduction software on the USGS network of minicomputers is speed-
ing up the data processing activity and improving accuracy by comprehensive quality control methods.

National Urban Stormwater Quality

   A paper in this conference by Nancy Driver of USGS, located in
Lakewood, Colorado, describes work in progress to statistically characterize regional patterns of urban-runoff quality. The research is
expected to produce predictive relationships for estimating stormwater
event loads for selected urban constituents. The statistical analyses
are making use of all available USGS data and also extensive data made
available through the Nonpoint Source Control Section, EPA. In addition, separate statistical procedures are being developed for estimation of long-term annual or seasonal stormwater loads. It is believed
that these predictive tools will complement the excellent screening-
level analyses made available by EPA (U.S. EPA, 1983).

   In particular, the USGS statistical prediction methods may be of
considerable utility, along with additional stormwater sampling, in
meeting the upcoming requirements of stormwater permitting.

Stormwater Detention

   One of the findings of the NURP studies (U.S. EPA, 1983) which confirmed earlier observations, was the apparent effectiveness of stormwater detention in improving urban stormwater quality. In particular,
it was suggested by EPA that dry ponds with outlets designed for
extended detention may possess removal rates close to those observed
in wet ponds. However, NURP data on such ponds was limited. USGS is
presently setting up several test sites in various parts of the United
States to improve our understanding of the operation, and assist in
proper design of detention systems for urban water-quality enhancement. At present, sites are in operation in Florida, Kansas, and New
York. New sites are expected to be installed in Wisconsin and
Washington. By careful monitoring of inflow and outflow loads over a
sequence of storm events, it is hoped that information useful for
urban planning and design will result. A report on studies in
Orlando, Florida (Martin and Smoot, 1985) is available to the conference participants.

   A key feature of the new USGS studies is the collaboration of an
ASCE Urban Hydrology Research Council Task Committee (TC) entitled TC
on the Use of Detention for Stormwater Quality Enhancement. The TC
members will provide guidance for the USGS-sponsored detention
research and ultimately will prepare written design criteria and
guidelines for stormwater detention pond systems. It is hoped that
the guidelines will maximize the effectiveness of such systems for
water-quality constituent reduction in addition to their hydrologic
peak-flow-reduction purposes. Other Federal and State agencies are
cooperating to provide all available data for use of the TC.

Urban Stormwater Gaging Networks

   USGS has operated hydrologic gaging networks in urban metropolitan
areas for many years in major U.S. cities. For example, a comprehensive network of 22 gaging stations with about 40 rain gages has been
providing information since 1964 in the Houston, Texas, metropolitan

area. Most of these networks now collect water-quality information in
addition to rainfall-runoff information. Most USGS interpretative
reports have focused on urban flood-frequency prediction. In a few
studies, USGS has used a simulation model (Alley, 1986), to extend
short gaged records prior to statistical regionalization of T-year
flood peaks. Discussions are under way to review and update the role
of USGS urban hydrology gaging networks and resulting analyses. It
has been suggested that a more significant use of simulation modeling
approaches, regionalization of design parameters, and more innovative
gaging networks may provide increased information for a wider range of
urban planning needs, including water-quality considerations. An ASCE
Urban Hydrology Council TC on Urban Gaging Networks has been proposed.

Example Study: Bellevue, Washington, Urban Catchment Studies

Twelve USGS NURP studies were performed in cooperation with U.S.
EPA and local agencies. In addition to accumulation of a valuable
national data base, the investigaions revealed valuable site-specific
information. Representative of the USGS investigations is the study
performed in Bellevue, Washington, during 1979-82. The studies were
in cooperation with the city of Bellevue. Basically, the studies
evaluated, using data for three catchments including quantity and
quality of urban runoff and chemical characteristics of atmospheric
deposition, the effects of street sweeping and stormwater detention on
quality of runoff.

Using two approximately 100-acre paired catchments with single-
family residential use, an elaborate street sweeping regimen was
imposed on the gaged catchments. Careful statistical analyses of runoff loads for about 25 storm events showed that for most constituents,
street sweeping had little effect on water quality. Also, rainfall
was frequently found to be the source of approximately one-third of
the total nitrogen in stormwater runoff. Such findings proved consistent with results from other NURP study areas.

The Bellevue study collected concentrations and flows for inflow
and outflow of an in-pipe and grassy depression detention system. The
studies indicated that this type of detention system was ineffective
in removal of water-quality constituents during the gaged period.

Apart from evaluation of stormwater management practices, the
Bellevue study also examined catchment runoff volume and peak flow
prediction by two methods--regression of peaks with total rainfall and
three-day antecedent rainfall and use of a calibrated deterministic
catchment model. Such studies help to ascertain the limitations of
catchment models and provide guidelines for appropriate use.

Finally, the Bellevue study examined in detail, using regression
analyses, the relationship of water discharge and constituent concentration in runoff as functions of time. These analyses led to an
innovative examination of the traditional "washoff" equation widely
used in urban stormwater models. Copies of the U.S.Geological Survey
Bellevue study (Prych and Ebbert, 1986) will be made available to
conference participants.

Future Investigations

Much progress has been made in understanding urban stormwater hydrology of the United States since publication of the ASCE Urban Hydrology Research Council report in 1969. Through cooperation with U.S. EPA and other agencies, USGS has compiled useful national urban hydrology data bases. It is suggested that intensive studies of the data by those interested in the issues of urban stormwater hydrology will produce tools to assist in workable solutions for urban storm-water problems. USGS wishes to cooperate fully with the Council, Federal and local agencies, universities and consultants to achieve such solutions.

Appendix - References

Alley, William M., "Summary of Experience With the Distributed Routing Rainfall-Runoff Model (DR₂M)" _in_ Proceedings, International Symposium on Comparison of Urban Drainage Models with Real Catchment Data, Dubrovnik, Yugoslavia, 1986.

American Society of Civil Engineers, "An Analysis of National Basic Information Needs in Urban Hydrology," ASCE Urban Hydrology Research Council, 1969.

Driver, N. E., Mustard, M. H, Rhinesmith, R. B., and Middleburg, R. F., "U.S. Geological Survey Urban-Stormwater Data Base for 22 Metropolitan Areas Throughout the United States," U.S. Geological Survey Open-File Report 85-337, 1985.

Kilpatrick, F. A., Kaehrle, W. R., Hardee, Jack, Cordes, E. H., and Landers, M. N., "Development and Testing of Highway Storm-Sewer Flow Measurement and Recording System," U.S. Geological Survey Water-Resources Investigations Report 85-4111, 1985.

Martin, E. H., and Smoot, J. L., "Constituent-Load Changes in Urban Stormwater Runoff Routed Through a Detention Pond-Wetlands System in Central Florida," U.S. Geological Survey Water-Resources Investigations Report 85-4310, 1985.

Prych, E. A., and Ebbert, J. C., "Quantity and Quality of Storm Runoff from Three Urban Catchments in Bellevue, Washington," U.S. Geological Survey Water-Resources Investigations Report 86-4000, 1986.

Sauer, V. B., Thomas, W. O., Jr., Stricker, V. A., and Wilson, K. V., "Flood Characteristics of Urban Watersheds in the United States," U.S. Geological Survey Water-Supply Paper 2207, 1983.

U.S. Environmental Protection Agency, "Results of the Nationwide Urban Runoff Program, Volume I - Final Report, Water Planning Division WH-554, 1983.

Modeling Urban Runoff Quality: State-of-the-Art

Wayne C. Huber,* M. ASCE

Abstract

Procedures used in urban runoff quality modeling are reviewed in the context of common objectives of urban runoff quality analysis. The need for calibration/verification data is emphasized for any model that attempts to predict absolute magnitudes of quality parameters.

Introduction

Within the past two decades, new responsibilities have arisen out of the recognition of the severe pollution potential of urban nonpoint runoff, especially from combined sewer overflows (CSOs) and to a lesser degree, from stormwater runoff (Field and Struzeski, 1972; Field and Terkeltaub, 1981; EPA, 1983b). With recognition of these quality problems (and federal funding for their control) has come the development of new analytical tools for their analysis. The resulting computer models coupled with large data aquisition programs have revolutionized the engineer's ability to perform a sophisticated analysis of complex quality problems. Yet in spite of these advances, it will be seen that the dependence upon measured data is as severe as ever for many of the typical engineering design activities.

Objectives of urban runoff quality analysis include the following:

1. Characterize the urban runoff.
2. Provide input to receiving water analysis.
3. Determine effects, sizes and combinations of control options.
4. Perform frequency analyses on quality parameters.
5. Provide input to cost-benefit analyses.

Objectives 1 and 2 characterize the magnitude of the problem, whereas objectives 3, 4 and 5 are related to the analysis and solution of the problem. Computer models allow some types of analysis, such as frequency and time series analysis, to be performed that could rarely be performed otherwise since periods of measurement are seldom long enough. It should always be borne in mind, however, that use of measured data is usually preferable to use of simulated data, particularly for objectives 1 and 2 for which accurate concentration values are needed. In general, models are not good substitutes for good field sampling programs.

*Department of Environmental Engineering Sciences, University of Florida, Gainesville, Florida 32611.

A model may be defined as any documented set of procedures for application to a problem. There are probably hundreds of models that would fit this definition, but there is only a much smaller subset of named models that are "operational." Operational means 1) the model is documented, 2) the model has been used widely, by more than just the model developer, and 3) the model has user support, often sponsored by a public agency. Probably the best example of models in this category is provided by those supplied by the Corps of Engineers, Hydrologic Engineering Center.

In attempting the overly ambitious task of describing the "state-of-the-art" in urban runoff quality modeling, the procedures used in the small subset of operational models will be reviewed, rather than the somewhat wider range of provisional procedures that may be found in the literature. To this subset must be added generic procedures such as regression and other statistical methods that are more universally applied. Model reviews are available from several sources, including Huber and Heaney (1982), Kibler (1982), EPA (1983a), and Whipple et al. (1983). A detailed review of physically-based urban runoff quality procedures is given by Huber (1985), from which portions of the following text have been abstracted.

Is Quality Modeling Necessary?

It is generally accepted that CSOs usually (but not invariably) cause receiving water problems (Field and Struzeski, 1972; Yousef et al., 1980) but the negative impacts of stormwater are not nearly so clear (Field and Turkeltaub, 1981; EPA, 1983b; Heaney and Huber, 1984). For instance, the extensive EPA Nationwide Urban Runoff Program (NURP) found few instances of impaired beneficial use of receiving waters (in the sense of violation of a standard or other criterion) in spite of the fact that the stormwater itself may have very high concentrations of pollutants (EPA, 1983b). Most stormwater-induced negative receiving water impacts result from temporarily high bacteria levels that may cause beach closings. The question then arises, is it necessary to be concerned about stormwater quality at all?

For example, stormwater quality regulations in Florida may be satisfied by providing for retention of the runoff from the first inch of rainfall (or from the first 0.5 inch of rainfall from areas less than 100 acres). In such cases there is clearly no benefit in conducting a water quality modeling exercise that may be both complex and useless. However, as receiving water quality standards become more conservative and environmentally sensitive, stormwater quality will assume a more important roll in drainage design (Field and Turkeltaub, 1981), especially since potentially chronic effects of heavy metals and other toxics are still mostly unkown. The moral is simply to avoid engaging in an involved stormwater quality modeling study unless the results are expected to make a difference and affect the design. Suit the analysis to the task.

The Essential Need for Data

There is an unavoidable and critical need for site-specific quality

(and ancillary quantity) data for calibration and verification of urban
runoff quality modeling procedures. In fact, the models are almost
worthless wihout such data whenever accurate concentrations and loads
are required, as in studies of receiving water impacts. There is somewhat more flexibility when only relative values are required, for instance, to determine the relative effects of control options. But in
any application in which absolute values are needed, all models require
site-specific data since there is such a large variability in such data,
even locally (Huber et al., 1981; EPA, 1983b). Generalized data from
other studies are suitable for rough estimates or "first cut" parameter
estimates, at best. To reiterate, predictions of absolute values of
concentrations and loads will not be credible without local, site-
specific data for calibration and verification. This is in marked
contrast to prediction of hydrographs, which are often reasonably accurate early in the calibration procedure just on the basis of initial
parameter estimates.

Required Temporal and Spatial Detail

    Receiving water concentrations are usually the final indicator of the
impacts of urban runoff and associated control measures. Fortunately,
in most cases of practical interest, receiving waters respond only
slowly to pollutant inputs, as indicated in Table 1. The implication is
that it is seldom necessary to consider more than just total pollutant
loads from storms for receiving water analysis, and for problems such as
lake eutrophication even annual loads might do. This is fortunate
because it is easier to predict toal storm loads than it is to predict
detailed pollutographs during a storm.

Table 1. Required Temporal Detail for Receiving Water Analysis.
         After Driscoll (1979) and Hydroscience (1979)

Type of Receiving Water	Key Constituents	Response Time
Lakes, Bays	Nutrients	Weeks - Years
Estuaries	Nutrients, DO(?)	Days - Weeks
Large Rivers	DO, Nitrogen	Days
Streams	DO, Nitrogen Bacteria	Hours - Days Hours
Ponds	DO, Nutrients	Hours - Weeks
Beaches	Bacteria	Hours

    On the other hand, short time increment pollutographs may be required
for studies of control options, the effectiveness of which is dependent
on the temporal sequence of loads and concentrations (e.g., capture of a
"first flush"). Real time control may also depend on intrastorm varia-

tions, but the effectiveness of most controls can usually be assessed simply through their effect on total loads. Again, the point is to match the level of analysis to the task.

Similarly, unnecessary spatial detail can often be avoided for quality modeling when only the concentrations and loads at the catchment outfall are desired. Only as much detail is needed in a simulation as is required to answer subsequent questions about control options or to ensure a realistic simulation. For instance, the effect of moving or "kinematic" storms cannot be simulated with a completely lumped system since variable rainfall must be distributed spatially.

Operational Model Examples

At the risk of being incomplete, examples of seven operational models are given in Table 2. These seven embody most of the options available for urban runoff quality prediction, except for pure regression methods. The several techniques and predictive components will be discussed.

An important observation is the fact that four of the seven models can be run continuously (and the statistical method is a form of a continuous response). Continuous simulation permits a frequency analysis on the parameter of interest, such as concentrations, loads, peak concentrations, etc., instead of relying on statistics of rainfall (or runoff) for frequency information. The frequency distributions of such parameters may be quite different (Geiger, 1984). Thus, historic rather than synthetic storms may be selected for detailed design purposes using single event simulation.

Predictive Methods

Introduction

Several methods routinely used for quality prediction will be discussed briefly. Methods related to source generation include 1) constant concentration, 2) a known frequency distribution for concentration, 3) regression equations and loading functions, 4) rating curves, 5) buildup-washoff, 6) land surface erosion and scour and deposition in sewers, and 7) other miscellaneous sources. Related processes include pollutant transport and storage and treatment.

Constant Concentration

Constant concentration is the simplest of all options, since loads can be generated easily as the product of runoff volume and concentration. In fact, the method is probably most powerful when used with a very sophisticated hydraulic model, such as the Extran Block of the SWMM model (Roesner et al., 1981). In other words, an accurate hydraulic analysis may be more important for load estimation than use of a more sophisticated but possibly hydraulically unrealistic water quality model. But what concentration value should be used? Concentration ranges may be found in many references (e.g., Manning et al., 1977; Huber et al., 1981a; Kibler, 1982; EPA, 1983b; Whipple et al., 1983); however, it is unfortunate that concentrations may not be clearly delineated on the basis of land use, location, hydrology, etc. (EPA, 1983b).

But the necessity for local data is a prerequisite to almost any method.

Table 2. Seven Operational Urban Runoff Quality Models

Model	Sponsoring Agency	Year Originated	No. Pollutants	Simulation Type*	References
DR3M-QUAL	USGS	1982	4	C,SE	Alley and Smith (1982)
FHWA	FHWA	1981	13	SE	Dever et al. (1983)
HSPF	EPA	1976	10	C,SE	Johanson et al. (1980)
QQS	EPA	1976	2	C,SE	Geiger and Dorsch (1980)
STORM	HEC	1974	6	C	Roesner et al. (1974), HEC (1977)
SWMM	EPA	1971	10	C,SE	Huber et al. (1981), Roesner et al. (1981)
Statistical	EPA	1976	Any	N/A	EPA (1976), Hydroscience (1979)

*C = Continuous simulation
SE = Single event simulation

Known Frequency Distribution

Event mean concentrations (EMCs) are the ratio of storm event mass loads to storm event runoff. It is a somewhat remarkable fact that EMCs are distributed lognormally for the overwhelming majority of nonpoint source pollutants, and for both stormwater and combined sewage (EPA, 1983b; Driscoll, 1986). If the runoff volumes are also lognormal, then the loads (the product of flow times EMC) will be lognormal. Finally, if receiving water flows are lognormal, a derived lognormal distribution for receiving water concentration can be obtained (Di Toro, 1984). This is the basis of the EPA statistical method (EPA, 1976; Hydroscience, 1979), which lends itself to simplified receiving water impact analysis of both stormwater (EPA, 1983b) and combined sewage (Driscoll and Assoc., 1981). However, because of its several assumptions and inability to simulate control alternatives explicitly, the method is probably best suited to broad surveys and may be inferior to simulation models (or direct measurements) for intensive, site-specific studies (Roesner and Dendrou, 1985).

Regression Analysis

Most studies in which water quality has been measured have attempted to relate the effluent data to catchment, demographic and hydrologic characteristics, usually through regression analysis. Such studies may range from loading equations based on land use, area etc. (McElroy et al., 1976) to pure multiple regression analysis (Miller et al., 1978). A recent review of regression formulations for highway runoff quality (Miracle, 1986) reinforces the usual caveat regarding regression analysis: such formulations are adequate only for the data base from which they were derived. It is hazardous to extend them to new locations.

Rating Curves

Rating curves are just a special case of regression analysis in which concentration or event load is regressed against flow rate or runoff volume, usually in a power function form, with no other independent variables used. Such a relationship can easily be built into a model (e.g., DR3M-QUAL, HSPF, SWMM) in place of more complex buildup-washoff methods and is relatively easy to calibrate since many urban runoff data are analyzed in this way. The method is especially useful for predicting total storm event loads, but it is not so easily adapted to simulation of control alternatives. Spurious correlation (Benson, 1965) must be noted between runoff loads (the product of concentration times volume) and volumes; event mean concentrations are usually only weakly correlated with runoff volume, if at all (Wallace, 1980).

Buildup and Washoff

The most common physically-based formulation used in urban runoff quality models is that of buildup and washoff. "Buildup" is a term that represents all of the complex spectrum of dry-weather processes that occur between storms, including deposition, wind erosion, street cleaning, etc. The idea is simply that all such processes lead to a net accumulation of solids and perhaps other pollutants, which are then "washed off" during storm events. The distinction between dry- and wet-weather processes is not always clear, especially for continuous modeling. Nonetheless, the concept of buildup and washoff is entrenched in urban quality modeling, in strong measure because of early urban data collection efforts that supported these ideas, notably APWA (1969) and Sartor and Boyd (1972). And the method can give very good results when calibrated (as is necessary for all quality prediction methods). (Default values found in original versions of SWMM and STORM are totally unreliable.) Furthermore, the method is attractive because it lends itself to the simulation of land-surface control measures, such as street sweeping. Although most data for buildup are strictly empirical, there have been some attempts to separate contributing factors such as atmospheric fallout, automobile related deposition, deicing compounds, construction, pavement degradation, etc. (Boregowda, 1985). The problem with such an approach is a need for even more varied data, such as traffic counts. Buildup formulations cover a range of linear and non-linear functions of dry-days prior to a storm event (Huber et al., 1981b), and different models accept different options (Huber, 1985).

Sartor and Boyd's (1972) classic measurements of simulated washoff
resulted in an "exponential washoff" formulation, in which pollutant
washoff rate (mass/time) is proportional to runoff rate and to remaining
pollutant load on the surface. These results were independently verified by Nakamura (1984). Once again, the use of early default values in
the washoff equations may be justifiably criticized (Sonnen, 1980).
More generalized formulations of the washoff relationship are easily
calibrated (Huber et al., 1981b) and avoid many of the pitfalls of the
original rigid assumptions (Metcalf and Eddy et al., 1971).

The idea of buildup and washoff is easiest to conceptualize for
solids. Separate parameters may be used for various pollutants (e.g.,
as in SWMM), or pollutant concentrations may be calculated as a fraction
of the concentration of "dust and dirt," a ubiquitous parameter measured
in Chicago by APWA (1969) and incorporated into many model formulations.
The pollutant fractions are also known as "potency factors" for use in
non-urban areas and for runoff quality predictions from pervious land
surfaces. The HSPF model estimates these fractions for pesticides on
the basis of a Freundlich isotherm, but most data sources (e.g., Manning
et al., 1977) ignore this possibility.

What of methods that better describe the true physics, such as sediment transport theory and methods based on rainfall energy? Rainfall
energy has been incorporated empirically into some models (e.g., HSPF)
and appears to be most important for predicting loads from pervious
areas, especially land surface erosion. Sediment transport theory has
not been implemented in detail for surface washoff because of the great
heterogeneity of urban surfaces and because of the general lack of field
studies of the physics of the processes involved.

Erosion, Scour and Deposition

The importance of rainfall energy in the prediction of erosion has
just been discussed, and it has been implemented in EPA nonpoint source
models (Donigian and Davis, 1978; Johanson et al., 1980) and others
(Solomon and Gupta, 1977). In these empirical formulations, detached
sediment is usually a power function of rainfall intensity. Erosion
predictions work best for long-term values (e.g., annual) and are very
erratic for storm events.

Scour and deposition within the drainage system is important wherever
natural channels form part of drainage network, and especially in combined sewers (Field and Struzeski, 1972; Geiger, 1984), in which material which has been deposited during dry weather flow can be scoured
during wet weather and form a "first flush" and also contribute the
majority of the solids during the storm event. Beyond basic sediment
tranport theory, few advances have been made for calculations directed
specifically at the sewer system. Theoretical considerations are reviewed by Shen (1981). Ackers (1978) presents a useful development that
can be used to estimate the depth of solids accumulation in a sewer with
attendant reduction in cross sectional area and need for higher hydraulic gradients, but his method has not been implemented formerly as part
of a model.

Probably the most ambitious attempt to apply sediment transport
theory for development of a scour and deposition model in sewers was
made by Sonnen (1977), who simulated bedload, suspended load and wash-
load using established relationships that incorporate critical shear
stress, friction and roughness interrelationships, and settling theory.
Unfortunately for the fate of this work, it was incorporated into the
Extran Block of SWMM (Roesner et al., 1981). Quality routines for this
block were eventually dropped on the basis that the state of the art of
urban quality modeling did not justify linkage with such a sophisticated
quantity model. Heuristic routines remain in the SWMM model (Huber et
al., 1981b) which may be calibrated and tend to behave in a "reasonable"
manner, but otherwise have little dependence on theory. In addition,
gross sediment deposition in combined sewers may be estimated on the
basis of studies in Boston and elsewhere (Pisano and Queiroz, 1977).

Other Sources

Other sources include precipitation, catchbasins and dry-weather
flow. Rainfall quality is usually modeled as a constant concentration
although there is evidence that there is variation during a storm
(Randall et al., 1981). Rainfall concentrations and loading data are
now widely available and are measured as part of most urban runoff
sampling programs. It is especially important to account for nutrient
concentrations in rainfall since they may be greater than those in
runoff (Kluesener and Lee, 1974; Mattraw and Sherwood, 1977). Regarding
urban snow quality data, a good review is given by Proctor and Redfern
and James F. MacLaren (1976).

Catchbasins are more likely to act as a source than as a sink for
pollutants due to their generally poor maintenance (Lager et al., 1977).
If catchbasin concentrations have been measured, they may be easily
modeled as a "reservoir" of pollutants at the beginning of a storm which
is flushed during the storm, but their contribution to total pollutant
loads is usually minor and may usually be safely neglected during simu-
lations (Huber et al., 1981b).

On an annual basis in combined sewers, dry-weather flow represents a
significant fraction of the total flow, although only 3 to 5 % of it is
lost from the system during overflows. CSOs are more influenced by
scour of deposited sediment and by the quality of entering stormwater
than by the mixture with dry-weather flow (Field and Struzeski, 1972).
Baseflow may also occur in storm sewers due to infiltration or seepage
from banks into unlined channels and be of low quality (Bedient et al.,
1980). Dry-weather flow or baseflow is simulated in most models as a
constant background source, which may be varied for combined sewers to
simulate diurnal and daily variations measured at treatment plants.
Treatment plant data can also be used to infer wet-weather quantities
and overflows (Meuller and Di Toro, 1983).

Pollutant Transport

Little attention is customarily given to routing of pollutants
through the urban drainage system because of the typically short residence time involved and because of the presence of complex hydraulic
structures with unknown mixing characteristics. When only total loads at

the outlet are required, this neglect is probably justified, but if time variations during a storm are needed, pollutant transport assumes more importance. Additionally, scour and deposition of solids in sewers may be important as discussed previously. Model implementations usually assume complete mixing within channels (e.g., FHWA, SWMM) or plug flow (e.g., DR3M-QUAL, QQS) in lieu of a solution of the complete advective-dispersion equation. Calibration of such routines is difficult since simultaneous upstream and downstream quality (and quantity) measurements are rare except in instances of velocity measurements by the dilution method.

Storage and Treatment Processes

Simulation of storage and treatment is a topic unto itself. As for the sewer system, routing may range from complete mixing to plug flow or a solution of the advective-diffusion equation (Nix et al., 1978; Medina et al., 1981; Ferrara and Harleman, 1981). The more challenging problem is the simulation of removal processes which may be done heuristically using empirical removal functions (e.g., SWMM) or on the basis of particle settling theory (e.g., DR3M-QUAL, SWMM). Although solids removal is to be expected in detention basins, removal of other parameters, especially nutrients, cannot be taken for granted; there is evidence of higher concentrations in the outflow than in the inflow (EPA, 1983b; Ferrara and Witkowski, 1983). Increasing amounts of data and literature are available for assessment of removals in detention and retention basins (e.g., McCuen, 1980; Degroot, 1982; EPA, 1983b).

Computing Requirements

As computing continues to become easier and more accessible, so does modeling and engineering analysis. With the widespread availability of microcomputers, there is hardly an excuse for any engineer not to be using some type of modeling procedure in urban hydrology. Among quality models, SWMM (James and Robinson, 1984) and STORM (Bontje et al., 1984) have been adapted to microcomputers, and additional preprocessors are under development using higher level languages (Aldrich and Rosener, 1986; Heaney and Miles, 1986). A mainframe preprocessor is available for HSPF and may also be suitable for other models (Lumb and Kittle, 1983). Even continuous simulation is possible on microcomputers if sufficient disk storage is available for the long time series involved (Bontje et al., 1984; Robinson and James, 1984). The goal of much of the current computer-related research is the development of expert systems for urban hydrology.

Case Studies

Models have been used many times to address urban runoff quality problems, which is not quite the same thing as saying that they have been used to model quality, per se. That is, in some instances the emphasis has been upon quantity modeling for definition of overflow events, etc., with no prediction of concentrations and loads. However, there are many instances of the full quality prediction routines being used. Several case studies of applications of various urban models are described by Kibler (1982) and Whipple et al. (1983). Examples of analysis, data collection and implementation of controls are presented by

Lynard et al. (1980). A recent bibliography of SWMM usage (Huber et al., 1985) lists eleven references describing quality predictions during case studies (and many more without). A recent application of STORM for generation of pollutant loads for input to a receiving water model is described by Najarian et al. (1986). The USGS has applied its DR3M-QUAL to some of its NURP sites (EPA, 1983b). Modeling and statistical analysis has been a part of various FHWA projects dealing with highway runoff quality (Kobriger et al., 1981; Dever et al., 1983; Miracle, 1986). And the EPA statistical method (Hydroscience, 1979; Di Toro, 1984) has been applied as a screening tool for all of the EPA NURP sites that involved discharge to rivers and streams (EPA, 1983b).

In short, quality models are being used. However, the validity of the quality predictions (i.e., concentrations and loads) depends strongly on the availability of calibration and verification data. In instances where a model is used only to assess relative effects of, say, one control option versus another, the data requirements are not as severe (although still important). But if absolute values of concentrations are loads are required, the requirement for site-specific calibration and verification data is unavoidable.

Summary of Modeling Capabilities and Limitations

Standardized procedures (models) are available for assessment of urban runoff quality problems, ranging from statistical summaries of data to full-fledged simulation models. For application to a given site in a given city, all quality models require data for calibration and verification of predictions of concentrations and loads. Physically based models are able to assess the relative magnitude of changes with a somewhat less stringent need for site-specific data. However, it should be remembered that the effectiveness of controls depends heavily on the nature of the stormwater or combined sewage. That is, characterization data (e.g., particle sizes, settling velocities, etc.) are still necessary for assessment of controls even if the absolute magnitude of loads and concentrations is not required.

Quality predictions in simulation models are made in a variety of ways. The main advantage of methods that are ostensibly physically based (e.g., buildup and washoff) is in their ability to assess control measures on the land surface. The writer knows of no instance in which accurate predictions of concentrations and loads in stormwater effluent were made solely on the basis of measurements of surface loads of "dust and dirt" and/or associated pollutants. In other words, physically-based methods, such as they are, must still be calibrated. The lack of field research on fundamental physical, chemical and biological processes as they affect urban runoff quality has been noted (Sonnen, 1980; Heaney, 1986). On the other hand, primarily through the NURP activities, a massive urban quality data base now exists for model calibration. Improved parameter estimates may follow.

Conclusions

Many methods and several operational models are available to predict hydrographs, pollutographs and statistical parameters of urban runoff. Accurate predictions of concentrations and loads may be made by several techniques, given adequate data for calibration. On the other hand, there are probably no methods available for such purposes without such data, although relative magnitudes (due to various control options or changes) might be assessed. In some instances (scour and deposition) it is doubtful that even a "pure" representation of the physics would help the modeling effort due to the unknown nature of the solids being modeled. With site-specific data, however, various techniques can be calibrated. The large influx of urban runoff quality data should make this increasingly possible.

Acknowledgements

The writer is grateful for support from the U.S. Environmental Protection Agency for several projects related to urban hydrology and water quality and for continuing support from colleagues at the University of Florida and elsewhere, particularly, Dr. James P. Heaney.

References

1. Ackers, P., "Urban Drainage: The Effects of Sediment on Performance and Design Criteria," Proceedings of the International conference on Urban Storm Drainage, University of Southampton, Pentech Press, London, Apr. 1978, pp. 535-545.

2. Aldrich, J.A. and Roesner, L.A., "PC-RUNOFF and dBASE-III for Stormwater Data Management, Planning and Design," Proceedings of the Stormwater and Water Quality Model Users Group Meeting, Orlando, FL, EPA Report (in press), March 1986.

3. Alley, W.M. and Smith, P.E., "Multi-Event Urban Runoff Quality Model," USGS Open File Report 82-764, Reston, VA, 1982.

4. American Public Works Association, "Water Pollution Aspects of Urban Runoff," Federal Water Pollution Control Administration, Contract WP-20-15, Washington, DC, 1969.

5. Bedient, P.B., Lambert, J.L. and Machado, P., "Low Flow and Stormwater Quality in Urban Channels, Journal of the Environmental Engineering Division, ASCE, Vol. 106, No. EE2, Apr. 1980, pp. 421-436.

6. Benson, M.A., "Spurious Correlation in Hydraulics and Hydrology," Journal of the Hydraulics Division, ASCE, Vol. 91, No. HY4, July 1965, pp. 35-42.

7. Bontje, J.B., Ballantyne, I.K. and Adams, B.J., "User Interfacing Techniques for Interactive Hydrologic Models on Microcomputers," Proceedings of the Conference on Stormwater and Water Quality Management Modeling, Burlington, Ontario, Report R128, Computational Hydraulics, McMaster University, Hamilton, Ontario, Sept. 1984, pp. 75-89.

8. Boregowda, S., "Modeling Stormwater Pollutants in Hamilton, Canada," Ph.D. Thesis, Dept. of Civil Engineering, McMaster University, Hamilton, Ontario, Sept. 1984.

9. DeGroot, W., Ed., "Stormwater Detention Facilities," Proceedings of the Conference, Henniker, NH, American Society of Civil Engineers, New York, Aug. 1982.

10. Dever, R.J., Jr., Roesner, L.A. and Aldrich, J.A., "Urban Highway Storm Drainage Model, Vol. 4, Surface Runoff Program User's Manual and Documentation," FHWA/RD-83/044, Federal Highway Administration, Washington, DC, Dec. 1984.

11. Di Toro, D.M., "Probability Model of Stream Quality Due to Runoff," Journal of Environmental Engineering, ASCE, Vol. 110, No. 3, June

1984, pp. 607-628.
12. Donigian, A.S., Jr. and Davis, H.H., Jr., "User's Manual for Agricultural Runoff Management (ARM) Model," EPA-600/3-78-080, Environmental Protection Agency, Athens, GA, Aug. 1978.
13. Driscoll, E.D., in "Benefit Analysis for Combined Sewer Overflow Control," Seminar Publication, EPA-625/4-79-013, Environmental Protection Agency, Cincinnati, OH, Apr. 1979.
14. Driscoll, E.D., "Lognormality of Point and Non-point Source Pollutant Concentrations," Proceedings of the Stormwater and Water Quality Model Users Group Meeting, Orlando, FL, EPA Report (in press), March 1986.
15. Driscoll and Assoc., "Combined Sewer Overflow Analysis Handbook for Use in 201 Facility Planning," Report to EPA by E.D. Driscoll and Assoc., Oakland, NJ, July 1981.
16. Environmental Protection Agency, "Areawide Assessment Procedures Manual," Three Volumes, EPA-600/9-76-014, Environmental Protection Agency, Cincinnati, OH, July 1976.
17. Environmental Protection Agency, "EPA Environmental Data Base and Model Directory," Information Clearinghouse (PM 211A), Environmental Protection Agency, Washington, DC, July 1983a.
18. Environmental Protection Agency, "Results of the Nationwide Urban Runoff Program," NTIS PB84-185552, Environmental Protection Agency, Washington, DC, Dec. 1983b.
19. Ferrara, R.A. and Harleman, D.R.F., "Hydraulic Modeling for Waste Stabilization Ponds," Journal of the Environmental Engineering Division, ASCE, Vol. 107, No. EE4, Aug. 1981, pp. 817-830.
20. Ferrara, R.A. and Witkowski, P., "Stormwater Quality Characteristics in Detention Basins," Journal of Environmental Engineering, ASCE, Vol. 109, No. 2, Apr. 1983, pp. 428-447.
21. Field, R. and Struzelski, E.J., Jr., "Management and Control of Combined Sewer Overflows," Journal of the Water Pollution Control Federation, Vol. 44, No. 7, July 1972, pp. 1393-1415.
22. Field, R. and Turkeltaub, R., "Urban Runoff Impacts: Program Overview," Journal of the Environmental Engineering Division, ASCE, Vol. 107, No. EE1, Feb. 1981, pp. 83-100.
23. Geiger, W.F., "Characteristics of Combined Sewer Runoff," Proceedings of the Third International Conference on Urban Storm Drainage, Chalmers, University, Goteborg, Sweden, June 1984, Vol. 3, pp. 851-860.
24. Geiger, W.F. and Dorsch, H.R., "Quantity-Quality Simulation (QQS): A Detailed Continuous Planning Model for Urban Runoff Control, Volume I, Model Description, Testing, And Applications," EPA-600/2-80-011 (NTIS PB80-190507), Environmental Protection Agency, Cincinnati, OH, March 1980.
25. Heaney, J.P., "Research Needs in Urban Storm-Water Pollution," Journal of Water Resources Planning and Management, ASCE, Vol. 112, No. 1, Jan. 1986, pp. 33-47.
26. Heaney, J.P. and Huber, W.C., "Nationwide Assessment of Urban Runoff Impact on Receiving Water Quality," Water Resources Bulletin, Vol. 20, No. 1, Feb. 1984, pp. 35-42.
27. Heaney, J.P. and Miles, S.W., "Application of Lotus Spreadsheet for a SWMM Preprocessor," Proceedings of the Stormwater and Water Quality Model Users Group Meeting, Orlando, FL, EPA Report (in press), March 1986.
28. Huber, W.C., "Deterministic Modeling of Urban Runoff Quality," Proceedings of NATO Worshop on Urban Runoff Quality, Montpellier,

France, Springer-Verlag, Germany, Aug. 1985.

29. Huber, W.C. and Heaney, J.P., "Analyzing Residuals Discharge and Generation from Urban and Non-Urban Land Surfaces," in Analyzing Natural Systems, Analysis for Regional Residuals - Environmental Quality Management, D.J. Basta and B.T. Bower, Eds., EPA-600/3-83-046 (NTIS PB83-223321), Environmental Protection Agency, Washington, DC, June 1982, Chapter 3, pp. 121-243.

30. Huber, W.C., Heaney, J.P., Aggidis, D.A., Dickinson, R.E. and Wallace, R.W., "Urban Rainfall-Runoff-Quality Data Base," EPA-600/2-81-238 (NTIS PB82-221094), Environmental Protection Agency, Cincinnati, OH, Oct. 1981a.

31. Huber, W.C., Heaney, J.P. and Cunningham, F.A., "Stormwater Management Model (SWMM) Bibliography," NTIS PB86-136041/AS, Environmental Protection Agency, Athens, GA, Oct. 1981.

32. Huber, W.C., Heaney, J.P., Nix, S.J., Dickinson, R.E. and D.J. Polmann, "Storm Water Managment Model User's Manual, Version III," EPA-600/2-84-109a (NTIS PB84-198432), Environmental Protection Agency, Cincinnati, OH, Nov. 1981b.

33. Hydrologic Engineering Center, "Storage, Treatment, Overflow, Runoff Model, STORM, User's Manual," Generalized Computer Program 723-S8-L7520, Corps of Engineers, Davis, CA, Aug. 1977.

34. Hydroscience, Inc., "A Statistical Method for Assessment of Urban Stormwater Loads - Impacts- Controls," EPA-440/3-79-023, Environmental Protection Agency, Washington, DC, Jan. 1979.

35. James, W. and Robinson, M., "PCSWMM3 - Version 3 of the Executive, Runoff and Extended Transport Blocks, Adapted for the IBM-PC," Proceedings of the Conference on Stormwater and Water Quality Management Modeling, Burlington, Ontario, Report R128, Computational Hydraulics, McMaster University, Hamilton, Ontario, Sept. 1984, pp. 39-52.

36. Johanson, R.C., Imhoff, J.C. and Davis, H.H., Jr., "User's Manual for Hydrological Simulation Program - Fortran (HSPF)," EPA-600/9-80-015, Environmental Protection Agency, Athens, GA, Apr. 1980.

37. Kibler, D.F., Ed., Urban Stormwater Hydrology, American Geophysical Union, Monograph 7, Washington, DC, 1982.

38. Kluesner, J.W. and Lee, G.F., "Nutrient Loading from a Separate Storm Sewer in Madison, Wisconsin," Journal of the Water Pollution Control Federation, Vol. 46, No. 5, May 1974, pp. 920-936.

39. Kobriger, N.P., Meinholz, R.L., Gupta, M.K. and Agnew, R.W., "Constituents of Highway Runoff, Volume III, Predictive Procedure for Determining Pollution Characteristics in Highway Runoff," FHWA/RD-81/044 (NTIS PB81-241911), Federal Highway Administration, Washington, DC, Feb. 1981.

40. Lager, J.A., Smith, W.G. and Tchobanoglous, G., "Catchbasin Technology Overview and Assessment," EPA-600/2-77-051 (NTIS PB-270092), Environmental Protection Agency, Cincinnati, OH, May 1977.

41. Lynard, W.G., Finnemore, E.J., Loop, J.A. and Finn, R.M., "Urban Stormwater Management and Technology: Case Histories," EPA-600/8-80-035 (NTIS PB81-107153), Environmental Protection Agency, Cincinnati, OH, Aug. 1980.

42. Lumb, A.M. and Kittle, J.L., "ANNIE - An Interactive Processor for Hydrological Models," Proceedings of the Conference on Emerging Computer Techniques in Stormwater and Flood Management, Niagara-On-The-Lake, Ontario, November 1983, American Society of Civil Engineers, New York, pp. 352-365.

43. Manning, M.J., Sullivan, R.H. and Kipp, T.M., "Nationwide Evalua-

tion of Combined Sewer Overflows and Urban Stormwater Discharges - Vol.
III: Characterization of Discharges," EPA-600/2-77-064c (NTIS PB-
272107), Environmental Protection Agency, Cincinnati, OH, Aug. 1977.
    44. Mattraw, H.C., Jr. and Sherwood, C.B., "Quality of Storm Water
Runoff from a Residential Area, Broward County, Florida," Journal of
Research, U.S. Geological Survey, Vol. 5, No. 6, Nov.-Dec. 1977, pp.
823-834.
    45. McCuen, R.H., "Water Quality Trap Efficiency of Storm Water
Management Basins," Water Resources Bulletin, Vol. 16, No. 1, Feb. 1980,
pp. 15-21.
    46. McElroy, A.D., Chiu, S.Y., Nebgen, J.W., Aleti, A. and Bennett,
F.W., "Loading Functions for Assessment of Water Pollution from Non-
Point Sources," EPA-600/2-76-151 (NTIS PB-253325), Environmental Protection Agency, Washington, DC, May 1976.
    47. Medina, M.A., Jr., Huber, W.C. and Heaney, J.P., "Modeling Storm-
water Storage/Treatment Transients: Theory," Journal of the Environmental Engineering Division, ASCE, Vol. 107, No. EE4, Aug. 1981, pp. 781-
797.
    48. Metcalf and Eddy, Inc., University of Florida, and Water Resour-
ces Engineers, Inc., "Storm Water Management Model, Volume I - Final Report," EPA Report 11024DOC07/71 (NTIS PB-203289), Environmental Protection Agency, Washington, DC, July 1971.
    49. Meuller, J.A. and Di Toro, D.M., "Combined Sewer Overflow Charac-
teristics from Treatment Plant Data, "EPA-600/2-83-049 (NTIS PB83-
224543), Environmental Protection Agency, Cincinnati, OH, June 1983.
    50. Miller, R.A., Mattraw, H.C., Jr., and Jennings, M.E., "Statisti-
cal Modeling of Urban Storm Water Processes, Broward County, Florida,"
Proceedings of the International Symposium on Urban Storm Water Management, University of Kentucky, Lexington, July 1978, pp. 269-273.
    51. Miracle, D.L., "Review of Existing Methods for Predicting Pollu-
tant Loads from Highway Runoff," Publication of Florida Water Resources
Research Center, University of Florida, Gainesville, 1986.
    52. Najarian, T.O., Griffin, T.T. and Gunawardana, V.K., "Development
Impacts on Water Quality: A Case Study," Journal of Water Resources
Planning and Management, ASCE, Vol. 112, No. 1, Jan. 1986, pp. 20-35.
    53. Nakamura, E., "Factors Affecting Stormwater Quality Decay Coeffi-
cient," Proceedings of the Third International Conference on Urban Storm
Drainage, Chalmers University, Goteborg, Sweden, June 1984, Vol. 3, pp.
979-988.
    54. Nix, S.J., Heaney, J.P. and Huber, W.C., "Revised SWMM Storage/
Treatment Block," Proceedings of the Storm Water Managment Model Users
Group Meeting, Annapolis, MD, EPA-600/9-79-003 (NTIS PB-290742/6BE),
Environmental Protection Agency, Washington, DC, Nov. 1978.
    55. Pisano, W.C. and Queiroz, C.S., "Procedures for Estimating Dry
Weather Pollutant Deposition in Sewerage Systems," EPA-600/2-77-120
(NTIS PB-270695), Environmental Protection Agency, Cincinnati, OH, July
1977.
    56. Proctor and Redfern, Ltd. and J.F. MacLaren, Ltd., "Storm Water
Management Model Study - Vol. II, Technical Background," Research Report
No. 48, Canada-Ontario Agreement on Great Lakes Water Quality, Environ-
mental Protection Service, Environment Canada, Ottawa, Ontario, Sept.
1976.
    57. Randall, C.W., Grizzard, T.J., Helsel, D.R. and Griffin, D.M,
Jr., "Comparison of Pollutant Mass Loads in Precipitation and Runoff in
Urban Areas," Urban Stormwater Quality, Management and Planning, Pro-

ceedings of the Second International Conference on Urban Storm Drainage, Urbana, IL, Water Resources Publications, Littleton, CO, June 1981, pp. 29-38.

58. Robinson, M.A. and James. W., "Continuous Variable Resolution Stormwater Modelling on a Microcomputer," Proceedings of the Conference on Stormwater and Water Quality Management Modeling, Burlington, Ontario, Report R128, Computational Hydraulics, McMaster University, Hamilton, Ontario, Sept. 1984, pp. 59-73.

59. Roesner, L.A. and Dendrou, S.A., Discussion of "Probability Model of Stream Quality Due to Runoff," by D.M. Di Toro, Journal of Environmental Engineering, ASCE, Vol. 111, No. 5, Oct. 1985, pp. 738-740.

60. Roesner, L.A., Nichandros, H.M, Shubinski, R.P., Feldman, A.D., Abbott, J.W. and Friedland, A.O., "A Model for Evaluatin Runoff-Quality in Metropolitan Master Planning," ASCE Urban Water Resources Research Program Technical Memorandum No. 23 (NTIS PB-234312), American Society of Civil Engineers, New York, Apr. 1974.

61. Roesner, L.A., Shubinski, R.P. and Aldrich, J.A., "Storm Water Management Model User's Manual Version III: Addendum I, EXTRAN," EPA-600/2-84-109b (NTIS PB84-198431), Environmental Protection Agency, Cincinnati, OH, Nov. 1981.

62. Sartor, J.D. and Boyd, G.B., "Water Pollution Aspects of Street Surface Contaminants," EPA-R2-72-081 (NTIS PB-214408), Environmental Protection Agency, Cincinnati, OH, Sept. 1981.

63. Shen, H.W., "Some Basic Concepts on Sediment Transport in Urban Storm Drainage Systems," Urban Stormwater Quality, Management and Planning, Proceedings of the Second International Conference on Urban Storm Drainage, Urbana, IL, June 1981, Water Resources Publications, Littleton, CO, pp. 495-501.

64. Solomon, S.I. and Gupta, S.K., "Distributed Numerical Model for Estimating Runoff and Sediment Discharge of Ungaged Rivers 2. Model Development," Water Resources Research, Vol. 13, No. 3, June 1977, pp. 619-629.

65. Sonnen, M.B., "Abatement of Deposition and Scour in Sewers," EPA-600/2-77-212 (NTIS PB-276585), Environmental Protection Agency, Cincinnati, OH, Nov. 1977

66. Sonnen, M.B., "Urban Runoff Quality: Information Needs," Journal of the Technical Councils, ASCE, Vol. 106, No. TC1, Aug. 1980, pp. 29-40.

67. Wallace, R.C., "Statistical Modeling of Water Quality Parameters in Urban Runoff," Master of Engineering Technical Report (unpublished), Dept. of Environmental Engineering Sciences, University of Florida, Gainesville, 1980.

68. Whipple, W., Grigg, N.S., Grizzard, T., Randall, C.W., Shubinski, R.P. and Tucker, L.S., Stormwater Management in Urbanizing Areas, Prentice-Hall, Inc., Englewood Cliffs, NJ, 1983.

69. Yousef, Y.A., Wanielista, M.P., McLellon, W.M. and Taylor, J.S., Eds., "Urban Stormwater and Combined Sewer Overlfow Impact on Receiving Water Bodies," Proceedings of the National Conference, Orlando, Florida, November 1979, EPA-600/9-80-056 (NTIS PB81-155426), Environmental Protection Agency, Cincinnati, OH, Dec. 1980.

Physical and Chemical Data Needs for Design

J Bryan Ellis*

ABSTRACT

The problems and deficiencies in the existing characterisation
and evaluation of urban stormwater runoff quality are examined through
discussion of adopted and proposed design criteria intended for
pollution control enhancement of the sewerage system. Conversion of
rainfall to sewer inflow is dependent on the selection of an appropriate storm intensity and return period and the potential benefits are
identified of including cost optimisation approaches for the quantification of damage functions in the chosen design criteria. The
pollutional significance of further refinements of initial losses on
design inflow volumes is discussed together with the potential extent
and effect of sediment deposition on the quality performance of the
sewer system. The need for appropriate design criteria and supporting hydrological and geochemical data to help resolve identified
deficiences and in up-grading measurement technology is emphasised and
suggestions made for further practical actions to realise urban water
quality enhancements.

INTRODUCTION

The urban sewered network is fundamentally designed for the rapid
and efficient hydraulic conveyance of stormwater runoff and, apart
from a basic and somewhat limited consideration of self-cleansing
velocity, does not incorporate any quality criteria in the design or
performance terms. This exclusion would appear to be shortsighted
given that transient non-point sources, which operate only some 2-6%
of the time, are alleged to be responsible for between 20 to 50% of
the total annual pollutant load to the receiving stream (Yousef et
al., 1980; Ellis, 1986). It is also undoubtedly true that most urban
water bodies are severely quality limited in terms of potential water
uses. However, there is an increasing awareness of and sensitivity to
uncontrolled, untreated wet-weather discharges within urban catchments
and a growing demand for the development of working methodologies for
evaluating receiving stream impacts from intermittent, non-point
discharges which might be feasibly utilised in project design and
appraisal. It is nevertheless true that many deficiencies still exist
in our corporate knowledge and understanding of the pattern and
process of pollutant routing and delivery through the sewerage system.
In particular, there are fundamental measurement gaps which currently

*Head of the Urban Pollution Research Centre, Middlesex Polytechnic,
Queensway, Enfield, London, EN3 4SF, UK.

prevent or limit the application of quality criteria in evaluating
system performance and efficiency in design terms.

INITIAL CONSIDERATIONS FOR QUALITY IMPACT DESIGN

Even if it could be incontrovertibly demonstrated that detailed
knowledge of urban runoff quality would not necessarily lead to an
improved sewer design protocol, it must be admitted that planning for
the control of urban water quality requires the ability to specify
water quality criteria (or dose-effect relationships) and to forecast
water quality improvements that might result from proposed mitigating
developments. Therefore, whilst extensive documentation exists within
US EPA, WHO or EEC Directives on the effects of quality characteristics on and criteria for the suitability of water for given uses, the
number of characteristics, their potential interactions and the target
organisms they affect are so varied and numerous that knowledge in
some areas is inevitably sparse. Much more is known about the acute
toxicity of pollutants than about their sub-lethal longer term effects
and there is a dearth of methods by which such effects can be inferred
from tests of acceptably short duration. It is not clear for example
how the results of the Ames test can be used to assess maximum acceptable concentrations. A new generation of methods needs to be developed to evaluate the persistent, chronic toxicity effects of urban
runoff. This might be achieved through the assessment of potential
pollutional stress in terms of particular physiological cell activity
and response or through exposure tests using synthetic resins which
can mimic pollutant diffusion across the cell membrane.

In a similar manner, the immediate water quality impacts of
wet-weather flows have received considerable attention in comparison
to the undefined, longer term delayed impacts resulting from the
resuspension and mobilisation of in-pipe (and in-stream) deposits of
contaminated runoff sediments. The results of the US EPA Nationwide
Urban Runoff Program (Torno, 1984), necessarily and singularly failed
to identify or recognise this potential longer term impact and
recovery problem.

This is a pervasive professional requirement and pressure to
address only those recognisable problems which are known or expected
to be significant in affecting the design criteria or in improving
measurement technology. Practical operational realities and
continuing financial constraints, often coupled with lack of manpower
and expanding job remits, are powerful arguments for rationalisation
and strict targeting of objectives. The expressed concern of bioenvironmental scientists for a more thorough understanding of such
mechanisms as the translocational or transformational pollutant
process through and between the sediment and water phases receives
short shrift from the professional engineer. Such processes
nevertheless, do have specific relevance for the quality performance
and operational efficiency of many conventional engineering structures
and a specification of quality criteria could well lead to improved
cost-effective investment ratios and enhance their public and
institutional acceptibility.

Sewer performance might additionally be evaluated through consideration of public health/flooding aspects but such an approach,as
in the case of structural upgrading, must apply cost-effective rather
than cost-benefit rationale as the latter equations are dominated by
difficult and contentious intangibles. The dimensioning of engineering controls might be improved through the identification and
determination of:

- quality based 'damage' functions
- efficient biomonitoring techniques and biological exposure times
- pollutant performance and efficiencies under design conditions for
  structures such as on-line storage tanks, overflows, detention
  ponds etc.,
- economic balance between various municipal pollution control
  operations such as sweeping, gully and sewer cleansing.
- pollutant routing and phase interactions within hydraulic
  structures.
- relations between changes in non-point pollutant discharges to
  stream recovery rates.
- exceedance values for impairment of beneficial urban water uses.

All of these areas involve physico-chemical considerations which have
implications, interactions and impacts with hydraulic design parameters. 'Correct' dimensioning and design of hydraulic and structural
performance needs to identify the location and causes of system deterioration and deficiency and incorporate where relevant quality measurements and criteria in the establishment of cost effective solutions.
It is within the context of system deficiency deterioration and impairment that stormwater runoff quality problems must be defined and
quantified if they are to be of use to public as well as to operational management and to the decision making process.

STORM EVENT - SEWER INFLOW DESIGN PARAMETERS

Pollutant washoff from impermeable urban surfaces, as well as
sediment entrainment, transport and re-working of adsorbed pollutants
below ground, is primarily a function of flow rate. The flowpaths
followed by stormwater runoff pollutants from source through
(temporary) sinks within the system to sewer outfall or overflow have
been summarised in numerous system diagrams such as those included in
Hall and Ellis (1985) or Geiger (1986). Considerable improvement in
existing design procedures might be achieved through a better understanding and definition of the rainfall-runoff-inflow process and its
influence on pollutant mass flows between the surface components of
the urban drainage system. The selection of an appropriate storm
intensity and return period and sewer inflow volume is of prime
importance in deciding on the final design of the pipe system and will
inevitably have implications for pollutant accumulation and routing.

Design Storm Interval

Application of the so-called WASSP-SIM or Wallingford Procedure

(DoE/NWC, 1981) now in fairly widespread use in the UK, shows that if
a return period of two years is varied down to one year or up to five
years, the effect is to decrease or increase the design flow
respectively by about 20%. The corresponding capital cost effect is
around 9/10%. The return period is ultimately chosen in relation to
catchment characteristics with the economic analysis finding the
lowest total (sewer + flood damage) cost. The existing level of performance (RI) - cost approach is fundamentally flawed in that it is
impossible to judge value for money when there is no minimum value
available for selection as the optimum choice of total costs for a
range of sewer performance levels. When considering the cost of extra
protection, the decision maker has to ask what it will buy in the way
of extra cost effectiveness. The answer must surely lie in extra
quality and flood protection and so in reduced 'damage' costs.   The
inclusion of pollutional cost valuations within overall flood damage
costs would allow an aggregation with sewer costs to derive total
costs for given return periods and location of their economic minima
(Fig. 1).

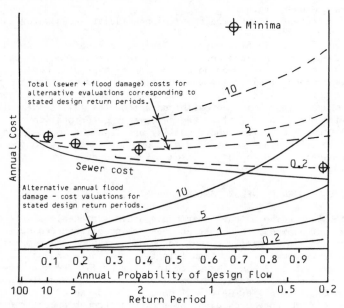

Figure 1.   Identification of Optimum Design

     Replacement of annual by total capital cost on the ordinate
would also allow the damage cost curve for a particular return period
and design flow probability to be assessed against graphed sewer
replacement or renovation cost curves - or even perhaps against
source control cost curves - thus enabling comparison of various rehabilitation and control options. A decision making matrix approach
combining flow conditions against allocated design return periods for
stated levels of risk/damage based on known or expected catchment
characteristics would improve the existing rather vaguely defined and
subjective criteria. Research intended to measure quality costings

and to widen the damage cost range in current system design criteria
would certainly help in the establishment of acceptable standards of
performance for sewerage systems. Therefore there would seem to be
considerable potential benefits in developing quality and public
health damage functions, using real rather than the relative costs
indicated in the general model presented above. At the very least it
would enable fine-tuning of designs through marginal optimisation to
eliminate such deficiencies as uneconomic throttle and flushing
points, overcapacity and deposition areas, rogue manhole surcharging,
all of which are out of line with the general system performance.

A source control approach to both the quality and flood problem
which works from an acceptance of some specified frequency of street
flooding (perhaps in residential and other low activity urban areas),
would also appear to be worthy of more detailed consideration.
Whilst accepting that the time of concentration is probably more
significant for the frequency of street flooding than the design
rainfall intensity, what is the lowest minimum design intensity
acceptable and what will be the effective storage depths between
pavement edges for given intensities and return periods but which
will not lead to basement flooding? What cost, maintenance and
social implications would such a design approach have for municipal
authorities and for their street cleaning operations? A cost
optimised system might be identified for any selected set of design
values allowing systems to be compared on the same basis.

Surface Losses and Design Inflow Volumes

There is an increasing confirmation and professional recognition
that initial rainfall losses over urban catchments can be very high
(Voortman, 1984; Ellis, Harrop and Revitt, 1986). Generalised depression storage relationships used in the WASSP-SIM model can
underestimate initial loss by up to 60% as well as overestimating
peak design volumes and predicting illusory early peak flows in the
storm profile. The introduction of such anomolies into design flow
behaviour will again have implications and knock-on effects for runoff quality parameters. The conversion of rainfall to sewer inflow
requires a further refinement of heat flux loss determinations for
urban surfaces. First order approximations for residential areas
using a modified Penman equation, would suggest that Eo can be 0.5 -
1.0 mm during summer periods, which would average to some 100 - 150
mm/yr for a W. European situation.

However, the predominant initial losses result from infiltration
which can account for 30 - 50% of the incoming precipitation volume.
Infiltration capacities for paved surfaces of between 5 - 20 mm/hr.
are quoted in recent literature with the rate varying linearly with
storm duration. When cumulative wetting and infiltration are sub-
tracted from cumulative precipitation, the resultant storage and
runoff volumes will inevitably be highly variable through the storm
event. What is the effect of such variations on the amount and form
of pollutants delivered as dissolved and adsorbed species to the
roadside sewer inlet? The sensitivity of the so-called pollutant
'availability factors' included within operational quality models
such as SWMM, STORM, DR3M-QUAL or FHWA to fluctuating losses and

water depths over the surface would certainly repay measurement in
this context. Comparison of the probability distributions of runoff
coefficients for differing storm profiles and surface types might
also help in the decoding of this rainfall-inflow transformation.

It is undoubtedly clear that inflow rather than rainfall data
should be used for determining the design storm as inflow depths can
be 20 - 70% smaller than comparable rainfall depths; the largest
differences occurring at short time intervals. However, the whole
field of initial losses and their quality implications requires
further attention, including the neglected issue of resuspension and
its effects upon and relations to conventional buildup rate equations. Finally, would inclusion of total initial losses lead to any
reduction of the theoretical overflow frequency and if it does, what
are the implications for this in terms of construction costs? What
would be the effects on storage capacity in the sewer system and on
'actual' overflow frequency?

The property of surface infiltration can potentially be of
advantage in terms of source pollution control as well as in attenuation of peak flows. The large scale use of permeable surfacing
materials still remains to be thoroughly tested. Pilot tests in
Scandinavia using a geotextile layer under a macadam bed which is
capped by pervious asphalt, have yielded encouraging results (Hogland
and Niemczynowicz, 1986) but the longer term problems of durability
to traffic loads, infiltration capacities, clogging, maintenance
procedures, groundwater pollution risks etc., need to be evaluated
against the possible long term benefits. It is my impression that
the substantial European belief in the potential quality control
effectiveness of porous surfacing is not shared or endorsed by
American experience although specific data is difficult to find.

IN-PIPE DEPOSITION AND SEWER DESIGN

The effects of subsurface sediment deposition and their pollutional consequences and impacts upon the sewer system performance has
long been a cause for concern but remains largely unresolved. The
sewer system is still very much a 'black box' as far as the nature,
form and strength of in-line pollution potential is concerned. It
may be that the issue has been over-emphasised simply through a basic
lack of knowledge but the extent of the 'problem' together with
possible remedies, needs to be urgently identified.

The effects of sediment deposition on hydraulic sewer
performance has received attention (Sonnen, 1977; Ackers, 1984) and
Figure 2 shows that for a sediment depth of about 30% the pipe full
discharge is roughly halved. This reduction in capacity for what
are only relatively modest increases in sediment depth is often the
explanation for hydraulic overloading of the system and for premature
overflow operation. It is also the resuspension and mobilisation of
these contaminated, cohesive sediments which is most probably
responsible for the pronounced 'first-foul flush' commonly observed
at sewer overflows and outfalls (Fig. 3) yet the geochemistry and

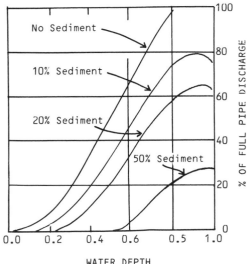

WATER DEPTH
(Proportion to Full Depth)

Figure 2. Pipe Flow
Reduction as a result
of Sediment Infill.

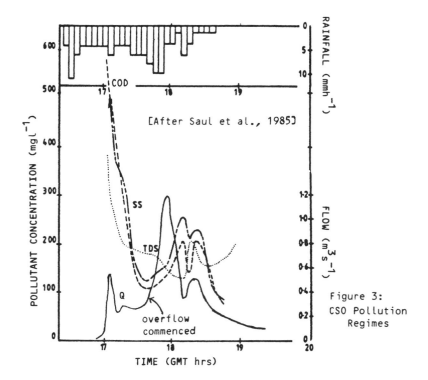

[After Saul et al., 1985]

Figure 3:
CSO Pollution
Regimes

TIME (GMT hrs)

transport mechanics of these sediment mats which accumulate on the
sewer invert are poorly understood. A better knowledge of the
sources, nature and behaviour of both solids and adsorbed pollutants
that are deposited within the sewer system is urgently needed if
progress is to be made towards identifying measures required to deal
with the problem.

   Given an empirical self-cleansing velocity of 0.7 - 0.9 m/s,
Ackers (1984) has shown that for pipe sizes above 750 mm diameter,
the requirements of the sediment transport capacity dictate the
design and steeper sewer gradients are necessary to achieve self-
cleansing velocities e.g. 1.2 times steeper for a 20/30% sediment
depth. However, the proposed design approaches only take into
account solids concentrations of up to 200 mg/l and particle
diameters of the order of 0.4 mm. The design implications of the
very much higher concentrations and agglomerated sizes typically
encountered during wet-weather flows still need to be worked out,
especially for older, oversized sewers with flat gradients and low
velocities. It may be that there is little hope of achieving
significant reductions in sedimentation within such older systems
except at prohibitively high cost, but there is still a need to
develop methods for rationalising operation and maintenance pro-
grammes which will result in a better use of existing resources.

   One area which has been largely ignored in urban water quality
hydrology is the vexed question of required overflow frequency and
the relation of such frequency to receiving water quality and to the
specification of water quality objectives. The differences in design
guidelines for overflow frequency adopted throughout Europe for example reflect national tradition and cannot be explained on the
grounds of national situation. Whatever these differences might be,
what would be the effect of fixing lowest allowable design criteria
on the quality performance of various overflows and in any case is
overflow frequency a design parameter that will allow an estimation
of CSO effects on surface waters?

   It is clear that the frequency of overflow operation is often
very much greater than that of the design storm and quality modelling
needs to consider this fact. It is equally apparent that the concept
of a single design storm does not give a clear indication of system
performance and the effective design of control structures such as
storage chambers must take into consideration time series rainfall
events as well as temporal variation in pollutant loadings. The
current subjective approach to the design calculation of storage
volumes in sewerage systems is certainly in need of revision if the
quality performance of overflows is to be improved.

   The nature of the biogeochemical processes operating below
ground which result in the production of septic, toxic sediments also
needs to be addressed through a combination of theoretical,
laboratory and field studies. The phase interactions and
mobilisation of pollutants at the kerbside-gullypot interface has
received some attention. Morrison et al (1986) have identified the
mechanisms by which pH, surface area, ionic strength and organic
carbon control the enrichment, mobilisation and bioavailability of

heavy metals delivered to and contained within roadside gully
chambers. This work certainly improves our understanding of the
controlling geochemical processes and provides a modelling approach
for the determination of toxic equilibrium conditions. Nevertheless
there is still a need to fully relate these mechanisms to storm and
hydraulic design parameters such as channel gradients, gully spacing
and size, as well as to set absolute standards for sweeping or gully
emptying; it is important to have known standard requirements which
can be monitored.

There is however, very little data available which relates to
in-pipe quality characteristics, their temporal variability or
hydraulic design criteria apart from limited information on size,
compositional and physical characteristics of suspended solids and
bacterial sludges found in separate sewers (Ellis, Hamilton and
Roberts, 1982). The organic, bacterially slimed and agglomerated
sediments which accumulate under oxygen deficient, reducing conditions below ground have received very little attention. Not only is
there a need to examine their effect on hydraulic roughness under
differing flow depths as well as changes in resistance brought about
by increases in sediment transport but there is also an urgent need
to develop adequate theory in respect of cohesive sewer sediment.
Existing theory is applicable only to non-cohesive particulate
materials and other sediment criteria such as sliming, septicity and
cohesion may well have important effects on design and pollution
control limits such as gradient, pipe size, first flush or overflow
quality efficiency.

It is only possible to speculate about the biogeochemical
processes operating both within the sewer sediment as well as at the
sediment-water interface. What is the exact nature and pollutional
significance of the ternary complex of available ions with the
amorphous, surface hydroxyl groups, with the ions simultaneously
interacting with natural humic ligands? The complexation is not
only dependent upon the conditional stability constants and concentrations of the reacting species but also upon the pH adsorption
edge, ionic strength and relative abundance of competing ions. The
properties and functions of polyelectrolyte-like humics in the
complexation of carcinogenic organics and toxic metal cations, which
seems effective even in the presence of high excesses of competing
ions, would seem to be well worthy of further study. The adsoprtion
properties of organic micropollutants have been primarily related to
the octanol-water partition coefficients and organic content of
specific sediment size fractions. However, there is growing evidence
that dissolved organic carbon/matter should be taken into account to
predict adsorption-desorption processes and it would be interesting
to see such considerations incorporated within toxic models such as
TOXIWASP or HSPF. The transformation of species within the
interstitial pore waters of the sedimented redox sequence is another
area requiring investigation. Are pollutant fluxes for example
determined by pore water precipitation - dissolution processes or by
adsorption - desorption phenomena? It is undoubtedly possible to
substantially improve our existing scant information and knowledge of
the partitioning, kinetics and transformational mechanisms of these
aspects of transport and sediment phenomenology. The availability of

good, thorough data on in-pipe sediment quality would certainly help
in the formulation, calibration and testing of efficient modelling
techniques for pollution control and sewer design.

WHAT GOES ON DOWN THERE?

The major limitations preventing an adequate evaluation of the
cost-effectiveness and performance efficiency of pollution control
structures in urban sewerage systems arise from the paucity of field
information about in-pipe conditions and their operational quality
controls during wet weather flow. A number of refinements and
possible approaches to the analysis of surface quality reservoirs
have been suggested, particularly those relating to the identification and enumeration of pollution damage functions and initial
losses. However, data information needs on pollutant transformations and pathways within the system remain the outstanding
priority. They are essential if the design performance and 'correct'
dimensioning of urban engineering structures, in water quality terms,
are to be evaluated and improved. In addition, it is the mobility
and bioavailabiliy of the pollutants in and between the sediment
water system that will determine their ecological and receiving
stream significance rather than their accumulative loading behaviour.

Therefore a better understanding of the physical and biogeochemical processes and their relations to hydraulic design criteria
and prevailing operational and catchment conditions is urgently
needed. This will only come about through the development of
integrated water quality models which utilise the expertise and
evidence of bioenvironmental scientists as well as the engineer. It
will not be cost-effectively achieved through repeated measurements
of truth about the runoff constituents themselves or through isolated
hydraulic analysis of potential control structures.

APPENDIX 1 - REFERENCES

Ackers, P., "Sediment Transport in Sewers and the Design Implicat-
ions". Planning, Construction, Maintenance and Operation of Sewerage
Systems, British Hydrodynamic Research Assoc., Cranfield, Bedford,
UK, 1984. 215-230.

Department of the Environment/National Water Council. "Design and
Analysis of Urban Storm Drainage - The Wallingford Procedure,"
DoE/NWC Standing Technical Committee, Report No. 29, HMSO, London,
1981.

Ellis, J.B., "Pollutional Aspects of Urban Runoff," Urban Runoff
Quality, H. C. Torno, J. Marsalek and M. Desbordes, eds., Springer-
Verlag, Heidelberg, 1986, 1-34.

Ellis, J.B., Hamilton, R.S. and Roberts, A.H., "Sedimentary
characteristics of suspensions in London Stormwater," Sediment.
Geology, 33, 1982, pp. 147-154.

Ellis, J.B., Harrop, D.O. and Revitt, D.M., "Hydrological Controls of
Pollutant Removal from Highway Surfaces," Water Research, 21, 1986.
(In Press).

Geiger, W.F., "Use of Field Data in Urban Drainage Planning," Urban
Runoff Quality, H.C. Torno, J. Marsalek and M. Desbordes, eds.,
Springer-Verlag, Heidelberg, 1986.

Hall, M.J. and Ellis, J.B., "Water Quality Problems of Urban Areas,"
Geojournal, 11 (3), 1985, pp. 265-275.

Hogland, W. and Niemczynowicz,J., "The Unit Superstructure During the
Construction Period," Science Total Environ., 49, 1986. (In Press).

Morrison, G.M.P., Revitt, D.M., Ellis, J.B. and Balmer, P.,
"Pollutant Transport Mechanisms and Processes in Roadside Gullypot
Systems," Env., Science & Tech., 21, 1986. (In Press).

Saul, A.J., Thornton, R.C. and Henderson, R.J., "The Flood Control
Characteristics of a Storage Volume in a Sewer System based on Field
Measurements and Computer Simulation," Hydraulics of Floods and
Flood Control, British Hydrodynamics Research Assoc., Cranfield,
Bedford, UK., 1985. pp 193-204.

Sonnen, M., "Abatement of Deposition and Scour in Sewers"," EPA
600/2-77-212, Env. Prot. Agency., Cincinatti, Ohio, 1977.

Torno, H.C., "The Nationwide Urban Runoff Program," Urban Storm
Drainage, Vol IV, P Balmer., P-A Malmquist and A. Sjoberg, eds.,
Chalmers Univ. Tech., Gothenburg, Sweden, 1984, 1465-1474.

Voortman, B.R., "The Monthly Water Balance of a Housing Area and a
Parking Lot in Lelystad," RIJP Report 35., Ijsselmeerpolders Dev.
Auth., Lelystad, Netherlands, 1984.

Yousef, A.Y., Wanielista, M.P., McLellon, S.M. and Taylor, J.S.
"Urban Stormwater and Combined Sewer Overflow Impact on Receiving
Water Bodies," eds., Proc. of National Conference, Orlando,Florida.
EPA 600/9/-80-056, EPA, Cincinatti, Ohio, 1980.

Toxicology and Chemistry of Metals in Urban Runoff

Patrick H. Davies*

ABSTRACT

The toxicity of metals to aquatic life is affected by a number of factors. Water quality characteristics such as inorganic and organic ligands, pH, and water hardness will reduce the toxicity of metals through different chemical or physiological mechanisms. Increases in water temperature tends to increase the toxic response of organisms. The roles of alkalinity, i.e. the bicarbonate-carbonate system, and water hardness in ameliorating acute and chronic toxicities of metals are discussed.

Factors such as organism sensitivity and life stage, ability to acclimate, and length of exposure also affect the toxicological responses of organisms to metals. Generally smaller organisms are more susceptible to metal impacts and, as the period of exposure increases, so will the toxic response. Embryonically exposed fish, i.e. during the egg stage of development, will acclimate to some metals and become less sensitive to the effects of metals than fish not embryonically exposed. Factors regulating the bioavailability of different metal forms, chemical equilibria, and chemical kinetics are discussed at length regarding the roles they play in affecting the toxicity of metals. Generally, it is the ionic fraction of metals that is toxic to aquatic life. This fraction can be profoundly affected by factors influencing chemical reaction rates and equilibria.

A discussion is given on different analytical methodologies and their appropriateness in measuring metal concentrations to assess potentially toxic impacts on aquatic life in natural waters. Recommendations are made regarding procedures and methods for measuring metal concentrations in urban run-off waters.

Introduction

The toxicity of metals to aquatic life is affected by a number of factors including various water quality characteristics, sensitivity and life stage of aquatic organisms, ability to acclimate to toxicants, time of exposure, and the bioavailability of metals as regulated by chemical equilibria and kinetics.

*Aquatic Toxicologist and Chemist, Colorado Division of Wildlife, 317 W. Prospect, Fort Collins, CO 80526. Supported in part by Federal Aid in Wildlife Restoration (Dingell-Johnson F-33-R).

Water Quality Characteristics

The water quality characteristics, which generally affect the toxicity of metals to aquatic life in natural waters include pH, inorganic and organic ligands, water hardness, and temperature. The role of naturally occurring organic ligands, such as humic substances, has not been studied very well, but with some metals, toxicity decreases with increased organic matter. Increases in pH, alkalinity, and water hardness have been found to decrease the toxicity of metals (Table 1). As water temperature increases, metal toxicity generally increases as a result of both increased chemical activity, and metabolism of the organism (Table 2).

Table 1. Effect of hardness and alkalinity on the acute
toxicity of zinc to rainbow trout of similar size[a].

Hardness mg/l	Alkalinity mg/l	96 hr LC50 mg/l
315	227	7.21
102	81	1.00
23	20	0.56

[a]Goettl et al. 1971.

Table 2. Effect of water temperature on the acute toxicity of
zinc to rainbow trout in soft water[a].

Temperature C	96 hr LC50 mg/l
6	0.83
10	0.41
15	0.24

[a]Goettl et al. 1971.

Alkalinity vs Hardness

Inorganic and organic ligands control the ability of natural waters to bind or tie-up metals, thereby controlling the bioavailability of metals which could potentially impact aquatic life. This ability to bind metals is defined in terms of the complexing capacity of a particular water. Complexing of metals by inorganic ligands in natural waters is primarily controlled by pH and the bicarbonate-carbonate system which is frequently measured by alkalinity determinations.

In most natural waters there exists a close relationship between alkalinity and water hardness. Whereas, alkalinity is a measurement of the bicarbonate-carbonate system, hardness is a measure of primarily the presence of calcium and magnesium ions. Alkalinity and hardness are expressed in terms of calcium carbonate ($CaCO_3$); hence, their paired relationship in natural waters.

From the standpoint of controlling the bioavailability of metals, water hardness does not play a role. Hardness, however, does play a role in reducing the toxicity of metals because of what has been termed as antagonistic mechanisms. The presence of calcium and magnesium is antagonistic to the uptake of toxic metals at the gill surface probably as a result of competition for uptake sites, such that the uptake of metals through the gills is reduced.

Hardness antagonism has been referenced for a number of years from toxicity tests which have shown decreased toxicity of some metals with increased water hardness. However, most of these tests have not distinguished between reduced toxicity resulting from increased hardness as opposed to reductions in toxicity occurring from increased complexation of metals by carbonate ligands.

Acute toxicity tests have been conducted in water of low carbonates, i.e. alkalinity, at increasing levels of calcium, i.e. hardness, and have demonstrated antagonistic properties of hardness to the acute (short-term) toxicity of zinc to fathead minnows (Judy and Davies, 1979). Acute toxicity is generally defined in terms of an LC50, i.e. a concentration lethal to 50% of the test organisms in a defined period of time. A question has existed as to whether the antagonistic mechanisms of hardness in acute tests would continue under conditions of long-term exposure or, would the long-term uptake of toxic metals eventually reach a point where toxic impacts would occur? Recent chronic, i.e. long-term, toxicity tests conducted at low alkalinity and increasing levels of hardness with rainbow trout exposed to cadmium have demonstrated only slight long-term antagonistic properties of water hardness, showing approximately a two-fold decrease in chronic toxicity between hardnesses of 50 and 400 mg/liter with chronic values of 1.4 versus 3.5 µg/liter, respectively (Table 3). These data indicate that use by EPA of water hardness as a means of relating acute and chronic toxicity to the complexing capacity of water may not be appropriate for developing criteria in low alkaline waters of elevated water hardness. In such waters the regression of toxicity on alkalinity would be more appropriate.

Sensitivity of Aquatic Life

The sensitivity of aquatic organisms to the toxicity of metals is highly varied depending on the species, life stage, and a particular metal. Some fish, both cold and warm water species, such as rainbow trout and fathead minnows, and cladocerans, such as Daphnia magna, are highly sensitive to metals. Macroinvertebrates on the other hand are generally insensitive. There are, however, no consistent "rules of thumb" since for both fish and invertebrate species alike, one may be particularly sensitive to a particular metal and not another. Generally smaller, i.e. younger, organisms in their earlier stages of development are more sensitive to the toxic effects of metals than are older, adult organisms (Table 4).

Table 3. Long-term effect of water hardness (as magnesium sulfate) on cadmium toxicity to rainbow trout in low alkaline waters.

Item	Exposures					
	1	2	3	4	5	C

Hardness - 400 mg/l, Alkalinity - 30 mg/l

Hardness	383	413	437	410	423	401 & 45
Cd, µg/l	16.6	8.4	5.0	2.5	1.5	< .5 < .5
% mortality	100	75.0	42.5 --- 0.0	0.0		0.0 0.0

*Chronic value - 3.5 µg/l[a]

Hardness - 200 mg/l, Alkalinity - 30 mg/l

Hardness	206	203	216	219	240	200 & 43
Cd, µg/l	16.4	8.4	5.2	2.5	1.2	< .5 < .5
% mortality	100	62.5	25.0 --- 2.5 --- 2.5			0.0 0.0

*Chronic value - 3.6 or 1.7 µg/l[a]

Hardness - 50 mg/l, Alkalinity - 30 mg/l

Hardness	46	45	47	46	45	47 & 40
Cd, µg/l	5.9	3.1	1.7	1.2	0.6	0.3 0.3
% mortality	100	40.0	7.5 --- 0.0	0.0		0.0 0.0

*Chronic value - 1.4 µg/l[a]

[a]A chronic value is calculated as a geometric mean of the no-effect/effect limits.

Table 4. Effect of fish size on the acute toxicity of zinc to rainbow trout in hard water at a temperature of 15C[a].

Length cm	Weight g	96 hr LC50 mg/l
11.9	18.3	4.52
5.6	2.0	1.19

[a]Goettl et al. 1971.

Acclimation

Research has shown that fish exposed to some metals during their embryonic stage of development have an ability to acclimate (Sinley, et al. 1974, Goettl and Davies 1976). Rainbow trout exposed embryonically to cadmium and zinc, under laboratory conditions, became acclimated, such that fish exposed during the egg stage can withstand higher concentrations without adverse effects than fish not embryonically exposed. The no-effect/effect range for fish embryonically exposed to cadmium was 3.4-7.1 µg/liter as opposed to a range of 0.7-1.5 µg/liter for fish not exposed as embryos (Table 5). The no-effect/effect ranges for rainbow trout exposed to zinc were

non-embryonically exposed fish, respectively (Table 6). In each case, acclimation provided approximately a four-fold (4X) decrease in sensitivity.

Table 5. Long-term toxicity of cadmium to rainbow trout for embryonic-cally exposed and non-exposed embryos in soft water.

Item	Exposures					
	1	2	3	4	5	C
		Eggs Exposed				
Percent mortality	43.2	6.6	4.7	2.5	2.1	2.5
Cd, μg/l	7.1 ↑	3.4	1.7	0.9	0.5	0.0
		no-effect/effect range				
		Eggs not Exposed				
Percent mortality	95	35	10	0	0	0
Cd, μg/l	5.6	2.7	1.5 ↑	0.7	0.4	0.0
			no-effect/effect range			

Table 6. Long-term toxicity of zinc to rainbow trout for embryonically exposed and non-exposed embryos in soft water[a].

Item	Exposure					
	1	2	3	4	5	6
		Eggs exposed				
Percent mortality	63.3	24.3	14.5	14.5	14.1	13.0
Zn, μg/l	547	260 ↑	140	71	36	11
		no-effect/effect range				
		Eggs not exposed				
Percent mortality	100	83	59	8	1	0
Zn, μg/l	547	260	140	71 ↑	36	11
				no-effect/effect range		

[a]Sinley et al. 1974.

Field testing of this embryonic acclimation phenomenon was performed in Georgetown Reservoir, a lake contaminated with 207 μg/liter of zinc from abandoned mine drainage. Eyed eggs were hatched and reared in the laboratory for 17 weeks in soft water (20 mg/liter alkalinity, as $CaCO_3$) containing a mean concentration of 478 μg/liter zinc. Eggs were also hatched and reared in a similar water containing an ambient zinc concentration of 16 μg/liter, to which no zinc was added.

In situ, bioassays were conducted with 25 zinc-acclimated fingerlings, which had been previously marked by an adipose clip; and 25 unacclimated, unmarked fingerlings in each of two almuminum cages suspended at one meter in the reservoir. Sixty-six percent of the unacclimated fish died within the first 4 days of a 14-day test period. No deaths occurred among the acclimated rainbow trout. Approximately 1,600 zinc-acclimated, adipose clipped fingerlings and 700 unacclimated, unmarked fingerlings with an average weight of 1.1 g were released to the reservoir following the bioassays. A year later two 125-feet experimental gillnets, set for 24 hours, recovered eight zinc-acclimated, adipose clipped rainbow trout with a mean weight and length of 62 g and 178 mm, respectively. No unacclimated, unmarked rainbow trout were recovered.

Additional research has shown that embryonic acclimation does not occur with all metals such as lead and silver. Also, such acclimation as resulted from embryonic exposure to cadmium and zinc in a low alkaline, soft water did not occur from embryonic exposure in more alkaline, harder waters. Other research has shown an ability of fish to acclimate to some metals when exposed to sub-lethal concentrations. However, this relationship has not been well defined.

Period of Exposure

Length of exposure of aquatic life to various metal concentrations affects the toxic response. Generally as the time of exposure increases, toxic effects from metals will be observed at lower concentrations (Table 7). Acute, short-term responses are generally defined in a time period of 24-96 hours. Acutely lethal effects to metals usually result from suffocation wherein oxygen can not be taken up by the gills due to a destruction or separation of the gill epithelium. Long-term, chronic effects of metals on aquatic life may take from a week to a year or more before being expressed. Such effects may be seen as long drawn out lethality, effects on reproduction and/or growth, and/or the development of physical or behavioral abnormalities, all of which result from some breakdown in physiological metabolism and other biochemical functions.

Table 7. Effect of exposure period on the acute toxicity of lead to rainbow trout of similar size in soft water of equivalent water quality characteristics[a].

Exposure days	Alkalinity mg/l	Fish size mm	LC50 mg/l
4	29	161	1.17
14	30	145	0.20

[a]Davies et al. 1976.

Bioavailability of Metals

Metals in natural waters exist in various forms, including ionic, complexed, particulate, and absorbed onto other particles. Aquatic life generally represents the most sensitive use being protected from potential impacts of metals. Yet, only a certain fraction of the total metal concentration in a water will be in a form that is biologically available, depending on the complexing capacity of the water. It is important that methodologies used to measure metal concentrations not overestimate the bioavailable fraction in streams or underestimate the potential bioavailable fraction in point and non-point source discharges. These methods should best reflect the potentially toxic relationships between metal concentrations in discharges and the ultimate concentration of the bioavailable fraction in the receiving water. This is important not only for protecting the aquatic life use of water, but also to minimize impacts on point source municipal and industrial discharges and non-point source discharges from agriculture and urban run-off in terms of waste water treatment costs and controls.

The toxicity of metals to aquatic life is generally related to the activity of the free metal ion (Davies et al. 1976 and Andrew et al. 1977). Studies conducted on the acute and chronic toxicity of lead to rainbow trout in soft and hard waters will be used to illustrate toxicity relationships to the form or speciation of metals in natural waters (Davies et al. 1976).

Lead was found to be highly toxic to rainbow trout in both hard water (hardness 353 mg/liter, as $CaCO_3$) and soft water (hardness 28 mg/liter). Analytical and toxicological results differed greatly depending upon the analytical methods used to measure the concentrations of lead in the two types of water. These differences are exemplified in the acute and chronic results reported for free or total lead concentrations.

Acute Toxicity

Two static toxicity tests in hard water gave 96-hour LC50's of 1.47 and 1.32 mg/liter free lead versus total lead LC50's of 471 and 542 mg/liter. In soft water the 96-hour LC50 was 1.17 mg/liter measured as either total or free lead (Table 8). Note the similarity of LC50 results when measuring free as opposed to total lead. The acute toxicity of lead in hard water (Tables 9 and 10) reveals the great discrepency in lead concentrations between total lead added and analytical results obtained for concentrations of lead measured by atomic absorption spectrophotometry (AA). These tests demonstrate that in hard, alkaline waters, lead is not acutely toxic until sufficient lead is added to overwhelm the bicarbonate-carbonate buffering system, such that lead is complexed and precipitated as lead carbonate until all the carbonate is tied-up in the water. In essence, highly alkaline water is reduced both in terms of pH and alkalinity to a low alkaline water by the precipitation of lead carbonate (Table 11) and analytical results by AA (which measures total available lead) and pulse polarography (PP) (which measures essentially free or labile lead) become comparable (Table 9).

Table 8. Effect of total versus free lead measurements on the
          96 hour LC50 results for rainbow trout in different water
          hardness[a].

| Hardness | 96 hr LC50 (mg/1) | |
mg/1	Total lead	Free lead
290	471	1.47
385	542	1.32
32	1.17	1.17

[a]Davies et al. 1976.

Table 9. Difference between total lead concentrations added and
          measured concentrations by tomic absorption spectrophotometry (AA)
          and pulse polarography (PP) from an acute toxicity test in a water
          hardness of 290 mg/liter[a].

| Item | Exposure | | | | | |
	1	2	3	4	5	C
Pb added, mg/1	500	490	480	470	460	0
Pb (AA), mg/1	7.56	5.05	2.85	1.30	0.25	0.00
Pb (PP), mg/1	7.18	4.79	2.77	1.26	0.29	0.00
Percent mortality	100	100	100	30	0	0

[a]Davies et al. 1976.

Table 10. Difference between total lead added and measured
           concentrations on the acute toxicity of lead to rainbow trout
           in a water hardness of 385 mg/liter[a].

| Item | Exposure | | | | | |
	1	2	3	4	5	C
Pb added, mg/1	580	560	540	520	500	0
Pb (AA) mg/1	6.54	5.29	0.79	0.48	0.97	0.00
Percent mortality	100	100	30	0	0	0

[a]Davies et al. 1976.

Lead added in excess of the carbonate buffering system or the
metal excess region, (i.e. to the right of point "A" in Figure 1),
would exist as free lead capable of causing an acutely toxic
response. When measuring lead by AA in the carbonate excess region
(i.e. to the left of point "A" in Figure 1), analytical results become
confusing in terms of corresponding toxicological responses. Note in
Table 9 that no lethality was observed at a total, added, lead concentration of 500 mg/liter which had a corresponding AA measurement of

0.97 mg/liter, whereas, at 540 mg/liter total lead and a measured lead concentration of 0.79 mg/liter (i.e. a lower concentration), 30% lethality was observed. This anomaly occurs as a result of AA measuring lead carbonate complexes in the ligand excess region which biologically is not available to produce a toxic response. Such complexed forms of lead would not be measured using pulse polarography.

Table 11. Effect of added lead concentrations on pH and alkalinity when added to hard water[a].

| | \multicolumn{6}{c}{Total lead added (mg/1)} | | | | | |
	500	490	480	470	460	0 (control)
pH	6.89	6.91	6.97	7.08	7.26	8.78
Alkalinity (mg/1)						
PHTH	0	0	0	0	0	9
M.O.	7	9	10	20	21	228
Hardness (mg/1)	300	300	300	300	300	290

[a]Davies et al. 1976.

Chronic Toxicity

The disparity between analytical results by atomic absorption spectrophotometry and pulse polarography in the ligand excess region are clearly demonstrated in Table 12. These results obtained from a long-term toxicity test in hard, alkaline waters show fairly comparable analytical results between nominal, added concentrations of lead and lead concentrations determined by atomic absorption spectrophotometry. The pulse polarographic results show lead concentrations considerably less than those measured by AA and reflect much more accurately the biologically available fraction of lead. Thermodynamic calculations on the speciation of lead in this alkaline water reveal at pH 8, a free ion, lead activity of $1.45 \times 10^{-7}M$ or 30 g/liter as illustrated in the species distribution diagram in Figure 2. The fact that the PP results in Table 12 exceed the calculated solubility of lead is not surprising considering the uncertainty of the equilibria calculations.

Table 12. Comparison of nominal lead concentration with analytical results obtained by atomic absorption spectrophotometry (AA) and pulse polarograph (PP) in the ligand excess region of a hard water containing 353 mg/liter hardness and 243 mg/liter alkalinity[a].

| Item | \multicolumn{6}{c}{Nominal lead concentrations (μg/1)} | | | | | |
	3240	1080	360	120	40	0
Pb (AA), μg/1	2310	850	380	190	100	0
Pb (PP), μg/1	64.2	41.2	31.6	18.2	10.2	0.5

[a]Davies et al. 1976.

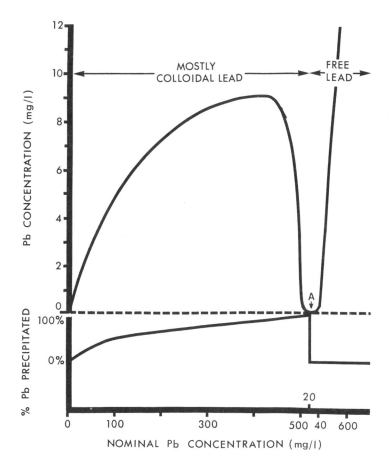

Figure 1. Graphic interpretation of the nature of lead in a hard, alkaline water when analyzed by atomic absorption spectrophotometry.

Long-term toxicity tests conducted with lead in hard and soft waters also show the importance of analytical methodologies in comparing and assessing toxicological results. From long-term toxicity tests for lead in hard water, the no-effect/effect range on rainbow trout was between 18.2 and 31.6 µg/liter free lead as determined by pulse polarography compared to a range between 120 and 360 µg/liter total lead (Table 13). In soft water the no-effect/effect range was between 7.2 and 14.6 µg/liter expressed as either free or total lead since lead was soluble in this water up to 500 µg/liter (Table 14).

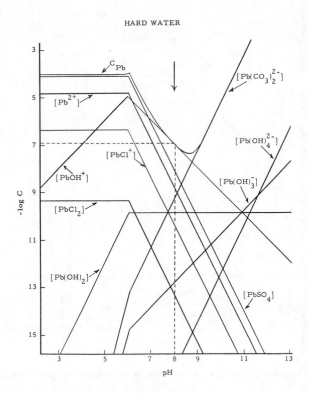

Figure 2. Solubility and species distribution for lead in a hard, alkaline water. The C_{Pb} curve gives the activity of the free Pb ion for different pH values.

Table 13. Long-term toxicity results on lead exposure to rainbow trout in hard water, based on pulse polarographic (PP) analyses[a].

Item	Nominal Pb concentration − ($\mu g/l$)					
	3240	1080	360	120	40	0
Pb (PP), $\mu g/l$	64.2	41.2	31.6	18.2	10.2	0.5
Percent mortality	5.7	0.0	0.0	0.0	0.0	0.0
Abnormality:						
blacktail	100	90	70	0	0	0
lordoscoliosis	100	60	10	0	0	0
eroded caudal	30	20	10	0	0	0
			no-effect/effect range			

[a]Davies et al. 1976.

Table 14. Long-term toxicity results from the exposure of rainbow
trout to lead in soft water[a].

Item	Nominal Pb concentration - (μg/1)					
	80	40	20	10	5	0
Pb, μg/1	61.8	31.2	14.6	7.2	3.6	0.5
Percent mortality	50.6	15.0	7.2	0.6	0.6	0.6
Abnormality:						
blacktail	100	84.5	41.3	0.0	0.0	0.0
lordoscoliosis	96.7	43.8	3.0	0.0	0.0	0.0
eroded caudal	45.4	38.2	6.3 ↑	0.0	0.0	0.0
			no-effect/effect range			

[a]Davies et al. 1976.

Comparing no-effect/effect range in soft water with the range for
total lead in hard water, the concentrations of lead needed to give a
toxicological effect are quite different; yet, when assessed on the
basis of free lead concentrations, the results are very similar. The
difference between the two ranges is probably the result of having
initiated the two tests with different size fish, i.e. trout fry in
the soft water test versus 80 mm fish in the hard water test.

In comparing PP analytical results with AA results in the long-
term tests conducted in hard water, lead concentrations found by AA
are much higher than the corresponding values obtained by PP (Table
12). Analytical results by AA become increasingly less meaningful
where water quality constituents facilitate the complexation of
vulnerable heavy metals, specifically in this study with reduced
solubility of lead with increased alkalinity.

Chemical Equilibria

As seen in the species distribution diagram for lead in Figure 2,
calculations on chemical equilibria can be used to estimate free ion
activities of metals under different conditions of pH, ionic strength,
and different ligands in natural waters. Such diagrams can be very
useful but must be prepared with care and proper consideration of the
various components which are used to construct the diagram. Such
diagrams are constructed from thermodynamic values determined from the
use of Gibb's free energy measurements. They represent the ultimate
state of chemical equilibrium and do not consider the kinetics or
rates of various chemical reactions. For example, in the book
"Aquatic Chemistry" by Stumm and Morgan (1981), they relate the
activity of the Cu(II) ion as being controlled by the stable phase of
the mineral malachite ($Cu_2(OH)_2CO_3(s)$) below pH 7. Above pH 7
tenorite ($CuO(s)$) would control the activity of the Cu(II) ion.
However, both of these stable mineral phases have formation rates
which are kinetically regulated and which may take many years to
form. Obviously, in natural water such reaction times have little
meaning and the control of CU(II) activity would be regulated by some
other metastable solid which forms much more quickly.

Figures 3 and 4 illustrate species distribution diagrams in which Cu(II) activity is governed by the solubility of tenorite ($CuO_{(s)}$) versus the solubility of copper hydroxide ($Cu[OH]_{2(s)}$), a metastable solid. Using these diagrams, the estimated solubility or activity of Cu(II) ion at pH 7 would be 48 μg/liter for control by tenorite and 505 μg/liter as governed by copper hydroxide. Therefore, the choice of the governing solid mineral can be very important, and as seen in this situation, provides more than a ten-fold difference in the concentration of Cu(II) ion.

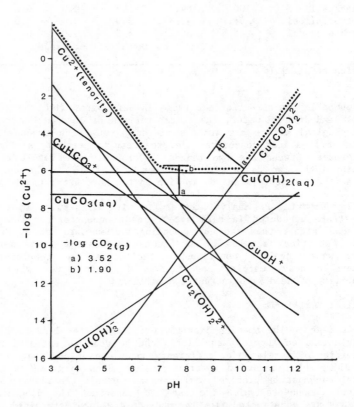

Figure 3. Solubility and species distribution diagram for complexes of copper in equilibrium with tenorite (CuO). The dotted line gives the solubility of Cu(II) ion at different pH values in natural waters.

Chemical Kinetics

As we have seen in the previous section, chemical kinetics or the rate at which chemical reactions occur can play an important role in calculating chemical equilibria. In performing toxicity tests, toxicologists have generally assumed relatively instantaneous kinetics and chemical equilibrium in their bioassay systems. Recent research on the toxicity and chemistry of cadmium in hard and soft waters has shown chemical kinetics are not instantaneous and can significantly affect bioassay results.

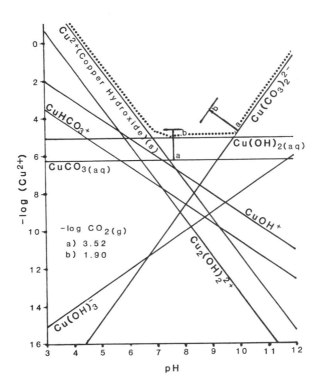

Figure 4.   Solubility and species distribution for complexed of copper in equilibrium with copper hydroxide $(Cu(OH)_{2(s)})$. The dotted line gives the solubility of the Cu(II) ion at different pH values in natural waters.

A chemical experiment was conducted to determine the time required for cadmium activity to reach equilibrium upon being added as cadmium sulfate to hard water (i.e. hardness 300 mg/liter and alkalinity 220 mg/liter). The decreased activity of cadmium over time was measured by differential pulse anodic stripping voltametry (DPASV) which measured the decrease in peak current (10^{-8} amps) as cadmium was being complexed in the alkaline water. Peak current is directly proportional to the cadmium ion activity. Chemical equilibrium was reached after 48 hours as determined by stabilized cadmium activity (Figure 5).

Two toxicity tests for unaged and aged hard water in which cadmium sulfate was added through Mount and Brungs (1967) proportional diluters. The flows from one diluter were split and delivered directly, unaged, to duplicate aquaria containing rainbow trout giving five different concentrations of cadmium exposure and a control. Flows from the second diluter were delivered at five concentrations and a control to large 269-liter aquaria. At a diluter flow rate of 10 liters per hour, this would give a 95% replacement time in 78 hours (Sprague 1969). This allowed cadmium activity to reach equilibrium prior to being delivered to duplicate aquaria containing rainbow trout.

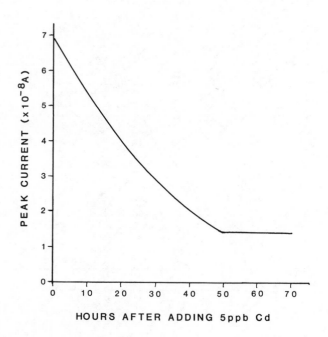

HOURS AFTER ADDING 5ppb Cd

Figure 5. Kinetic equilibrium of cadmium in a hard, alkaline water is shown by the reduction in peak current over time as measured by differential pulse anodic stripping voltametry (DPASV) which is directly related to cadmium ion activity.

As seen in Table 15, cadmium concentrations (based on cadmium added by the diluter and measured in the fish tanks) and mortality results differed significantly in unaged and aged water as seen from the percent of cadmium recovered in the tanks. In the unaged water, lethality and cadmium tank concentrations were significantly higher based on added concentrations, than those found in the aged water since additions of ionic cadmium did not have time to be complexed and come to equilibrium prior to fish exposure. This was true even though added concentrations of cadmium were significantly higher in the aged versus unaged hard water. This would suggest that toxicity tests on metals performed in alkaline or other complexing waters would tend to overestimate the degree of mortality, i.e. percentage of dead fish, but does not substantially affect the no-effect/effect limits as defined by the calculated chronic values (Table 16). On the other hand, the other side of this coin would suggest that toxicity tests conducted in metal effluents with higher complexing capacities than the receiving waters to which they discharge would underestimate the toxicity of metals.

Table 15. Effect of chemical kinetics and measured cadmium concentrations and mortality results of rainbow trout in unaged versus aged hard water.

Item	Exposure					
	1	2	3	4	5	C
Unaged hard water						
Added Cd, mg/l	30.2	14.7	8.4	5.1	2.5	0.0
Measured Cd, µg/l	24.4	13.9	6.2	3.4	1.4	< 0.3
% recovered in tanks	88.4	91.6	82.5	55.7	55.4	
% mortality	90.0	75.0	2.5 ↑	0.0	0.0	0.0
		no-effect/effect range				
Aged hard water						
Added Cd, µg/l	45.8	25.0	12.4	7.3	5.6	0.0
Measured Cd, µg/l	5.5	3.3	1.7	1.0	0.4	< 0.3
% recovered in tanks	12.0	13.3	13.5	13.2	7.1	
% mortality	37.5	2.5 ↑	0.0	0.0	0.0	0.0
		no-effect/effect range				

Table 16. Effect of chemical kinetic on chronic values derived from the long-term toxicity of cadmium to rainbow trout in unaged and aged hard water.

Item	Hard water	
	Unaged	Aged
No-effect/effect range, µg/l	3.4-6.2	1.7-3.3
Chronic value[a], µg/l	4.6	2.4

[a]Calculated as the geometric mean of the no-effect/effect limits.

Analysis of Metals in Urban Runoff

Considering the information discussed above, the question is now raised as to how metals analyses should be performed to assess the potentially toxic effects of metals in urban runoff waters?

Currently, metal concentrations in natural waters are determined on the basis of acid soluble or total recoverable metals, where acid soluble refers to the acidification of a water sample to a pH < 2. The "total recoverable" procedure involves an acid digestion which is less stringent than that employed in total metal analysis. Both the acid soluble and total recoverable procedures frequently give analytical results from natural waters which exceed metal concentrations reported as safe to aquatic life. Such elevated levels are frequently the result of metals being released from suspended and particulate matter in the stream which are not biologically available. As a result of acidification of a water sample to preserve the sample until it is analyzed, metals are leached from the suspended and settleable matter into the sample, to give erroneously high metal concentrations which, from a biological standpoint, do not exist in an available state in streams or lakes.

The average concentration of several metals in soils throughout the United States have been reported as: 5,000 µg/liter (cadmium); 30,000 µg/liter (copper); 10,000 µg/liter (lead); and 300,000 µg/liter for zinc (Lindsay 1979). It is obvious that soils contain relatively high metal concentrations which are bound to and/or within the matrix of soil particles. For example, the average concentration of copper in soils is 30,000 ppb. The toxicity of copper to aquatic life ranges from 5 to 50 ppb. Consequently, if only a small fraction of metals bound within the matrix of suspended and settleable solids is released and made soluble as a result of adding acid to a water sample, it is not surprising that erroneously high metal concentrations could be reported.

Toxicity data on aquatic life generally indicate that the ionic fraction of metals constitutes the primary toxic form. There are only a few analytical methodologies capable of measuring the ionic fraction of metals and these are further limited by: 1) the low levels of detection needed in aquatic toxicology; 2) interference problems; and 3) a host of other analytical problems.

The ion selective electrode for copper has been used successfully in measuring ionic concentrations of copper in natural waters, but it is limited in its detection capability and subject to interferences. Differential pulse anodic stripping voltametry and differential pulse polarography are other electrochemical techniques which show promise in measuring ionic metal concentrations. However, in addition to ionic species of metals, polarographic methods measure other labile forms, are subject to non-electroactive species interference, and are limited in the number of metals that can be analyzed, with analytical methodologies yet to be developed for most of these. A third procedure that may also show promise is the use of ion exchange resins, and/or ion chromatography which are capable of separating various metal forms. However, analytical procedures are still being developed and will need to be experimentally validated.

The problem arises from not being able to directly measure these bioavailable or toxic fractions of metals using currently available and accepted methodologies. Consequently, we need to utilize those methodologies that: 1) best define those metal fractions which are potentially toxic to aquatic life; and 2) are acceptable to regulatory agencies.

Since the total and total recoverable methods greatly overestimate the bioavailable concentrations of metals to aquatic life, I do not think they should be used. Of current methodologies available, the dissolved method most closely approximates a means by which the bioavailable, i.e. toxic, fractions of metals in natural waters can be identified. Dissolved metal analysis consists of filtration of a water sample at a site through a 0.40 or 0.45 micron membrane filter, followed by acidification to a pH < 2 for sample preservation using nitric acid.

The use of dissolved methods to measure metal concentrations in effluents for NPDES compliance cannot be justified, since the dissolved method reports only those metals that will pass through the filter and prohibits analysis of larger metal complexes and precipitates which could be released to the receiving water.

Effluents, unlike receiving waters, are generally highly complexing with most metals existing as complexes or precipitates. Upon being released to a less complexing receiving water, the metals could be transformed into biologically available forms which would not be measured using the dissolved metal method and which could impact aquatic life. Therefore, some analytical method intermediate to dissolved and total recoverable methods is needed to identify metal concentrations in the effluent which are potentially available upon being discharged to the receiving water.

I would recommend that the determination of metals concentrations in effluents and for measuring compliance with NPDES permit limits be based on the "potentially dissolved method." The analysis of potentially dissolved metals requires the acidification of an effluent sample to pH < 2 with nitric acid followed by a minimum delay of 8 to 96 hours prior to sample filtration through a 0.40 or 0.45 micron membrane filter. This delay in filtration and analysis of the sample is needed to allow potentially dissolved metals to reach a state of equilibrium such that potentially available metals have sufficient time to be released to the sample which is a kinetically regulated process.

Which method is most appropriate for measuring metals concentrations in urban runoff? If urban runoff waters have similar water quality characteristics as the receiving water into which they are discharged, especially for pH, alkalinity, hardness, and total organic carbon (TOC), then the dissolved method would be appropriate. Generally, however, urban runoff would be more complexing than the waters into which they are discharged and metals should be measured using the potentially dissolved method.

LITERATURE CITED

Andrew, R.W., K.E. Biesinger, and G.E. Glass. 1977. Effect of inorganic complexing on the toxicity of copper to Daphnia magna. Water Res. 11. Pp. 309-315.

Davies, P.H., J.P. Goettl, Jr., J.R. Sinley, and N.F. Smith. 1976. Acute and chronic toxicity of lead to rainbow trout, Salmo gairdneri, in hard and soft water. Water Res. 10. Pp. 199-206.

Goettl, J.P., Jr. and P.H. Davies. 1976. Water pollution studies. Study of the effects of metallic ions on fish and aquatic organisms. Colo. Div. Wildl. Job Prog. Rep., Fed. Aid. Proj. F-33-R-10, Job 6. Pp. 6-54.

Goettl, J.P., Jr., J.R. Sinley, and P.H. Davies. 1971. Water pollution studies. Study of the effects of metallic ions on fish and aquatic organisms. Colo. Dept. Game, Fish, and Parks. Job Prog. Rep., Fed Aid. Proj. F-33-R-6, Job 6. Pp. 49-128.

Judy, R.D., Jr. and P.H. Davies. 1979. Effects of calcium addition as $Ca(NO_3)_2$ on zinc toxicity to fathead minnows, Pimephales promelas, Refinesque. Bull. Env. Contam. Tox. 22. Pp. 88-94.

Lindsay, W.L. 1979. Chemical equilibria in soils. John Wiley and Sons, New York. 449 p.

Mount, D.I. and W.A. Brungs. 1967. A simplified dosing apparatus for fish toxicological studies. Water Res. 1. Pp. 21-29.

Sinley, J.R., J.P. Goettl, Jr., and P.H. Davies. 1974. The effects of zinc on rainbow trout (Salmo gairdneri) in hard and soft water. Bull. Env. Contam. Tox. 12(2). Pp. 193-201.

Sprague, J.B. 1969. Measurement of pollutant toxicity to fish - I: Bioassay methods for acute toxicity. Water Res. 3. Pp. 793-821.

Stumm, W. and J.J. Morgan. 1981. Aquatic chemistry. John Wiley and Sons, New York. 780 p.

DISCIPLINARY INTEGRATION: THE SOLUTION

Edwin E. Herricks*

Introduction

The decade of the 60's found water quality regulation shifting from state to federal control with an emphasis on the development of water quality criteria and standards. The decade of the 70's established a firm federal hold on water quality regulation and found the implementation of a comprehensive effluent control strategy. The decade of the 80's is seeing another shift in regulatory emphasis. Although effluent controls are firmly in place, the nature of those controls is being defined and refined by water quality based analyses (EPA, 1985). The changing nature of water quality regulation is changing the role of engineers and bioenvironmental scientists in environmental management. With water quality based approaches there is a shift away from the regulation of conventional pollutants (BOD, TSS, DO, etc) to an emphasis on toxic pollutants and other environmental contaminants. Improvements in analytical procedures (gas chromatography, gas chromatography-mass spectrometry, etc.) combined with advances in living system analyses (e.g Ames testing for mutagenicity and advanced carcinogenicity testing procedures) acted as a catalyst in water quality based programs. There is an increased emphasis on monitoring techniques and designs which include analysis of conventional and toxic pollutants and the biological integrity of the receiving system (GAO, 1981; EPA, 1985). Monitoring must now include suspected mutagens or carcinogens. With the shift away from an emphasis on conventional pollutants, engineers have been faced with a reevaluation of treatment processes, particularly the removal of a range of contaminants which don't behave like conventional pollutants.

Engineers are now faced with using their training and history of practice to deal with environmental problems which are poorly defined and possibly intractable. This is particularly true in dealing with urban runoff. The "treatment" for urban runoff includes a large dose of prevention and careful use of retention. The use of conventional treatment for urban runoff often has little effect on contaminant levels in the receiving system. Yet, engineers are called on to "fix" the problem. With clients and regulators calling for solution to urban runoff problems engineers have turned to bioenvironmental scientists for assistance and answers. What they have found is limited assistance, few answers, many evasions, and often more questions.

*Associate Professor of Environmental Biology, Department of Civil Engineering, University of Illinois at Urbana-Champaign, 208 N. Romine, Urbana, IL 61801

The role on bioenvironmental scientists in environmental regulation and management has grown over the past three decades, the growth
in environmental science paralleling the growth in environmental
engineering. The 60's found an emphasis on public health. The
increased environmental awareness of the general public in the 70's
and 80's redefined the role of bioenvironmental scientists to include
the responsibility for maintenance of the interconnections of
ecosystems and environmental integrity. Today the consequences of
contaminant addition to the environment are identified by toxicologists, assessed in the field by ecologists, fisheries biologists and
other natural scientists, and interpreted by regulatory agencies
which have large staffs of environmental scientists. The initial
stages of contaminant effect analysis depend on prediction or
extrapolation from a limited data base. Validation of predictions is
difficult if not impossible because a comprehensive experimental
analysis of contaminant effects is limited by cost and practicality.
Yet, from the extrapolations of some bioenvironmental scientists come
the concerns for treatment which burden engineers.

In the past, the interactions between engineers and bioenvironmental scientists has been cordial, separated by limited mutual
understanding and a small measure of antagonism. New pressures
demand bridging the gulf and an end to antagonism. As a bioenvironmental scientist with some engineering training, I have observed
interactions between engineers and scientists for over 15 years. I
suggest that there should be an honest reappraisal of roles of
engineers and bioenvironmental scientists in environmental management. Both groups should recognize that the fundamental changes in
management and regulatory philosophy occurring in the 80's require
development of effective engineering designs based on implementation
of data collection programs which are dependent on skills provided by
a range of scientific and technical disciplines.

Bridging gaps and ending antagonism is not a simple process. A
common approach is mediation. In mediation, fixed positions of two
parties are examined carefully and some middle ground is reached
where both parties accept an outcome. The mechanisms of mediation
span the range from gentle persuasion to binding arbitration; third
parties are often essential. Unfortunately, although a middle
ground may be reached, fundamental differences are not effectively
resolved and deep seated problems often remain. Mediation solutions
are also temporary. The position of the parties in conflict do not
change; mediation forces accommodation to a position which is
uncomfortable for both parties. If mediation produces a cessation of
hostilities, the quiet should only be considered temporary truce.
Mediation does not necessarily provide sound long term solutions to
the conflicts, particularly those between developers and environmentalists.

The long term solution to antagonism requires the gap between
disciplines to close. An alternate to mediation is implementation of
programs which seek a fundamental change in the positions of both
parties through education. In this approach, a forum is established
where information is exchanged. The exchange of information leads to
an understanding of positions, illuminating the causes of conflicts.

Both parties have the time and opportunity to alter their positions. An unforced change in position encourages a balance which is missing in mediation or arbitration. This paper adopts this approach, seeking to increase the understanding of engineering by bioenvironmental scientists and an increase understanding of bioenvironmental sciences and scientists by engineers.

The objective of this paper is to encourage a careful review of the interactions between engineers and bioenvironmental scientists (biologists, ecologists, and ecotoxicologists) as they attempt to deal with urban runoff problems. This review begins by assessing the differences in tradition and training between engineers who deal almost exclusively with physical systems and the bioenvironmental scientists who deal almost exclusively with living systems. The differences in data, data variability, and the interpretation of data used by engineers and bioenvironmental scientists will be discussed. Lastly, this paper will review data collection activities which are appropriate for engineers and bioenvironmental scientists and briefly discuss acceptable standards of performance for each discipline.

Tradition and Training

Tradition - The differences in tradition between engineers and bioenvironmental scientists is significant. The scientific tradition for engineers has its origin in the natural philosophy of Socrates and Plato (active from 450 to 350 BC). Their students emphasized empirical and practical science leading to the Alexandrian school of engineering (dating from around 250 BC). The reasoning of these early engineers was deductive, following the example of Archimedes. Deductive science was advanced by Descartes in the early seventeenth century. Descartes used mathematical arguments to support his contention that all salient features of the natural world were revealed by deductive science. Deductive sciences were advanced by Galileo (1564-1642) to isolate phenomena from their natural environment, identify the role of mathematics in the scientific method, and establish modern approaches to mechanics. With a tradition founded on deductive science engineers depend on exact mathematical description applied to constructs isolated from the natural environment. The engineering disciplines have developed a sound body of theory based on established physical and chemical principles. By using quantitative, deductive approaches supported by well developed theory, engineers carry to their profession a fundamental confidence in the quality, accuracy, and applicability of their work.

Where engineers are uncertain they have developed sound empirical methods to adjust the sensitivity of their mathematical analysis techniques. Limits of accuracy, safety factors, and other constraints placed on the analysis are well described. An engineer, when asked to make a prediction is able to draw upon a history of good practice and make a prediction with confidence. In addition, engineers are able to make clear and understandable predictions of consequence based on their quantitative, deductive analysis approach. Lastly, engineers are able to communicate their predictions simply.

In contrast to engineering traditions, the scientific tradition of the bioenvironmental sciences is founded on inductive, qualitative analysis. Bioenvironmental sciences have their origin in Greek history but are founded on the philosophy Aristotle which differs from his contemporary Plato. Aristotle's approach to science depended on observation. This observational approach to science was the foundation for connections between empirical studies and the theoretical interpretation of nature which developed in sixteenth century England. Francis Bacon (1561-1626), unlike Galileo viewed the scientific method as experimental, qualitative, and inductive. He distrusted the deductive logic of mathematics even though he used mathematics as a tool in scientific inquiry. Bacon's impact on scientific thinking was not fully felt until the nineteenth century when inductive approaches led to the development of evolutionary geology and biology. During this period scientists roamed the world, collecting facts, and generating theories by inductive reasoning. By the end of the nineteenth century the qualitative-inductive method was broadly accepted (as evidenced by Darwin's theory of evolution).

Because the bioenvironmental sciences depend on observation, description, and qualitative analysis few standard methods exist, and the body of theory which has developed is still being refined. In many bioenvironmental sciences theoretical constructs are still immature because the sciences are extremely young. For example, ecology is less than 50 years old and has only recently entered the stage where mathematical models are supporting and sometimes replacing strict observational analysis. Unfortunately, observations made by individual bioenvironmental scientists seldom contribute to a body of knowledge which will support model construction. Empirical validation of model predictions is rare because the absence of detailed information forces the development of general models which cannot withstand application to specific sites without major alteration. As technology advances, bioenvironmental sciences are fundamentally challenged by new insights and observations. Unlike engineers who depend on new insights to refine theory and improve practice, bioenvironmental scientists find their theories challenged and models invalidated. In the absence of well developed and refined theories or consistent empirical data, bioenvironmental scientists qualify responses to problems often raising more questions than they answer. Unlike engineers, bioenvironmental scientists lack confidence in the results of their work.

Where engineers work with simplified constructs, separate from the natural environment, the focus of bioenvironmental investigations are complex natural systems which defy exact mathematical description. Simple cause and effect relationships do not exist in natural systems. Multiple, if not an infinite number, of outcomes are possible for any change to input variables in natural systems. In addition natural systems have the capacity to independently make changes in fundamental characteristics. The capacity exists to change over short time periods within the genetic scope of individual organisms (termed acclimation) while species can modify their genetic scope over longer time periods through adaptive processes. Bioenvironmental scientists have developed qualitative observational skills and quantitative analysis methods which reflect the need for

constant adjustment to change. Empiricism is of minimal value in
most living systems analysis because the characteristics of a species
or the composition of an ecosystem constantly changes. Bioenvironmental scientists cannot depend on a history of good practice to
support their predictions because observations are only valid at the
time of the observation. Bioenvironmental scientists are not
trained to use the practice and skill of their predecessors. They
are trained to develop individual and specialized knowledge, seldom
using tools supplied by generations of their predecessors.

Bioenvironmental scientists do make predictions but predictions
are either narrowly focused and precise, or general with little
precision. Predictive accuracy is only possible for the simplest
natural system. To illustrate this point, bioenvironmental scientists can be classified based on the level of biological or ecological organization of their specialty area, Figure 1. It may be
possible to predict biochemical or enzymatic activity with accuracy.
Unfortunately, determining the effect of a change in biochemical
activity or enzyme function on higher levels of organization is
problematic. In environmental analysis, operating in the ecological
spectrum of the hierarchy, similar difficulties accompany extrapolation from single species effects to impacts on ecological systems.
Communicating these limitations in a positive sense is extremely
difficult. The result is that engineers and non-scientists responsible for regulation and management receive no simple answers from
bioenvironmental scientists. Bioenvironmental scientists, unlike
engineers, cannot communicate the results of their analyses simply.
No absolute predictions of consequence are generally made.

Figure 1.

Biological and Ecological Organization Hierarchies

BIOLOGICAL HIERARCHY

Enzyme --> Cell --> Organ --> Organ-System --> Organism

ECOLOGICAL HIERARCHY

Organism --> Species/Population --> Community --> Ecosystem

Training - Associated with the vastly different scientific
tradition between engineers and bioenvironmental scientists is a
difference in training which often interferes in the communication
between both groups. Engineering training is quantitative in the
sense that the dependence on mathematical analysis pervades the
standard engineering curriculum. Engineers are trained to effectively use the practice and skill developed by generations of engineers. Curricula are well defined and disciplinary divisions well

established. An engineer is trained to use a set of tools extremely
well. As science and technology advance, the quality of those tools
improves. An important feature is that the training an engineer
receives reinforces successful empirical observations. Engineering
practice is improved with experience. The extensive record of
achievement and success in engineering supports a tradition of
excellence.

Although the training of bioenvironmental scientists is often
specific, the specialty descriptions are not well understood by the
general public. Typically a limnologist (specialist in the study of
lakes), an ichthyologist (specialist in fish), a taxonomist (a
specialist in the identification organisms), and a geneticist (a
specialist in genetic characteristics and relationships) are all
termed biologists. Even more confusing is the title "ecologist." In
each of the disciplines identified above, the presence of a few
courses on a transcript allows an individual to call himself an
ecologist.

Although this and following discussions might benefit from more
exact definition, by specialty, of the training of biologists and
ecologists, I will continue to use "bioenvironmental scientist" with
the understanding that a range of disciplines with vastly different
training are included in this classification. In the training
programs for bioenvironmental scientists the development of mathematical skills is usually minimal. Mathematical training of most
biologists and ecologists will usually emphasize statistics, not
calculus. Although biochemistry, molecular biology, and many aspects
of toxicology require advanced mathematics, similar to the mathematical skills required of chemists, quantitative skills in biologists
and ecologists are usually poorly developed.

If we compare the training received by biologists and ecologists
to the training of engineers and chemists, a single critical difference is evident. Engineering coursework programs are well defined
and evaluated regularly by accreditation groups. Programs in biology
and ecology do not have the advantage of accreditation. Although
societies (Cairns 1980) are providing validation of professional
qualifications, no formal system of professional qualification exists
for biology or ecology in general.

In summary, tradition and training of engineers and bioenvironmental scientists are so different that they constitute a major
barrier to effective interdisciplinary approaches to solving urban
runoff problems. The challenge lies in the effective integration of
these two vastly different disciplines. One approach requires
effective information transfer between the two disciplines. Improving information transfer requires a careful evaluation of the types
of data produced by engineers and bioenvironmental scientists,
followed by assignment of collection responsibility to the discipline
most capable of meeting data collection and analysis requirements.

Characteristics Of Data

The objective of the following section is to explore in detail
the characteristics of data collected by both engineers and bioenvironmental scientists. As a preamble to that analysis it is important
to recognize that the objective of urban runoff analysis is the
development of information, not the generation of data. In the
following discussions data will be differentiated from information.
Data, as generally defined, are facts or principles on which an
argument is based. Specifically, urban runoff data may include
contaminant concentration, the presence and abundance of a species,
or the measure of contaminant effect on a species.   Information
provides knowledge. Knowledge is developed from a body of facts and
the ideas inferred from those facts. Information is the product of
the analysis of data using techniques of correlation and comparison.

Variable identification - Urban runoff data can be classified by
variable characteristics.   Quantitative data are continuous variables. Concentrations, species abundances, or specific test results
(e.g. toxicity testing) are examples of continuous variables. The
definition of quantitative data is independent of the collection
technique; both quantitative and qualitative methods can produce
quantitative data as defined in this context. A second type of
variable is binary data. The presence or absence of a species or the
detection or non-detection of a contaminant provide binary data.
Binary data are often considered inferior to quantitative data
although binary data may be preferable in some instances. Green
(1979) discusses situations where the variability of quantitative
data introduces noise to the system decreasing the sensitivity of an
analysis.   Binary data are regularly used in biology in correlation
and cluster analysis (Romesburg, 1984).

A third type of variable is the rank. Ranking methods are often
used to transform quantitative data for later analysis. Ranking is
commonly used whenever there is nonlinearity in a relationship
between two variables. Rank correlation is commonly used in simple
nonparametric statistical analyses (Green, 1979). The final type of
variable is a derived variable. Indices, ratios, and rate parameters
are all derived variables. Derived variables are commonly used to
simplify complex data sets. This simplification generally results in
statistical intractability. Sokal and Rohlf (1973) summarize the
disadvantages of ratios as: 1)increased variability when compared
with the inherent variability of individual metrics, 2) biased
estimation of the mean of the ratio, 3) the development of intractable distributions, and 4) obscuring intervariable relationships.

In the assessment of impacts from urban runoff, continuous data
are generally preferred.   The typical data collection program will
begin with the selection of the parameters to be measured. Tables 1,
2, and 3 present proposed measurements for different water quality
monitoring purposes. Table 1 lists the water quality characteristics
designated by the U. S. Environmental Protection Agency for
monitoring at network stations under its basic water monitoring
program.   The list of parameters is straightforward with the only
"biological" analyses a fecal coliform count and representative fish

Table 1

List of Parameters Measured
USEPA Water Monitoring Network Stations*

Parameter	Sampling Frequency	
	Rivers and Streams	Lakes
Flow	monthly	seasonally
Temperature	monthly	seasonally
Dissolved oxygen	monthly	seasonally
pH	monthly	seasonally
Conductivity	monthly	seasonally
Fecal coliform	monthly	seasonally
Total Kjeldahl nitrogen	monthly	seasonally
Nitrate plus nitrite	monthly	seasonally
Total Phosphorus	monthly	seasonally
Chemical oxygen demand	monthly	seasonally
Total suspended solids	monthly	seasonally
Representative fish/ shellfish tissue	annually	annually
Transparency, secchi disk		annually

* Basic Water Monitorng Program, USEPA, 1976

and shellfish tissue analysis. Table 2 identifies the water quality characteristics monitored at the U. S. Geological Survey national stream quality accounting network (NASQUAN). Note that the emphasis is still on physical and chemical water quality parameters, but biological analyses have been expanded to include analysis of phytoplankton species present and a measure of phytoplankton abundance (phytoplankton biomass and chlorophyll concentrations). Table 3 lists the parameters analyzed when performing a use attainability analysis. In this listing there is a shift in the emphasis from a focused water quality analysis to the inclusion of measures of physical habitat, the analysis of a wide range of aquatic organisms, and specification for development of derived variables.

The differences in the parameters monitored among the EPA monitoring network, NASQUAN, and use attainability studies are due to the different objectives of each sampling effort. Monitoring water quality follows defined guidance. Use or condition analysis must be modified to meet site specific conditions. I suggest that the monitoring program designs in Tables 1 and 2 are engineering designs-engineering designs in the sense that the intent is the development of an empirical data base which will support deductive analyses of receiving system state or condition when compared with established criteria or standards. The data base is also designed to support modeling efforts (e.g., wasteload allocation, USEPA, 1983). The program design in Table 3 has a bioenvironmental sciences emphasis. The intent is the development of a complete description of a stream or lake, to support an inductive analysis of state or condition.

Table 2

Water Quality Characteristics Monitored at USGS NASQUAN Stations

Characteristic	Frequency
Field determination	
discharge	continuous
water temperature	continuous, daily/ or monthly[1]
specific conductance	continuous, daily/ or monthly[1]
pH	monthly
fecal coliform bacteria	monthly
fecal streptococcus bacteria	monthly
Common constituents (dissolved)	
bicarbonate, carbonate, total hardness, non-carbonate hardness, calcium, magnesium, flouride, sodium, potassium, dissolved solids, silica, turbidity, chloride, and sulfate	monthly or quarterly[2]
Major nutrients	
total phosphorus	monthly
total nitrite plus nitrate	monthly
total Kjeldahl nitrogen	monthly
Trace elements (total and dissolved)	
arsenic, cadmium, chromium, cobalt copper, iron, lead, manganese, mercury, selenium, and zinc	quarterly
Organic and biological	
total organic carbon	quarterly
total phytoplankton	monthly
three co-dominants of phytoplankton	monthly
periphyton, biomass dry and ash weight	quarterly
periphyton, chlorophyll a and b	quarterly
Suspended sediment	monthly

[1]Continuous or daily based on station equipment and monitoring schedule. Monthly measurements made at stations with long-term records.

[2]Quarterly or monthly, depending on established relationship between conductance and concentrations of various parameters

*   USGS Circular 717 The National Stream Quality Accounting Newtork (NASQUAN)

Table 3

Data Collected for Typical Use Attainability Analyses*

PHYSICAL EVALUATIONS   CHEMICAL EVALUATIONS
Instream parameters   Dissolved oxygen
    size (mean width/depth)   Toxicants
    flow/velocity   Nutrients
    total volume   nitrogen
    reaeration rates   phosphorus
    gradient/pools/riffles   Sediment oxygen demand
    temperature   Salinity
    suspended solids   Hardness
    sedimentation   Alkalinity
    channel modifications   pH
    channel stability   Dissolved solids

Substrate composition
Substrate characteristics
Channel debris
Sludge deposits
Riparian characteristics
Downstream characteristics

BIOLOGICAL EVALUATIONS
    Biological Inventory
        fish
        macroinvertebrates
        microinvertebrates
        phytoplankton
        macrophytes

    Biological Condition/Health Analysis
        diversity indices
        HSI models
        tissue analyses
        recovery index
        intolerant species analysis
        omnivore-carnivore analysis

    Biological Potential Analysis
        reference reach comparison
*   from USEPA Water Quality Standards Handbook (1982)

Data Variability - Variability is introduced during both analysis
and sampling. Analytical errors are small and can be controlled by
maintaining laboratory quality control programs. Variability
introduced by sampling includes the variability in the concentration
of analytes between samples, the inherent variability of the sampling
procedure, and an interpretative bias produced by the number of
samples collected. In the typical monitoring program the greatest
variability is introduced during sampling with sampling errors an
order of magnitude greater than analytical errors (Herricks, et al.,
1985).

Sampling procedures selected to reduce variability introduce bias to the data set. Schaeffer, et al., (1980) have shown that grab and composite sampling may be comparable, but analysis of a composite sample will reduce variability between samples and may not adequately identify dangerous concentration excursions. Interpretative bias is also introduced by the number of samples in an analysis set. Loftis and Ward (1980) showed that if greater than 30 samples are collected per year, serial correlation will bias interpretation; if fewer than 10 samples are collected per year seasonal variation will bias analyses.

Different types of data will also have different characteristic variability. Physical data, such as flow, will have high variability, although flow variability is well described and related to standard stochastic models. Chemical data is more predictable, if not less variable. Conservative chemical variability is not caused by the inherent variability of the element or compound, but to source variability and variability in receiving system conditions which may control constituent chemistry (solubility, equilibria, etc). Distributional characteristics of conservative chemicals are likely to be normal or log-normal (Herricks, et al., 1985). Non-conservative chemical elements or compounds will have higher inherent variability with poorly defined distributional characteristics. The state of a non-conservative chemical will depend on complex interactions between the chemical, its environment, and possibly a biological system which transforms or degrades a compound. Stochastic events may dominate variability at one time and biological function may dominate at another.

The variability of biological data is much greater than the expected variability of physical or chemical data. Biological systems are complex and, by definition non-conservative, varying through both time and space. Within a fixed genetic scope, organisms have the capacity to alter their response to environmental conditions to operate effectively in an environment which would normally be lethal. This capacity for acclimation may vary between individuals. Organisms also have the capacity to change genetic scope through evolution, adapting to changing physical, chemical, or biological conditions.

Biological variability is also due to the complexity of living systems. Organisms are prepared to do the same thing different ways. Response to a single stimulus may vary depending on ambient conditions, previous history of exposure, or species characteristics. Biological variability may be impossible to quantify. The distributional characteristics of biological variability are highly non-parametric.

Sampling and bias are related. Engineers should recognize that a shift from parameters in Tables 1 and 2 to those in Table 3 require different expectations. The inherent variability of the data will control analysis possibilities (Herricks and Schaeffer, 1985) and constrain information extraction from a data set. Both engineers and bioenvironmental scientists should recognize that different types of data, with different inherent variability will support different

approaches to problem solving. Data with low variability will
support empirical deductive analyses and satisfy engineering
expectations. Data with high variability will not satisfy
engineering expectations. Interpretation of highly variable data
will follow inductive paths and involve bioenvironmental scientists.

Data Interpretation - Analysis and interpretation of data,
including preparation of reports and communication of results to
decision makers, is the final step in data collection. Data analysis
and interpretation are selective processes beginning with the choice
of sampling design and ending with the selection of data analyses
procedures. Analysis begins with an assessment of data quality and
is followed by development of relationships between independent and
dependent variables in the data set. Analysis may include calculation of derived values, ratios, and indices and involve the use of
models and advanced statistical techniques. The number of analysis
approaches is limitless.

Previous sections argued my contention that engineers and
bioenvironmental scientists collect different types of data and
analyze that data differently based on differences in scientific
tradition and training. Since data analysis and interpretation is a
selective process, suggesting that engineers and bioenvironmental
scientists will draw different conclusions from the same data set
should come as no surprise. Differences in interpretation are
greatest when engineers and bioenvironmental scientists collect
"their" data when solving the same problem.

Engineers will be more consistent in their interpretation of
environmental data. Although both engineers and bioenvironmental
scientists can choose from an unlimited set of analysis approaches,
engineers depend on a limited set of analyses proven effective and
useful by practice. By applying deductive approaches engineers
isolate phenomena from their natural environment, identify simplified
mechanisms of control based on known physical and chemical principles, and develop empirical models for analysis. Consistent interpretation also results from the reference to handbooks which standardize model coefficients and may specify procedures for analysis.
Engineers apply a limited set of tools consistently and extremely
well.

Bioenvironmental scientists are inconsistent in their interpretation of environmental data. This inconsistency arises from the
limitless analysis possibilities and the different data analysis
approaches used by scientists from various bioenvironmental disciplines. Bioenvironmental scientists approach data analysis statistically, assuming all things in the environment are related. A major
analytical focus is correlation. Although analytical expediency
requires isolating elements of the natural system, inductive approaches are used to build relationships within and between elements of
the natural system. Few handbooks exist to guide analysis because
the relationship between dependent and independent variables may
change with the time reference adopted for the analysis (Schumm and
Lichty, 1965). When models are used by bioenvironmental scientists,

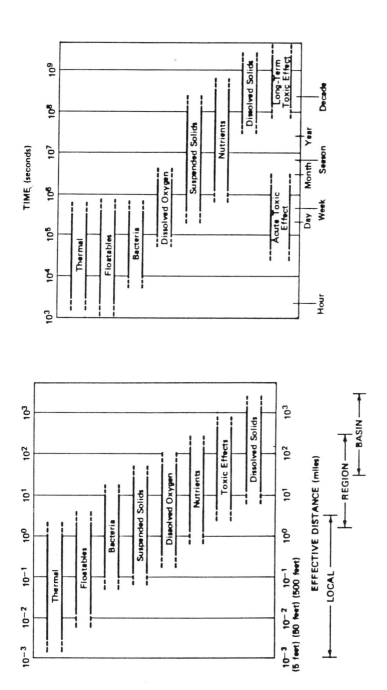

Figure 2. Time and space scales for assessment of water quality problems (from USEPA Technical Guidance for Performing Waste Load Allocations – Book II, Streams and Rivers, 1983)

the absence of empirical data and the inherent complexity of natural systems forces the proliferation of simplifying assumptions with uncertain validity. The resulting models are complex constructs of differential equations. Model calibration is based on site specific conditions limiting transportability because handbooks or historical practice do not provide constants or coefficients for model application to other areas. Analysis and interpretation of environmental data by bioenvironmental scientists is an individual process, drawing on analytical successes and experience of the individual, not the profession.

The causes of differences in analysis and interpretation which arise from independent analysis of the same problem can be developed from Figure 2. Time and space scales differ for measurements used to assess water quality problems and a range of values for time and distance exist for each commonly used measurement. Assessing urban runoff effects may include several measurements which are operative over time and space scales which do not overlap.

Engineers emphasize distance relationships. Their concern is identification of the location of maximum (or minimum) concentration. Water quality sampling designs emphasize local, regional, or basin analyses. In contrast, bioenvironmental scientists emphasize time relationships. The effect on living systems is controlled by both concentration and the length of exposure. Increasing average concentrations of a contaminant slightly may have greater effect on an ecosystem than reducing maximum concentration at some location. With a different view of the same problem, independent analyses by engineers and bioenvironmental scientists result in different sampling designs, analytical approaches, and eventually, result interpretation. Each design, data collection, and analysis approach will have strengths and weaknesses. Interpretations may be contradictory but still valid.

Conclusions

The effective integration of engineering and bioenvironmental disciplines can occur if effective interdisciplinary approaches to problem solving, not multidisciplinary programs which perpetuate and accentuate differences in scientific tradition and training are developed. The strength of the engineering approach is deductive problem solving supported by engineering practice. The strength of the bioenvironmental approach is inductive analyses which identifies relationships and connections. The major weakness of the engineering approach is a narrow focus which dissociates a problem from the natural environment. The major weakness of the bioenvironmental sciences is the lack or an organized empirical and quantitative approach to identifying cause and effect. With the recognition of these strengths and weaknesses it is possible to identify activities which are appropriate for engineers and bioenvironmental scientists in environmental management.

Engineers should assume the responsibility for the collection of data illustrated in Tables 1 and 2. They should continue to develop models and test the sensitivity of those models under varying environmental conditions. Bioenvironmental scientists should continue to evaluate the condition and state of the environment, using living systems and correlative and statistical analyses to establish cause and effect relationships between contaminant presence and living system effects. Neither group should become so involved with their responsibilities that the other group is ignored. Engineering effort is wasted if single focus modeling ignores issues of major environmental consequence. Connections between cause and effect are only useful if presented by bioenvironmental scientists in a manner which clearly identifies the importance of the expected effect. Neither discipline can operate with complete independence in the present climate of environmental concern.

The acceptable standard of performance for engineers and bioenvironmental scientists must change. Simply demonstrating that a maximum concentration will not be reached or that the presence of a contaminant may affect some organisms in the receiving system is no longer acceptable. Engineers must recognize connections and bioenvironmental scientists must quantify predictions.

Acknowledgements

The exploration of the differences in tradition between engineers and bioenvironmental sciences began with a Plenary Session presentation by Prof. Donald O'Connor at the 1980 meeting of the North American Benthological Society. Critical reviews by David Schaeffer, Mark Rood, and Michael Sonnen are acknowledge and appreciated.

References

Cairns, J. Jr., "Certification, Standard Methods And Criteria," Fisheries, Vol 5, 1980, p.10-11.

Herricks, E. E., Schaeffer, D. J. and Kapsner, J. C., "Complying With NPDES Permit Limits: When Is A Violation A Violation?" J. Water Pollut. Control Fed., Vol 57, 1985, p 109-114.

General Accounting Office, "Better Monitoring Techniques Are Needed To Assess The Quality of Rivers and Streams - Volume 1" CED-81-30, April 30, 1981, 121 pp.

Green, R. H., "Sampling Design and Statistical Methods for Environmental Biologists" John Wiley & Sons, New York, 1979, 257 pp.

Herricks, E. E. and Schaeffer, D. J. "Can We Optimize Biomonitoring?" Environ. Manage. Vol 9, 1985, p. 487-492.

Loftis, J. C. and Ward, R. C. "Water Quality Monitoring - Some Practical Sampling Frequency Considerations" Environ. Manage. Vol 4, 1980, pp 521-526.

Romesburg, H. C., "Cluster Analysis For Researchers" Lifetime Learning Publications, Belmont, CA 1984, 334 pp.

Schaeffer, D. J., Kerster, H. W., Bauer, D. R., and Rees K., "Composite Samples Overestimate Wasteloads" J. Water Pollut. Control Fed., Vol 55, 1983, p 1387-1392.

Schaeffer, D. J., Kerster, H. W. and Janardan, K. G. "Grab Versus Composite Sampling: A Primer For The Manager And Engineer" Environ. Manage., Vol. 4, 1980, p 157-163.

Schumm, S. A., and Lichty, R. W., "Time, Space and Causality in Geomorphology" Amer. J. Sci, 1963, Vol 263, p. 110-119.

Sokal, R. R. and Rohlf, F. J., "Biometry" Freeman, San Francisco, 1973

United States Environmental Protection Agency, "Basic Water Monitoring Program" EPA 440/9-76-025, 1977.

United States Environmental Protection Agency, "Water Quality Standards Handbook" Office of Water Regulations and Standards, Washington, D.C., 1982.

United States Environmental Protection Agency, "Technical Guidance Manual for Performing Waste Load Allocations, Book II Streams and Rivers" EPA-440/4-84-020, 1983.

United States Environmental Protection Agency, "Technical Support Document for Water Quality-based Toxics Control" Office of Water, September 1985, 75 pp.

United States Geological Survey, "The National Stream Quality Accounting Network" Circular 719.

REVIEW OF DATA NEEDS AND COLLECTION TECHNOLOGY

Michael B. Sonnen[*]

My daughter, a new holder of a valid driver's license, drove me to the airport to start my journey to this conference. When I first travelled to New England to an Engineering Foundation Conference to discuss "Urban Runoff Quality, Its Impacts and Quality Enhancement Technology" or the equivalent, she was not yet born.

Here we are again, discussing whether urban runoff quality is a threat to anybody or anything, whether and how that can be proved, and what if anything we as an intelligent species can or should do about it. Nothing -- with respect to urban runoff quality information or resolve -- appears to have changed since 1968. The three preceding papers have me convinced now that little is going to change in this regard in my lifetime, or my daughter's. Still, many things have changed and many problems have been resolved in the intervening years of my professional lifetime since I first came here, and I have participated in solutions to those problems. The difference has been a political resolve to get on with solving those other problems, which I will describe later herein. These three papers, however, all markedly different from one another, make a plain and singular statement:

> The quality -- or pollutional effect -- of urban
> runoff has not attained a societal level of import-
> ance sufficient to support understanding it, much
> less controlling it.

That may come as an arguable revelation to some, particularly those who have made and wish to continue professional lifetimes devoted to urban runoff and little else.

It is unarguable, however, that these three papers contain exactly the same catalog of data insufficiencies that a number of the pundits in this audience and on this week's program were cataloging at such conferences in 1968 and before.

Be that as it may, let us look at the three papers.

---

[*]Manager, Water Resources & Utilities, URS Corporation, 412 West Hospitality Lane, Suite 208, San Bernardino, CA 92408, USA.

THE PAPER BY BRYAN ELLIS

There are many reasons for me, personally, to like this paper, even preferentially over the other two. First, it seems addressed to engineers, and I am an engineer. It talks about 'damage' functions, cost-effectiveness, hydraulic structures, exceedance values, annual and capital costs, SWMM, and 'overflow frequency' -- things I think about and grasp as an engineer. Secondly, as a reviewer, I appreciate the author's listing for me explicitly what the remaining data needs are to improve the dimensioning of engineering controls for urban runoff. These appear on the third page of Ellis' paper, and I reiterate them here for effect, innocuously edited.

   o   Quality based 'damage' functions.
   o   Efficient biomonitoring techniques and biological exposure times.
   o   Performance efficiencies for structures such as on-line storage tanks, overflows, and detention ponds.
   o   Economic comparisons between and among control options such as street sweeping, manhole cleaning, and sewer flushing or rodding.
   o   Pollutant routing through, and phase interactions within, hydraulic structures.
   o   Relations between changes in nonpoint pollutant discharges and stream recovery rates.
   o   Exceedance values for impairment of beneficial urban water uses.

Despite this being a reworded list of what we engineers have been saying were the data deficiencies for two decades, and despite the fact that it is an almost impossible list to achieve according to Mr. Davies and Mr. Herricks, it is nonetheless a short, tidy list that Ellis has provided to my benefit.

Thirdly, Ellis has the charming distinction from among the three authors of being British. That has useful qualities for my purposes, which I choose to expand from mere reviewer to a once-more, last-time-and-I'm-gone iconoclast trying to stir American technocrats and politicians to action. Here is Ellis -- a man who talks about "gully pots" and who spells "mobilization" with an "s" (which means he serves adequately as the often-invoked objective observer from Mars) -- saying that EPA's NURP study "necessarily and singularly failed" to "identify or recognise" long-term mobilization and resuspension phenomena related to potential-pollutants attached early in their travels to runoff-carried sediments. Now, America, that's pretty plain. It was nobody's fault of course, the study was simply too short, so it "necessarily" had to fail to find long-term effects. But that still means it observed less than needs to be known.

Fourthly, I judge Ellis' presentation superior because he had the good sense to cite my own (1977) work, which nonetheless was too difficult for me ever to be permitted to tackle alone, but which I

have not found to be repeated or advanced in ten years. Scour and
deposition transport equations for purely cohesionless soil particles, not including any physical chemistry of adherence to or
absorption within them of other constituents, is no place for this
world to have left that inquiry.

Additional Martian-like, objective observations of Ellis that I
find particularly adroitly put and yet decades old are these, which
are worth repeating:

o   "...many deficiencies still exist in our corporate know-
    ledge and understanding of the pattern and process of
    pollutant routing..."

o   Urban sewer network design, "apart from a basic and
    somewhat limited consideration of self-cleansing velo-
    city, does not incorporate any quality criteria in the
    design or performance terms."

o   "The sewer system is still very much a 'black box' as far
    as the nature, form and strength of in-line pollution is
    concerned."

o   "...it is the mobility and bioavailability of the
    pollutants in and between the sediment water system that
    will determine their ecological and receiving stream
    significance rather than their accumulative loading
    behavior."

I have seen no evidence in 20 years, Professor Ellis, that American
agencies at any level have held more than a passing, grudging
interest in engineered runoff control system behavior on other than
an average-annual, tons-per-year basis. Talk of interevent or even
singular-event or design-event behavior of things like 'chemicals'
is considered idle, academic, and generally uncooperative. What
that means is, talk of chemical behavior is tantamount to suggestion that such behavior be altered, which is talk of stormwater
treatment; and it is intuitively obvious to large numbers of people
that treatment would be outlandishly expensive, which your own cost
curves (even without numbers on the ordinate) demonstrate conclu-
sively enough, thank you very much.

THE PAPER BY PATRICK DAVIES

The paper by Patrick Davies is exciting to me because it is so
mysterious; and, I predict, it will raise trepidation in many of my
engineering and agency friends who have been assigned the responsibility of doing something about urban runoff.

Engineers are not going to want to hear about a 'differential pulse
anodic stripping voltameter,' because they don't have one in the
backs of their trucks. It sounds like an expensive thing to buy.

And they can't be certain, but they're pretty sure the crew members they have in the maintenance department today do not include anybody who could run one. Are they going to have to hire somebody with a masters degree in something? What do those kids make right out of school today? How much is that with overhead added on? There goes the budget. Maybe next year.

To most engineers, 'ligands' sound like things they ripped years ago in a football injury. They are not going to be pleased to hear that they are in runoff as well. Ligands, in fact, are groups, ions, or molecules bound mysteriously to a central, controlling atom in a 'complex.' A complex in turn is a group of constituents more intimately associated than in a simple mixture. They act together in a new and different way than they act alone or than they would act in a mixture if they didn't get together. A chelate is a special type, in which metals are bound together in a ring structure with other molecules, usually organic ones, to form an available, soluble-like conglomerate that results in the metal being somewhat available to organisms, being essentially soluble, and being able to pass through a filter; whereas without the ligand or chelating stuff there, the metal would be either completely soluble and very available or rendered insoluble, unavailable, and filterable from the remaining chemical properties of the water.

Engineers generally are not going to want to know about things like that. That's going to mean they will have to measure for those things. And engineers are plenty smart enough to know that ligands are just the sort of things that aren't going to be there every time, but they will be there enough of the time that they will have to be looked-for every time. Engineers don't like to measure things that might not be there but matter.

Engineers are not going to be receptive to the idea that different life forms or stages of various aquatic critters have different toxicity responses to different metals. They want to know if they have to remove zinc, period. They aren't interested that fingerlings are going to be more susceptible to zinc than adult fish. The things engineers build protect babies and adults alike. What they want chemists and toxicologists to tell them is: Should I slow down urban runoff and store it, or should I whistle it downstream to a big river or an estuary as fast as I can on an almost frictionless cushion of concrete? Decide. Decide for me. You went to the right schools to know those things; I didn't. So tell me.

Engineers -- right here in this room -- are upset with chemists and toxicologists already. This conference was put together by Ben Urbonas largely because he was personally troubled by data being reported on 'metals' in runoff. Were these dissolved metals? Total metals? Chelated metals? Available metals? Were these the same kinds or sorts of soluble or insoluble metals in this data report as they were in the last one? Did it matter? Did it matter a lot? Was there a standard somewhere that could be and should be applied? Ben wanted answers; so do others of us.

So, the engineers among us are not going to be happy to hear from
Davies that there are still controversies and uncertainties among
the chemists and toxicologists themselves about what to measure and
how to measure it. Didn't Pasteur and Arrhenius figure all this
out a century ago? Or was it van der Waals or van't Hoff? Maybe
van Gogh. Whoever it was, what have you people been doing for a
hundred years?

EPA is about to tell us engineers that we have to take metals out
of storm runoff and to prove we did it. Some of us are going to
have to measure metals at hundreds of places throughout our urban
area. That's expensive. We would like to know that we are proving
something worthwhile. We would be especially proud if we could
prove to EPA that the expense wasn't worth it; but we will be
equally proud of ourselves if we did a right and good thing. We
hear Davies when he says that the thing to be measuring is not
soluble metals, not total metals, but "potentially soluble metals."
But "potentially" anything sounds wishy-washy and unclear, and we
didn't miss the part of Davies' presentation where he said, "of
current methodologies available," the dissolved method comes
closest to being right. That means the "potentially dissolved
method" doesn't exist or isn't approved for use. Great. Another
hundred years.

Just to satisfy Davies' curiosity about metals, though, he implies
strongly that we need to be measuring the following things -- from
place to place and from event to event, at least for a while:

> pH
> alkalinity
> hardness
> temperature
> zinc
> cadmium
> life stages of various organisms
> time (of exposure)
> lead
> toxicity data from bioassays
> copper
> total organic carbon.

These things need to be measured both at the site of a detention or
controlled-release point and in the receiving water. They are
directed to metals alone.

THE PAPER BY HERRICKS

It is perhaps comforting for Professor Herricks to know that a week
will acutally come in his life -- and this is it -- when a large
group of people will decide whether he is Saint Genius or the Devil
incarnate.

What he has told us is: We have met the enemy, and he is ... everybody.

What he has told us is: Urban storm runoff is the most complex natural water on the planet.

What he has told us is: Nobody can tell another body what the 'right' thing to do with urban runoff is, and therefore, perforce, everything anybody has done with it up to now has been 'wrong.'

What he has told us is: The impacts of urban runoff quality are to be felt within minutes to decades of its passing by a point and within microns to miles of a given position in a stream or sewer.

What he has told us is: The largely chemical, highschool-freshman General Science litanties of materials in his Tables 1 and 2 differ from the largely biological, graduate-course zoology and toxicology list in his Table 3 like daydream and nightmare. Guess who he says have been measuring Tables 1 and 2 and who should go on measuring them? Engineers, right.

Professor Herricks has produced the first useful revelation about urban runoff quality and what to do about it in my 20 years of coming here to ruminate over it.

That revelation is this:

> It is incidental to society that urban storm water achieves certain controllable depths, speeds, or flotsam loads, my Engineer friends; what is compelling is that the stuff is <u>alive</u> or affects people and other creatures who are.

Corollaries of that revelation are these:

1) You engineer-boys have done a fine job of getting urban runoff into underground sewers or over to the side of our development to a slick channel so it won't flood our homes, but we scientists haven't figured out yet what that stuff is doing to people and fish and such who have to drink it downstream. Just wait; we'll get back to you, or somebody will.

2) You engineers are lucky you've had a few demagogues like Manning who told you what to do; in the pure sciences, we're all egomaniacs who insist on deciding for our-selves, so there is no consistent help we can give you. Maybe you ought to ask a politician what to do, for whom the word 'demagogue' was invented.

3) Tables 1 and 2 are your baliwick, and it is embarrassing to scientists how well you measure and use those things; Table 3 is ours, and it may be embarrassing to you to share the planet with eggheads like us who measure those

things; but remember we measure our things instantaneously and you get a month or a season or a year to
measure yours. You can't expect us to tell you what will
happen right here a month from now or what ever did or
will happen over there. This is where we measured and
this is what was going on when we were here.

Herricks has made the choice for us engineers very simple. We can
rest and await useful developments in the scientific and political
realms; or we can go mad. We can be serene and smugly out ahead,
or we can insist that urban runoff control is our God-given area of
responsibility and become supinely frustrated because neither God
nor a scientist will tell us what to do with it. If it is clear
that we can't measure or change things with instruments smaller
than a forklift, and if we start trying to measure things like life
stages of a microinvertebrate, no-one will believe our answers
anyway and no-one should. So we'll just wait.

Still, Herricks is quite right when he says that engineers and
bioenvironmental scientists should start talking and otherwise
communicating with one another. The place to start is for drainage
engineers to tell EPA's scientists to direct county and city health
departments and fish-and-game departments to measure metals and
diversity indices at 200 places; don't send the bill to the Public
Works Department.

HOW DO OTHER SCIENTIFIC PROBLEMS GET SOLVED?

Just a few years ago, wildlife scientists discovered that selenium
was being flushed from soils in the San Joaquin Valley of California
in quantities sufficiently large to cause deformities among waterfowl's offspring and dermatitis-like annoyances to few enough human
beings to consitute mere epidemiological curiosities. Nonetheless,
the political decision was made, fairly rapidly and without undue
fanfare, that irrigated agriculture in one of the most diverse and
abundant areas on the planet would not be sacrificed, but that the
selenium-laden discharge would be handled appropriately. In less
than a year, feasible alternatives for collection, treatment,
and/or deep-well injection of these wastewaters were found.
Farmers, considered to be the loudest cry-babies about environmental protection imperatives, did not cry and accepted the financial burden, such as it was, with no noticeable strain. I worked
on the deep-well disposal option, and I enjoyed the experience.
Something got done. Scientists are still arguing about which
enzyme it is in each of countless species that chelates selenium.

Six years ago, trichloroethylene (TCE) and perchloroethylene (PCE)
showed up in municipal water supply wells near where I live. The
State set standards for these things in drinking water. Since
then, 14 wells have been closed. Groundwater is virtually the only
source of supply. A year ago, the State of California hired our
firm to seek the original sources of the contamination, so
"responsible parties" could be found and so the sources could be
cleaned up.

We sampled a network of 100 points over a 15-square-mile area of the city, using soil pore gas analyses. We found PCE at every single site. TCE we found only sporadically; but these solvents were both throughout the area in no particular pattern. Every time we put the gas probe up in the air to get a background reading, we found PCE present. The stuff was ubiquitous. With one possible exception, not a single identifiable source was found. These materials are solvents or parts of solvents that were used all over town. They are consequences of life in an urbanizing area over the past 40 years. They are being mushed around our underground alluvial aquifer now by percolated urban runoff as much as by anything else. So what was the solution? Municipalities and water districts are adding stripping towers at noticeable but bearable costs, and the state is following up on pursuit of the one source we tentatively identified. I was a part of that work, and I enjoyed the experience. Something got done. Scientists to this day will not tell me if TCE at 4 ppb or PCE at 5 ppb will cause cancer in humans.

Three years ago, the U.S. Air Force finally decided to base its M-X missiles (the Peacekeepers) in existing Minuteman silos in Wyoming and Nebraska. Congress decided that an Environmental Impact Statement should be produced, but that it should not address the "impacts" of nuclear war, since the likelihood of such an event was so small and since "the project" had as its goal the prevention of nuclear war. So I worked on that EIS, leading team's of engineers to determine if water mains in Cheyenne or Scottsbluff were large enough to absorb the demands of new construction workers in the area or to determine whether storm or combined sewers were large enough to accept added flows from new developments. The EIS took up 13 volumes and cost over 20 million dollars. But it was done by January 31, 1984, the date Congress set for its completion. I started on the project on May 1, 1983. I enjoyed that work; something got done, because decisions got made.

I recently managed a project for General Motors Corporation in which we were the environmental consultants, monitoring the closure and demolition of a 2,000,000-square-foot auto assembly plant. Ninety "units" containing potentially hazardous materials were sampled by our team before and after removal of their contents to approved places and decontamination of the sumps, tanks, and other containers. Monitoring wells were sunk and sampled, and other clean-up steps were followed according to RCRA-imposed "closure plans." We didn't have to determine whether and to what degree anything found in any of these tanks would harm people or wildlife. These things had been administratively, politically determined in advance. If the contents found were on a certain list, they should be considered hazardous and dealt with accordingly. I enjoyed that work; the whole 90 acres will be a grassy field by next February, as GM had it scheduled from the outset.

Urban runoff pollution problems will eventually be dealt with in a similar fashion. Neither engineers nor pure scientists will decide when or where to measure various properties or constituents of urban runoff or what those characteristics should be. When the threat to people of urban runoff reaches a level noticeable by the U.S. Congress, Congress will tell EPA, and EPA will tell the rest of us. If Ben Urbonas gets told to measure heavy metals at 200 places around Denver -- at his own District's expense, he can do that or he can change his Congress-persons. That's the way it works. That's the way it works whether the metals data tell Ben anything useful or not. That's the only way urban runoff control (which means measurement) is going to work, whether Ben's data are meaningful to a scientist or not.

If we engineers and scientists want to make suggestions to EPA or the Congress about what to have us look for, that's fine.

I personally told an ASCE audience in 1979 (Sonnen, 1980) that I was using an awful lot of pesticides and fertilizers on my lawn that nobody was measuring on urban watersheds. These seemed like the dangerous things to me. None of our speakers has talked about source control very much at all. But it seems to me if we are ever to control the quality of urban runoff, we are going to have to control it (which means measure it) before it is in a storm sewer or whooshing down a prismatic concrete channel. And it seems to me that we won't be told to control urban runoff quality until Congress decides it's been killing people. A GAO report released in May of this year is alleged (UPI, 1986) to have warned the Congress and the rest of us that pesticide risks in the urban environment are worth worrying about, despite the lack of scientific certainty about health risks. CBS Evening News on May 21, 1986, included a segment on this report's findings and announced a separate investigation of its own which found that several hundred to a thousand people die each year in this country as a result of acute toxic effects from home and public (i.e., lawn, park, and golf course) use of pesticides. Pesticide data appear to me to be an essential 'data need' to be added to any worthwhile list.

REFERENCES

1. Sonnen, Michael B., "Urban Runoff Quality: Information Needs," Journal of the Technical Councils, ASCE, Vol. 106, No. TC1, Proc. Paper 15611, August 1980.

2. UPI, Washington, "Pesticide Dangers Unknown for Weekend Gardeners," Daily Facts newspaper, Redlands, California, May 25, 1986, p. A-11.

Discussion at Session 2:   Data Needs and Collection Technology

Question: [for Pat Davies]   What does one do with the metals accumulated in a stormwater detention pond?

Answer: The accumulated sediments and other materials should be sampled for metals first, before deciding.   If the concentrations, particularly the soluble or 'potentially soluble' metals concentrations are high, they should be treated as toxic materials, because they are. If the metals are low, the accumulated material could be sent to a less stringently controlled disposal site.   Sample first, then handle these materials accordingly.

Ben Urbonas: Based on what Pat Davies told us tonight, it is likely that all the metals data reported for the last 20 years about urban runoff should be scrapped.   Most of what we have is micrograms per liter of 'zinc' or 'cadmium' or whatever.   We have no idea from the reported data, and the investigators probably didn't either, whether these are 'available' and hence damaging amounts of these metals or not.   It seems, from what Pat told us, that the total amounts of metals found and reported are often if not usually much higher concentrations or loads than are actually available or potentially available to be harmful to any aquatic creatures or man.   I think we would all be upset to find ourselves mandated by regulators to measure metals in all our storm sewers or channels (and I would have to monitor at hundreds of places)

if the likelihood of dangerous metal concentrations or masses in urban
runoff were actually very low.

[Extended discussion ensued, mostly in agreement. Engineering and
managerial knowledge of metals chemistry and toxicology in general is
rudimentary and perhaps incorrect. Ed Herricks reinforced this
conclusion by pointing out that single-valued lethal concentrations to
50 percent of a population (LC_{50}'s) are 'a moving tartet,' because a
level of concentration or mass of a metal, in particular, depends on
alkalinity and other chelating or binding materials in each water which
render metals more or less available to harm aquatic organisms.
Moreover, the levels of these toxicity-interfering 'liqands' or
complexes in water can fairly obviously vary with time, redox
conditions, and other factors at a single point.]

Question: [for Pat Davies] Aren't most toxicological measurements made
in a laboratory under controlled conditions and with 'indicator' or
'test' species which may not even exist in the 'natural' water in
question?

Answer: Yes, most toxicological work is performed in the laboratory.
But, when it is done correctly -- and it usually is, the toxicology
experiments take the field conditions into account. Much of aquatic
toxicology has to do with basic water chemistry, and the toxicologist to
be helpful has to know that the chemistry of the water in the lab is
equal to or approximates that to be found in the field. If the
toxicologist gets the chemical and kinetic information correct to
reflect the field conditions, the lab data will be 'right.' This is one

reason I stressed the chemical kinetics and phase relationships for
metals. If soluble metals enter a detention pond with a 3-hour
detention time and basic kinetics of reactions tells us that it would
take 12 hours for 50 percent of the metals to be complexed, and that
they will not be complexed or adhered to solids instantaneously, then
the implications of that data should be clear -- whether measured in a
lab or in the field. If, on the other hand, lab chemistry alone tells
us that less than one percent of the metals in a given water could
possibly be available or potentially available to organisms, that is
useful information as well.

Sources of Urban Pollutants - Do We Know Enough?

Michael L. Terstriep, M. ASCE[1]
Douglas C. Noel,[2] and
G. Michael Bender, M. ASCE[2]

Abstract

The non-USGS data from the NURP program are summarized in terms of their availability and adequacy for decision making and modeling. Results of selected projects are reviewed and related research needs are discussed.

Introduction

Data were collected by 28 projects during the Nationwide Urban Runoff Program (NURP), USEPA (1983-A). The types of samples collected included rainfall, runoff, wetfall, dryfall, in-lake samples, and samples related to the best management practice (BMP) being investigated by the individual project. Of these 28 projects, 14 were managed completely by the local NURP agency, and 5 had USGS participation for the collection of rainfall, runoff, and washoff data. The remaining 9 were managed wholly by the USGS. This paper will deal with the 19 projects in which a non-USGS agency collected all or part of the data.

The NURP agency projects are:

Durham, NH	Knoxville, TN
Lake Quinsigamond, MA	Lansing, MI
Mystic Lake, MA	Ann Arbor, MI
Lake George, NY	Champaign, IL
Washington, DC	Austin, TX
Winston Salem, NC	Little Rock, AR
Tampa, FL	Kansas City, MO

Those with USGS participation include:

Denver, CO	Long Island, NY
Bellevue, WA	Irondequoit Bay, NY
Baltimore, MD	

---

[1]Head, Surface Water Section, Illinois State Water Survey, 2204 Griffith Drive, Champaign, IL 61820

[2]Associate Engineer, Illinois State Water Survey, 2204 Griffith Drive, Champaign, IL 61820

Project Summaries

Several projects have been selected for brief presentation to illustrate the types of goals that were important in various parts of the country. These project descriptions also demonstrate a commonality in the problems identified and in the conclusions. These similarities resulted in many cases despite problems encountered in the collection and analysis of data.

Champaign, Illinois

This project was carried out in two phases. The first, described by Terstriep et al. (1982), was an evaluation of street sweeping as a management practice for storm runoff quality. No distinct water quality benefit was discernible from sweeping at frequencies as high as twice per week.

The second phase of the project, described by Bender et al. (1983), included sampling at two points on an urban drainage channel and three points on an agricultural stream well above, just below, and several miles downstream from the urban contribution. The results of this study indicated that urban runoff affected the receiving stream by raising concentrations of metals, nutrients, and suspended solids well above background levels, and above ambient water quality standards for several metals. In general the elevations of concentrations were of short duration.

Other conclusions of note were that wet fallout was the source of large fractions of the ammonia, nitrate, and copper observed in the storm runoff, and that most metals were largely associated with solids, while most nutrients were predominantly dissolved.

Predictive equations for event mean concentrations and event loads of six constituents were developed from the second phase of the study. The rainfall parameters of total volume, duration, and maximum 5-minute intensity had the greatest influence on the concentrations and loads.

Bellevue, Washington

The City of Bellevue Storm and Surface Water Utility coordinated the efforts of several agencies in their project, Pitt and Bissonette (1984). The University of Washington compared biological and chemical conditions of one rural and one urban stream. The Municipality of Metropolitan Seattle looked at toxic pollutants at their sources and in receiving streams. The U.S. Geological Survey monitored urban runoff quantity and quality from three residential areas, identified contributions from atmospheric fallout, and evaluated the effectiveness of a detention basin in runoff quality management. The City of Bellevue collected baseflow and storm runoff samples from two residential basins for over 300 storms and evaluated street sweeping as a management practice.

It was concluded that one impact of urbanization is a degradation of stream habitat, including greater variation in flow and temperature between dry and wet weather periods and deposition of settleable solids, with associated contaminants, on the stream bottoms. Impervious areas in a watershed are the source of more than 60% of the runoff volume from storms whose total volume exceeds 0.1 inch. Lead, zinc, and chemical oxygen demand in runoff originate mainly from streets, while phosphorus and Kjeldahl nitrogen are washed from all paved surfaces. Total solids, however, appear to be carried from pervious surfaces as well as impervious areas. Good control of street load is achieved by sweeping three times per week, and vacuum-assisted sweepers are better removers of smaller particles. No improvement in water quality was found in storm runoff from swept areas. Regular semiannual cleaning of catch basins can reduce lead and total solids concentrations in runoff up to 25%, and zinc, nitrogen, phosphorus, and COD concentrations up to 10%.

A comparison of annual load values for runoff with those estimated for the watersheds from atmospheric sources shows that wet fallout loads account for major portions of the runoff loads of COD, nitrate, ammonia, Kjeldahl nitrogen, and organic carbon. Smaller but significant fractions of phosphorus and lead loads also may come from precipitation.

Denver, Colorado

The goals of this project were to characterize urban runoff and its associated problems and to evaluate detention basins and percolation pits as potential control measures, Denver Regional Council of Governments (1983) and Ellis and Mustard (1985). In the conclusions, urban runoff was declared to be a major source of total suspended solids whether or not there were exposed erodible land disturbances in a drainage basin. Fecal coliform oxygen-demanding substances, metals, and nutrients were also named as urban runoff pollutants with significant impact on receiving streams. Detention basins and percolation pits were determined to be effective in reducing pollutant loads in urban runoff, and the need for design specifications addressing the water quality benefits afforded by these structures was stated.

Winston Salem, North Carolina

The goals of this project were to characterize urban runoff and to evaluate the effectiveness of street sweeping as a best management practice, North Carolina DNR (1983). The primary conclusion of the study was that street sweeping was not effective as a BMP. The street sweeper was shown to perform much better in removing large particles than small ones. Frequent sweeping resulted in good control of nuisance street load, but no appreciable improvement in storm runoff quality. Rainfall was identified as a major contributor of runoff loads of ammonia, nitrate, Kjeldahl nitrogen, and phosphorus. Dry fallout was shown to be a significant source of cooper, zinc, lead, and mercury. Storm runoff sampling demonstrated heavy loads and criteria-exceeding concentrations of metals, ammonia, and nitrate. The effects of the degradation of quality these substances cause in receiving waters was documented in biological evaluations of the larger streams. The study acknowledged, however, that much of this load appeared uncontrollable by any means short of treatment.

Durham, New Hampshire

The goals of this project were to assess existing runoff conditions and to evaluate grassed swales and vacuum-assisted street cleaning as management practices, Oakland (1983).

High concentrations of metals, especially copper and zinc, were observed in storm runoff, exceeding standards and approaching acute toxic criteria. Receiving stream levels were lower because of dilution and sedimentation of solids. No denial of freshwater use was associated with storm runoff, but loss of shellfish harvest in the estuary due to elevated coliform counts represented a true impairment of use.

Evaluation of control practices suggested that grassed swales are good for removing COD, inorganic nitrogen, total residue, and total and dissolved metals, but poor for removing BOD, turbidity, dissolved solids, organic nitrogen, and total phosphorus. Runoff through the test swale showed increases in suspended residue, dissolved phosphorus, and bacteria. Vacuum-assisted street cleaning was shown to have good removal of large material and poor removal of small material. Some reduction of BOD and fecal streptococci in runoff samples indicated a degree of control from the better capture of large particles by the sweeper. Lake sampling of the freshwater impoundments revealed low dissolved oxygen and abundant plant life, indicating retention of nutrients. Inflow and outflow monitoring and mass balance calculations showed that the freshwater pond is also a sink for total and fecal coliforms, nitrate, phosphorus, zinc, and total residue.

Kansas City, Missouri

The goals of this project were to characterize urban runoff, to relate runoff loads to land use, and to address impacts of runoff and methods of controlling it, Mid America Regional Council et al. (1983). The conclusions of the study stated that erosion competes with washoff from impervious areas as a source of runoff solids. Land use has less effect on erodibility than slope and drainage pattern. High intensity land uses, with heavy traffic or development, are the sources of large washoff loads of nitrogen, oxygen demanding substances, zinc, copper, and lead. Impacts of urban runoff on receiving streams include bacterial contamination, dissolved oxygen depletion, and altered benthic population (toward more tolerant species). Runoff volumes were identified as crucial to constituent loads; impervious areas yielded low flow-weighted concentrations but high volumes, making them the major source per unit area. An unusual result was that the metals from the high intensity land uses were mostly in the dissolved phase.

Austin, Texas

The goals of this project were to characterize urban runoff from two residential land use areas, to evaluate a detention basin, and to define the impact of urban runoff loads on two urban lakes, City of Austin et al. (1983). Monitoring of the lakes indicated some short-term degradation of water quality due to storm runoff, with constituents such as TOC, BOD, COD, total nitrogen, ammonia, nitrate, phosphorus, suspended solids, and fecal coliform. Toxics were not seen to pose any real problem since only lead and zinc were measurable. Short-term effects of runoff on lake quality were observed, but not long-term effects. The question remains as to the stability of the pollutant-enriched bottom sediments of the lakes.

Lake Quinsigamond, Flint Pond, Massachusetts

The purposes of this project were to define the current lake quality, to determine sources of pollutants and their relationship to lake quality, and to recommend control actions to be taken, McGinn (1982).

A main conclusion was that urban runoff affects the lakes by raising concentrations of total and dissolved phosphorus and total and fecal coliform. Estimates of 1980 loads to the lakes state that surface runoff carried in 87% of the total phosphorus, 67% of the dissolved phosphorus, 96% of the suspended solids, and 49% of the total nitrogen. The remainder was attributed to base flows of tributaries and atmospheric fallout. Nutrients are the great concern because of certain problems of eutrophication which arise from them. Large metal loads enter the lake sediments but their recycling or other effects are not known. High bacterial counts are also a problem but the source is uncertain because of the numerous possibilities. The lake exhibits a great capacity to absorb the loads, which disguises the extent of the potential problem.

Little Rock, Arkansas

The purpose of this project was to clarify the problems of Fourche Creek and to evaluate management practices for technical effectiveness, cost effectiveness, and community benefit from their implementation, Metroplan (1983). Fourche Creek and its tributaries drain 90% of the Little Rock metropolitan area before discharging into the Arkansas River. Water quality problems of Fourche Creek include low levels of pH and dissolved oxygen and high levels of fecal and total coliform, suspended solids, metals, and phosphorus.

Results of first-year sampling showed that urban runoff caused high levels of BOD, COD, suspended solids, total and Kjeldahl nitrogen, and fecal coliforms in Fourche Creek. Sampling results also indicated that urban runoff concentrations of metals and solids were reduced as flow passed through the wetlands of the creek bottoms. However, Kjeldahl nitrogen and phosphorus concentrations were greater in the outflow from the wetlands than the inflow during storm runoff periods.

The primary conclusion of the project was that control of elevated levels of BOD, suspended solids, Kjeldahl nitrogen, and phosphorus was not feasible unless it was achieved as part of flood control management. It was recommended that stormwater management plans include extensive use of grassed drainage paths and detention/settling basins.

Extent and Availability of Data

The total volume of data collected for the 19 projects considered here was substantial. There were 237 basins (sampling stations) for which 588,650 rainfall/runoff observations were recorded and 102,720 samples were collected and analyzed. These samples included not only in-stream data, but also some atmospheric and street dirt samples.

Each of the 14 projects which collected their own rainfall, runoff, and instream water quality data monitored at least 5 storm events, and some monitored 80 or more events. For those projects that dealt with flows in storm sewers and urban receiving streams, a good record of rainfall and the associated runoff exists. The majority of these projects collected flow-weighted composite samples for water quality analysis but a few collected discrete samples through the course of the events. These discrete samples were generally taken at a preset time interval, such as once every 5 or 10 minutes, but some were collected on the basis of real-time evaluation of the volume of flow that had passed the monitoring station (one for every X cubic feet).

An important part of the NURP data base is the fixed site data. This data set provides the time invariant or slowly varying data from each site. Included is catchment information such as the area, population, slope, land use, and percent sewered. The length and slope of the main channel is provided as well as information on annual rates of fertilizer application and area under construction. The length, type, and condition of streets is also provided. Not all of the above information is available for all projects.

The primary data base on which the non-USGS NURP data reside is the USEPA STORET Data Base. Each project was responsible for providing USEPA with data tapes formatted for this particular data base system. A series of records were provided for each data set to serve as identification of the type of data to be stored in the data set. The program also allowed comment cards with which to describe the data, collection procedure, site, etc., if so desired.

Although the raw data from non-USGS projects are available directly from STORET, the data will also be available from the Illinois State Water Survey. Through a contractual arrangement with USEPA, the Water Survey has obtained all of the data and supporting documentation for the 14 non-USGS projects. This information will be reviewed and reformatted for consistency with the USGS project data. It will then be made available, for the cost of copying, on magnetic tape or 5-1/4 inch floppy diskettes. In addition to the actual data, a companion manual will provide fixed site data and any available maps showing location, topography, land use, and drainage.

Variability of the Data

An extensive list of chemical constituents of interest was developed by USEPA and USGS, but each project was allowed to emphasize its own list of constituents.

In general, each non-USGS project used a different laboratory and different sample collection and handling techniques. Although efforts were made to standardize procedures and each lab had its own quality control, some variability of results was introduced into the program by these differences.

In order to access the magnitude and variability of the non-point problem on a nationwide basis, a short list of 12 water quality constituents which were sampled by most projects was compiled. This list, referred to as the fast track data base, USEPA (1983-B) was used as a means of evaluating the questions of whether or not a significant problem existed on a national scale, and if so, whether it was a problem with a manageable solution. The following list identifies the constituents included in the fast track data:

Total Suspended Solids, TSS	Total Coliforms
Chemical Oxygen Demand, COD	Fecal Coliforms
Biochemical Oxygen Demand, BOD	Total Phosphorus, Tot.P
Total Copper, Cu	Soluble Phosphorus, Sol.P
Total Lead, Pb	Total Kjeldahl Nitrogen, TKN
Total Zinc, Zn	Total Nitrate Nitrogen, NO2+3

The fast track information is listed in terms of event mean concentration (EMC) of each constituent by event, followed by the site mean and coefficient of variation.

Figures 1 through 6 illustrate the high degree of variability in the constituents of interest. The limited amounts of data for high density residential and industrial land use make it difficult to compare the values directly. The results shown are based on 37 low density residential sites, 3 high density residential sites, 10 commercial sites, and 2 industrial sites.

Figures 2 through 6 indicate that the EMCs of the constituents shown are highest for high-density residential land use. Since only three basins were included in the high-density sample, this is not a valid conclusion.

With the exception of coliforms, the coefficient of variation for low density residential ranges between 0.45 and 0.61 for BOD, COD, Tot.P, Sol.P, TKN, and Pb. For TSS, NO2+3, Cu, and Zn, however it ranges between 1.09 and 1.53. For the ten commercial sites, the coefficient of variation is clearly lower with only Sol. P and Zn exceeding 0.60 at 0.75 and 0.86 respectively. The remaining constituents range between 0.22 and 0.60.

Suitability For Modeling

The value of the existing urban non-point source data base for modeling is highly subjective and is a function not only of the available data and their geographic distribution, but also the specific model to be used. For the purpose of this discussion, two rather broad classifications of urban runoff/washoff models will be considered.

Statistical Models

The models in this classification are basically stochastic models or regression models. They may predict either event or annual loads as a

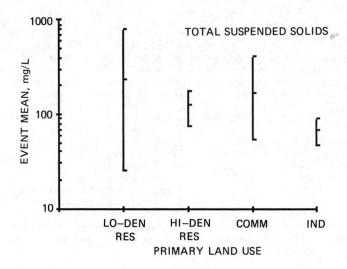

Figure 1.   Maximum, minimum, and mean concentrations of
total suspended solids

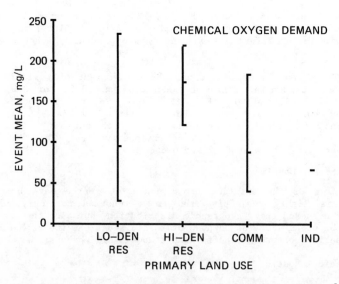

Figure 2.   Maximum, minimum, and mean concentrations of
chemical oxygen demand

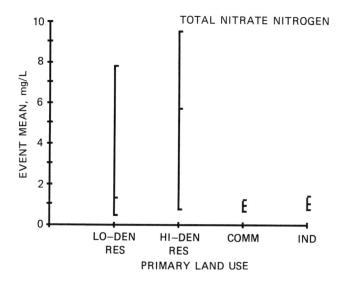

Figure 3.   Maximum, minimum, and mean concentrations of
total nitrate nitrogen

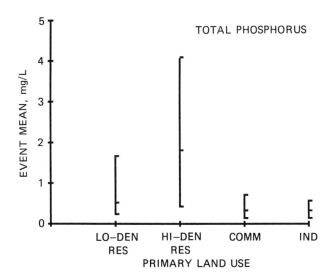

Figure 4.   Maximum, minimum, and mean concentrations of
total phosphorus

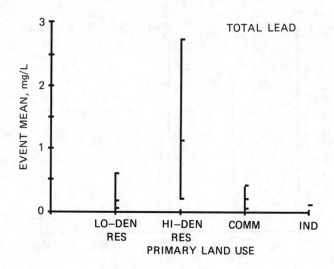

Figure 5.   Maximum, minimum, and mean concentrations of
total lead

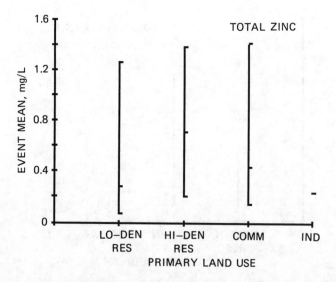

Figure 6.   Maximum, minimum, and mean concentrations of
total zinc

function of climatic or basin factors. Other forms may predict the
frequency of excursions beyond some given concentration. These models
are not extremely data intensive, requiring only minimal information on
the basin itself, a moderate number of event or annual loads (>5
samples, preferably >10), and rainfall associated with the event.

Physically Based Models

The models in this category attempt to simulate the actual
runoff/washoff phenomena by reducing the physical processes involved to
mathematical functions. They require considerably more data than do
statistical models, in terms of both physical data to describe the
basin and its drainage network, and the hydrometeorologic data
required. In terms of physical data needs, these models require that
each sub-catchment be described by unique surface runoff
characteristics such as impervious and pervious areas, flow path
lengths, flow path slopes, and (depending on the model) surface
depression storage estimates, soil types, canopy, and surface
roughness.

These models also require detailed information on the drainage for
each sub-catchment, including such parameters as channel length, slope,
cross-sectional roughness, and possibly storage volumes in the reach.

The hydrometeorologic data needed to calibrate and verify these
models include rainfall data, which serve as the primary input; flow
data, which are used to calibrate and verify the channel parameters and
effective contributing areas; wetfall/dryfall data to generate a
surface loading function for various pollutants; and water quality
data to calibrate and verify the washoff function of the model.

In analyzing the utility of the data available from the 14 non-USGS
NURP projects relative to modeling, the physical model classification
was further divided into two sub-classifications: single event models
and continuous simulation models. The criteria for judging the
modeling capabilities of the available data on a per project basis are
described below.

1. Statistical Models: at least 5 events, land use and basin area,
    rainfall/runoff totals, channel slope, and composite or discrete
    water quality samples.

2. Event Models: at least 10 events, total rainfall, discrete runoff
    measurements, surface loading curves, discrete W.Q. samples,
    detailed physical basin parameters.

3. Continuous Simulation Models: at least 20 events continuously
    sampled for rainfall, runoff, and water quality (discrete samples
    only), atmospheric deposition information, detailed basin physical
    characteristics and particle size distribution of surface load and
    washoff load (depending on the model).

Table 1 lists the information available for each of the 14 projects,
followed by the type of model(s) for which the data are minimally
sufficient. The limiting factor for each project is underlined on the
table.

Table 1. Suitability of Data for Modeling

Project	No. of Events	Wet/dry data (Y,N)	Fixed site (C,P,N)	Rain/ Runoff (Y,N)	WQ (D,C)	Model (S,E,C)
Ann Arbor, MI	6	Y	C	Y	D	S
Austin, TX	10	N	C	Y	C	S
Champaign, IL	85	Y	C	Y	D	SEC
Durham, NH	34	Y	C	Y	C	S
Kansas City, MO	17	Y	C	Y	C	S
Knoxville, TN	12	Y	C	Y	C	S
Lake George, NY	32	Y	C	Y	C	SEC
L.Quinsigamond, MA	8	N	C	Y	C	S
Lansing, MI	22	Y	C	Y	C	S
Little Rock, AR	20	N	C	Y	D*	SE
Mystic River, MA	6	N	C	Y	C	S
Tampa, FL	12	?	N			-
Washington, DC	45	Y	C	Y	C	S
Winston-Salem, NC	90	Y	C	Y	D	SEC

*discrete sampled, composite computed and reported

Fixed site - C = complete, P = partial, N = none available
Water quality - C = composite sampled, D = discrete sampled
Model - S = statistical, E = event, C = continuous
Wet/dry data and Rain/runoff - Y = yes, N = no

Priority Pollutants

A portion of the NURP program was devoted to an assessment of the significance of priority pollutants in urban storm runoff, Frederick and Healy (1982) and Cole et al. (1984). The priority pollutants are a group of 129 toxic chemicals or classes of chemicals which were identified as substances of serious concern in the Clean Water Act of 1977. The pollutants fall into ten groups: pesticides, metals and inorganics, PCBs (polychlorinated biphenyls), halogenated aliphatics, ethers, monocyclic aromatics, phenols and cresols, phthalate esters, PAHs (polycyclic aromatic hydrocarbons), and nitrosamines and other nitrogen-containing compounds. The priority pollutant monitoring program in NURP was designed to identify which pollutants might be found in urban runoff, how frequently, and at what concentrations, and to evaluate their potential impacts on aquatic life and water uses.

Nineteen of the 28 NURP project sites participated in the priority pollutant sampling program. A total of 121 flow-weighted composite samples representing entire runoff events were analyzed. They were collected at 61 sites, all of which were already storm runoff sampling sites in the conventional pollutant sampling program of NURP. The watersheds draining to the sites were residential, commercial, or mixed land uses and their sampling locations had no base flow. No runoff from industrial areas was analyzed for priority pollutants. Each participating project made its own arrangements for analysis of its samples, subject to quality assurance procedures supplied by NURP headquarters.

In all, 77 priority pollutants, including 14 inorganic and 63 organic pollutants, were found at least once in the NURP urban runoff samples. Two priority pollutants, asbestos and dioxin, were excluded from direct analysis and the results for seven more pollutants were termed invalid upon completion of the program.

The 14 inorganic pollutants, 13 metals plus cyanides, were the most prevalent group of priority pollutants in the samples. All 14 were found at least once and 11 were found in at least 10% of the samples. The most frequently found inorganic pollutants were copper, lead, and zinc, all occurring in at least 91% of the samples. Comparisons of individual constituent results to EPA water quality criteria and drinking water standards showed that lead exceeded its drinking water standard in 73% of the runoff samples, that lead and copper often exceeded freshwater acute criteria, and that lead, copper, zinc, and cadmium regularly exceeded freshwater chronic criteria.

Organic priority pollutants were generally found less frequently and at lower concentrations than the inorganics. One phthalate ester and one pesticide were found in over 20% of the runoff samples. Another 11 organics were found in 10 to 20% of the samples. Fifty more organics were found in 1 to 9% of the samples. Four organic priority pollutants were found in street dirt at one project site (Bellevue, Washington) but not in the runoff samples from that or any other project.

Criteria exceedances were less common with the organic priority pollutants. A single observation of one phenol and two observations of one pesticide exceeded freshwater acute criteria. Freshwater chronic criteria were exceeded by the same phenol in 11 samples, by the same pesticide in 17 samples, by two other pesticides in 8 and 10 samples, and by one phthalate ester in 22 samples. The remaining exceedances fell in the human health/carcinogenic category. Three pesticides and three PAHs were observed in concentrations exceeding those associated with various risk levels for human exposure. It should be noted that several organic priority pollutants have water quality criteria which are lower than the detection limits of the routine analytical methods employed in this study. Therefore, the fact that these pollutants were not detected in the analysis of these runoff samples does not mean that they were not present, possibly even in concentrations above their criteria.

From the standpoint of human health, organic priority pollutants appear to pose little threat. No organic pollutants were found, even in undiluted runoff, at levels exceeding noncarcinogenic human toxicity criteria. With regard to aquatic life, only two organic pollutants were observed even rarely in levels exceeding freshwater acute criteria, and only five were found to exceed freshwater chronic criteria, at different frequencies.

The greatest unanswered question related to the priority pollutants is the fate and effects of those pollutants, both organic and inorganic, known to be bound to sediments. Pollutant-enriched sediments carried by urban runoff to receiving waters may be deposited in any stream channel, reservoir, or lake. Very little is known about the effects such sediments have on aquatic life at the site of deposition or on the uses of the water body. Furthermore, the

potential of deposited materials as sources of these constituents, due
to migration or resuspension of sediment or recycling of pollutants
into solutions, remains unknown. Through their residence in the
sediments, priority pollutants may represent an entirely different
threat to human or aquatic life than current standards and criteria
consider.

Summary

It should be remembered that this paper is based primarily on the
non-USGS NURP data and that other data sets are available. The project
descriptions presented demonstrate that local goals have often been met
and questions answered by well designed data collection programs.
Collectively the projects have also successfully evaluated some BMPs.
We know, for example, that street sweeping will not generally improve
water quality but that detention has promise. It has also been clearly
demonstrated that metals and nutrients occur in storm water runoff in
concentrations as high as any point sources, but are of short duration.

Clearly we have learned a great deal about urban non-point
pollution, but many of the old questions remain and new ones have been
raised. The NURP priority pollutant study did not raise serious
alarms, but it did demonstrate that organic and inorganic pollutants of
concern are common in stormwater runoff. More recent studies have
shown toxic accumulation in sediments even when water samples are
negative.

Several projects identified surprisingly high pollutant levels in
wet and dry fallout with little hope of control. We need to know much
more about the fundamental processes of atmospheric deposition
including the release of metals related to acid rain.

Models offer us the means of transferring our knowledge from
instrumented basins to other areas. The reliability of these models is
therefore a measure of our knowledge of the processes involved. At
this point, for example, runoff models are seen to be reliable on
ungaged basins. This is not the case with water quality models. Most
modelers would agree that calibration data is required for the best of
our runoff quality models. This is perhaps the best indicator that we
do not know enough about the sources, transport, and fate of urban
pollutants.

Appendix - References

Bender, G.M., Noel, D.C., and Terstriep, M.L., "Nationwide Urban Runoff
Project, Champaign, Illinois: Assessment of the Impact of Urban Storm
Runoff on an Agricultural Receiving Stream," Contract Report 319,
Illinois State Water Survey, Champaign, Illinois, June 1983.

Cole, R.H., Frederick, R.E., Healy, R.P., and Rolan, R.G., "Preliminary
Findings of the Priority Pollutant Monitoring Project of the Nationwide
Urban Runoff Program," Journal of the Water Pollution Control
Federation, Vol. 56, No. 7, July, 1984. pp. 898-908.

Ellis, S.R., and Mustard, M.H., "A Summary of Urban Runoff Studies in the Denver Metropolitan Area, Colorado," Water-Resources Investigations Report 84-4072, U.S. Geological Survey, Lakewood, Colorado, 1985.

"Final Report of the Nationwide Urban Runoff Program in Austin, Texas," City of Austin and Engineering-Science, Inc., Austin, Texas, January 1983.

"Fourche Creek Urban Runoff Project," Metroplan, Little Rock, Arkansas, 1983.

Frederick, R.E., and Healy, R.P., "NURP Priority Pollutant Monitoring Program, Volume I: Findings," Monitoring and Data Support Division, U.S. Environmental Protection Agency, September 1982.

McGinn, J.M., "Watershed Management Plan for Lake Quinsigamond and Flint Pond," Office of Planning and Program Management, Massachusetts Department of Environmental Quality Engineering, and Lakes Section, Technical Services Branch, Massachusetts Division of Water Pollution Control, April 1982.

"Nationwide Urban Runoff Program, Kansas City Area Project," Mid-America Regional Council and F.X. Browne Associates, Inc., Kansas City, Missouri, January 1983.

"Nationwide Urban Runoff Program, Winston-Salem, North Carolina," Division of Environmental Management, North Carolina Department of Natural Resources and Community Development, Raleigh, North Carolina, October 1983.

Oakland, P.H., "Summary Report, Durham Urban Runoff Program," New Hampshire Water Supply and Pollution Control Commission, Concord, New Hampshire, June 1983.

Pitt, R., and Bissonnette, P., "Bellevue Urban Runoff Program, Summary Report, "City of Bellevue, Washington, August 1984.

"Results of the Nationwide Urban Runoff Program," Volume I, Final Report, Water Planning Division WH-554, U.S. Environmental Protection Agency, December, 1983-A.

"Results of the Nationwide Urban Runoff Program," Volume III, Data Appendix, Water Planning Division WH-554, U.S. Environmental Protection Agency, December, 1983-B.

Terstriep, M.L., Bender, G.M., and Noel, D.C., "Nationwide Urban Runoff Project, Champaign, Illinois: Evaluation of the Effectiveness of Municipal Street Sweeping in the Control of Urban Storm Runoff Pollution," Contract Report 300, Illinois State Water Survey, Champaign, Illinois, December 1982.

"Urban Runoff Quality in the Denver Region," Denver Regional Council of Governments, Denver, Colorado, September 1983.

ESTIMATION OF URBAN STORM-RUNOFF LOADS

Abstract   Nancy E. Driver* and David J. Lystrom, M. ASCE**

Urban planners and managers need to determine the quantity and quality of runoff in their cities and towns if they are to adequately plan for the effects of various land and water uses on storm-runoff quality from urban watersheds. As a result of this need, regression relations are being determined for estimating storm-runoff constituent loads, including suspended solids, dissolved solids, chemical oxygen demand, total nitrogen, and total ammonia plus organic nitrogen, using basin and climatic characteristics. The United States was divided into three regions, on the basis of mean-annual rainfall, to decrease the variability in storm-runoff constituent loads and to improve regression relations with basin and climatic characteristics. Multiple-regression analyses, in progress, are being refined to determine the best regression models for each of the storm-runoff constituent loads in each of the three regions. These techniques, when finalized, can be used to estimate storm-runoff constituent loads for gaged and ungaged urban watersheds. The preliminary standard errors of estimate for five constituents examined to date ranged from 54 to 223 percent, and the coefficients of determination (r^2) ranged from 0.39 to 0.94. Total storm rainfall and total contributing drainage area appear to be the most significant independent variables in the regression models. This paper is a progress report on preliminary results of estimating storm-runoff constituent loads for ungaged watersheds.

Introduction

The U.S. Geological Survey (USGS) and the U.S. Environmental Protection Agency (USEPA), in cooperation with State and local governments, have conducted programs to collect and analyze storm rainfall, runoff, and water-quality data in numerous cities throughout the United States to provide needed data for planning, zoning, and design. However, with increasing urbanization, city planners and managers need techniques to estimate discharge-weighted storm-runoff constituent loads (hereinafter referred to as storm-runoff loads) and mean-seasonal or mean-annual loads where little or no data exist. Because data collection and analysis of urban-hydrology data are both expensive and time-consuming, a regional method is needed to estimate the effects of basin and climatic characteristics on storm-runoff quality and to transfer those effects to ungaged urban watersheds.

*Hydrologist, U.S. Geological Survey, Lakewood, Colo.
**Hydrologic Studies Chief, U.S. Geological Survey, Lakewood, Colo.

For this study, two major data bases were used. The USGS national urban-stormwater data base contains data for as many as 18 water-quality constituents (converted to storm-runoff loads), 15 storm characteristics, and 32 basin characteristics, including 14 land-use categories, for each of 98 watersheds in 21 metropolitan areas monitored by the USGS. The USEPA data base contains data for as many as 12 water-quality constituents (converted to storm-runoff loads), 3 storm characteristics, and 9 basin characteristics, including 5 land-use categories, for most of 75 watersheds in 15 metropolitan areas (USEPA, 1983). These two data bases were combined to enhance the statistical analysis and to provide geographical coverage of 31 metropolitan areas (Fig. 1).

Purpose and Scope

The objectives of this study are to develop techniques for estimating storm-runoff loads for urban areas, using basin and storm characteristics. A regionalization approach will be developed to transfer storm-runoff-load data to ungaged watersheds.

This report describes the approach and preliminary results of the first phase of the project, which involves developing the best regression model to predict a set of storm-runoff loads at selected gaged or ungaged watersheds on a regional basis. Five storm-runoff loads, out of 11 storm-runoff loads, have been analyzed to date. In this analysis, the United States is divided into three regions based on divisions of mean-annual rainfall (Fig. 1). For each region, a predictive equation is developed for each water-quality constituent using basin and storm characteristics to estimate the water-quality load for a given storm. Coefficients of determination (r^2) and standard errors of estimate are presented to provide indicators of variability and accuracy of estimates. Actual regression equations are not published in this report because of the preliminary status of the results.

The second phase of this project (not discussed further in this report) involves estimating values of mean-seasonal or mean-annual loads for a particular site, and developing regional-regression models which will be of potential use to city planners for estimating seasonal or annual loads entering receiving water in urban areas.

Data Base

The USGS data base consists of two complementary data bases, in various stages of completion, which provide part of the input to this regional analysis. Driver and others (1985) compiled a national urban-stormwater data base containing time-series values of rainfall and runoff, water-quality analyses, and basin characteristics for 99 watersheds monitored by the USGS. In a related effort, watershed maps showing land uses and storm sewers are being compiled for most of the same urban watersheds (M.E. Jennings, USGS, oral commun., 1986). Data presently (1986) are being compiled, comprised of computed storm-runoff loads and characteristics of rainfall, runoff, basin, and antecedent conditions for 98 USGS urban stations, where streamflow, stream-water quality, precipitation, and occasionally precipitation-quality data were collected. This final data base includes data on 1,123 storms for 98 stations in 21 metropolitan areas.

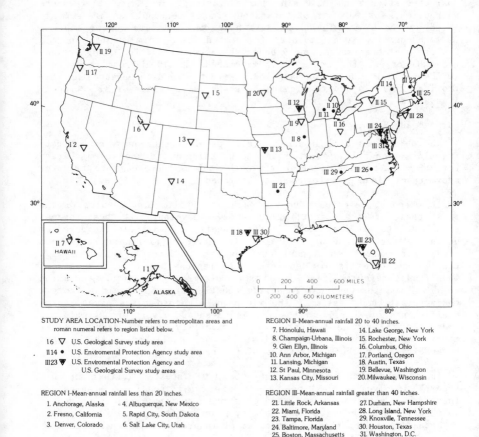

Figure 1.--Locations of urban-stormwater study areas and
mean-annual-rainfall regions in the United States.

A report by the USEPA (1983) describes an urban data base complementary to the USGS data base. This report has data on 1,690 storms for 75 urban stations in 15 metropolitan areas. Storm-runoff loads were computed by the USGS using published values of total storm runoff and event mean concentrations. Information for a USEPA station was included in the combined data base for joint analysis if adequate data for one or more storms at each station existed. The minimal data included (1) storm-runoff concentration values; (2) total rainfall and storm-duration values; and (3) total contributing drainage-area, impervious-area, and land-use values.

By combining the USGS and USEPA data bases, a common set of water-quality constituents were: total suspended solids, biochemical oxygen demand, chemical oxygen demand, total phosphorus, soluble phosphorus, total ammonia plus organic nitrogen, total nitrite plus nitrate, fecal coliform, total copper, total lead, and total zinc. Total nitrogen was calculated by adding total ammonia plus organic nitrogen and total nitrite plus nitrate. Common storm characteristics included total rainfall, total runoff, and storm duration. Common basin characteristics included total contributing drainage area, population density, basin slope, percent impervious area, and five categories of land use: residential, commercial, industrial, open, and other.

The USEPA data base was compared to the USGS data base where stations were present in both data sets. Comparisons were made for storm-runoff loads and storm characteristics for storms that were common to both data sets. Basin characteristics also were compared for these stations. In most instances, there was little difference between the two data sets.

Approach

The regional-regression relations discussed in this report are based on results of preliminary regression models that relate storm-runoff loads to easily measured climatic and basin characteristics. The storm-runoff load (dependent variable) is regressed against a selected set of climatic and basin characteristics (independent variables). Accuracy of the estimates of loads (standard error of estimate) is a function of the difference between the measured and estimated storm-runoff loads.

In a simplistic assessment, storm-runoff loads could be estimated from mean values of storm-runoff loads for each region or from an average yield (expressed in pounds per acre per inch of rainfall) for each region. However, in a regionalization approach, more accurate estimates of storm-runoff loads can result by using multiple-regression analysis and basin and climatic characteristics. Regional analysis accounts for spatial variations in storm-runoff loads that are caused by regional differences in characteristics directly or indirectly affecting storm-runoff loads. Accuracy of the storm-runoff-loads regression models for each region is dependent on the accuracy of both the dependent and independent variables (data error) and the ability of the independent variables in the regional-regression models to account for the statistical variation in the dependent variable (model error).

All storm-runoff loads and climatic and basin characteristics were transformed to log units (base-10) prior to regression analysis to provide the best means of meeting the assumptions of regression analysis. The assumptions of regression analysis are: (1) Errors are normally distributed about the regression model; (2) errors about the regression model have a constant variance; (3) relation between dependent and independent variables is linear; (4) errors have zero mean; and (5) errors are uncorrelated (Draper and Smith, 1981).

Multiple-regression relations, based on logarithmic transformations of the variables, are in the following form:

$$\log Y = B_0 + B_1 \cdot \log X_1 + B_2 \cdot \log X_2 + \ldots + B_n \cdot \log X_n; \qquad (1)$$

or, taking antilogs,

$$Y = B_0' \cdot X_1^{B_1} \cdot X_2^{B_2} \ldots X_n^{B_n}; \qquad (2)$$

where Y = storm-runoff load (dependent variable);
B_0, B_1, B_2, B_n = regression coefficients;
$B_0' = 10^{B_0}$;
$X_1, X_2, \ldots, X_n$ = basin or climatic characteristics (independent variables); and
n = number of basin and climatic characteristics in the model.

Description of Selected Variables

Regional-regression relations developed to date are for five storm-runoff loads. The five storm-runoff loads, expressed in pounds, are chemical oxygen demand, suspended solids, dissolved solids, total nitrogen, and total ammonia plus organic nitrogen. Additional analyses are in progress for total phosphorus, dissolved phosphorus, total cadmium, total copper, total lead, and total zinc. Dissolved-solids loads are available only in the USGS data base. Values for each of the storm-runoff loads are included in a comprehensive summary of data for the national urban water-quality data base in preparation (1986).

The dependent variables (storm-runoff loads) were selected based upon the frequency of the variable in the data base as well as the general importance of the variable in urban planning. Although one of the assumptions of regression analysis is that the errors are uncorrelated, some storm-runoff loads may be slightly correlated due to some storms being sampled consecutively in a watershed. This correlation in the dependent variable is assumed to be negligible in this analysis, since most storms were sampled in a random fashion.

Independent variables used in this report include the following:

Basin characteristics:
1. Total contributing drainage area, in acres;
2. Impervious area, as a percent of total contributing drainage area;
3. Population density, in people per square mile;
4. Industrial land use, as a percent of total contributing drainage area;
5. Commercial land use, as a percent of total contributing drainage area;
6. Residential land use, as a percent of total contributing drainage area;
7. Non-urban land use, as a percent of total contributing drainage area.

Climatic characteristics:
1. Total rainfall for each storm, in inches;
2. Duration of each storm, in minutes;
3. Mean-annual rainfall, in inches;
4. Maximum 24-hour precipitation intensity having a 2-year recurrence interval, in inches;
5. Mean-annual nitrogen-precipitation load, in pounds of nitrogen per acre; and
6. Mean-minimum January temperature, in degrees Fahrenheit.

Highly correlated independent variables were identified so that these variables would not be combined in the same model. Independent variables also were selected based upon the frequency of the variables in the data base, upon the ease of measurement by urban planners, and upon the assurance that the various combinations of independent variables were physically logical.

Definition of Homogeneous Regions

The objective of this analysis was to relate individual storm-runoff loads for all sites to basin and climatic characteristics, on a storm-event basis. Initially, all data were analyzed together, and the best regression models were selected for each constituent. Then the data were analyzed on a regional/stratified basis to evaluate whether the models could be improved.

The best regional divisions were selected after testing the following possible regionalizations: physiographic divisions, geographic divisions, total contributing drainage areas, impervious areas, 2-year 24-hour rainfall, mean-minimum January temperatures, and mean-annual rainfall. The resultant regionalized models were compared with the models representing all the data. Regionalization improved the accuracy of the models. The regional breakdown providing the best regression results, according to the lowest standard errors of estimate, was based on mean-annual rainfall. Further subdivisions of the regions based on mean-annual rainfall were attempted, but statistical relations were not improved. Analysis of covariance was performed on data in regions based on mean-annual rainfall to determine if the regions were significantly different from one another. All three regions were

statistically different from one another at a 99-percent or better
significance level, according to an F-test. The coefficients for each
variable in the models differed significantly between regions. This
test further substantiated that regionalization improved the models.

The United States was divided into three regions (Fig. 1) representing areas having mean-annual rainfall of less than 20 inches
(region I), mean-annual rainfall of 20 to less than 40 inches
(region II), and mean-annual rainfall of greater than or equal to
40 inches (region III). Geographically, metropolitan areas in region I
included all the stations in the western United States, excluding
Hawaii, Oregon, and Washington; metropolitan areas in region II
included the northeastern inland stations, the northwestern stations,
and Hawaii; and metropolitan areas in region III included the southern
United States as well as the coastal stations in the northeastern
United States. Mean-annual-rainfall regions are not drawn on the map
because too many local variations occur in the United States to depict
accurately on a map of this scale; mean-annual-rainfall values can be
determined from the National Oceanic and Atmospheric Administration
publication (1980).

Regression Analysis

Following the selection of regions, the best regression model for
each constituent in each region was determined. Regression relations
were determined using stepwise regression procedures written by the
Statistical Analysis System (SAS Institute, 1985, p. 763-774).
Initially, all selected dependent and independent variables with a
reasonable number of values in a region were regressed. Then a series
of models with different combinations of significant independent variables were run to determine the best relation. Regression analysis was
tried using the untransformed data and using logarithmic and square-
root transformations. Residuals, the differences between what actually
is observed and what is predicted by the regression equation, were
plotted for each model with these different transformations. Residual
patterns can reveal whether or not the assumptions of regression
analysis are violated. For example, certain abnormal residual patterns
indicate a need for alternate statistical approaches to the model
(Draper and Smith, 1981). Examination of the residual patterns for the
models of these different transformations verified that the best transformation for the five storm-runoff-loads models was a logarithmic
transformation. Examination of standard errors of estimate supported
the findings from the residual plots.

Stepwise regression was used to eliminate independent variables that
did not significantly explain the variation in storm-runoff loads.
Many statistics were examined in selecting the best model for each
storm-runoff load in a region. Models generally were selected with the
highest r^2, the lowest standard error of estimate, significance levels
greater than 95 percent, and the Mallows' Cp statistic that was closest
to the number of coefficients in the model (Draper and Smith, 1981,
p. 299-302). The coefficient of determination, r^2, indicates the
proportion of the total variation of the dependent variable that is
explained by the independent variables. The standard error of estimate
squared is an estimate of the variance about the regression; therefore,

the smaller it is, the more closely the estimated values agree with the observed values. F-tests with 95-percent significance levels allow only the most significant independent variables to enter the equation in stepwise regression. The Mallows' Cp statistic identifies the model that is both unbiased and has minimum variance. Another consideration in selecting the best equation was to determine the lowest number of independent variables. By dropping the less significant variables from these equations, the amount of data and effort required for application is greatly reduced.

After the best model was selected, the residuals were plotted to determine if the assumptions of regression were violated. All residuals for storm-runoff loads in each region generally produced randomly scattered plots along a horizontal band, thereby satisfying regression assumptions. The predictive capabilities of the regression relations will be verified when the models are finalized.

Discussion of Regression Relations

The preliminary results, in the process of being finalized, are summarized in Table 1. Three equations are given for each storm-runoff load--one equation for each of the three mean-annual-rainfall regions. The negative and positive signs under the independent variables in Table 1 are the signs of the coefficients for the preliminary equations. The general format for the equations is discussed in the approach section.

Regional equations generally were based on data for metropolitan areas shown for each region in Figure 1. Some metropolitan areas and stations were not used because of missing data. However, the total numbers of stations and storms (observations) listed in Table 1 generally were adequate for the development of regional equations. The regional equation for dissolved solids in region III was omitted because only one metropolitan area was represented. One metropolitan area in a region is not considered adequate for the development of a regression equation because five of the independent variables (mean-annual rainfall, 2-year 24-hour rainfall, mean-annual nitrogen-precipitation load, and mean-minimum January temperature) had only one common value for all watersheds in a metropolitan area.

Total rainfall and total contributing drainage area were predominant variables in every equation. Each of these independent variables was separately and independently correlated to the dependent variable at a 99-percent or better significance level, according to an F-test. These two variables always were the first to enter the equation in a forward-stepwise regression. In addition to these two variables, the 14 equations generally included a combination of land uses or impervious area.

Mean-annual rainfall, 2-year 24-hour rainfall, mean-annual nitrogen-precipitation load, and mean-minimum January temperature were cross-correlated; correlation coefficients ranged from 0.70 to 0.94. As a result, equations were restricted to only one of these independent variables; selection of the independent variable depended on how much it improved the model. Population density and duration of rainfall were used less because these variables were available only in some areas.

Table 1.--Summary of preliminary regression relations

(COD = Chemical oxygen demand; SS = Suspended solids; DS = Dissolved solids;

lb = pounds; in. = inches; % = percent; min = minutes;

Storm-runoff constituent load (lb)	Region number (see Figure 1)	Number of stations	Total rainfall (in.)	Sign of coefficients for independent variables						
				Total contributing drainage area (acres)	Impervious area (%)	Land use, industrial (%)	Land use, commercial (%)	Land use, non-urban (%)	Land use, residential (%)	
COD	I	21	+	+		+	+	-		
COD	II	51	+	+		+	+		+	
COD	III	39	+	+		+	+	-		
SS	I	19	+	+	+			+		
SS	II	44	+	+						
SS	III	33	+	+		+	+	-		
DS	I	16	+	+	+					
DS	II	19	+	+			+	-	+	
TN	I	15	+	+		+	+	-		
TN	II	44	+	+		+	+	+		
TN	III	40	+	+	+					
AN	I	23	+	+		+	+	-		
AN	II	63	+	+	+					
AN	III	39	+	+				-		

Signs of the coefficients for each of the equations generally were logical in explaining cause-effect processes; however, signs sometimes are difficult to interpret in multiple-regression relations because some correlation between independent variables exists. Correlations between independent variables in these models are small; therefore, general trends in the signs of the coefficient are presented. Coefficients for total rainfall, total contributing drainage areas, impervious areas, industrial land uses, commercial land uses, residential land uses, 2-year 24-hour rainfall, mean-annual nitrogen-precipitation loads, and population density always were positive. A positive relation with loads for all these variables would be expected. Non-urban land use has a negative relation with loads for most equations. Mean-annual rainfall has a negative relation to loads for all of the equations, which may indicate that longer periods between storms in drier climates allow more residue to build up on impervious surfaces; therefore, a smaller mean-annual rainfall would produce greater storm loads. Precipitation intensity (2-year 24-hour rainfall) has a positive relation to storm-runoff loads. The concept that higher intensity storms would produce higher loads seems reasonable because the pollutant washoff from impervious areas would be large in high-intensity storms.

for storm-runoff-load regionalization.

TN = Total nitrogen; AN = Total ammonia plus organic nitrogen;

$^\circ F$ = degrees Fahrenheit; mi^2 = square mile)

Sign of coefficients for independent variables

Mean-annual rainfall (in.)	2-year 24-hour rainfall (in.)	Mean-annual nitrogen-precipitation load (lb of nitrogen/acre)	Duration of rainfall (min.)	Mean-minimum January temperature ($^\circ$F)	Population density (persons/mi^2)	R^2	Standard error of estimate (%)	Coefficient of variation (%)	Number of observations
−						0.76	85	226	216
	+					.64	107	269	779
						.51	155	223	567
	+		−			.77	129	335	171
				−	+	.55	185	335	972
						.56	223	387	528
−						.93	75	351	175
						.73	168	198	286
−						.94	54	399	121
						.54	111	183	583
−						.42	69	113	619
		+				.86	57	479	188
		+				.67	85	364	849
−						.39	69	128	613

The duration of rainfall has an inverse relation with loads in region I because the shorter storms in the West generally are more intense thunderstorms with greater rainfall that would produce higher loads. Mean-minimum January temperatures have an inverse relation to loads for region II for suspended-solids. This inverse relation may be due to road salting in this region.

The coefficients of determination (r^2) in Table 1 for the equations range from 0.39 to 0.94. Standard errors of estimate range from 54 to 223 percent. These ranges indicate that some of the predictive equations have significant unexplained variability and corresponding high error. The coefficient of variation is the standard deviation of the untransformed dependent variable divided by the mean of the dependent variable, expressed in percent. This statistic generally indicates how well the dependent variable could be predicted using only the mean value, without any regression relation. Comparison of these two columns shows that substantially more variability is explained by the regression equation than could be explained by the mean of the dependent variable.

Summary

    Regression relations for estimating storm-runoff loads are being
developed for urban areas in the United States. Preliminary regression
relations were determined for five storm-runoff loads--chemical oxygen
demand, suspended solids, dissolved solids, total nitrogen, and total
ammonia plus organic nitrogen. The United States was divided into
three mean-annual-rainfall regions to decrease the variability in
storm-runoff loads caused by differences in basin and climatic characteristics. Data compiled by the USGS and the USEPA were used to determine regression relations for the three regions. Preliminary results
from fourteen regression models are presented with relevant statistics.

    Total storm rainfall and total contributing drainage area are the
most significant variables in all of the storm-runoff-load relations.
Other significant variables in the regression relations are impervious
area, industrial land use, commercial land use, residential land use,
non-urban land use, mean-annual rainfall, 2-year 24-hour rainfall,
mean-annual nitrogen-precipitation load, mean-minimum January temperature, population density, and duration of rainfall. Each of the
preliminary regression relations includes at least the following
variables: total rainfall, total contributing drainage area, and two
other characteristics.

    This paper is a progress report on preliminary results of storm-
runoff-load regionalization. Further analysis on the storm-runoff
loads is in progress (1986), and predictive relations on annual (or
seasonal) loads of selected water-quality constituents will be
developed.

References

Draper, N.R., and Smith, Harry, 1981, Applied regression analysis,
    2d ed.: New York, John Wiley, 709 p.
Driver, N.E., Mustard, M.H., Rhinesmith, R.B., and Middelburg, R.F.,
    1985, U.S. Geological Survey urban-stormwater data base for
    22 metropolitan areas throughout the United States: U.S.
    Geological Survey Open-File Report 85-337, 219 p.
National Oceanic and Atmospheric Administration, 1980, Climates of the
    States, 2d ed.: Detroit, Gale Research Company, 2 v.
SAS Institute, Inc., 1985, SAS user's guide, Statistics: Raleigh,
    N.C., 956 p.
U.S. Environmental Protection Agency, 1983, Results of the nationwide
    urban runoff program: U.S. Environmental Protection Agency Final
    Report, 4 v.

METRICS

Conversion factors for measurements in this article:

1 acre=0.4047 hectare;
1 inch=25.40 millimeters;
1 pound=0.4536 kilogram;
1 square mile=2.590 square kilometers;
°F=9/5°C+32.

Urban Runoff and Water Quality Criteria

John L. Mancini*
Alan H. Plummer*

Introduction

The need to treat or reduce the loading from urban runoff can be determined, in part, by the characteristics of the urban runoff, by receiving water responses, and the water quality criteria employed to assess the impacts of this type of discharge. Each of these factors are discussed in this paper.

Water quality impacts from urban runoff are controlled, to a large extent, by local conditions such as runoff characteristics, water body type, geometry, flow, and chemistry. In spite of the importance of local conditions, it is possible to examine the general water quality impacts from urban runoff and identify the important issues as well as suggest methods which could be employed to develop regional or national wet-weather water quality criteria. The significance of water quality impacts from urban runoff could be judged on the basis of existing water quality criteria developed to control continuous point source discharges. Wet-weather criteria could provide one input into decisions on the water quality importance of urban runoff and requirements for controls.

Characteristics of Urban Runoff

Three primary characteristics of urban runoff, which potentially make the water quality impact different from treated point sources, are 1) the intermittent nature of the loadings which are usually of relatively short duration with a longer time separating events, 2) the variability within and between events, and 3) the relatively high suspended solids concentrations in the discharges.

*Author, John Mancini Consultants Inc., 12 Ginger Cove Road, Valley, NE 68064.

*Author, Alan Plummer and Associates, Inc., 841 West Mitchell, Arlington, Texas.

Table 1 illustrates the intermittent nature of rainfall. Event durations average approximately 6 hours for many locations. The interval between storms which average 80 hours is on the order of ten times longer than the rainfall durations. An indication of the variability of storm duration and interval between storms is also provided.

The rainfall process is highly variable in both time and space. The intensity of rainfall at a location can vary from minute to minute. The intensity at any time can be different at several locations in the same urban area. Phenomena such as urban runoff and associated contaminant concentrations which are driven by the rainfall process are also highly variable in both time and space.

Most urban areas contain networks of drainage systems which collect and discharge urban runoff into one or more receiving water bodies. Since rainfall, runoff, and contaminant concentrations all vary in space and time, it is impossible to determine the sources or causes of short time scale receiving water quality changes by measurement, calculation or a combination of these activities.

Although very short duration exposures (in terms of minutes) to very high concentrations of toxics can have environmental consequences for aquatic organisms, it is likely that, for the concentrations encountered in urban runoff, exposure in terms of hours have the highest possibility of causing adverse environmental impacts. This is, in part, a consequence of the mixing in natural systems and the averaging of numerous sources which have different means and variabilities of both concentration and flows.

In view of the above, an appropriate and convenient time scale for analysis and evaluation of urban runoff loads, concentrations and effects is the event duration. The average concentration of contaminants, on this time scale, can be represented by the total constituent mass discharged, during an event, divided by the total runoff volume of the event. This concentration is defined as the event mean concentration (EMC). The EMC can also be used to compute loadings on the annual time scale associated with long-term water quality impacts.

Examination of EMC data indicates that this concentration varies from storm to storm at a location and also varies from location to location both within an urban area and between urban areas. Figure 1 presents information illustrating the variation of the EMC for total copper at a site and between sites (USEPA, 1983). The difference between the dashed line and the solid line is a measure of variations between events at the same sites. The coefficient of variation generally ranges between 0.5 and 1.0. The change in concentration as a function of probability (i.e., the variation along the solid or dotted line) is an illustration of the variation from site to site. The site-to-site variation tends to be larger than the variation at a site. The ratio of the median to 90 percent value for site-to-site variability is 2.7 for copper.

TABLE 1   AVERAGE STORM AND TIME BETWEEN STORMS FOR
SELECTED LOCATIONS IN THE UNITED STATES

Location	Average Annual Values in Hours	
	Storm Duration	Time Between Storm Midpoints
Atlanta, GA	8.0	94
Birmingham, AL	7.2	85
Boston, MA	6.1	68
Caribou, ME	5.8	55
Champaign-Urbana, IL	6.1	80
Chicago, IL	5.7	72
Columbia, SC	4.5	68
Davenport, IA	6.6	98
Detroit, MI	4.4	57
Gainesville, FL	7.6	106
Greensboro, SC	5.0	70
Kingston, NY	7.0	80
Louisville, KY	6.7	76
Memphis, TN	6.9	89
Mineola, NY	5.8	89
Minneapolis, MN	6.0	87
New Orleans, LA	6.9	89
New York City, NY	6.7	77
Steubenville, OH	7.0	79
Tampa, FL	3.6	93
Toledo, OH	5.0	62
Washington, DC	5.9	80
Zanesville, OH	6.1	77
Mean[1]	6.1	81
Denver, CO	9.1	144
Oakland CA	4.3	320
Phoenix, AZ	3.2	286
Rapid City SD	8.0	127
Salt Lake City, UT	7.8	133
Mean	6.5	202
Portland, OR	15.5	83
Seattle, WA	21.5	101
Mean	18.5	92

Note: Typical values.

	Average hours	90% hours
Storm duration	6	15
Interval between storm midpoints	80	200

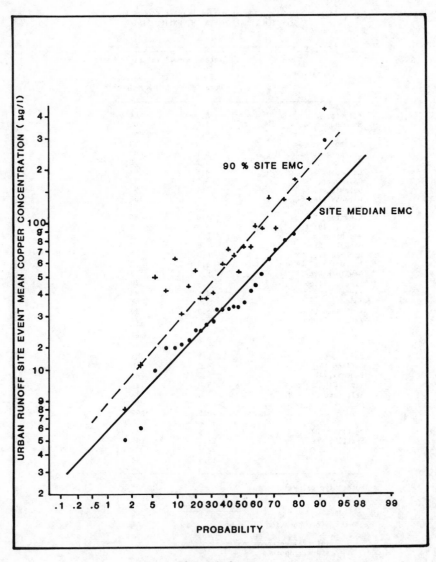

Figure 1
SITE PROBABILITY BASED UPON EMC

Table 2 contains information (USEPA, 1983) on the concentration characteristics of urban runoff for a number of constitutents. The information presented illustrates site-to-site variations and event-to-event variations at a site.

Water Column Constituent Transport and Water Quality Impacts

There are three types of water quality impacts which can be associated with urban runoff. The first is characterized by short-term changes in water quality during and shortly after storm events. An example would be aquatic organism mortality as a result of increases in the concentrations of toxics during storm events. The short-term impacts from urban runoff are the primary focus of this presentation.

A second type of water quality impact can be caused by contaminants associated with suspended solids that settle and by nutrients which enter receiving waters with long detention times. The common characteristic of these types of water quality impacts is that annual urban runoff loadings and time scales are important. These long-term impacts from urban runoff can be manifested during critical periods normally considered in point source control analysis. Examples are bottom sediment oxygen demand, lake eutrophication, and non-lethal impacts from toxics. Limited discussions of these types of impacts will be included.

A third type of impact from runoff is associated with scour and resuspension of sediment and the associated pollutants. These types of impacts will not be examined.

Figure 2 illustrates a discharge event from a runoff site. The idealized situation shown employs a constant upstream flow and a pulse input of contaminant. At location "A", in the vicinity of the discharge, the flow and concentration is shown as a function of time. At location "B" which is remote from the discharge, the river flow and concentration are also shown. In principal, the flow increase will travel as a wave downstream with a velocity in excess of the rate of travel of the mass of contaminant. This is illustrated for location "B" on Figure 2 by the earlier appearance of the flow spike at "B" as compared to the appearance of the mass spike. One way of thinking of this is that a downstream volume of clean water is displaced out of the system to make room for the contaminated water that has been introduced at the discharge location and after some time period the system returns to the original volume.

Water quality impacts and constituent transport are determined by:

1. The spatial extent of the spike of contaminated water "Tw" is determined by the river flow at the time of the discharge event and the duration of the discharge.

TABLE 2 WATER QUALITY CHARACTERISTICS OF URBAN RUNOFF

Constituent	Event-to-Event Variability in EMCs (Coef Var)	Site Median EMC	
		For Median Urban site	For 90th Percentile Urban site
TSS (mg/l)	1-2	100	300
BOD (mg/l)	0.5-1.0	9	15
COD (mg/l)	0.5-1.0	65	140
Total P (mg/l)	0.5-1.0	0.33	0.70
Solid P (mg/l)	0.5-1.0	0.12	0.21
TKN (mg/l)	0.5-1.0	1.50	3.30
NO_{2+3}-N (mg/l)	0.5-1.0	0.68	1.75
Total Cu (ug/l)	0.5-1.0	34	93
Total Pb (ug/l)	0.5-1.0	144	350
Total Zn (ug/l)	0.5-1.0	160	500

TABLE 3 EPA HEAVY METALS WATER QUALITY CRITERIA

Metal	Hardness	Fresh water ug/l	
		$CMC^{(1)}$ (Acute)	$CCC^{(2)}$ (Chronic)
Copper[3]	50	9.2	6.5
	100	18	12
	200	34	21
Lead[3]	50	34	1.3
	100	83	3.2
	200	200	7.7

Notes: [1]Criterion Maximum Concentration - Averaging period 1 hour. This is also exposure duration in stormwater context.

[2]Criteria Continuous Concentration - Averaging period 4 days. This is also exposure duration in stormwater context.

[3]EPA, 1985 Criteria FR-50, 145. July 29, 1985.

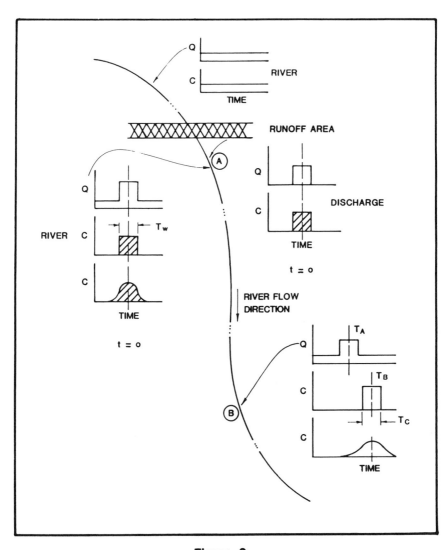

Figure 2

**ILLUSTRATION OF FLOW
AND MASS TRANSPORT**

2. The time required for the spike of contaminated water to reach any location, such as "B", is determined by the flow and dynamics both during and after the discharge event.

3. The time required for the spike of contaminated water to pass any location "B" is controlled by the flow and dynamics after the event and during the time interval "Tc" centered about time "Tb".

4. The time "Tc" can be longer, shorter, or equal to the storm runoff duration.

5. Any reaction rates (such as reaeration rate) that are dependent on velocity or stream geometry are controlled, in part, by the flow history after the event has ended.

Potential Water Quality Impacts of Urban Runoff

As indicated in Table 1, an average storm duration of 6 hours and a 90 percent value of 15 hours are typical. As illustrated in Figure 3, the time to reach a minimum DO as a function of the purification rate (Ka/Kd) varies from about 3/4 to 7 days. Most situations would require from 2 to 5 days to develop the minimum DO. The fairly large travel times required provide opportunities for dilution from tributaries, dilution from subsequent storm events, and settling of organics. Very unusual situations are required for there to be urban runoff related dissolved oxygen depressions which are not controlled, in part, by the flow, transport, and reaeration coefficient after the end of a storm event.

While there is little direct supporting data, the largest dissolved oxygen impact from urban runoff could be associated with bottom oxygen demand or in some situations scour rather than the direct oxidation of organic contaminants during and shortly after the runoff event. Limited data (Driscoll, 1985) on settling velocities of particles in urban runoff support this and suggest that about 50 percent of the particle mass has settling velocities that are in the range of those normally associated with sand or larger silt particles. The remainder of the mass has smaller settling rates that are normally associated with smaller silt and clay size particles. The information on settling velocities suggest that a large percentage of the particle mass either is associated with small diameter particle size and/or low density particles (possibly organic particles or organic coatings on particles). This suggests that a large percentage of the particles in urban runoff could be active in terms of either contributing to bottom oxygen demand and/or adsorption sites for toxics. Direct observational data on bottom deposition rates and quality is not available to examine this possibility. The potential impact of urban runoff on sediments and ultimately on water quality should be one of the areas examined in the future. There are no criteria relating sediment quality in the water column or bed to water usage. This area will also need to be examined.

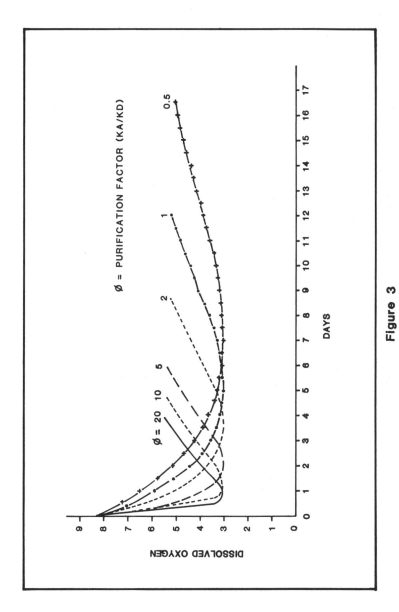

Figure 3

DISSOLVED OXYGEN CONCENTRATION IN A SLUG OF
WATER AS A FUNCTION OF TIME

The analysis of toxic impacts in the water column, from the discharge of urban runoff, should first address the near field impacts which are associated with the time during and shortly after an event. If protection from toxic impacts is available on this space and time scale, then larger space and time scales could and probably will be protected due to removals by adsorption, complexing, and settling.

EPA has expended significant effort (USEPA, 1985a, b; USEPA, 1980) recently to upgrade and revise water quality criteria for toxics. This effort is one of the steps being taken in what appears to be an increased emphasis on control of toxics through the permitting process. Other efforts have addressed the use of whole effluent bioassay data in the permitting process. The EPA now encourages the use of chemical specific and/or "whole effluent toxicity" information in the permitting process. There is a very small amount of data on the toxicity of urban runoff samples (Mote, 1984). Because of the highly variable nature of urban runoff, it will be necessary to generate urban runoff bioassay data on a very large number of events and sites before the "whole effluent toxicity" approach can be used with any confidence. This would, however, be very desirable since urban runoff has high concentrations of several metals as well as solids which are organic or have large surface area to mass ratios and could be active in adsorption of toxics. For the present, there is an adequate data base for chemical specific analysis of heavy metals. The EPA has recently published water quality criteria (USEPA, 1985a) for copper and lead.

Criteria for the two metals are presented in Table 3. The criteria consist of two concentration numbers each of which has an associated averaging period which, for intermittent discharges, can also be considered as an exposure duration. The recent criteria for copper and lead consider the exposure duration of 4 days for criterion continuous concentration (CCC) (chronic concentration) and 1 hour for the criterion maximum concentration (CMC) (acute concentration). The recent criteria suggest return frequencies of 3 to 10 years depending on the level of environmental stress.

The criteria are presented in a manner which makes them appear to be applicable to urban runoff. There are a number of characteristics of urban runoff that are different from continuous discharges. Urban runoff is characterized by event durations on the order of 6 hours with periods between events on the order of 80 hours. The difference in urban runoff and continuous discharges is in the time of exposure and the interval between exposures. The handling of these time issues, in the criteria development, is essentially directed towards continuous discharge concerns. The methods used to develop the criteria, when viewed in the context of urban runoff, did not fully employ the concept of dose-response relationships when establishing the allowable concentration and averaging period. The two components, concentration and exposure duration, that combine to determine the dosage were assigned independently; and the response, (mortality) was assumed to apply to the new dosage. From a technical standpoint the

promulgated criteria can not be considered as completely appropriate
for use in evaluation of the impacts from intermittent discharges such
as urban runoff.

Consideration of the intermittent nature of urban runoff loads
would tend to yield less stringent water quality criteria. If urban
runoff violates existing water quality criteria, then development of
criteria for intermittent wet-weather discharges could be considered.
If urban runoff does not violate the promulgated criteria, the
criteria for intermittent discharges would not change water quality
management decisions and are not needed.

Computations were developed using the statistical methods which
EPA has indicated are appropriate for examination of receiving water
concentrations of toxics (EPA, 1985b). The concentrations and
coefficient of variation of the heavy metals (for an average site),
urban runoff flow, and base stream flow indicated on Figure 4 were
used to calculate the heavy metals concentration, and mean recurrence
interval for various ratios of the urban drainage area to the stream
drainage area (DAR).

Figures 4a and 4b contain the results of these calculations for
recurrence frequencies between .1 and 10 years (assuming 100 storm
events per year). The EPA criterion maximum concentrations CMC from
Table 3 for each heavy metal is also indicated on these figures.
Criteria lines A, B, and C on these figures are CMC values for
hardness concentrations of 50, 100, and 200 mg/l respectively.
Examination of the information shown for each of the heavy metals
indicates that urban runoff metals concentrations exceed the EPA CMC
criteria for all the metals. Copper is the controlling toxicant. For
copper instream concentrations are calculated to exceed the allowable
CMC concentration for drainage area ratios (DAR) of 1000 to 1.
Assumptions included in these calculations are: 1) the stream
concentration of the heavy metal was assumed zero, 2) the total metals
concentration was compared to the allowable CMC, and 3) the CMC
criteria apply to exposures of no greater than 1 hour and the average
event duration is approximately 6 hours for urban runoff. For the
controlling metal, copper, the soluble concentration is approximately
50 percent of the total concentration. The effects of this assumption
can be examined by increasing the allowable CMC for urban runoff by a
factor of 2. When this is done, the instream concentration of copper
exceeds the revised CMC for drainage area ratios of 100 to 1. This
drainage area ratio could include almost all urban runoff discharges
since many discharges are into small drainage tributaries which carry
the runoff to the main receiving water. The exposure duration is
6 times the EPA duration associated with the CMC. This further
suggests that urban runoff at almost all locations will exceed
promulgated criteria and could require treatment.

Decisions on the need for treatment of almost all urban runoff
discharges may be changed by development of water quality criteria
which consider the characteristics of wet-weather intermittent

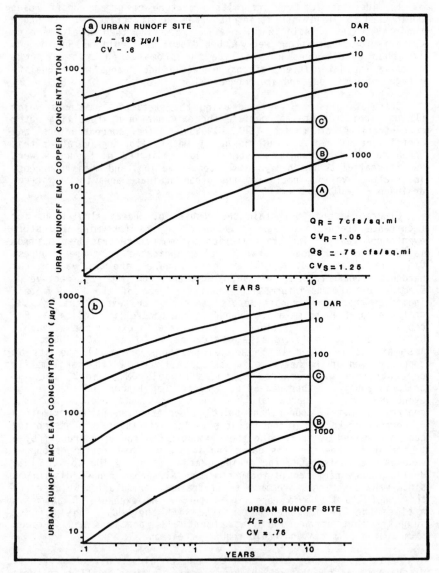

Figure 4
MEAN RECURRENCE INTERVAL YEARS
(BASED UPON 100 STORM/YR)

discharges. Consideration of the effects of intermittent exposures might reduce the concentrations which would cause mortality by factors of three to seven. It, is prudent to consider investigations to determine appropriate water quality criteria for controlling wet-weather intermittent loadings. These investigations should consider:

1. Exposure durations and intervals between events.
2. Chemical forms of the toxicant.
3. Genus and/or species to be protected.
4. Toxicity employing bioassays using urban runoff.

Wet-Weather Criteria

The following is a brief discussion of technology (Mancini, 1983, 1985) that can be considered for use in development of wet-weather water quality criteria. A unique feature of this technology is that it can be, and has been, tested in the laboratory, and therefore quantitative estimates of the strengths and weaknesses of the approach can be developed.

Wet-weather discharge criteria for urban runoff can be computed considering the suggested EPA CMC and a sequence of exposures which represent a possible, yet extreme, wet-weather condition. The suggested sequence of exposures is shown on Figure 5. Equation 1 can be used to calculate a site or regional specific wet-weather criteria (CWW) for the situation shown considering the EPA CMC from Table 3.

$$CWW = CMC*[(1-EXP(Kr*96))/(1-EXP(Kr*T3))]$$

$$-[CWM*(1-EXP(Kr*T1))*EXP(Kr*(T2$$

$$+ T3))/(1-EXP(Kr*T3))] \hspace{2cm} (1)$$

where:

T1	=	expected value of the duration of runoff (hours)
T2	=	expected value of the interval between storms (hours)
T3	=	an extremely long runoff duration
CWW	=	site or regional specific wet-weather criteria
CMC	=	EPA criteria from Table 3
CWM	=	expected concentration of the constituent in the stream
Kr	=	detoxification rate for the contaminant
96	=	exposure duration of original laboratory experiments (hours)

The site or regional specific wet-weather discharge criteria calculated for the situation shown on Figure 5 and using Equation 1 considers the carryover effects from sequences of wet-weather exposures. The first term in Equation 1 accounts for the intermittent

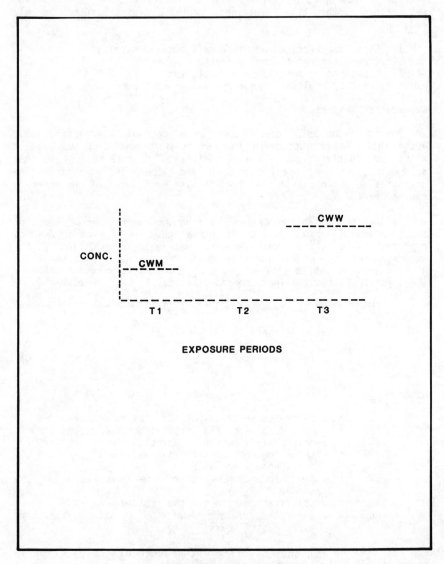

Figure 5
EXPOSURE SEQUENCE

nature of runoff exposures and can consider an extreme exposure
duration at the 90 percent or greater level. The second term in
Equation 1 reduces the wet-weather criteria due to the carryover
effects from previous wet-weather exposures.

An examination of the available information on the value of the
detoxification rate (Kr) indicates that the average rate is 0.036 per
hour and is similar for lead, copper and zinc. This is illustrated on
Figure 6 for the 74 data sets available. Kr is normally distributed
with a variance of 0.018 (cv = .5).

Figure 7 has been prepared to indicate the relative effects of the
two parts of Equation 1 on the wet-weather criteria considering the
mean detoxification rate of 0.036 per hour. The right curve shows the
influence of the first term of Equation 1 which accounts for the
intermittent nature of the exposure. The left curve illustrates the
effects of the carryover from prior exposures. The carryover effects
from previous exposures can be small in many situations.

Wet-weather criteria which are carefully developed may not
eliminate the need for treatment of urban runoff. (Though preliminary
indications are that this will be the result.) At a minimum, any
required treatment will be based on an applicable technical
evaluation.

Conclusions and Recommendations

1. Short-term reductions of dissolved oxygen concentrations as a
    result of oxidation of the contaminants in urban runoff has a
    low probability of occurrence.

2. Comparison of concentrations of heavy metals with promulgated
    EPA criteria indicate that either treatment of urban runoff is
    required in virtually every situation or the criteria are not
    applicable to urban runoff. Since the criteria development
    procedures did not consider the exposure times and intervals
    between exposures in a way that is consistent with the urban
    runoff situation, it is likely that the criteria are not
    applicable to urban runoff. It is suggested that development
    of criteria for effects from intermittent discharges be
    considered.

3. Some possible procedures and considerations for development of
    criteria for intermittent discharges have been identified and
    presented. These techniques consider the duration of runoff
    events and the interval between events.

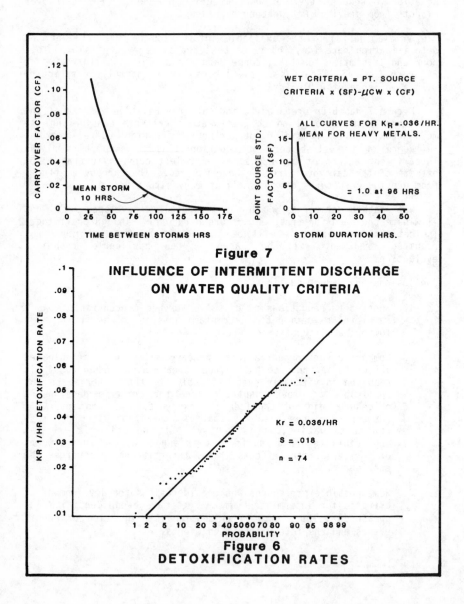

Figure 7

INFLUENCE OF INTERMITTENT DISCHARGE ON WATER QUALITY CRITERIA

Figure 6

DETOXIFICATION RATES

REFERENCES

Driscoll, E. D. Performance of Detention Basins for Control of Urban
    Runoff Quality, 1983 Internship Symposium on Urban Hydrogen
    Hydraulics and Sediment Control, University of Kentucky, July
    1983.

Mancini, J. L., A Method for Calculating Effects on Aquatic Organisms
    of Varying Concentrations, Water Resources, Vol. 17, No. 10, pp.
    1355-1362, 1983.

Mancini, J. L., "Heavy Metals Criteria," Federal Highway
    Administration memorandum to E. D. Driscoll, Manager of Federal
    Highway Project on Urban Runoff, April 1, 1986.

Mote Marine Laboratory. Biological and Chemical Studies on the of
    Stormwater Runoff Effects Upon the Biological Community of the
    Hillsborough River, Tampa, Florida, Submitted to the Tampa
    Department of Public Works, March 1984.

U.S. Environmental Protection Agency, Water Quality Criteria,
    Federal Register, Vol. 45, No. 231, pp. 79318-79, November 28,
    1980.

U.S. Environmental Protection Agency, Results of the Nationwide Urban
    Runoff Program, Vol. 1, Final Report, December 1983.

U.S. Environmental Protection Agency, Water Quality Criteria,
    Federal Register, Vol. 50, No. 145, pp. 30784-96, July 29, 1985a.

U.S. Environmental Protection Agency, Technical Support Document for
    Water Quality - Based Toxics Control, September 1985b.

POLLUTION SOURCES AND POTENTIAL IMPACTS--
NEXT STEPS

Larry A. Roesner, Ph.D., P.E., M. ASCE*

Introduction

The previous three papers have dealt with different but related aspects of pollution sources and potential impacts of pollutants in urban runoff on receiving waters. Based upon the findings of these papers and the discussion that followed the presentation of each paper, two major conclusions can be drawn:

1. We still have much to learn about what determines the magnitude and variability of pollutant loads in urban runoff; and

2. With the exception of nutrient enrichment, experts cannot agree whether or not the pollution loads carried to receiving waters by urban runoff are of sufficient magnitude and duration to adversely affect the aquatic ecosystem of the receiving waters.

The next section of this paper summarizes the findings of the previous three papers and the discussion that followed their presentation. My opinions of why we find ourselves where we are and what we should do about it are addressed in the last two sections.

Review of Papers and Discussion

"Sources of Urban Pollutants - Do We Know Enough?" M. L. Terstriep, et al., (1986)

Terstriep, et al. (1986) summarized what we know about urban runoff pollution sources based upon a review of 19 National Urban Runoff Program (NURP) project sites. These include all NURP sites except 9 which were managed wholly by the U.S. Geological Survey. Based on these data, the authors concluded that sufficient data abound to estimate the event mean concentration (EMC) for many water quality constituents on the basis of land use. However, the range of the EMC from event to event and from site to site is large, with coefficients of variation ranging from 40 percent to over 150 percent, depending upon the constituent.

Discussion related to this finding centered around the usefulness of this information for prediction since the variability is so high. Terstriep noted it's the best we have for practitioners and it is valuable for estimating the expected load and probable range of the load from existing and alternative land use plans. Discussants indicated most practitioners today estimate urban runoff pollution loads

*Vice President and Regional Director of Water Resources, Camp Dresser & McKee Inc., 555 Winderley Place, Maitland, FL 32751.

POLLUTION SOURCES AND IMPACTS 151

on the basis of land use and EMC or annual load (e.g., lbs/ac/yr) data. Discussants had differing opinions on whether event-to-event variability was less than site-to-site variability.

When queried whether using data gathered in the 208 studies might have improved the findings of the study, Terstriep replied that the data from these studies are generally unreliable because so many agencies were just learning to do wet weather sampling and sampling protocols were still being developed.

The extent of the data collected in these 19 NURP studies was substantial (102,720 samples at 273 sampling stations). Yet the only useful information we have obtained are event mean concentrations and coefficients of variation by land use. In only 4 of the 19 studies was data collection adequate to calibrate or test a physically based mathematical model. Data gathered at the other sites are suitable only for statistical analysis.

Based upon priority pollutant analysis, 121 flow-weighted composite samples from 61 stations within 19 of the NURP project sites, Terstriep concluded that "organic priority pollutants (in the dissolved state) appear to pose little threat. . . The greatest unanswered question related to the priority pollutants is the fate and effects of these pollutants, both organic and inorganic, known to be bound in the sediments." This conclusion was strongly supported by the audience.

"Estimation of Urban Storm-Runoff Loads," Nancy E. Driver and David J. Lystrom (1986)

This study is a progress report on a USGS project to develop a multi-parameter regression model to estimate event loads expressed in pounds. The nationwide data base includes data on 2,800 storms from 150 watersheds in 31 metropolitan areas. Statistical analysis of the data showed that mean annual runoff significantly affects storm runoff loads. Thus the data base was subdivided into three subsets corresponding to mean annual rainfall: (1) less than 20 inches per year, (2) 20-40 inches per year, and (3) greater than 40 inches per year.

For these three data subsets, regression analysis was performed on storm runoff data for total suspended solids, chemical oxygen demand, dissolved solids, total nitrogen and ammonia nitrogen. Basin characteristics used in the regression analysis were: (1) contributing drainage area, (2) percent impervious, (3) population density, and (4) land use. Constant climate characteristics were: (1) annual rainfall, (2) maximum intensity for 2-year storm, (3) annual nitrogen precipitation load, and (4) minimum January temperature. Storm variable characteristics were total rainfall and storm duration.

Total rainfall and total drainage area were predominant variables in the analysis. One discussant suggested that since first flush is

important, using initial rainfall intensity would significantly
improve the regression mode. Comparison of the coefficient of variation of the raw data to the standard error of estimates shows that
about 50 percent of the variance in the raw data can be explained by
the regression equations. But even so, the standard error of estimate
is still 55 to 220 percent of the true value.

In this regard, one discussant pointed out that the best available
deterministic models of highway runoff cannot predict storm loads
within 300 percent of the actual value. Another discussant believes
that the physically based models would be more accurate if data
collection efforts were directed more toward model development than
toward measuring catchment runoff.

"Urban Runoff and Water Quality Criteria," John L. Mancini and
Alan H. Plummer (1986)

In this paper Mancini and Plummer address wet weather water quality
criteria for streams. A statistical methodology is proposed that uses
runoff load statistics and acute toxicity data to compute an allowable
wet weather mean concentration of a pollutant. The methodology takes
into account the probable time that the ecosystem will be exposed to a
given concentration level and the frequency of the exposure. Although
the method is simplistic, it is a significant step forward in relaxing
the EPA's long-term criteria to something more reasonable. The
authors point out that these criteria are for in-stream dissolved
concentrations and that the criteria computation does not take into
account the potential impact of urban runoff on sediments and ultimately on water quality.

A great deal of discussion was generated around the question of how
we get the basic biological data to establish wet weather criteria.
One biologist pointed out that the EPA laboratory in Duluth,
Minnesota, responsible for all of the water quality criteria work for
toxic compounds, has only recently "discovered" the concept of return
frequency. Further discussion noted that Duluth tends to build safety
factors into their water quality criteria. It was generally agreed
that this should not be done, rather the biologist should develop the
biological cause–effect relationships and let the engineers and
policy-setters build in the safety factors (risk). Many discussants
lamented our lack of knowledge on the effects on aquatic biota of
toxic pollutants in urban runoff; e.g., the effects of exposures to
high concentrations for short periods (2-8 hrs), the effects of
repeated short period exposure to sublethal concentrations of a
pollutant, and the lack of data relating chronic effects of pollutants
in the dissolved form versus those attached to solids. Finally, one
discussant noted that society is moving ahead with the promulgation of
runoff pollution control requirements regardless of our lack of understanding of the level of control required to protect/enhance our
aquatic ecosystem.

How Did We Get Into This Situation?

Twelve years ago, the Urban Water Resources Research Council of ASCE held its first conference of URBAN RUNOFF QUANTITY AND QUALITY. I think it is worth quoting from the report of the workgroup on Water Quality Aspects of Urban Runoff [see B. B. Berger (1974)]:

> The work group believes the attention given at the meeting to water quality aspects of urban runoff represents a desirable, but a belated and inadequate recognition of an important problem, whose magnitude is still poorly understood. The problem is highly complex; but this complexity is not reflected in a comprehensive and well-supported program of research directed to providing the information that is urgently needed. The problem of pollution in urban runoff is significant, since national goals of water clean-up cannot be realized until practicable methods of control are developed. Regulatory water pollution control programs that do not provide for problem prediction and control are defective. Without adequate prediction and control, public expectations resulting from large investments in end-of-pipe treatment plants cannot be realized. The harm that may be done by unfulfilled promises (unfulfillable promises based on existing knowledge and techniques) may produce consequences that could discredit the total water quality management program.

A statement from the discussion following the workgroup report is also worth quoting:

> The main thrust of the 70's is building waste treatment plants. The main thrust of the 80's is apt to be treatment of secondary source of pollution, mainly urban runoff. We must be prepared for this next big move with adequate data, technology and planning. Concepts will change. Unless we know, we won't be ready.

A prophecy come true. Just how we managed to get ourselves into this predicament is academically interesting but pragmatically deplorable. It is my opinion that neither the Congress of the United States nor the Presidents who have been in office since 1972 understand the complexity of the urban runoff pollution issue. They do not understand the source of urban runoff pollutants and their contamination of urban runoff, nor do they comprehend the utter lack of knowledge that exists with respect to intermittent exposure of aquatic biota to these pollutants, particularly toxic pollutants. Apparently we scientists and engineers have not communicated these problems known 12 years ago to the people in these august positions. As a result, neither Congress nor the President has seen fit to fund a national research program to understand and simulate urban runoff pollution phenomena. For lack of leadership at the federal level, and lack of funding from anywhere else, little new research into the pollution

sources or their effects on aquatic ecosystems has been done over the
last 12 years. But now, under pressure from the National Environmental Defense Fund, Congress and the courts are being told that a
problem exists and to fix it. So what do we do?

Next Steps

We are shortly going to be required to implement runoff water
quality control measures in urban areas, but we do not know what
levels of control are required since receiving water impacts cannot be
quantified. To solve this dilemma, I propose a three-front attack.
The attack needs to be carried out simultaneously on all fronts, but
the priority for immediate effort and funding is as follows:

1. Education and training of persons who will design these urban
    runoff water quality control devices;

2. Development of design and performance criteria for the various
    control measures; and

3. Quantification of the response of receiving water ecosystems to
    urban runoff pollutants, particularly toxic compounds.

The suggested approach to each of these action items follows.

Education and Training

The designers of the urban runoff control facilities are primarily
drainage engineers who work for developers. Most of them have had
little training in water quality processes, either landside or
receiving water impacts. As a result, most of the water quality
control devices presently installed around the country perform primarily as hydraulic control devices to retain, detain or retard runoff; if they reduce the pollution load in the runoff, so much the
better. Education can be accomplished in the following ways:

1. Introduce the topic into the undergraduate civil engineering
    curriculum, including it in the traditional water and waste-
    water engineering courses.

2. Offer water quality control in continuing education courses as
    part of runoff control or stormwater management.

3. Offer workshops sponsored by regulatory agencies to familiarize
    designers with the runoff water quality regulations and various
    ways these regulations can be implemented to maximize the cap-
    ture of pollution in runoff.

An integral part of this education is to acquaint the designers
with the physio-chemical-biological processes that occur in various
runoff control devices. Armed with this understanding, the designer
will be able to use his own ingenuity to maximize the capture of runoff pollutants in any particular design situation.

Development of Design Criteria for Runoff Quality Control Devices

Although it is difficult to quantify removal efficiencies of runoff quality control devices, we have a substantial body of qualitative information on the physio-chemical-biological interrelationships that occur in the commonly used control devices. This knowledge could be collected into a "design guidelines" book to guide facility designers to take maximum advantage of the pollution removal phenomena that occur in the various runoff quality control devices. It would include such ideas as baffling in detention devices, permanent pool volumes to be used in wet detention facilities, effective use of swales, O&M requirements for various control practices.

Since we know that nutrient enrichment in receiving waters occurs from urban runoff, we should concentrate our efforts on control or removal of phosphorus and nitrogen from the runoff. Because this requires removal of nutrients in both the suspended and dissolved form, any device that maximizes the capture of nutrients will undoubtably capture most other pollutants in urban runoff, particularly the toxic compounds, which tend to attach to solids.

It must be emphasized to designers that quality control devices and quantity control devices must be separated unless it can be demonstrated that the quality control devices perform equally well when combined with the quantity control devices. The problem is that when the 25-year event comes through a quality control device designed to capture/"treat" the 1-year storm, it washes all the pollutants captured in previous storms into the receiving waters, essentially negating the previous capture effectiveness of the device.

Receiving Water Effects of Urban Runoff

It is time to take a fresh approach to quantifying receiving water impacts of urban runoff. First, it is necessary to develop research techniques that reflect the dosing phenomena that occur in the receiving water with respect to frequency, intensity, and duration of dosing. For toxic pollutants, maybe LC50 curves could be developed that are analogous to rainfall intensity-duration-frequency curves. Compounds used in the laboratory experiments must be similar to those to which the organism is exposed in the field. For example, a field measurement of "dissolved" zinc will include those ions that are attached to colloidal solids and pass through the filter media as well as the free ions. Do these two forms of zinc exhibit the same toxicity? If not, laboratory studies using dissolved ions will never reproduce field behavior.

Summary

The papers and discussion of this session reveal that sufficient information exists to estimate average pollution loads from urban runoff on the basis of land use. But, from event to event the estimates are very approximate ($\pm$100-300 percent). This information can be used in land use planning to qualitatively compare the relative changes in runoff loads that occur from different plans, and may produce some guidance in where to require more or less stringent runoff quality controls.

Receiving water impacts of urban runoff are poorly understood because of the variability of the loads, and times of exposure and their intermittent nature. The effect on the aquatic ecosystem of toxic pollutants attached to sediments is unknown. The lack of demonstrated adverse impacts has led many to conclude that urban runoff is not a threat to receiving water quality. Even so, the public perceives that it is; thus, there will be (and already are in three states) regulations requiring control of pollutant loads in urban runoff.

It is up to us as professionals in the urban water resources field to ensure that the regulations that are developed are realistic and can be implemented, and that the most cost-effective pollution control strategies are implemented, based on our knowledge of sources and efficiencies of control devices. We can do this most effectively by promoting the education of drainage engineers with respect to runoff quality control measures and by developing design guidelines. Simultaneously, we must push the federal government to sponsor receiving water impact studies to determine the degree of runoff quality control required to protect our aquatic ecosystems.

References

Berger, B. B., "Workshop Report – Water Quality Aspects of Urban Runoff" Proceedings of a Research Conference on Urban Runoff Quantity and Quality, Franklin Pierce College, Rindge, NH, August 11–16, 1974, ed. William Whipple, Jr., ASCE, 1974, page 250 ff.

Driver, Nancy E. and David J. Lystrom, "Estimation of Urban Storm Runoff Loads," these proceedings.

Mancini, John L. and Alan H. Plummer, "Urban Runoff and Water Quality Criteria," these proceedings.

Terstriep, Michael L., Douglas C. Noel, and G. Michael Bender, "Sources of Urban Pollutants – Do We Know Enough?" these proceedings.

POTENTIAL IMPACTS ON RECEIVING WATERS

ABSTRACT   Robert K. Bastian*

As a discrete source of water-borne pollutants that are discharged to receiving waters, urban stormwater runoff can be and has been in specific instances a source of water quality problems. Insight into where urban runoff fits among the sources of water pollution and potential water quality impacts that may result from urban runoff, as well as reactions to some of the scientific and regulatory implications that may well face the management of urban runoff in the future, are discussed in relation to experience with other programs aimed at controlling water pollution.

Introduction

While their amount, form, timing and duration can all be very important, it generally makes little difference from a water quality standpoint if the sources of excessive pollution (be they conventional pollutants or toxics) finding their way into receiving waters come from traditional point sources, urban stormwater runoff, atmospheric sources, agricultural runoff runoff or other nonpoint sources. As a result, many of the water quality problems and concerns and the resulting management objectives associated with controlling other point and nonpoint sources must also be faced when addressing the management of urban runoff. Therefore, we need to keep in mind the lessons learned from other programs that have been undertaken to control the various sources of water pollution as we make what Earl Jones and Ben Urbonas refer to in their objectives of this conference as a "thoughtful re-examination" of what should be appropriate responses to the current pressures to "do something" to control urban stormwater runoff quality.

The basic characteristics that we generally associate with urban stormwater runoff - periodic occurrence, variable quality and quantity, and regional (or even local) severity - are not unknown to other sources of water pollution. While these characteristics may be more similar to certain non-point sources, POTWs receiving seasonal industrial discharges (e.g., certain food processors) or slug loads from sanitary sewer sources or illegal discharges often suffer from similar conditions. The pollutants of major concern in urban runoff (i.e., conventional and priority pollutants in soluble and insoluble forms; sediment; coliforms, Salmonella and other pathogens) are quite similar to those present in other point and nonpoint sources. Data

---

* Environmental Scientist, U.S. Environmental Protection Agency, Office
  of Municipal Pollution Control (WH-595), Washington, D.C. 20460

available which characterize urban runoff stormwater quality show
that in certain areas it is nearly equal to domestic wastewater in
concentration of some parameters (see Table 1). Finally, many of the

Table 1. Comparison Some of Water Quality Parameters in
Urban Runoff with Domestic Wastewater(mg/l)*

Constituent	Urban Runoff Separate Sewers		Domestic Wastewater before treatment		after secondary
	Range	Typical	Range	Typical	
COD	20 - 275	(75)	250 - 1000	(500)	80
TSS	20 - 2890	(150)	100 - 350	(220)	20
Total P	.02 - 4.30	(.36)	4 - 15	(8)	2
Total N	.4 - 20.0	(2.0)	20 - 85	(40)	30
Lead	.01 - 1.20	(.18)	.02 - .94	(.10)	.05
Copper	.01 - 0.40	(.05)	.03 - 1.19	(.22)	.03
Zinc	.01 - 2.90	(.20)	.02 - 7.68	(.28)	.08
F. coliforms per 100 ml	400 - 50x10^3		1x10^6 - 1x10^8		200

* data used from EPA reports including the National Urban Runoff
Program Final Report, Fate of Priority Pollutants in POTWs
Final Report, and other sources

general effects associated with degraded water quality due to the
pollutants in urban runoff - impairment or denial of beneficial uses
(e.g., drinking water, fishing and swimming), violations of water
quality standards, negative public perceptions, etc. - are similar to
those resulting from other water pollution sources.

Receiving Water Impacts from Urban Runoff

The intermittent nature and relatively short duration of urban
runoff in many areas (especially larger streams and well-mixed lakes)
will generally allow the natural pollutant assimilative capacity of
receiving waters to buffer (or at least dilute) these pollutant
loadings to a considerable degree. Streams, lakes and estuaries and
other aquatic ecosystems have a finite ability to remove, convert,
transform or otherwise treat or process pollutants present in urban
stormwater and other sources (Benforado & Bastian, 1985), similar to
land treatment systems (Page et al, 1984). However, as with other
sources of intermittent discharges, if ambient water quality levels in

a particular receiving water are already near threshold levels, the added increment provided by urban runoff may well be all that is required to realize significant receiving water impacts.

Clearly, existing models and monitoring techniques make it difficult in many cases to differentiate among the many potential sources of pollutants and to provide accurate estimates of the mass balances of inputs and outputs associated with surface waters. Whether to blame the resulting impacts on the intermittent discharges, the ambient sources, or a combination of sources and how to focus efforts to clean up such polluted water bodies often becomes a matter of serious debate during regulatory proceedings.

The dramatic changes that occurred in Lake Erie during the late 1960s and then again in the late 1970s/early 1980s can serve as a good example of this situation. While much of the available nitrogen and phosphorus data were apparently difficult to interpret, Beeton (1969) noted that data from a number of open-lake studies of the western basin of Lake Erie indicated that ammonia-N increased fivefold and total nitrogen increased about threefold between 1930 and 1958. Total phosphorus concentrations appear to have doubled between 1942 and 1958. Severe oxygen depletion and blooms of blue-green algae were appearing in certain parts of the lake by the late 1960's. In 1966 about 65 percent of the central basin suffered from severe oxygen depletion. Fish kills became common, and many of the beaches which weren't closed due to high bacteria counts were not used because of objectionable algal slime. Probably as a result of the effects of excessive nutrient and other pollutant loads from both point and nonpoint sources created by the greatest population growth among the Great Lakes (the population in the Lake Erie watershed increased from about 3 million in 1900 to about 10.1 million in 1960; the current Lake Erie watershed has a population/area ratio of 567 people per square mile), by the mid 1960s Lake Erie's high quality commercial and sport fishery had nearly completely collapsed. While Lake Erie continued to produce about 50 million pounds of fish per year (which was about 50 percent of the total Great Lakes production), the species composition of the catch had changed markedly, with the greatest degree of change occurring after 1940 (see Figure 1). What once had been a high quality commercial fishery based on lake herring (cisco), blue pike, yellow perch, sauger, whitefish, and walleye had converted to fishery dominated by yellow perch, smelt, sheepshead and carp, with whitebass, catfish and walleye playing a minor role.

Efforts to reduce the noxious algae blooms and revive a more desirable fishery in Lake Erie have been focused on the reduction of phosphorus and other pollutants through a combination of phosphate detergent bans and strict point source controls (e.g., with typical discharge limits of 0.5mg/l Total P), plus efforts to modify tillage and fertilization practices to reduce soil erosion and phosphorus losses from agricultural runoff. Probably because the lake has only a 2.6 year water detention time (the shortest of all the Great Lakes), these efforts have resulted in a dramatic, improvement in water quality in Lake Erie (in 1975 only about 6 percent of the central basin suffered from severe oxygen depletion) and the re-establishment

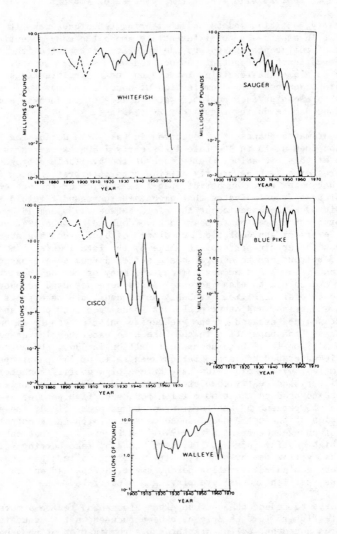

FIGURE 1   Commercial production of blue pike, cisco (lake herring), lake trout, sauger, walleye, and whitefish in Lake Erie. Broken lines represent production during periods when annual data were not available.

from Beeton, 1969

of a highly successful sport fishery, bringing in more than $50
million annually (second only to Lake Michigan). The major species
currently found in the lake are carp, catfish, white bass, yellow
perch and a walleye population that is considered one of the finest in
the world. A recent Michigan Natural Resoures Magazine devoted to the
Great Lakes (1986) referred to Lake Erie's ecological recovery as
being as dramatic as its previous degradation.

The receiving water impacts resulting from urban stormwater on a
small urban lake or stream can be nearly as dramatic as the Lake Erie
example. Numerous examples exist where severe hydraulic scouring has
effectively eliminated desirable stream habitat or where high sediment
loadings and water quality degradation have resulted from urban
stormwater discharges into such receiving waters, resulting in
extensive sediment build-up, noxious algae blooms and die-off of
desirable game fish, creating conditions where only hardy less
desirable species can survive. When faced with the desire or mandate
to maintain or re-establish recreational boating, swimming and fishing
in such areas, communities have often been faced with undertaking
extensive measures to control the sediment and nutrient levels
resulting from urban runoff inputs. Situations also occur where high
Fecal coliform or toxic chemical levels in urban runoff (possibly due
to illegal connections or discharges, sanitary sewer overflows, or
even animal wastes from pets or large concentrations of waterfowl)
lead to or contribute significantly to closures of harvestable
shellfish beds or swimming beaches in poorly circulated receiving
waters.

More often, technical violations of water quality standards in the
receiving waters have occurred as a result of urban stormwater runoff
inputs. In cases where this has occurred and fish populations in the
receiving waters appear unaffected, serious questions have been raised
as to the appropriateness of applying current water quality standards
to the control of urban runoff. Still, such examples can and do serve
as a basis for some states to regulate or otherwise require the
control of urban stormwater runoff at least under certain
circumstances. Whether to encourage or require the use of BMP's or to
establish a more formalized regulatory approach to avoid these and
other situations has become a matter of considerable controversy.

Federal and State Assessments

The results of the extensive U.S. EPA and U.S.G.S. national urban
runoff database evaluations discussed elsewhere during this conference
have lead to the general conclusion that urban stormwater runoff is
not usually considered a major source of national water quality
problems. But it is clear that water quality problems do result in
specific situations and are currently being dealt with at a state and
local level.

A difference in Federal vs State attitudes regarding the role of
urban runoff in affecting receiving water quality also is apparent
when reviewing the results of several recent surveys. The results
of a survey of EPA Regions concerning what activities are affecting

near coastal waters suggest that those activities most likely to
contribute to urban runoff are not widely viewed as "major" sources of
pollution in near coastal waters (especially when compared to
activities such as industrial and municipal discharges, dredging and
agriculture). Yet there appears to be considerable concerns associated
with the potential for impacting habitat loss/alteration and changes in
biota as a result of surburban/tourist development which may contribute
significantly to urban runoff problems.

However, the results of two recent surveys (ASIWPCA, 1984 &'85)
by the Association of State and Interstate Water Pollution Control
Administrators (ASIWPCA) of the impact of point and nonpoint sources
on water quality, could be read to suggest a somewhat different
reaction to the role of urban runoff relative to water pollution.
ASIWPCA's surveys indicated that since 1972, control of point and
nonpoint sources of water pollution have helped restore or at least
maintain many of the nation's surface waters despite an 11 percent
increase in population and expanded industrial and recreational use of
these waters. They further indicated, as shown in Tables 4-7, that
urban runoff (including CSOs) is the primary "nonpoint" source causing
impacts on:

o   972,000 lake acres
o   8,000 river miles, and
o   1,000 sq. mi. of estuaries

While the ASIWPCA survey results indicated that the States clearly
find agriculture to be the leading source of nonpoint source impacts
on receiving waters, a substantial percent of the waters impacted by
nonpoint sources (5% of river miles, 12 % of lake acres, and 18% of
estuary square miles assessed) was attributed primarily to urban
runoff. Also, while a significant number of States rated urban runoff
plus construction as the most or second-most widespread cause of
surface water quality problems, far fewer States indicated urban
runoff to be a known source of groundwater contamination than all
other categories listed (e.g., agriculture, leaking storage tanks,
land disposal, septic tanks, spills, etc.).

Table 2. ASIWPCA Assessment of "Nonpoint" Sources

	River (mi)	Lake (ac)	Estuaries (sq mi)
Total	1,800,000	39,400,000	32,000
Assessed	404,000	15,400,000	19,000
Impacted	165,000	8,100,000	5,400
Impaired	117,000	4,400,000	2,400

Impacted = uses severely or moderately impaired or
                 threatened
Impacted = interference with designated uses

Table 3. Primary "Nonpoint" Sources in Impacted Waters

	Rivers	Lakes	Estuaries
Agriculture	64%	57%	19%
Urban Runoff	5%	12%	18%
Construction	2%	4%	--

Table 4. Number of States Reporting as
Most Widespread Cause of Problems

	Most Widespread	2nd Most Widespread
Rivers:		
Agriculture	27	10
Urban Runoff	3	8
Construction	1	4
(# states)	(46)	(43)
Lakes:		
Agriculture	24	10
Urban Runoff	4	10
Construction	2	2
(# states)	(41)	(38)

Table 5. Known or Suspected Sources of
Groundwater Contamination

	Known	Suspected
Agriculture	33	5
Leaking Storage Tanks	25	4
Land Disposal	23	6
Septic Tanks	20	6
Spills	19	1
Industry	16	1
Mining	14	2
Urban Runoff	7	2

Insights from Other EPA Programs

It appears that the issue of whether urban runoff is or is not a significant source of water pollution boils down to site-specific conditions, which is also true of many other potential point and nonpoint sources. In certain parts of the country water of almost any quality is viewed as a valuable resource and may even carry property rights value. Even domestic wastewater is often recycled for its nutrients and/or water supply value through irrigation and groundwater recharge projects. In reality, the goals of the CWA do not differentiate among sources of water pollution. But the experiences that have been gained as well as the directions being taken by other EPA programs relating to water pollution control (see Figure 6) may provide some useful insights to managers of urban runoff.

Table 8. EPA Water Pollution Control & Related Programs

Cleanup Programs:
Construction Grants
Lake Restoration
Estuarine Protection
CERCLA (Superfund)

Regulatory Programs:
Water Quality & Standards
NPDES Permits
UIC, Groundwater & Drinking Water
404 Dredge & Fill
Sewage Sludge & Septage Mgnt.
RCRA/HSWA

Construction Grants Program. Under its mandate in the CWA, EPA's Construction Grants Program has been providing Federal funding (well over $40 billion since 1972) and technical assistance to municipalities to assist in the planning, design and construction of municipal wastewater treatment systems and has encouraged greater use of "innovative and alternative" technologies for recycling municipal wastewater. In some cases, urban runoff is being viewed in a similar manner, and some of the same treatment and recycling concepts used for municipal wastewater management (e.g., pond treatment, land treatment by spray irrigation, overland flow, rapid infiltration; wetlands treatment) can and in some cases are being applied to urban runoff. A considerable information base has been developed over the years concerning these types of wastewater treatment systems, including design manuals, operations experience, and monitoring data on their effects on water quality that should be of considerable assistance to designers of projects considering similar techniques to manage urban runoff.

Clean Lakes & Estuaries Programs. The Clean Lakes and Estuaries
Programs also provide Federal funds to assist in the coordination,
development, and, in some cases, clean up of contaminated lakes and
estuaries across the country. In some cases urban runoff controls may
be identified as a significant cause of the water quality problems of
these receiving waters and lead to specific controls being required as
a part of cleanup or post cleanup efforts.

CERCLA (Superfund) Program. The Agency's relatively new, high-
visibility program under the Comprehensive Environmental Response,
Compensation, and Liability Act (CERCLA) for cleaning up abandoned
hazardous waste sites may well help reduce urban runoff contamination
in the localized areas around individual Superfund sites. Also, a
number of the sites listed for eventual cleanup (including sites in
estuaries) are areas that have received numerous types of waste
inputs, including urban runoff, for years.

Water Quality Criteria & Standards Program. Clearly, the Agency's
efforts to establish both freshwater and marine water quality
criteria, to set treatment standards and have the States establish
both receiving water quality standards and designated uses to be
maintained have considerable influence on urban runoff management.
Debates over the validity of applying water quality standards which
are based on laboratory LD50 data derived for continuous sources to
intermittent sources, such as urban runoff, will likely continue for
years to come, especially as more State permitting and enforcement
programs are put into place. Similar debates can also be expectd
regarding the use of Fecal coliform tests for shellfish bed or bathing
beach closures.

Whether existing standards can be modified for urban runoff, or
whether this would even be appropriate, should be worth considering.
The traditional 30/30 plus 85 percent removal secondary treatment
standards established by EPA in the early 1970s have since been
modified several times to allow States an opportunity to set
considerably looser standards for wastewater treatment pond
discharges, allow for section 301(h) waivers from secondary treatment
requirements for marine discharges, and more recently to remove the 85
percent removal requirement for combined sewers and to define existing
trickling filter effluents as meeting secondary treatment
requirements. As for the use of lab vs field data to establish
criteria and standards, there is a similar debate going on concerning
the establishment of requirements for land application of sewage
sludge (i.e., whether to base requirements on data generated using
metal salts additions to greenhouse and field plot studies or to limit
consideration to field studies using sludge-borne contaminants only).
Further, there have always been different approaches taken in handling
municipal end-ofpipe treatment requirements vs industrial discharge
standards, which allow for mixing zones prior to meeting water quality
standards.

NPDES Program. A continued series of court cases and agreements
reached as a result of these cases may lead to a requirement for
National Pollution Discharge Elimination System (NPDES) permits of

some type being required for urban runoff discharges to surface
waters. While a controversial subject at best, this situation may
well lead to an opportunity for comprehensive urban area planning and
permits that would allow for trade-offs between treatment requirements
placed on POTW discharges and urban runoff discharges into the
receiving water segment in an effort to allow for the implementation
of the most cost-effective means of meeting loading limits.

The control of toxics has become a growing focus of the EPA NPDES
program. This has occurred in part because of problems with residual
toxicity below outfalls (after meeting discharge requirements for
conventional pollutants), and has resulted in Agency efforts to
promote tighter source control programs at the local level and to add
a new "no toxics in toxic amounts" provision to newly issued discharge
permits. It has been suggested that in some areas urban runoff may be
playing a role in these residual toxicity problems. In addition,
biological monitoring, involving sensitive local species, below
permitted outfalls is now becomming a common requirement as a means to
detect residual toxicity. As a result of such biological monitoring,
changes to water quality criteria and stream standards might become
more possible. In any case, as indicated by the Agency's National
Municipal Policy, which calls for municipalities to meet their
discharge permit standards by July 1, 1988, it is clear that the
Agency will be pressing hard to reach the Clean Water Act's
fishable/swimmable goals and to maintain designated beneficial
receiving water uses in the years to come.

UIC, Groundwater and Drinking Water Programs. To date the Agency's
Underground Injection Control (UIC) and Groundwater Programs have
focused on the development of State plans and programs to protect
groundwater aquifers, while the Drinking Water Program has focused on
establishing safe drinking water standards and advisories. Although
groundwater contamination by infiltration of urban runoff has not been
shown to be a serious problem to date, it is probably advisable to
keep a close eye on new groundwater regulations and policies (e.g.,
non-degradation policies) that may limit certain urban runoff
management practices or establish further treatment requirements for
their use.

404 Dredge & Fill Program. This program is focused on the protection
of aquatic habitat in wetlands and other receiving waters from the
impacts of dredge and fill activities. Because of the value being
placed on preserving natural wetland habitats and the growing interest
in using wetlands to help manage urban runoff, the 404 Program
requirements could come into play in certain urban runoff management
project and practices, especially where high silt loads may occur.

Sewage Sludge and Septage Management. In many ways the management of
urban runoff and other nonpoint sources has been handled in a manner
similar to sewage sludge and septage. State and local control
utilizing best management practices rather than comprehensive Federal
regulatory requirements and permits has been the approach usually
followed. While States have developed full-blown regulatory programs,
others have done little to require controls over sewage sludge and

septage, or urban runoff management practices. Until recently, many
POTW operators knew little about the concentration of pollutants
present in their sludges. Even less effort has been made to
characterize septage quality.

However, the situation for sewage sludge (and probably septage) is
changing rapidly. As a result of interest by Congress and several
environmental groups, comprehensive technical regulations to generate
health-based criteria for all major sewage sludge use and disposal
practices are currently under development by EPA that will address a
long list of pollutants. Regulations requiring States to develop
State Sludge Management Programs to assure that Federal sludge
criteria are followed have already been published for public comment.
The pending CWA Amendments will likely require permits to be issued to
control sewage sludge management practices, either by the States or
EPA directly.

RCRA/HSWA. Under the CWA, when considering the problems associated
with toxic chemicals entering receiving waters, our attention has been
focused on the Consent Degree List of 126 toxic chemicals. However,
the hazardous waste control program established under the Resource
Conservation and Recovery Act (RCRA) and its recent Hazardous Solid
Waste Amendments (HSWA) is focused on a list of nearly 400 hazardous
constituents (listed in Appendix VIII of 40 CFR Part 261). Clearly
the maintenance of urban runoff control systems will result in
sediment residues that fall under the broad definition of "solid
waste" provided in RCRA. As a result, this residue material is
subject to the requirements of proper management and disposal as
either a non-hazardous or hazardous solid waste, depending upon
whether or not it exhibits any of four "characteristics" exhibited by
hazardous solid wastes.

Few residuals from urban runoff control projects have ever been
evaluated to determine if they exhibit any of the characteristics of a
hazardous waste. Since some of the pollutants present in urban
stormwater are similar in concentration to those in municipal
wastewater, the fact that few of the sewage sludges tested to date
have been found to be hazardous wastes is good news. However, many
POTW officials are now concerned that their sewage sludges may
possibly fail the revised testing procedure called for under HSWA
which was recently proposed for determining when a waste exhibits the
"toxicity" characteristic of a hazardous waste. Since the cost of
running the new toxicity characteristic leachate procedure (TCLP) can
amount to as much as $5,000 per sample, just paying for the analyses
involved in demonstrating that a solid waste is not a hazardous waste
is no longer a simple undertaking, let alone handling the expense of
waste disposal if the material is found to be a hazardous waste.

The HSWA Amendments to RCRA place new requirements on existing
hazardous waste disposal sites which are expected to result in the
closure of something like two-thirds of the existing sites. Along
with a change in the small-quantity generator exemption provision
(which lowered the volume of hazardous waste generated from 1000 kg/mo
to 100 kg/mo - approximately one half of a 55 gallon barrel), the

closure of so many existing hazardous waste disposal sites could well
lead to more illegal dumping into sewers and drainage systems,
resulting in more hazardous substances ending up in POTWs and urban
runoff, as well as in sewage sludges and urban runoff control
residues.

Implications for Urban Runoff Management

When considering the potential for urban runoff to impact
receiving waters in light of the other EPA programs designed to
protect our receiving waters, the following conclusions can be drawn:

1. In the future, any source of water pollution may become subject
to permits and control.

2. There is a clear movement toward site-specific and
biologically-based permit standards and monitoring requirements.

3. There are some problems with the current water quality
criteria, or at least how they are being used to establish stream
water quality and discharge standards applied to urban runoff.

4. The concept of using habitat loss criteria to address
sedimentation or stream scour problems to control urban runoff
discharges should be well received by regulatory officials -
once the concerns over nutrient and toxics control are addressed.

5. While local control and use of BMPs may work well, regulation-
based approaches involving risk-based standards are generally
preferred by Congress and lawyers.

6. Residuals management will likely become an issue to be
addressed at urban runoff control facilities.

7. As a result of the developments noted above, renewed interest
in the following may occur:

o increased use of constructed wetlands for detention and
   treatment of urban runoff;
o instream treatment concepts;
o analysis of all sources of water pollution and evaluation
   of the most cost-effective solutions to reduce loads,
   allowing trade-offs between point and nonpoint source
   controls;
o a rethinking of designated uses for urban streams and
   possibly of appropriate water quality criteria and
   standards to apply to urban runoff.

REFERENCES

ASIWPCA, 1984. America's Clean Water: The States' Evaluation of
Progress 1972-1982. Prepared by the Assoc. of State & Interstate
Water Pollution Control Admin's., Washington, D.C. 16 pp summary
report and detailed appendix.

ASIWPCA, 1985. America's Clean Water: The State's Nonpoint Source
Assessment 1985. Prepared by the Assoc. of State & Interstate
Water Pollution Control Admin's., Washington, D.C. 24 pp summary
report and detailed appendix.

Benforado, J. and R.K. Bastian, 1985. Natural Waste Treatment.
IN: McGraw-Hill Yearbook of Science & Technology. McGraw-Hill
Book Co., New York, NY. p. 32-49.

Beeton, A.M., 1969. Changes in the Environment and Biota of the
Great Lakes. IN: Eutrophication: Causes, Consequences,
Corrections. National Academy of Sciences, Washington, D.C.
p. 150-187.

Michigan NDR, 1986. A Tribute to the Great Lakes. Michigan Dept.
of Natural Resources Magazine. 55(3):18.

Page, A.1., T.L. Gleason, III, J.E. Smith, I.K. Iskandar and L.E.
Sommers (eds), 1983. Proceedings of the 1983 Workshop on
Utilization of Wastewater and Sludge on Land. Univ. of
California-Riverside, CA. 480 pp.

ASSESSING BIOLOGICAL EFFECTS OF CONTAMINANTS IN SITU

Kenneth D. Jenkins[1,2] and Brenda M. Sanders[1,3]

ABSTRACT: This paper presents a monitoring strategy for assessing the effects of anthropogenic contaminants on aquatic organisms. This strategy takes advantage of our increased understanding of the mechanisms which underlie stress metabolism as a basis for assessing stress in native organisms in situ. General stress responses which react to a wide range of environmental factors are used to initially screen for deleterious biological effects due to contaminants. If data from this initial screening indicate that organisms are stressed, stressor-specific responses which are elicited by specific contaminants or classes of contaminants would be measured to identify the causative factors. When these data are taken together it is possible to determine both the extent of biological stress in native organisms in situ and to identify the environmental factors responsible for the observed effects.

INTRODUCTION

This paper proposes a monitoring strategy for assessing the health and fitness of an ecosystem in situ. This strategy is based on the physiological mechanisms by which organisms deal with stress. Stress in this context is a biological response and is defined as a measurable alteration of a physiological steady-state that is brought about by an environmental variable, and renders the organism more vulnerable to further environmental change (Bayne, 1975). Factors which elicit this stress response are referred to as stressors.

Contaminant-induced stress responses have been observed at every level of biological organization. Initially contaminants interact with biological systems at the molecular level (Figure 1). These interactions may result in physiological perturbations at the cellular and organismal levels such as reductions in growth, reproduction or survival (Sanders et al., 1983).

----

[1]Molecular Ecology Institute, California State University, Long Beach, CA 90840
[2]Department of Biology, California State University, Long Beach, CA 90840
[3]Duke University Marine Laboratory, Beaufort, NC 28516

Ultimately these toxic effects may propagate upward and
impact the population and community levels.

When assessing the effects of contaminants on an
ecosystem we are ultimately concerned with perturbations
at the population and community levels. However, the time
course for expression of toxic effects at the community
level is highly variable. It may be on the order of years
if toxicant concentrations are sublethal (Mearns et al.,
1982). On the other hand, if reproduction is impaired,
adverse effects may be rapidly translated to the community
and ecosystem levels (Slobodkin, 1961). Also, since
community stability is often regulated by one or several
"keystone species" (Herricks and Cairns, 1982) subtle
stress-induced changes in the reproductive success of
these species may have profound and rapid effects on the
community and ecosystem. The variations in response time
from initial molecular interactions to population and
community effects and the natural variability in the the
structure and productivity at these higher levels make it
difficult to distinguish stress-induced changes from
natural fluctuations.

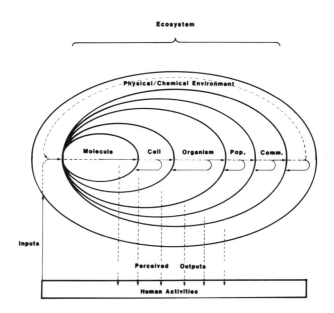

Figure 1. The levels of ecological organization are
depicted as a nested series of ovals. The outermost oval
represents the physical-chemical environment.
Anthropogenic inputs will initially interact with
biological systems at the molecular level and the effects
of these interactions will propagate to higher levels of
biological organization. Biological stress responses
(outputs) can be observed at each level of organization.

Therefore, cause and effect relationships between stressor action and stress responses can be monitored most effectively at the organismal level (Moriarty, 1983). If organismal stress cannot be detected by sensitive indicators, the population and community will not normally be affected (Moriarty, 1983). Alternatively, if organismal stress is detected and can be attributed to anthropogenic inputs, the significance of this stress to the population and community must be assessed.

A number of factors complicate the assessment of stress in native organisms from anthropogenic activities. Under natural conditions, the range of stressors to which an organism is exposed will vary greatly and can include both anthropogenic and natural stressors (e.g., temperature and salinity). In addition, such natural variables as food availability, life stage and physiological condition can alter an organism's capacity to cope with a particular suite of stressors (Stebbing, 1981a). Thus, both natural and anthropogenic changes in the environment contribute to the "total stress load" of an organism and are integrated into their stress response (Stebbing, 1981a). Since organisms have only a finite capacity to adapt, the effects of a particular contaminant, or group of contaminants, must be viewed within the context of these variables.

A wide range of indicators have been used to measure stress at the organismal level. They can be classified into two categories. The first involves general stress responses that are elicited regardless of the nature of the stressor. These responses provide an estimate of the integrated stress load to which an organism is exposed in its environment. Because of their lack of specificity, general stress responses are of little use for identifying the causative agents. The second category of stress responses are stressor-specific; they respond to a specific stressor or group of stressors. Although this latter group provides less integrative information, they can facilitate the establishment of cause and effect relationships. In the following sections we will discuss both general and specific stress responses and their integration into a monitoring program in which general stress responses are used for initial screening, and specific stress responses are used to help define the nature of the stressors.

GENERAL STRESS RESPONSES

Organisms can use several strategies to minimize detrimental effects of environmental stressors (Wedemeyer et al., 1984; Jenkins, 1986b). They may elicit avoidance responses, activate repair or stabilization mechanisms, and synthesize detoxication enzymes or binding ligands. All of these processes require energy which can only be obtained by diverting energy from other cellular

processes. As the stress load increases, there will be a
threshold at which this diversion disturbs important
physiological processes such as growth and reproduction.
Since inhibition of growth and reproduction reflect this
diversion of energy to counteract the detrimental effects
of a stressor, they can be used as indicators of stress
(Widdows, 1985). Scope for growth (Warren and Davis,
1967), growth inhibition (Sanders and Jenkins, 1984), and
hormesis, perturbations in the regulation of growth
(Stebbing, 1981a,b; Laughlin et al., 1981; Sanders et al.,
1985) have all taken advantage of this principle and have
been used successfully as sensitive general indicators of
stress at the organismal level.
     In the absence of a mechanistic understanding of
general stress physiology, these indices have been
valuable for evaluating stress. However, they have
several major limitations: (1) they are not based on the
mechanisms which underlie the relationship between general
stress physiology and toxicity and, therefore, measure
stress indirectly; (2) they function at the organismal
level and lack the sensitivity of cellular parameters; (3)
they are only applicable to situations in which organisms
are exposed to a stressor for days or weeks to evoke a
measurable response, thus limiting their versatility; and,
(4) they cannot be used easily to measure stress in native
organisms exposed in situ. Thus, there is a need to find
sensitive, rapid, and direct measures for evaluating the
total stress load in organisms exposed in the laboratory
and in situ. Such a "diagnostic" tool will have the
greatest predictive value and widest application to new
conditions and other organisms if it is based on the
molecular mechanisms involved in physiological
adaptation.
     The recently discovered heat-shock or stress proteins
response (SPR) is the basis for one of the most promising
approaches for evaluating general stress. The SPR is a
general response to stress at the cellular level that
increases an organism's tolerance to subsequent stress
(Tanguay, 1983). When a cell is stressed it synthesizes a
suite of specific stress proteins which appear to be
intimately involved in the cells physiological adaptation
to stress. The patterns of accumulation and tissue
distribution of these stress proteins are the direct
result of modification of gene expression in response to
changes in the environment. Therefore, the SPR has the
potential to be used to as a diagnostic tool to evaluate
the degree to which an organism is stressed in situ.
Also, since the SPR is expressed differentially in tissues
depending upon the nature of the effector, the SPR may
provide additional information on the types of stressors
to which an organism has been exposed.
     The stress proteins response can be considered a
general stress response because it can be elicited by a
wide variety of stressors. Although initially discovered

in cells as a response to heat-shock, the SPR can be
induced by hormones (Ireland et al., 1982; Caggese et al.,
1983; Kasambalides and Lanks, 1983), and by stressors with
different chemical and physical characteristics (Hammond
et al., 1982) including: trace metals (Levinson et al.,
1980; Heikkila et al., 1982; Courgeon et al., 1984; Leone
et al., 1985); water stress (Bewley et al., 1983); amino
acid analogs (Thomas and Mathews, 1984); anoxia, cold
shock, and viral infections (Guttman et al., 1980; Adams
and Rinne, 1982; Courgeon et al, 1984).

Since the stress proteins response is found in
prokaryotes, lower eukaryotes, higher plants,
invertebrates and vertebrates, it could be used as a
monitoring tool in a wide range of environmental
situations (Alahiotis, 1983; Black and Bloom, 1984).
Moreover, genes encoding stress proteins and the proteins
themselves are remarkably well conserved (Lowe et al.,
1983) and several major stress proteins are usually found
in common among various phylogenic groups (Atkinson et
al., 1983). Most species and tissues have stress proteins
in the 60-70 and 80-90 kD range with greater variability
in the other size classes. Antibodies to the 70 and 89 kD
stress proteins cross react with organisms ranging from
yeast to flies to mice (Schlesinger et al., 1982).
Consequently a common stress protein assay could be used
to measure the SPR in a wide range of phylogenic groups
and would have excellent potential for evaluating the
total stress load of native organisms exposed to stressors
in their environment.

STRESSOR-SPECIFIC RESPONSES

    After stress has been demonstrated in an aquatic
environment, the next challenge is to identify the
stressor(s) that are responsible. At first glance it
might appear that we could simply identify the nature of
the stressor by measuring the concentrations of
contaminants in tissues of stressed organisms. However,
relationships between contaminant concentrations in an
organism and its toxic effects are complex and, thus,
difficult to establish (Jenkins and Brown, 1984). A major
reason for this difficulty is that organisms have specific
metabolic mechanisms which modify, sequester,
compartmentalize, and excrete contaminants. Therefore,
the potential toxicity of a stressor will depend upon both
the amount that has been accumulated and how effectively
the organism can metabolize it. A more accurate approach
for identifying the causative agents involves examining
the patterns of metabolism for each class of contaminants
to determine which are having the greatest impact on the
organism. These stressor-specific responses have been
used to monitor the effects of both trace metals and
xenobiotic organic compounds (Jenkins et al., 1982a;
1982b).

Trace metal toxicity is primarily the result of the nonspecific binding of metals to proteins and other macromolecules (Friedberg, 1974). This nonspecific binding can modify the shape and function of macromolecules and adversely affect biochemical and physiological processes. Most organisms regulate the distributions of essential and nonessential metals at the tissue, cellular and subcellular levels to minimize nonspecific binding (Mason and Simkiss, 1982; Mason et al., 1984 and, Sanders et al., 1983; Sanders and Jenkins 1984). This regulation is mediated through soluble and insoluble metal ligands that optimize the specific binding of essential metals to appropriate macromolecules and act as sinks for excess metals (Simkiss et al., 1982). The ability of a given species to regulate metal metabolism will be a major factor in determining the relationship between metal accumulation and toxicity. As a consequence, the more subtle aspects of metal toxicity in aquatic organisms can be estimated more precisely by examining the distribution of metals within the subcellular ligand pools (Bayne et al., 1980).

We have examined the relationships between subcellular trace metal distributions and toxicity in several species of marine invertebrates. We found that at low copper exposures, crab larvae are able to regulate their accumulation of Cu (Sanders et al., 1983; Sanders and Jenkins, 1984). However, at Cu concentrations greater than those found in their environment, this ability to regulate appeared to break down, Cu accumulated in the metallothionein (MT) and very low molecular weight ligand pools (VLMW), and growth was inhibited. Similar correlations were found between increased relative accumulation of metals (cadmium) in the MT and VLMW pools and perturbations in growth and reproduction in experiments with the polychaetous annelid, Neanthes arenaceodentata (Jenkins and Sanders, 1986; Jenkins, 1986a). These data suggest that accumulation of metals in the MT and VLMW pools may reflect modifications in metal metabolism in response to metal-induced stress. The strong correlation between these alterations in metal metabolism and reduced growth and reproduction suggest that accumulation of metals in these ligand pools may serve as a good indicator of metal toxicity.

Metallothioneins are cysteine-rich metal-binding proteins whose synthesis can be induced by metals such as copper, cadmium, zinc and mercury (Richards and Cousins, 1976; Hildebrand et al., 1979). They have been isolated from vertebrates, invertebrates, and plants and are involved in metal uptake, metabolism and detoxication (Kagi and Nordberg, 1979). A number of early studies focused on metal-metallothionein interactions as a monitoring tool for assessing metal toxicity in situ in fish (Jenkins et al., 1982a; Roch and McCarter, 1984) and marine invertebrates (Jenkins et al., 1982b).

More recent studies have shown the importance of the
VLMW ligand pools in assessing metal metabolism and
toxicity (Sanders and Jenkins, 1984; George, 1982; Mason
and Nott, 1981; Simkiss and Mason, 1983; Mason et al.,
1984). This pool may also represent a regulated class of
metal-binding ligands. Frazier and George (1983) found
that metals accumulated in the VLMW pool in oysters in
response to high metal loading. Also, the synthesis of
VLMW ligands can be induced by cadmium in plants (Grill
and Zenk, 1985). An alternative explanation of these
data, however, is that metals accumulate in this pool due
to a breakdown in normal metal metabolism and
compartmentalization. Regardless of the actual mechanisms
that are involved it appears that metal accumulation in
the VLMW pool can serve as a biochemical indicator of
metal stress in a wide range of species.
     Stressor-specific responses have also been used to
evaluate the effects of xenobiotic organic compounds on
aquatic organisms. Much of this research has focused on
the enzymes that are involved in the metabolism of these
compounds, such as the mixed function oxidases (Spies et
al., 1984), aryl hydrocarbon hydroxylases (Davies et al.,
1984), epoxide hydrolayse, glutathione-S-transferase, and
UDP glucuronyl transferase (Andersson et al., 1985). This
research is based on the premise that information on the
organism's prior exposure to xenobiotics and its capacity
to metabolize various classes of xenobiotics can be
obtained by either measuring the activity of these enzymes
or the synthesis of new stressor specific isoforms of the
enzymes. Since the covalent binding of xenobiotic
metabolites with macromolecules are a major mechanism of
xenobiotic toxicity, a more direct measure of toxic
effects would involve examining the accumulation and
subcellular distribution of specific xenobiotic
metabolites (Brown et al., 1982; Jenkins and Brown, 1984)
This approach would provide a more integrated picture of
the potential impact of accumulated xenobiotics on the
organism (Jenkins, 1986b).

INTEGRATED BIOLOGICAL MONITORING

     The specific parameters for assessing stress
presented in this paper have several advantages: (1) they
measure stress directly since they are based on the
mechanisms which underlie the organisms' response to
stressors; (2) they are rapid and sensitive because they
represent the first level of response to the stressor; and
(3) they are particularly amenable to measuring stress in
native organisms exposed in situ. Thus, these parameters
provide the basis for a sensitive, rapid, and direct
assessment of the total stress load in organisms exposed
to stressors in the laboratory and in situ.
     To summarize, this monitoring strategy uses our
increased understanding of the underlying mechanisms of

stress metabolism to assess stress in native organisms in
situ. General stress responses would be measured in
native organisms as an initial screening for biological
stress. If these data indicate that native organisms are
stressed, stressor-specific responses would be measured to
help define the nature of the stressor(s).

ACKNOWLEDGMENTS

We wish to thank Stavros Howe, Andrew Mason and
Patricia Sullivan for reviewing earlier drafts of this
manuscript and Joyce Algranti for preparation of the final
manuscript. This work was funded by grants from the
Physiological Ecology Program, Division of Ecological
Research, Department of Energy to California State
University at Long Beach and Duke University. This is
contribution JS-86-001 of the Molecular Ecology Institute.

APPENDIX.-REFERENCES

1. Adams, C., and R.W. Rinne. "Stress protein formation:
   Gene expression and environmental interaction with
   evolutionary significance". Int. Review of Cytology,
   79:305-315, 1982.
2. Alahiotis, S.N. "Heat shock proteins. A new view on
   the temperature compensation". Comp. Biochem.
   Physiol., 75B:379-387, 1983.
3. Andersson, T., M. Personen, and C. Johansson.
   "Differential induction of cytochrome P-450-dependent
   monooxygenase, epoxide hydrolase, gluathione
   transferase and UDP glucuronyl transfersae activities
   in the liver of the rainbow trout by -napthoflavone
   or clophen A50". Biochem. Pharmacol., 34:3309-3314,
   1985.
4. Atkinson, B.G., T. Cunningham, R.L. Dean, and M.
   Somerville. "Comparison of the effects of heat shock
   and metal-ion stress on gene expression in cells
   undergoing myogenesis". Can. J. Biochem. Cell Biol.,
   61:404-413, 1983.
5. Bayne, B.L. "Cellular and physiological measures of
   pollution effect". Mar. Poll. Bull., 16:127-128,
   1975.
6. Bayne, B.L., D.A. Brown, F.L. Harrison, and P.P.
   Yevich. "Mussel health". In: The International
   Mussel Watch, Report on a Workshop at Barcelona,
   Spain, December 1978. E.D. Goldberg, ed. National
   Academy of Science, Washington, D.C., pp.163-235,
   1980.
7. Bewley, J.D., K.M. Larsen, and J.E.T. Papp. "Water-
   stress-induced changes in the pattern of protein
   synthesis in maize seedling mesocotyls: A comparison
   with the effects of heat-shock". J. Exp. Bot.
   34:1126-1133, 1983.

8. Black, R.E., and L. Bloom. "Heat shock proteins in
    Aurelia (Cnidaria, Scyphozoa)". J. Exp. Zool.
    230:303-307, 1984.
9. Brown, D.A., R.W. Gossett, and K.D. Jenkins.
    "Contaminants in white croakers Genyonemus lineatus
    (Ayres, 1855) from the Southern California Bight:
    II. Chlorinated hydrocarbon
    detoxification/toxification". In: Physiological
    Mechanisms of Marine Pollutant Toxicity   (Vernberg,
    W.B., A. Calabrese, F.P. Thurberg and F.J.
    Vernberg, eds.). pp. 197-213. Academic Press, Inc.,
    New York, 1982.
10. Caggese, C., M. Bozzetti, G. Palumbo, and P.
    Barsanti. "Induction by hydrocortisone-21-sodium
    succinate of the 70K heat-shock polypeptide in
    isolated salivary glands of Drosophila melanogaster
    larvae". Experientia, 39:1143-1144, 1983.
11. Courgeon, A.M., C. Maisonhaute, and M. Best-Belpomme.
    "Heat shock proteins are induced by cadmium in
    Drosophila cells". Exp. Cell Res., 153:515-521,
    1984.
12. Davies, J.M., J.S. Bell, and C. Houghton. "A
    comparison of the levels of hepatic aryl hydrocarbon
    hydroxylase in fish caught close to and distant from
    North Sea oil fields". Mar. Environ. Res., 14:23-45,
    1984.
13. Frazier, J.M. and S.G. George. "Cadmium kinetics in
    oysters - a comparative study of Crassostrea gigas
    and Ostrea edulis". Mar. Biol., 76:55-61, 1983.
14. Friedberg, F. "Effects of metal binding on protein
    structure". Q. Rev. Biophys., 7:1-33, 1974.
15. George, S.G. "Subcellular accumulation and
    detoxication of metals in aquatic animals". In:
    Physiological Mechanisms of Marine Pollutant
    Toxicity, (Vernberg, W.B., A. Calabrese, F.P.
    Thurburg and F.J. Vernberg, eds.). pp. 3-53.
    Academic Press, Inc., New York, 1982.
16. Grill, E., E.-L. Winnacker and M. H. Zenk.
    "Phytochelatins: the principal heavy-metal
    complexing peptides of higher plants". Science,
    230:674-676, 1985.
17. Guttman, S.D., C.V.C. Glover, C.D. Allis, and M.A.
    Gorovsky. "Heat shock, deciliation and release from
    anoxia induce the synthesis of the same set of
    polypeptides in starved T. pyriformis". Cell 22:299-
    307, 1980.
18. Hammond, G.L., Y.K. Lai, and C.L. Markert. "Diverse
    forms of stress lead to new patterns of gene
    expression through a common and essential metabolic
    pathway". Proc. Natl. Acad. Sci. USA 79:3485-3488,
    1982.
19. Heikkila, J.J., G.A. Schultz, K. Iatrou, and L.
    Gedamu. "Expression of a set of fish genes following
    heat or metal ion exposure". J. Biol. Chem.
    257:12000-12005, 1982.

20. Herricks, E.E. and J. Cairns, Jr. "Biological monitoring. Part III - Receiving system methodology based on community structure". Water Res., 16:141-153, 1982.

21. Hildebrand, C.E., R.A. Tobey, E.W. Campbell, and M.D. Enger. "A cadmium-resistant variant of the Chinese hamster (CHO) cell with increased metallothionein induction capacity". Ex. Cell. Res., 124:237-246, 1979.

22. Ireland, R.C., E. Berger, K. Sirotkin, M.A. Yund, D. Osterbur, and J. Fristrom. "Ecdysterone induces the transcription of four heat-shock genes in Drosophila S3 cells and imaginal discs". Dev. Biol. 93:498-507,1982.

23. Jenkins, K. D. "Relationships between perturbations in reproduction and cadmium accumulation and subcellular distributions in Neanthes". Submitted to Mar. Environ. Res., 1986a.

24. Jenkins, K.D. "Tolerance limits in aquatic organisms: A mechanistic basis". In: New Approaches to Water Quality Research. In press, 1986b.

25. Jenkins, K.D. and D.A. Brown. "Determining the biological significance of contaminant bioaccumulation". In Concepts in Marine Pollution Measurements, (White, H.H., ed.). Maryland Sea Grant College, 1984.

26. Jenkins, K.D., D.A. Brown, G.P. Hershelman, W.C. Meyer. "Contaminant in white croakers Genyonemus lineatus (Ayers 1855) from the Southern California Bight: I. Trace metal detoxification/toxification". In: Physiological Mechanisms of Marine Pollutant Toxicity (Vernberg, W.B., A. Calabrese, F.P. Thurberg and F.J. Vernberg., eds.). pp. 177-196. Academic Press, Inc., New York, 1982a.

27. Jenkins, K.D., D.A. Brown, P.S. Oshida, E.M. Perkins. "Cytosolic metal distribution as an indicator of toxicity in sea urchins from the Southern California Bight". Mar. Poll. Bull., 13:413-421, 1982b.

28. Jenkins, K.D. and B.M. Sanders. "Relationships between free cadmium ion activity in sea water, cadmium accumulation and subcellular distribution, and growth in polychaetes". Envir. Health Persp., 65:205-210, 1986.

29. Kagi, J.H.R., and M. Nordberg. Metallothionein. Birkhauser Verlag. Basel, Boston, Stuttgart, 1979.

30. Kasambalides, E.J., and K.W. Lanks. "Dexamethasone can modulate glucose-regulated and heat shock protein synthesis". J. Cellular Physiol. 114:93-98, 1983.

31. Laughlin, R.B., J. Ng, and H.E. Guard. "Hormesis: A response to low environmental concentrations of petroleum hydrocarbons". Science, 211:705-707, 1981.

32. Leone, A., G.N. Pavlakis and D.H. Hamer. "Menkes'
     disease: Abnormal metallothionein gene regulation in
     response to copper". Cell, 40:301-309, 1985.
33. Levinson, W., H. Oppermann and J. Jackson.
     "Transition series metals and sulfhydryl reagents
     induced the synthesis of four proteins in eukaryotic
     cells". Biochim. Biophys. Acta., 606:170-180,
     1980.
34. Lowe, D.G., W.D. Fulford, and L.A. Moran. "Mouse and
     Drosophila genes encoding the major heat shock
     protein (hsp 70) are highly conserved". Mol. Cell.
     Biol., 3:1540-1543, 1983.
35. Mason, A.Z. and J.A. Nott. "The role of
     intracellular biomineralized granules in the
     regulation and detoxification of metals in gastropods
     with special reference to the marine prosobranch
     Littorina littorea". Aquat. Toxicol., 1:239-256,
     1981.
36. Mason, A.Z. and K. Simkiss. "Sites of mineral
     deposition in metal-accumulating cells". Exp. Cell.
     Res., 139:383-391, 1982.
37. Mason, A.Z., K. Simkiss, and K. Ryan.
     "Ultrastructural localization of metals in specimens
     in Littorina littorea (L.) from polluted and non-
     polluted sites". J. Mar. Biol. Ass. U.K., 64:699-
     720, 1984.
38. Mearns, A.J., E. Haines, G.S. Kleppel, R.A. McGrath,
     J.J. McLaughlin, D.A. Segar, J.H. Sharp, J.J. Walsh,
     J.Q. Word, D.K. Young, and M.W. Young. "Effects of
     nutrients and carbon loadings on communities and
     ecosystems". In: Ecological Stress and the New
     YorkB: Science and Management (Mayer, G.F., ed.).
     pp. 53-66. Estuarine Research Federation, Columbia,
     South Carolina, 1982.
39. Moriarty, F. Ecotoxicology, The Study of Pollutants
     in Ecosystems. 233 pp. Academic Press, Inc., New
     York, 1983.
40. Richards, M.P. and R.J. Cousins. "Influence of
     parenteral zinc and actinomysin D on tissue zinc
     uptake and the synthesis of a zinc-binding protein".
     Bioinorg. Chem., 4:215-224, 1976.
41. Roch, M. and J.A. McCarter. "Metallothionein
     induction, growth, and survival of Chinook salmon
     exposed to zinc, copper, and cadmium". Bull.
     Environ. Contam. Toxicol., 32:478-485, 1984.
42. Sanders, B. M. and K.D. Jenkins. "Relationships
     between free cupric ion concentrations in seawater
     and copper metabolism and growth in crab larvae".
     Biol. Bull., 167:704-712, 1984.
43. Sanders, B.M., K.D. Jenkins, W.G. Sunda and J.D.
     Costlow. "Free cupric ion activity in seawater:
     Effects on metallothionein and growh in crab larvae".
     Science, 222:53-55, 1983.

44. Sanders, B., R. Laughlin, and J.D. Costlow. "The regulation of growth in larvae of the mud crab, Rhithropanopeus harrisii". In: Crustacean Issues. Vol. 2: Crustacean Growth, (Wenner, A.M., ed.). Balkema Press, 1985.

45. Schlesinger, M.J., G. Aliperti, and P.M. Kelley. "The response of cells to heat shock". TIBS 3:222-225, 1982.

46. Simkiss, K. and A.Z. Mason. "Metal Ions: Metabolic and Toxic Effects. In: The Mollusca, Vol. 2. Environmental Biochemistry and Physiology". (Hochachka, P.W. and K.M. Wilbur, eds.). pp 101-164. Academic Press, Inc., New York, 1983.

47. Simkiss, K., M. Taylor, and A.Z. Mason. "Metal detoxification and bioaccumulation on molluscs". Mar. Biol. Letts., 3:187-201, 1982.

48. Slobodkin, L.B. Growth and Regulation of Animal Populations. 184 pp., Holt, Reinhart, and Winston, New York, 1981.

49. Spies, R.B., J.S. Felton and L. Dillard. "Hepatic mixed-function oxidases in California flatfishes are increased in contaminated environments and by oil and PCB ingestion". Mar. Environ. Res., 14:412-413, 1984.

50. Stebbing, A.R.D. "The kinetics of growth control in a colonial hydroid". J. Mar. Biol. Ass. U.K., 61:35-63, 1981a.

51. Stebbing, A.R.D. "Hormesis-stimulation of colony growth in Campanularia flexuosa (hydrozoa) by copper, cadmium and other toxicants". Aqua. Toxicol. 1:227-238, 1981b.

52. Tanguay, R.M. "Genetic regulation during heat shock and function of heat-shock proteins: A review". Can. J. Biochem. Cell Biol. 61:387-394, 1983.

53. Thomas, G.P. and M.B. Mathews. "Alterations of transcription and translation in the Hela cells exposed to amino acid analogs". Mol. Cell. Biol., 4:1063-1072, 1984.

54. Warren, C.E. and G.E. Davis. "Laboratory studies on the feeding, bioenergetics and growth of fish". In: The Biological Basis of Freshwater fish Production (Gerking, S.D., ed.). pp. 175-214. Blackwell Scientific, Oxford, 1967.

55. Wedemeyer, G.A., D.J. McLeay, and C.P. Goodyear. "Assessing the tolerance of fish and fish populations to environmental stress: The problems and methods of monitoring". In: Contaminant Effects on Fisheries (Cairns, V.W., P.V. Hodson and J.O. Nriagu, eds.). pp. 164-195. John Wiley an Sons, Inc., 1984.

56. Widdows, J. "Physiological responses to pollution". Mar. Poll. Bull., 16:129-134, 1985.

Impacts of Urban Runoff on Estuarine Ecosystems

William E. Odum*
Mark E. Hawley*

INTRODUCTION

The importance of non-point source runoff from urban, suburban, and rural areas to the pollution of estuaries has been recognized for at least the past decade. For example, the U.S. Environmental Protection Agency's Chesapeake Bay Study noted that almost one third of the phosphorous and two thirds of the nitrogen entering the bay came from non-point sources.

Unfortunately, scientists working in estuaries have generally not focused on urban runoff per se. As a result our knowledge of the impacts of urban runoff on estuaries is not great and the actual role of the urban contribution to non-point source inputs remains relatively undefined.

In this paper we have first attempted to characterize the types of pollutants which could be expected to enter an estuary from urban runoff. Then, based on existing knowledge of the impacts of various types of pollutants on estuarine organisms and ecosystems, we speculate concerning the potential impact of urban runoff on estuaries. Finally, we discuss some of the critical research questions which must be addressed in order to ameliorate the impacts of urban runoff.

SOURCES AND CHARACTERISTICS OF URBAN RUNOFF POLLUTANTS

The pollutants contained in urban runoff are often complex in composition and occur in highly variable concentrations depending upon location, land use, time of the year, time since last rainfall event, duration of precipitation, and a variety of other factors. They originate largely from the land surface and particularly

*Department of Environmental Sciences, Clark Hall,
 University of Virginia, Charlottesville, Virginia 22903

from impervious surfaces such as parking lots, streets and buildings. Sources listed by Roesner (1982) include: dirt, oil, tire, and exhaust residues from automobiles; fallout of air pollution particles; fecal droppings from dogs, cats, birds, and other animals; remnants of household refuse dropped during collection or scattered by animals or wind; debris dropped or scattered by individuals; debris and pollutants deposited on or washed into streets from yards, roofs, and other indigenous open areas; and wastes and dirt from building and demolition. Obviously, the list could go on and on.

As shown in Table 1, the pollutant components of urban runoff can be highly varied and complex in composition. Under certain conditions, the loadings of BOD, COD, suspended solids, total nitrogen, total phosphorous, and lead can be greater in urban runoff than in sewage loads (Sheaffer et al. 1982). In fact, on an annual basis non-point source pollution loadings from urban runoff can contribute more suspended solids, nutrients (especially phosphorous), and lead to nearby bodies of water than any other pollution source (Sheaffer et al. 1982).

In an attempt to assess the impact of pollutants in urban runoff on estuarine ecosystems, we have reduced the list of potential pollutants to a more manageable size (Table 2). We have chosen those constituents of urban runoff which appear to be (a) most universal, (b) most concentrated, and (c) most potentially destructive to natural ecosystems. Certainly, there are materials (e.g. ethylene glycol) which have been omitted from Table 2 which may cause significant problems at certain locations. These materials, however, most likely will be introduced through special mechanisms (spills, unusual land use practices, etc.).

TABLE 1.   Composition of Pollutants Found in Urban Runoff
           (modified from Sheaffer et al. 1982)

I.   Large-sized/biologically insignificant

      A.   Bulk cellulosic matter (twigs, leaves, paper,
           cellophane, etc.)
      B.   Bulk metals and alloys of construction and
           containerization (steel, iron, aluminum,
           magnesium, etc.)
      C.   Fabric, packaging, and construction plastics
      D.   Natural processed animal fibers

II.   Variable-sized/biologically insignificant

      A.   Soil conditioners
      B.   Basic soil constituents
      C.   Inorganic dust falls from air pollutants

III. Variable-sized/biologically nutritive/water-soluble

    A. Natural and compounded fertilizers (ammonium, nitrate, phosphate, etc.)
    B. Deicing compounds (sodium hexametaphosphate, urea, etc.)
    C. Soluble air pollutants (sulfur oxides, nitrogen oxides, etc.)
    D. Phosphate-based detergents
    E. Lawn and garden ash

IV. Variable-sized solids or solutions/biologically inhibiting/water-soluble

    A. Deicing compounds (sodium chloride, calcium chloride, etc.)
    B. Air pollutants (carbon monoxide, sulfides, ozone, etc.)
    C. Antifreeze compounds (methonal, ethylene glycol, etc.)
    D. Roadway hydrocarbons (some highly oxygenated bitumens)
    E. Water-based paint solutions

V. Variable-sized/immiscible or suspendable/ biologically inhibiting/water-insoluble

    A. Vehicular and roadway hydrocarbons (oils, greases, bitumens, etc.)
    B. Hydraulic fluids (propylene glycol diricinoleate, etc.)
    C. Water-insoluble air pollutants-hydrocarbons
    D. Pesticide/herbicide carriers

VI. Variable-sized solids or solutions/biologically toxic-water-soluble

    A. Common pesticides, herbicides (lead, malathion, phenol, etc.)

VII. Variable-sized solids, liquids, or suspensions/ biologically toxic/water-insoluble

    A. Common pesticides, herbicides (chlordane, 2,4-D, parathion, organo-mercury compounds, etc.)

VIII. Variable-sized culture media/biologically active/ water-suspendable life forms

    A. Animal excretions, fecal chloriforms, fecal streptococci, etc.
    B. Human excretions (fecal chloriforms, fecal streptococci, etc.)
    C. Dead animals (fecal chloriforms, non-fecal chloriforms, etc.)

D. Vegetation (biological nutrient source)
E. Food wastes (biological nutrient source)
F. Soil (biological nutrient source)

TABLE 2. Principle Pollution Components of Urban Runoff

*I.   Suspended solids

*II.   Metals (Pb, Fe, Hg, Cd, Zn, etc.)

*III. Nutrients (N, P, Ca, etc.)

IV.   Petrochemicals (oils, greases, other hydrocarbon
      compounds, etc.)

V.   Non-metallic toxics (pesticides, PCB's, benzine,
      etc.)

* = probably the most damaging and widespread components
    to urban runoff

IMPACTS ON ESTUARIES

The effects of human alterations on estuarine
organisms and estuarine ecosystems are well documented
(e.g. Cronin 1967, Odum 1970, Olausson and Cato 1980). A
great deal of research and published literature has been
devoted to the adverse effects of heavy metals, BOD and
COD loadings, lowered dissolved oxygen, toxic chemicals,
petroleum compounds and so forth. Various researchers
have addressed the effects of single perturbations such as
dredging, oil spills, agricultural runoff, and point source
inputs of sewage, pulp wastes, toxic chemicals, etc.

Unfortunately, although most scientists are aware of
the potential problems, very few studies have focused
solely on the impact of urban runoff to estuaries. One
reason for this is that in large estuaries urban runoff
effects are inexorably and synergistically associated with
the effects of dredging, chemical spills, point-source
contaminants and other serious alterations. To separate-
out the impact of urban runoff is difficult and, perhaps,
artificial. Another problem is that the impact of urban
runoff is discontinuous; episodes of heavy runoff with
high pollutant levels are interspersed between long periods
with little or no runoff.

In spite of these difficulties, research on the impacts
of urban runoff on estuaries is essential. Without an
idea of the relative impact of urban runoff, it is
impossible to formulate comprehensive planning for urban
areas which impinge upon estuarine systems (Harrill 1985).
For example, if the impact is relatively minor, then it may
not be necessary to take expensive measures to reduce the

impact. On the other hand, if the impact can be relatively
serious, as we suspect, then understanding can lead to
better designed methodology to intercept the most
destructive components of the runoff.

Organismal Versus Ecosystem Impacts

In analyzing the impacts of urban runoff, it is
important to discriminate between effects on individual
organisms and upon entire ecosystems (Table 3). Effects
on organisms range from outright lethal effects to more
insidious sub-lethal effects. Lethal effects are
noticeable through events such as fish or invertebrate
kills or long term declines in the numbers of individuals
of a species or declines in species diversity. Causative
factors in urban runoff include high concentrations of
toxic compounds, heavy metals, and petrochemical compounds;
high BOD loadings leading to decreased oxygen concentrations; increased turbidity; and synergistic interactions
of two or more of these factors.

Sub-lethal effects are caused by the same set of
factors but are often more difficult to detect because the
effects are delayed over a longer period of time and may
be more subtle. For example, long-term exposure to
contaminants in urban runoff may gradually weaken an
organism rendering it more susceptible to disease, climatic
change or the action of other stresses. Reproduction,
growth, and survival may ultimately be affected.

TABLE 3. Adverse Effects of Urban Runoff

Effects on Organisms

sub-lethal effects on biota
lethal effects on biota

Effects on Ecosystems

increased turbidity

decreased oxygen concentrations

increased sedimentation rates (and associated geo-
    morphological change)

decreased species diversity

increased rates of eutrophication

increased or decreased primary production

increased or decreased secondary production

Both lethal and sublethal effects can lead to long-term changes in ecosystems. Examples include changes in the species composition of plant, invertebrate, and vertebrate communities, and declines in primary and secondary production which are often reflected in lowered sports and commercial fishery yields.

Other types of ecosystem change which may result from urban runoff include (1) increased sedimentation and associated changes in geomorphology (from suspended sediment loads), (2) increased rates of eutrophication (from nutrient loadings), and (3) long-term declines in dissolved oxygen (from BOD and nutrient inputs).

Short-term Versus Long-term Effects

In attempting to analyze the effects of urban runoff on aquatic systems, it is important to differentiate between short-term and long-term effects. For example, during the peak discharge portion of the hydrograph, the so-called "first flush phenomenon" (Lazaro 1979) may result in unusually high concentrations of toxic compounds and suspended solids for short periods of time. This may result in localized lethal effects such as fish kills and high turbidity. Long-term effects may occur weeks or even months after the precipitation event; examples include sub-lethal effects on animal populations, altered geomorphology due to changes in sedimentation patterns and rates, increased eutrophication, and continued depressed oxygen concentrations due to settling-out of the high BOD fraction of the suspended solids. The impacts of short-term and long-term effects may vary from site to site depending upon local conditions such as tidal flushing, water quality, and other inputs of pollutants.

EXAMPLES OF ESTUARIES DEGRADED BY URBAN RUNOFF

There are virtually no published studies which definitively show the degradation of a significant estuarine area as a result of urban runoff. As we have emphasized previously in this paper, this lack of evidence is due to (a) the tendency for urban runoff and its effects to be interrelated with a host of other pollutant sources and their effects and (b) a lack of recognition by estuarine scientists of the potential threat from urban runoff pollution.

In spite of the lack of hard evidence, there is a considerable body of circumstantial evidence pointing to urban runoff as a serious pollution source. In studies of the south portion of San Francisco Bay (Conomos 1979, Luoma and Cain 1979) there is a suggestion that metal contamination of benthic organisms can be traced to urban runoff. This section of the estuary is particularly vulnerable

because it is less well flushed by either ocean or river
water than the northern portion of San Francisco Bay.
Studies of Chesapeake Bay (Bieri et al. 1982) show that as
much as 20% of the lead and 10% of other metals entering
the Bay come from urban runoff. Furthermore, the U.S.
Environmental Protection Agency's Chesapeake Bay Study
suggests that significant inputs of BOD, sediments, and
nutrients enter the Bay through urban runoff inputs to its
tributaries, particularly through the Potomac and
Susquehanna Rivers and Baltimore and Norfolk Harbors.

There are similar examples along all coasts of the
United States in which damage from urban runoff is
occurring but has not been well documented. Examples
include the Tijuana estuary in California, Tampa Bay and
Biscayne Bay in Florida, Charleston Harbor in South
Carolina, the tidal Delaware River adjacent to Philadelphia,
and New York and Boston Harbors. In each case the impact
of urban runoff is masked by a variety of other pollution
inputs.

PROPOSED FUTURE RESEARCH

Throughout this paper we have emphasized the paucity of
research results to guide us in assessing the impact of
urban runoff on estuaries. The single most critical factor
has been the inability to separate the effects of urban
runoff from other sources of pollution. Two apparent lines
of research exist for the future, one oriented to the
field and one to the laboratory.

A Field Research Approach

In order to untangle urban runoff from other pollution
sources, a study should be designed at a site which
receives only urban runoff. Such a site should be
relatively small and not particularly well-flushed (i.e.
have only a modest input of freshwater from sources other
than urban runoff and a small tidal fluctuation). Ideally,
two nearby locations could be studied, one which is
relatively pristine and one which is impacted solely by
urban runoff. Variables to be monitored could include
patterns and rates of benthic and wetland sedimentation,
dissolved oxygen concentrations, suspended solids concentrations, species diversity of a variety of animal
and plant groups, and estimates of primary and, if possible,
secondary production. It would also be important to
monitor both sites closely during and for several weeks
after extreme storm events. A study of this type, if
properly designed and executed, should provide great
insight to the degree of severity of urban runoff effects.

Laboratory Studies

A great deal of expertise exists in measuring the effects of a variety of pollutants (pesticides, heavy metals, etc.) on representative estuarine organisms (i.e. killifish) in the laboratory. The extensive work at the EPA's Gulf Breeze, Florida, laboratory is a good example. We suggest utilizing samples of typical urban runoff water as experimental treatments in the laboratory in the same way that single pollutants have been used in the past. Field-collected urban runoff water would contain all of the usual pollutants (metals, BOD, toxics, etc.) in normal ratio's to each other. The results of this type of laboratory toxicity study would automatically incorporate synergistic effects between the different types of pollutants. Ecosystem effects could be studied with mesocosms such as the MERL apparatus presently in use in Rhode Island (Nixon et al. 1984). Admittedly, these studies would suffer from the highly variable composition of urban runoff and the attendant problem with reproducibility of experimental results. There should be ways to get around this problem, however, such as utilizing and storing very large samples of water to insure reasonable consistency over a number of replications.

Experimental Factors to Emphasize

In spite of our lack of knowledge about the impact of urban runoff on estuaries, there are certain questions which are clearly of top priority.

(1) Are suspended solids, metals, and nutrients the most damaging components of urban runoff as we have suggested in this paper?

(2) Is it practical to attempt to remove these three components from runoff before it enters the estuary?

(3) Are other toxic compounds of only occasional (not of general) importance in urban runoff?

(4) Do sediment loads in urban runoff seriously alter sedimentation patterns and geomorphology in estuaries and estuarine wetlands? (It may be possible to tackle this question with carefully designed studies at a variety of sites in otherwise complex polluted environments such as Boston Harbor and the Potomac River in the vicinity of Washington, D. C.)

(5) Are estuaries with restricted circulation (low tidal amplitude or modest river inputs) more susceptible to damage from urban runoff than well-flushed estuaries?

(6)   Are the short-term effects (during the early portion
       of storm-induced runoff) more severe than long-term
       effects?

(7)   Are long-term sub-lethal effects of urban runoff
       pollution more destructive to organisms than short-
       term lethal effects?

(8)   Are the effects of urban storm water runoff more
       severe at high ambient water temperatures?

(9)   Are the effects of urban runoff more destructive on
       a local scale (tidal urban rivers and wetlands) or
       on a large scale (regional bodies of water such as
       San Francisco or Chesapeake Bays)?

(10)   Which groups of animals and plants are most
       susceptible to urban runoff? For example, we might
       hypothesize that post larval and juvenile fishes
       and invertebrates would be particularly sensitive to
       components of urban runoff such as suspended solids
       and dissolved metals.

    These are, of course, only an example of the degree of
imperfection of our knowledge concerning urban storm water
effects on the world's estuaries. Clearly, a considerable
amount of research remains to be done.

REFERENCES

Bieri, R., O. Bricker, R. Byrne, R. Diaz, G. Helz, J. Hill,
R. Huggett, R. Kerhin, M. Nichols, E. Reinharz, L.
Schaffer, D. Welding and C. Strobel. 1982. Toxic
substances. IN: Chesapeake Bay Program Technical
Studies: A Synthesis. E. G. Maclaster, D. A. Barker
and M. E. Kasper, eds. U.S. E.P.A. Washington, D. C.

Conomos, T. J. 1979. San Francisco Bay: the urbanized
estuary. Pacific Division of the Am. Assoc. Adv. Sci.
San Francisco, Calif. 493 pp.

Cronin, L. E. 1967. The role of man in estuarine
processes. IN: Estuaries. G. H. Lauff, ed. Am.
Assoc. Adv. Sci. Pub. No. 83: 667-689.

Harrill, R. L. 1985. Urbanization, water quality and
stormwater management: a Maryland perspective.
Wetlands of the Chesapeake. Environmental Law Inst.,
Washington, D. C. 246-253.

Lazaro, T. R. 1979. Urban hydrology. Ann Arbor Science,
Ann Arbor, Michigan. 249 pp.

Luoma, S. N. and D. J. Cain. 1979. Fluctuations of
copper, zinc, and silver in Tellenid clams as related
to freshwater discharge - South San Francisco Bay.
IN: San Francisco Bay: the Urbanized Estuary. T. J.
Conomos, ed. Pacific Div. Am. Assoc. Adv. Sci. San
Francisco, Calif. 231-246.

Nixon, S. W., M. E. Q. Pilson, C. A. Oviatt, P. Donaghay,
B. Sullivan, S. Seitzinger, D. Rudnick and J. Frithsen.
1984. Eutrophication of a coastal marine ecosystem -
an experimental study using the MERL microcosms. IN:
Flows of Energy and Materials in Marine Ecosystems:
Theory and Practice. M. J. R. Fasham, ed. Plenum
Press, New York: 105-135.

Odum, W. E. 1970. Insidious alteration of the estuarine
environment. Trans. Am. Fish. Soc. 99: 836-847.

Olausson, E. and I. Cato. 1980. Chemistry and biogeo-
chemistry of estuaries. John Wiley and Sons, New
York. 452 pp.

Roesner, L. A. 1982. Quality of urban runoff. IN: Urban
Stormwater Hydrology. D. F. Kibler, ed. Am. Geoph.
Union Water Resources Monograph No. 7: 161-187.

Sheaffer, J. R., K. R. Wright, W. C. Taggart and R. M.
Wright. 1982. Urban storm drainage management.
Marcel Dekker, Inc. N.Y. 271 pp.

URBAN RUNOFF IMPACTS ON RECEIVING WATERS
By: Jonathan E. Jones*

ABSTRACT

Urban stormwater runoff contaminants affect the principal receiving water uses of: (1) public water supply,
(2) recreation, (3) protection of aquatic life forms,
(4) agricultural and industrial water supply, and (5)
groundwater protection in diverse ways. Through exploration of impacts to aquatic ecosystems, the paradoxes
and uncertainties of the urban runoff quality phenomenon
become apparent. Key questions must be answered when
assessing the impacts of urban runoff constituents on
receiving water uses.

INTRODUCTION

"Most river quality processes are so complex that the scientist is
never sure of the reliability of his quantitative results." (1)

"Our ability to model water quality is limited by inadequate knowledge of aquatic systems." (2)

Over $100 million dollars (3) has been invested over the past fif-
teen years to characterize urban stormwater runoff quality. The National Urban Runoff Program (NURP) and other studies now provide typical ranges of constituent concentrations in urban stormwater runoff.

Design guidance for various techniques to reduce constituent concentrations, such as extended sedimentation time in detention ponds,
rapid infiltration, overland flow and other approaches also exists.
Moreover, countless studies are available which describe the impacts
of constituents often found in urban runoff on aquatic life forms.
Although few of these studies are strictly oriented to urban runoff
contaminants, study results can be extrapolated to preliminarily
project potential impacts of urban stormwater runoff.

One would think that with: (1) volumes of urban runoff quality
data, (2) proven technologies to reduce constituent loading, and (3) a
broad array of studies which assess the fate of contaminants in aquatic environments, the impacts of urban stormwater runoff on receiving
water quality could be delineated. Such is not the case. A comprehensive assessment of the ways in which urban runoff contaminants
affect receiving water uses is not available. Although the information required to conduct most assessments probably exists in raw form,

*Principal; Wright Water Engineers, Inc., Denver, Colorado 80211

it has not been systematically collected, reviewed, organized, interpreted, summarized, and presented in a manner understandable to practicing professionals who are faced with the challenges of implementing
regulatory programs or designing runoff management facilities intended
to meet water quality objectives.

The U.S. Geological Survey, in its river quality assessment of the
Willamette River in Oregon, summarized the critical need for better
definition of the components of impact assessment, as follows (4):

> "Achievement of desirable river quality at acceptable
> cost requires that management decisions be based on
> sound impact assessments, not on arbitrary assumptions.
> Thus, the vital link between resource development plans
> and management decisions is scientific assessment to
> predict the probable impacts of each planning alterna-
> tive. At present, the impact assessment link is a stum-
> bling block to the overall process. The difficulty in
> appraising impacts results from: (a) absence of rational
> framework for structuring such work; (b) absence of
> well-developed, ready to use assessment methods; and (c)
> scarcity of reliable data."

The subject of impact assessment is explored herein, via three
major topics:

1. Delineate classifications (uses) of receiving waters and des-
    cribe the ways in which urban runoff quality influences these
    classifications.

2. Discuss the uncertainties, ambiguities, and paradoxes asso-
    ciated with predicting the impacts of runoff on receiving
    waters by focusing on impacts to aquatic ecosystems.

3. Provide key questions to be considered during impact assess-
    ment studies.

EFFECTS ON RECEIVING WATER USES

Under the auspices of the U.S. Environmental Protection Agency,
states have developed and enforce water quality classification systems
for nearly all waters within their jurisdictions. Such systems typically establish classifications (uses) of the particular water body
and specify water quality standards which assure that the designated
classifications will be maintained.

Typical water classifications include:

1. Drinking water,
2. Recreation,
3. Protection of fisheries and other aquatic life forms,
4. Agriculture,
5. Industrial water supply,
6. Groundwater supply

Of basic importance are the following:

1. Classifications and water quality standards are established on a reach by reach basis for each waterway (or lake) in question.

2. State governments establish that there are legitimate, identified zoning uses for waters of the state, under both existing and proposed conditions.

3. Classifications and standards are established to maintain these designated uses.

4. The goal of water quality management programs is to fulfill designated classifications and standards. This requires regulation of polluters, with focus traditionally on point sources. In many states, non-point sources are not regulated presently.

Prior to assessing the impacts of urban runoff constituents on receiving waters, the salient classifications and standards and their implications must be understood. Urban runoff affects water classifications in various ways, examples of which follow:

Drinking Water

Constituents in urban runoff that potentially pose concern from the standpoint of human health include heavy metals, various organic pollutants and coliform bacteria.

The cost of municipal water treatment is increased by stormwater contaminants. Nutrient inputs to raw water reservoirs are of concern, in light of problems related to chlorinated organics and eutrophication. Municipal water providers dictate that only particular kinds of development will be acceptable in basins tributary to public water supply lakes, and mandate that runoff control programs capable of reducing nutrient loads from developing areas will be implemented.

Dillon Reservoir, located in Summit County, Colorado and adjoined by various towns serves as a example of present governmental response to the potential adverse impacts of urban runoff on a public drinking water facility. To attain the recommended lake total phosphorus standard, local governments have agreed to limit phosphorus inputs from both point and non-point sources. If a municipality in the Dillon Reservoir basin determines that it is more cost effective to reduce phosphorus concentrations in urban stormwater runoff than in sewage effluent, that municipality can claim credit for phosphorus removal from non-point sources and apply that credit against the quantity of phosphorus which would otherwise have to be removed from the municipality's sewage. This example of "trading" phosphorus removal between non-point and point source inputs to a receiving water body represents a sensible means of addressing a politically sensitive issue, and may be implemented elsewhere advantageously.

Although public water systems can economically reduce urban runoff (and other) contaminant concentrations to acceptable levels through sophisticated monitoring and treatment, such may not be the case for individual water users. In a Jefferson County, Colorado District Court case entitled McCormick vs. Genesee Land Company, the owner of two shallow wells and an infiltration gallery successfully sued a developer for the effective loss of his water system due to the fact that a previously undeveloped mountain basin (which historically served as the water supply to the plaintiff's facilities) was transformed into an urbanized basin by the construction of approximately 150 town-homes and condominiums less than 1/4 mile upstream from the plaintiff's wells and infiltration gallery. The plaintiff contended that urban runoff constituents along with the ever present possibility of chemical spills into the drainageway by residents had rendered his water supply unfit for human consumption without implementation of a sophisticated monitoring and treatment program. A jury agreed with the plaintiff and awarded him nearly $300,000 as a result of the loss of his water system. Many other small water users who have historically had the benefit of relatively clean raw water supplies face this problem, given the proliferation of upstream residential and commercial developments. Increasing litigation in this area is inevitable.

The outcome of an ongoing federal court case in Boston will set a major precedent with respect to human health risks of contaminants in drinking water. The plaintiffs are families who claim that water supplies contaminated by two industries induced leukemia and other serious illnesses, and they intend to present studies which will designate specific chemicals as the cause(s) of the observed illness. Courts have traditionally sided with victims of unique environmental health problems, such as asbestosis, where the cause could be unequivocally traced to a specific pollutant (5). But efforts to prove damages from toxic wastes have failed for lack of evidence directly tying the suspect chemical to a specific illness or death (5). The plaintiffs' doctors in this case claim that they have established an irrefutable connection between chemicals in the water supply and the observed illnesses, and their testimony will be based on studies which show that toxins damage the human immune system.

Recreation

Urban runoff impacts recreation in three major ways: (1) increased coliform concentrations immediately after runoff, (2) eutrophication, and (3) impacts to aquatic life.

NURP data indicate that coliform bacterial counts frequently exceed state criteria for primary and secondary body contact after runoff events. The significance of this finding is unclear in that body contact sports are not prevalent immediately after runoff events. Based on the soon-to-be finalized non-point source NPDES permit that Bellevue, Washington will operate under (where swimming is common in urban streams) and other similar cases, it will be increasingly typical to apply coliform restrictions to urban runoff discharges.

Concern for lake water quality has induced many communities to initiate programs which sharply curtail allowable inputs of urban runoff contaminants (nutrients) into lakes. Denver, Colorado is comprehensively managing urban runoff inputs to lakes, principally to assure that the lakes will continue to provide attractive recreational features. Cherry Creek Reservoir, one of Denver's most heavily utilized parks, has been subjected to increasing phosphorus inputs due mainly to widespread urbanization in the basin tributary to the lake. The Colorado State Water Quality Control Commission established a chlorophyll a standard for Cherry Creek Reservoir of 0.017 mg/l, with a corresponding total phosphorus standard of 0.035 mg/l. Accordingly, local governments in the Cherry Creek basin have joined together to require that all new development within the basin will implement runoff control measures that will reduce total phosphorus levels in on-site discharges by 50 percent.

The ultimate "fail-safe" solution to the urban quality problem was recently conceived for a large lake at a development known as Highlands Ranch in south Denver. The focal point of Highlands Ranch is the reservoir, and the developers believe that maintaining excellent water quality is of paramount importance. Therefore, a ditch around the perimeter of the lake will be constructed to assure that all runoff from surrounding residential areas will be intercepted and discharged downstream. Orlando, Florida, with over 80 high quality lakes within its boundary, provides another excellent example of intensive management of non-point source pollution to maintain the visual appeal of reservoirs.

Impacts to Aquatic Life Forms

Given the: (1) myriad of life forms in aquatic environments and their inherent complexity, and (2) innumerable combinations of urban contaminants and their dynamic behavior within these ecosystems, site specific environmental assessments are mandatory. Nevertheless, study results from innumerable studies can be extrapolated (with varying levels of confidence) to project the probable general impacts of urban runoff contaminants on life forms. Odum and Hawley (6) provide the following discussion regarding impacts to life forms:

In analyzing the impacts of urban runoff, it is important to discriminate between effects on individual organisms and entire ecosystems (Table 1). Effects on organisms range from outright lethal effects to more insidious sub-lethal effects. Lethal effects are noticeable through events such as fish or invertebrate kills or long-term declines in the numbers of individuals of a species or declines in species diversity. Causative factors in urban runoff include high concentrations of toxic compounds, heavy metals, and petrochemical compounds; high BOD loadings leading to decreased oxygen concentrations; increased turbidity; and synergistic interactions of two or more of these factors.

Sub-lethal effects are caused by the same set of factors but are often more difficult to detect because the effects are delayed over a longer period of time and may be more subtle. For example, long-term exposure to contaminants in urban runoff may gradually weaken an organism, rendering it more susceptible to disease, climatic change or the action of other stresses. Reproduction, growth, and survival may ultimately be affected.

TABLE 1
ADVERSE EFFECTS OF URBAN RUNOFF
ON AQUATIC LIFE(6)

Effects on Organisms

Sub-lethal effects on biota
Lethal effects on biota

Effects on Ecosystems

Increased turbidity
Decreased oxygen concentrations
Increased sedimentation rates (and associated geo-morphological change)
Decreased species diversity
Increased rates of eutrophication
Increased or decreased primary production
Increased or decreased secondary production

Jenkins and Sanders (7) note that organisms employ various physio-logical mechanisms to deal with stress, with stress defined as a mea-surable alteration of a physiological steady state that is brought about by an environmental variable, and renders the organism more vul-nerable to further environmental change (7). Jenkins and Sanders (7) provide discussion regarding the basic levels of ecological organiza-tion, as depicted by a nested series of ovals, which progress from the molecule to the cell to the organism to the population to the commu-nity to the overall physical/chemical environment. Anthropogenic in-puts initially interact with biological systems at the molecular level and the effects of these interactions will propagate to higher levels of biological organization. Biological stress responses can be ob-served at each level of organization. Jenkins and Sanders (7) note that the time course for expression of toxicity at the community level is highly variable. It may be on the order of years if toxic concen-trations are sublethal or, if reproduction is impaired, adverse ef-fects may be rapidly translated to the community and ecosystem levels.

A number of the effects noted in Table 1 merit elaboration.

o   Urbanized areas produce substantial concentrations of sus-pended solids, predominantly of fine grain size. Fine grained sediments impose a number of adverse impacts includ-ing disruption of spawning beds, change in the oxygenated zone at the interface between water and substrate and de-creased transmission of sunlight. Literature typically indi-cates that undeveloped lands produce suspended solids con-centrations comparable to concentrations from urbanized areas during rainfalls of approximately the same duration and mag-nitude, and thereby downplay the significance of suspended solids inputs from urban areas. It should be recognized, however, that: (1) fine grained suspended solids seem to be indigenous to urban areas, whereas coarser sediments are associated with undeveloped lands, and (2) the frequency of measurable runoff and sediment inputs is higher in developed than undeveloped lands. Sediment inputs in urban runoff may blanket reaches of river bottom (substrate) that historically consisted of materials of various sizes with uniformly graded material, thereby decreasing the probable fish diversity in the particular reach. Fish cope poorly with an unstable, shifting substrate, another factor aggravated by urban runoff. Finally, runoff suspended solids concentrations may be high enough to directly affect fish. Sediment impacts to aquatic ecosystems are discussed extensively in many texts, and are not discussed further herein.

o   Urban runoff is variable both temporally and spatially. There is ample indication that the surge nature of loading imparts unusual stresses within receiving waters. Similarly, urban runoff poses both short- and long-term impacts. For example, unusually high concentrations of toxic substances are often characteristic of the "first flush" portion of the runoff event, and such concentrations may be immediately lethal on a localized basis. Long-term effects are more difficult to detect, but include bioconcentration of contaminants, altered substrate, eutrophication, etc. A complicating factor is the "seasonality" normally associated with aquatic environments.

o   Bioconcentration of metals and organics has been observed to occur. There is great variation and uncertainty associated with this phenomenon, a fact which renders intuitive judgments inappropriate. As one example, although filter feeders are highly susceptible to metal and pesticide ingestion, they also have adopted highly specialized coping mechanisms.

o   Metals tend to function non-selectively. Rather than obliterating particular species and leaving others unaffected, metals reduce numbers of nearly all species. The NURP summary for 78 sites nationally indicates that metal concentrations exceed EPA's water quality criteria and drinking water standards.

o   Nutrient inputs associated with urban runoff quality can affect the trophic status of lakes and reservoirs.

o   Urban runoff can introduce substantial organic loads to receiving waters and affect the dissolved oxygen regime of such waters. Heavy organic inputs generally tend to depress a broad range of life forms, while at the same time increasing the population of a given species (often an undesirable species) and increasing the total biomass.

o   Although many aquatic plants have the capability to withstand high contaminant concentrations, the ability is not ubiquitous. The U.S. Environmental Protection Agency, for example,

        attributes the decline of sea grasses in the Chesapeake Bay,
        in part, to urban stormwater runoff inputs.

o   Various immobilization mechanisms (adsorption to sediment,
        precipitation, etc.) minimize potential adverse impacts of
        contaminants. Conversely, resuspension and disruption of
        redox conditions, both of which can be caused by urban run-
        off, enhance mobilization.

    Specific examples of these and other phenomena will be presented
in more detail herein.

Agricultural Impacts

    Only infrequently does the question of how urban runoff contami-
nants affect agriculture arise. Concern normally focuses on the adverse impacts of farmland runoff on receiving waters. In the western
United States, few irrigation companies are willing to unconditionally
accept urban runoff into their ditches. Typically, in return for
ditch reconstruction, lining, or flume replacement, an irrigation company will allow a developer to discharge runoff into a canal. In excessive concentrations, trace elements such as barium and boron can be
toxic to particular crops; therefore, it is conceivable that under unusual circumstances, urban runoff could contain concentrations of constituents that might either impair plant/crop growth, or collect in
plants which are then consumed by livestock. Generally, the tangible
impacts of urban runoff on agricultural uses of water will be few.

Impacts on Industrial Use

    The principal concern of industry with respect to urban runoff is
that costs to treat raw water prior to inplant use are increased.
Discretization of industrial water treatment costs by category to
account for urban runoff is impractical for many reasons.

    Industries have developed programs to minimize urban runoff inflow
to their raw water sources. The Adolph Coors Company of Golden, Colorado for example, has a general policy which forbids the discharge of
urban runoff into all Coors Reservoirs. Additionally, a 400-acre
Coors commercial park complex is being designed to assure that runoff
for events of up to the 10-year return frequency will be detained on-
site for a minimum of 24 to 36 hours prior to release to downstream
properties.

Impacts to Groundwater

    Nationally, the implications of infiltration of urban stormwater
runoff into subsurface water supplies have not been well established.
Although many studies document historic changes in groundwater quality
and estimate the surface loading required to induce such changes, the
role that urban runoff plays is rarely segregated and quantified.
Heany (3) states that based on two NURP studies (Fresno, CA and Long
Island, NY) and a USGS study in Orlando, FLA. groundwater aquifers do
not appear to be threatened directly by urban runoff.

Nevertheless, it is clear that many localities have concern about potential degradation of groundwater due to infiltration of urban run-off. For example, members of the New Hampshire and Maine Geological Surveys presented papers at the 1985 Eastern Regional Conference of the National Water Well Association which describe adverse impacts to groundwater posed by salt-laden drainage from highways. Bouwer (8) provides discussion of the same subject.

The Miami, Fort Lauderdale, and West Palm Beach Metropolitan areas utilize the highly productive Biscayne Aquifer, a sand/limestone aqui-fer 50 to 200 feet thick and immediately below the ground surface for their water supply. The aquifer is recharged by rainfall, outflow from the Everglades, infiltration of surface water from drainage canals, and wastewater and surface runoff discharged directly into the ground at numerous locations. There has been increasing evidence in recent years that some of the drinking water supplies in this region are contaminated with synthetic or significant levels of synthetic organic chemicals. Of about 250 public water supply wells sampled, nearly 20 percent were found to be contaminated with one or more vola-tile organic chemicals (9). One of the sources of these volatile organic chemicals is urban runoff.

The owners of small, private water systems based on shallow wells have increasing cause for concern due to commercial and residential development on lands upstream of their wells. This problem is parti-cularly acute in small drainage basins where little dilution water is available. Hydrogeologic studies conducted for homeowners along Swede Gulch, in the mountains approximately 15 miles west of Denver, indi-cate that the urban runoff from a proposed 70 acre development located in the headwaters of a small drainage basin could migrate into the fractured bedrock and alluvial aquifers and contaminate dozens of wells on the gulch. The developer has agreed to implement a sophisti-cated drainage system to reduce outflow constituent concentrations and has agreed to provide ongoing monitoring of downstream wells. An in-teresting question associated with this case is to what extent the developer will be required to cleanse his stormwater runoff prior to returning it to the stream. Should the treated stormwater meet stream standards (after allowing for suitable dilution)? Alternatively, should treated stormwater contaminant concentrations not exceed those concentrations characterized by the basin in its predevelopment (his-toric) condition? How will "historic" concentrations be defined? Assessments of urban runoff impacts on groundwater can take advantage of excellent literature regarding wastewater effluent reuse.

Summary of Impacts to Receiving Waters

The foregoing represents a brief overview of impacts of urban stormwater runoff on water uses. Potential impacts are wide ranging. Little consensus has emerged as to the demonstrable effects of urban runoff contaminants as distinguished from those other sources. As demonstrated by the following discussion of impacts to aquatic eco-systems, attempting to predict impacts on a site specific (rather than generalized) basis can be frustrating.

IMPACTS TO AQUATIC ECOSYSTEMS -- HOW MUCH DO WE KNOW?

The difficulty of extrapolating generalized non-point source impacts to specific aquatic ecosystems is striking. The following considerations -- all of which are important components in the impact assessment process -- are, in themselves, far from straightforward. Examples of such considerations include:

o   Life forms within aquatic environments,
o   Forms of contaminants,
o   Pulse loading of urban stormwater runoff,
o   Complex mixtures of contaminants,
o   Physical behavior of receiving waters,
o   Bioassay limitations,
o   Modeling limitations,
o   Mechanisms of life forms to cope with contaminants, and
o   Sampling and statistical methods.

Life Forms Within Aquatic Environments

Undoubtedly, the greatest impediment to properly assessing impacts to life forms centers on the size and complexity of aquatic ecosystems themselves; failure to recognize, understand and account for this complexity on a localized basis will often lead to runoff management programs that produce unintended results. Factors such as age of the organism, life cycle stage, stress response to indigenous stressors (temperature, salinity, etc.) and other influence susceptibility of organisms to urban runoff contaminants.

Forms of Contaminants

Just as aquatic ecosystems are complex, the forms that contaminants assume upon entering the aquatic environment are diverse and complex. The toxicity of substance depends, first of all, on its chemical form. For example, chlorine in the elemental form (a gas) is highly toxic, whereas chlorine compounds may be relatively harmless, as is sodium chloride (common salt). Conversely, elemental arsenic is not toxic, although some arsenical compounds are highly toxic.

The toxicity of a substance is also determined by the dosage, that is, the amount, frequency and duration of administering the substance to the organism (10). To be toxic, a substance must be available to plants or animals -- that is, it must exist in a form that can enter tissues of the organism either in solution (generally aqueous), as a gas, or (uncommonly) as a solid; or it must emit ionizing radiation (10). Total amounts of a toxic element in the environment are not relevant to an adequate estimation of the toxicity hazard that may be present unless it can be shown that the element exists in, or is likely to assume, an available form under the environmental conditions in which it occurs.

The substance chromium, which is considered nonessential for plants yet an essential trace element for animals, provides an excellent example of how a substance's form affects impacts. The hexavalent form of chromium (+6) may be 100 times more toxic than the trivalent form (+3)(10).

Daphnia Magna was studied by Beisinger, et al (11) as to the accumulation and loss of inorganic and organic mercury in flow–through tests. Mercury as methylmercuric chloride was found to have 20 times the uptake as mercury added in the form of mercuric chloride (12). Weis and Weis (13) demonstrated that the embryonic killifish adapted more successfully to mercury in the form of $HgCl_2$ than they did to methylmercury (12).

Adverse effects are often dependent upon ambient pH. For example, Van der Put et al (14) examined the toxic effects of hexavalent chromium to rainbow trout and found that the chromium was more toxic at pH 6.5 than at pH 7.8 in all life stages studied. Miller and MacKay (15) found that the ability of trout mucus to bind to copper was pH dependent; lowering the pH to 3.6 from 7.3 decreased the ability of the mucous to bind cupric ion (12).

Zamuda and Sunda (16) determined the effect of complexation on the accumulation of dissolved copper by a species of oyster and found the accumulation of copper to be related to the cupric ion activity and not the concentration of chelated copper (12). They also found that labile Cu and Zn, rather than total Cu and Zn, provided selection pressure from metal tolerance in three species of diatoms from a polluted estuary (12).

Research into the impacts of hydrocarbons on life forms has become quite sophisticated. For example, Walker, et al (17) completed a histopathological study of soft shell clams located in 17 sites between Nova Scotia and the Chesapeake Bay that had varying degrees of exposure to petroleum. Statistical analysis enabled the authors to postulate that crude oils and heavy metals had less effect on the incidence of various pathological conditions than do the more refined petrochemicals (12).

In summary, the forms that contaminants assume upon entering aquatic environments, along with the chemical characteristics of the receiving waters, affect toxicity.

Pulse Loading of Urban Stormwater Runoff

One aspect of urban runoff which complicates assessment is its sporadic nature, with respect to both quantity and quality. Although it may be reasonable to project long–term trends under some conditions, impacts to receiving waters over periods of even one to two years may not be possible. Heany (3) listed the establishment of bioassay procedures to account for short–term, intermittent exposure to urban runoff contaminants as one of the principal research needs in the field.

The impacts of urban runoff constituents are striking, given the relatively small percentage of time that runoff is discharged to receiving waters. For instance, a five year study on the island of Oahu by Doty, et al (18) indicated that 90 percent of total suspended sediment load to the receiving water was produced during less than 2 percent of the time. Bieri et al (19) indicates that as much as 20 percent of the lead and 10 percent of other metals entering Chesapeake Bay come from urban runoff.

The results of many bioassay tests can be evaluated in the context of surge-type loading rather than long-term exposure. For example Bluzat, et al (20) exposed fungi to high levels of the fungicide, thiram. One batch of thiram was cured for 1 hour, another for 48 hours and another for 96 hours. Based on organism mortality, toxicity decreased 71 and 45 percent, respectively, in the 48 and 96 hour old suspensions.

Trevors, et al (21) used a bacterial assay to demonstrate that toxicity results were affected by the sequence of exposure to pentachlorophenol (PCP) and 2, 3, 4, 5, tetrachlorophenol (TCP), including both the concentration used and sequence of chlorophenol addition. Cell suspensions treated with PCP and subsequently removed from exposure were not affected by a second PCP dose; if the second dose was TCP the test species was sensitive to TCP (12).

An adequate methodology for accounting for the unpredictable sequencing of non-point source inputs is not presently available.

Complex Mixtures of Contaminants

Countless antagonistic and synergistic chemical relationships exist among the constituents in urban stormwater runoff and receiving waters. Transformations can render toxic substances harmless, and harmless substances toxic. Consider some examples.

Hendrix, et al (22) assessed, through use of a microcosm, system response to nutrient loading and chronic versus acute perturbations in response to cadmium exposure. Cadmium treatment of a mixed species microcosm generally resulted in a decrease in the abundance of grazing crustaceans and a subsequent increase in community respiration, suggesting a change in community structure from a grazing to a detritus food chain (12). The results suggested that nutrient enrichment may have reduced the toxic effects of cadmium, possibly through immobilization of the metal in large amounts of organic matter present in the highly enriched microcosm (12).

Attar and Maly (23) determined the acute toxicity of zinc, cadmium and their mixtures to Daphnia Magna. Daphnia was very sensitive to low concentrations of cadmium and zinc, whereas a mixture of the two substances at relatively high concentrations adversely affected only a small percentage of the population.

Tests on an Indian pond snail involving lethal dosages of copper, zinc, chromium, cadmium and nickel indicated that: (1) when sublethal concentrations of selenium were established, cadmium toxicity to the snail was reduced by approximately 50 percent, and (2) sublethal concentrations of cadmium prevented mortality of the snail from high concentrations of selenite and selenate (12).

The acute toxic effects of pentachlorophenol, cadmium and magnesium, low pH, high pH, salinity, and high temperature on mixed cultures of two kinds of worms were investigated (12). Comparisons of LC50 values between mixed cultures and individual cultures of the two species revealed that pentachlorophenol, Mg and Cd were significantly less toxic to mixed cultures (12).

These examples demonstrate that: (1) it is generally inappropriate to assess impacts of constituents individually, and, (2) extrapolating results from the laboratory to actual aquatic environment must be done with caution.

Physical Behavior of Receiving Waters

Urban runoff impacts vary depending upon the physical characteristics of the receiving water. There are obvious differences between constituent dynamics in estuaries, streams, lakes, and oceans; but at a more localized scale, a contaminant can adversely impact given areas of the receiving water body while leaving others unaffected. Examples of physical parameters which influence susceptibility of aquatic life forms to urban contaminants are the following:

o   Magnitude of flow in river, or lake volume,
o   Mixing characteristics of water body,
o   Seasonal variations,
o   Density layers,
o   Advection and dispersion,
o   Substrate
o   Hydrologic character of waterway due to man's activities (releases and inflows to reservoir, ditch diversions from and return flows to river, return flows of industrial cooling water, etc.),
o   Discharge locations of urban runoff,
o   Cyclic sedimentation and resuspension of settleable solids.

These factors, and others, are often difficult to account for in water quality analyses, and further complicate the assessment process.

The U.S. Geologic Survey in its comprehensive assessment of water quality in the Willamette River, Oregon (4) determined that the primary controller of algal growth in the river was not the concentration of nitrogen and phosphorus, but was water detention time. This finding resulted in savings of tens of millions of dollars that would otherwise have been allocated for the construction of tertiary wastewater treatment facilities and non-point source control facilities designed to remove nitrogen and phosphorus. The USGS notes that (4):

> "This example illustrates that rigid nationwide standards and regulations are likely to result in unneeded expenditures in some basins and in unachieved standards in others. The proper balance can be attained for each river only through an intensive, coordinated assessment that is key to local problems and conditions."

Standley Lake, located in a Denver, Colorado suburb, demonstrates anomalous behavior attributable to its physical characteristics. Although growing season total phosphorus concentrations are typically 70 to 90 micrograms per liter, chlorophyll a concentrations are typically 2 to 4 micrograms per liter, values associated with high mountain, oligotrophic lakes. Total phosphorus concentrations of 70 to 90 micrograms per liter are sufficient to produce eutrophic lake conditions with chlorophyll a concentrations 5 to 10 times those actually found in Standley Lake. Based on lake temperature data, coupled with the facts that: (1) the sole outlet for the 100-foot deep reservoir is at the lake bottom, and (2) releases are made year-round for municipal raw water supply, it has been postulated that the residence time of phytoplankton above the level of compensation within the reservoir is sufficiently short to hinder phytoplankton growth because the phytoplankton spend substantial time in the absence of sunlight. Constructing non-point source pollution control systems to reduce phosphorus inputs to Standley Lake may represent questionable expenditures given the behavior of the lake.

Another curious pattern of lake behavior was observed by Haufmann, et al (24) who studied the aquatic impacts of deicing salts. Elevated chloride levels were found in streams following wintertime applications of salt to major freeways, and one small lake was found in which a chloride-induced chemicline was sufficiently strong to stabilize a temperature inversion.

The location of constituents of concern within the water column is of importance. For example, the toxicities of pesticides to a shrimp were 80 to 100 times less in sediment than in water (26), and it was concluded that compounds adsorbed to sediment contributed little toward toxicity (12). Forney (25) found 50 percent growth inhibition when atrazine was applied to wild celery, redhead grass, watermilfoil, and elodea. When low atrazine concentrations were present in both water and soil, the water concentration determined the toxic effect. The author concluded that atrazine concentrations detected in Chesapeake Bay were not likely to have caused the observed decline of submerged plants in the Bay (12). These examples serve to indicate that violations of water standards attributable to loadings of urban contaminants may be irrelevant if the standards are designed to protect life forms that reside in sediments; conversely, concentrations of constituents within sediments at seemingly excessive levels may be of little significance because the constituents remain immobilized and are not available to aquatic life forms.

In summary, it is essential to develop a comprehensive understanding of the physical characteristics of the receiving water, both to assess impact under existing conditions, and to determine discharge locations best suited to minimizing ecological stress.

Bioassay Limitations

The most common means of establishing the impacts of water quality contaminants on life forms is via bioassays. Unfortunately, extraordinary limitations exist when extrapolating bioassay data from the laboratory to the actual aquatic environment. Aquatic ecosystems are so complex that it is virtually impossible to say with assuredness that "x" milligrams per liter of a particular substance will effect species "y" in designated ways.

Innumerable combinations of test conditions can be associated with any given bioassay. For example, the chemical composition of water used for the bioassay can be changed. The duration for which the constituent of concern is allowed to remain in the water before subjecting the organism to the constituent is variable. Measured effects can range from the most subtle abnormality to death. Depending upon the combination of variables adopted for a bioassay procedure, strikingly different conclusions can be drawn. Consider some examples of recent bioassay studies.

Determination of organic compound biodegradability has obvious implications for environmental toxicology. The reliability of the river die-away test (RDA) for establishing biodegradability of chemicals was assessed for reproducibility (27). RDA test results were not reproducible for two acids in replicated tests with Missouri River water. The author suggested that RDA test biodegradation measurements are too variable and too dependent on laboratory treatment of samples to be applied directly to aquatic environments (12).

Field studies do much to allay fears regarding the applicability of bioassay results. Consider, for example, an evaluation of the relationship between body contaminants and bone development for young of the year striped bass from the Hudson River and other East Coast locations. Mechanical properties of striped bass vertebrae were analyzed for strength, stiffness, toughness, and rupture (28). Fish from sites contaminated with PCB, DDT, DDD, DDE, and chlordane displayed vertebrae with the least strength, stiffness, toughness and rupture under lowest force, compared to hatchery reared fish (12).

Key properties with regard to the ultimate environmental fate of compounds and aqueous solutions depend on such variables as vapor pressure, water solubility, adsorption and desorption phenomena, partition coefficient, volatility, hydrolysis, and photochemical reactivity (29). These variables, and others, are exceedingly difficult to reasonably represent in bioassay procedures.

Modeling Limitations

Given the difficulty of delineating the impacts of urban stormwater runoff on aquatic ecosystems at even a rudimentary level, it is not surprising that comprehensive modeling of the ecological impacts of urban runoff constituents is extraordinarily difficult. By comparison, the state of the art of projecting constituent concentration in receiving waters is quite advanced.

Most current modeling studies emphasize the importance of uncertainty and risk in water quality management. For example, Walker (30) used first order error analysis to examine errors in a model relating land use to lake water quality. In an application of the procedure, he found the prediction error was comparable in magnitude to the year to year variability in lake water quality (12). In separate analyses, Mueller (31) and Mahama and Bhagat (32) evaluated the accuracy of selected simple empirical phosphorus models for lakes. Although both studies were concerned with Western U.S. lakes, the conclusions differed as to the model of best fit.

Jewell and Adrian (33) express concern over the inability of existing stormwater simulation models to accurately predict the quality of urban runoff. Using a large data set, they examined the fit of simple statistical models; from this it was concluded that models should be developed for a particular basin using site specific data

for calibration and verification. Krenkle and French note that our
ability to model water quality is not so much limited by the computer
as by inadequate knowledge of aquatic systems (34).

A literature review of non-point source models indicates that the
majority of models focus on predicting the magnitude of inputs of various constituents to waterways, based on land uses within particular
study areas. Models designed to evaluate impacts to life forms are
not nearly as numerous. Onishee, et al, (35) reported on development
of a procedure to predict the occurrence and duration of both dissolved and particulate pesticide concentrations to assess potential
acute and chronic damage to aquatic biota (12). Such a model carries
us to within one step of actually assessing impacts. Similarly,
Hubbard, et al, (36) measured and sampled runoff continuously from two
small watersheds over a two year period and found that 70 to 95 percent of the nitrogen and runoff and 90 to 98 percent of the phosphorus
was carried in sediment, except during winter months when up to 80
percent of the nitrogen 33 percent of the phosphorus were in solution
(12). This model would be of great value for projecting potential
eutrophication of reservoirs within the subject watersheds.

Another model which serves as an excellent management tool, even
though it does not project impacts to components of the ecosystem, is
a mathematical simulation of the role of sediment in Kepone transport
in the James River estuary (37), performed by applying the sediment
contaminant transport model, FETRA, to an 86 kilometer river reach between Bailey and Burnwell Bays. Results of the model indicated that
in the most optimal case, the Kepone concentration could be reduced by
up to 50 percent through cleaning the river bed of the 22 kilometer
reach in the midpoint of the estuary (12).

The U.S. Geological Survey, after concluding its comprehensive
modeling study of the Willamette River in Oregon, reached important
conclusions with respect to the usefulness of modeling. The following
excerpt from the USGS (4) should be borne in mind:

> "We found that there were several river quality problems
> that currently are too poorly defined to model in a
> practical and useful manner. Such problems include
> trace metal distribution and the relation between nutri-
> ents and algal growth. The project assessed these prob-
> lems through the development of qualitative, descriptive
> approaches. The results clearly demonstrated that qual-
> itative approaches can provide adequate and reliable in-
> formation for the management of certain river quality
> problems."

Mechanisms of Life Forms to Cope With Pollutants

Many organisms have developed capabilities to live successfully
despite the presence of high concentrations of toxins. An understanding of these coping mechanisms is necessary before impacts can be
suitably defined. Consider the following examples.

The mechanism of copper elimination by the digestive gland cells
of a mussel was investigated by Viarengo, et al (38). Mussels were

exposed to 40 mg/l for three consecutive days, followed by detoxification in copper-free sea water for three, six and twelve days (12).
The data indicated that digestive gland cells undergo the neosynthesis
of thioneine-like copper binding proteins which may represent a protective mechanism to reduce the toxic effects induced by copper (12).

Mason and Nott (39) investigated intracellular, mineralized granules located in the soft tissues of gastropod mollusks, finding that
they can be categorized into two types, each with a different location, structure, and composition that reflect distinct differences in
function (12). Both contain calcium and magnesium, but they can be
divided on their anionic content into carbonate and phosphate rich
varieties; only phosphate granules sequester other cations such as
zinc, copper, and manganese and represent a system for detoxification
(12).

In light of these examples, the question arises as to how a contaminant of concern will affect a given life form in the aquatic environment of interest. Roch, et al (40) noted that, ideally, measures
of biological response should be based on the intracellular mechanisms
by which a fish responds to heavy metal exposure, especially if the
toxic effects can be related to the perturbation of a particular biochemical process (12). Roch discovered that a low molecular weight
protein synthesized in the livers of mammals on exposure to cadmium,
copper, zinc and mercury was detected in livers of rainbow trout from
a metal contaminated river system (12). The concentrations of the
protein were directly related to pollutant concentrations in the water
(12).

Jenkins and Sanders (7) present a monitoring strategy for assessing the effects of anthropogenic contaminants on aquatic organisms, as
follows:

> "The monitoring strategy for assessing effects of con-
> taminants takes advantage of our increased understanding
> of the mechanisms which underlie stress metabolism as a
> basis for assessing stress in native organisms in situ.
> General stress responses which react to a wide range of
> environmental factors are used to initially screen for
> deleterious biological affects due to contaminants. If
> data from this initial screening indicate that organisms
> are stressed, stress or specific responses which are
> elicited by specific contaminants or classes of contam-
> inants would be measured to identify the causative fac-
> tors. When these data are taken together it is possible
> to determine both the extent of biological stress in
> native organisms in situ and to identify the environ-
> mental factors responsible for the observed effects."

A procedure developed by Mason (41) for assessing the impacts to
aquatic life of surface mining contaminants may lend itself to application in the urban runoff quality field. The advantages of this
approach and others of similar nature (Margalef, Simpson, Shannon-
Weaver, Bullouin, Biotic Condition Index and others) are expediency
and relatively low cost. Mason notes that data collection, analysis
and evaluation efforts aimed at defining impacts can be significantly

reduced by using short cut methods. These methods contain hidden sophistication; i.e., they conform to commonly accepted biological survey procedures but are condensed and in easy-to-use form (41). Observed diversities are obtained by simple, on-site collection and analysis procedures, and are compared against the expected diversities for the particular environments in question (41). Chadwick and Canton (42) state that based on a study of the Dolores River in Colorado, diversity indices were inadequate for assessing non-selective stress. More research into the applicability of diversity indices for assessing urban runoff impacts is merited.

Sampling and Statistical Methods

Ultimately, water quality and biotic sampling and surveys are the foundation upon which runoff quality management programs are based. Uncertainties associated with sampling and data interpretation programs are numerous and merit careful consideration. Odum and Hawley (6) note that:

> "Although most scientists are aware of the potential problems posed by water pollutants, very few studies have focused solely on the impact of urban runoff to estuaries. One reason for this is that in large estuaries, urban runoff effects are inexorably and synergistically associated with the effects of dredging, chemical spills, point-source contaminants and other serious alterations. To separate out the impact of urban runoff is difficult and, perhaps, artificial. Another problem is that the impact of urban runoff is discontinuous; episodes of heavy runoff with high pollutant levels are interspersed between long periods with little or no runoff."

Randall and Grizzard in their chapter entitled "Runoff Pollution" from the publication Stormwater Management in Urbanizing Areas (43) provide discussion regarding sampling methods, including the following:

> "Because of the transient nature of urban runoff phenomena, the random collection of grab samples does not allow a true representation of pollutant transport to be constructed. Even if grab sampling programs are modified to concentrate on storm events, the potential for error still remains quite high because of the large variations in pollutant concentrations which occur during runoff events."

Randall and Grizzard propose alternative sampling methods (composite sampling and sequential discrete sampling) to increase reliability.

A paradigm sampling procedure for evaluating a major reservoir is provided by Lewis, in his publication entitled Eutrophication and Land Use, Lake Dillon, Colorado (44). Lewis describes the methods that he employed for such tasks as lake and stream sample collection; analysis of chemical constituents, phytoplankton and zooplankton; temperature;

conductance; transparency; precipitation sampling; discharge measurements; morphometry; geology, and a host of other factors. Recognizing the range of error associated with defining each of these parameters, Lewis provides discussion regarding precision and accuracy. Through such techniques as judicious selection of multiple lake stations, collecting large numbers of duplicate samples, providing variance analysis to test for statistical significance leading to the establishment of confidence intervals, and others, Lewis casts his findings not in terms of absolute numbers, but rather in terms of probable ranges of values. Rarely are studies with this level of sophistication conducted, yet studies of lesser magnitude often result in land use decisions with sweeping implications and/or the expenditure of substantial sums of money.

It is essential to recognize the potential multiple sources of error associated with all sampling and analysis, and to account for these uncertainties when results are presented.

Summary of Uncertainties Associated with Establishing Impacts to Life Forms of Urban Stormwater Runoff Contaminants

Through discussion of only a limited number of the factors which influence impacts of runoff contaminants on biota, it is apparent that attempts to define impacts require sophisticated, site-specific analysis. Certain life forms are killed by a contaminant, while others can store the same contaminant internally with no ill effect. Metals may be harmful when in a certain form, and innocuous in another. A given substance may be lethal when found singly, while in combination with other toxins, the substance may pose no harm. Bioassay results obtained in the laboratory must be applied with slight confidence to the "real world". Contaminants in the water column may be of great concern while the same contaminants in sediment may pose no risk. Simple qualitative analyses may produce more reasonable results than complex models can. In short, the validity of projecting aquatic biotic impacts by simply comparing water quality criteria against constituent concentrations for the waterway in questions may oversimplify an extraordinary complex problem.

KEY QUESTIONS WHEN ASSESSING THE IMPACTS OF URBAN STORMWATER RUNOFF ON RECEIVING WATER USES

The complexity associated with urban runoff impacts on receiving water uses mandates that thorough, site-specific impact assessments be conducted, and that results be presented in the context of probabilities rather than absolute values. Among the more important key questions in the impact assessment process are the following:

Basis of Impact Assessment Study

   o   What potential impacts will be studied (i.e., drinking water, recreation, industrial use, etc.) and why?

   o   How do existing classification and standard systems affect the proposed study?

   o   To what extent will goals be focused on current vs. projected conditions?

o   How will impacts be defined; that is, in terms of dollars,
      environmental consequences, risks to public health, lost rec-
      reation days, etc.? What type of economic evaluation process
      reasonably reflects the intangible, non-quantifiable aspects
      of water uses?

o   Why is the assessment being conducted and by whom? What are
      the goals, objectives, policies, and criteria that guide the
      study?

o   Are there factors that may bias study results? What are the
      probable consequences of slanted conclusions?

Implications of Assessment Study

o   What entities will be affected by the study and how?

o   What is the likely fate of the study? For example, how will
      study results and recommendations influence regional devel-
      opment, housing prices, recreational opportunities, tax
      rates, intergovernmental relationships and other factors?

o   Will those entities impacted by the study challenge its con-
      clusions and recommendations? How can the study be defined
      and conducted to minimize susceptibility to future chal-
      lenges?

o   How will the specific study of potential impacts of urban
      stormwater runoff fit into the broad context of river basin
      or lake watershed management?

o   How will the relative significance of urban runoff on receiv-
      ing water quality be contrasted with impacts from other
      sources?

Nature of Impact Assessment Study

o   What will be the extent of the study area (i.e., short reach
      of river, entire river, portion of river affected by tides,
      river as defined by political or planning boundary, etc.)?
      Although the study may be conducted for an extensive reach of
      a major river, the study should be sufficiently discretized
      to account for localized ecologic, hydrologic, political and
      other characteristics.

o   What problems are posed by extrapolating results from other
      areas when resources are not available for local analysis?
      To what extent are generalizations appropriate?

o   What are the governmental and political implications of
      studies which encompass multiple jurisdictions as opposed to
      single jurisdictions?

o   What resources are available for commitment to the study, and
      what are the implications of various levels of effort with

respect to reasonableness of study results? A relatively
modest expenditure could nevertheless result in a "preliminary level" report that has resounding implications for local
or regional water quality management, despite the fact that
major questions will have been addressed incompletely, if at
all. Conversely, are large expenditures justifiable for
quantification of complex phenomena that do not lend themselves to quantification?

o   How accurate should study results be, and why? What level of
     confidence should be associated with study results?

o   What legal implications are associated with accuracy of re-
     sults? To what extent is speculation on the part of those
     conducting the study reasonable given potential implications
     of the study?

o   Along these same lines, under what conditions are qualitative
     as opposed to quantitative studies appropriate? Many pheno-
     mena are too poorly defined to quantify in a practical and
     useful manner. Qualitative approaches often provide adequate
     and reliable information for the management of certain river
     quality problems.

o   To what extent is modeling appropriate? For example, are
     sufficient data available to justify modeling, or do the
     available data mandate nothing more than a qualitative as-
     sessment?

o   What historic water quality conditions are associated with
     the river or lake in question? Are certain trends evident
     respect to lake quality? Recent studies of Lake Erie, for
     example, have demonstrated that dissolved oxygen depletion
     was a routine occurrence in portions of the lake long before
     man discharged pollutants into the lake. Similarly, irres-
     pective of man's influence, some lakes are destined to be
     eutrophic and will consistently fail to provide aesthetically
     appealing recreational facilities for the public. Historical
     perspective may change the strategy of an impending impact
     assessment.

Technical Considerations of Impact Assessment Study

o   What hydrologic regime will be studied? For example, are
     7-day, 10-year mean daily flows appropriate, or should a
     higher or lower number be chosen? Why?

o   During what times of the year will be study be conducted, and
     for what seasons will results be projected?

o   What assumptions will be made regarding the ambient character
     of the waterway or lake prior to exposure to urban runoff?

o   What assumptions will be made as to the nature of urban run-
     off (i.e., frequency, quantity, locations of discharge, dis-
     tribution within the river or lake, etc.)?

o   What dispersion mechanisms will be assumed for the urban run-
     off in the receiving water? What mixing characteristics are
     associated with a lake?   What withdrawal or release pattern
     is associated with a lake?

o   What life forms will be studied?   Will studies be highly
     sophisticated or will simple diversity-based studies be
     acceptable as a general indication of potential problems?
     Given the availability of numerous bioassays for particular
     constituents of concern, how will the results of these tests
     be utilized for the waterway in question?

o   Will contaminants be assessed individually, or will the
     synergistic and antagonistic relationships among those con-
     stituents within complex mixtures be accounted for?   How?

Developing and Evaluating Management Strategies

o   Who will interpret the significance of the impact assessment
     study?   What will be basis for this interpretation?

o   In light of the impact assessment study findings, what kind
     of management strategies be potentially be studied?   Who will
     design such management strategies?

o   How will the management strategies be evaluated?

o   Once one or a number of management strategies are implement-
     ed, how will their implementation be administered?   How will
     effectiveness be characterized?

o   How will non-point source management programs be interrelated
     with control programs related to point sources of pollution
     and river basin management generally?

o   What will constitute acceptable results for the management
     strategies implemented?   Will occasional exceedence of stream
     standards be acceptable?   What price is appropriate for ob-
     taining desirable results?

Consideration of these kinds of questions will hopefully facilitate an understanding of the probable impacts of urban stormwater runoff constituents on receiving waters.

REFERENCES

1. Rickert, David A., and Hines, Walter G., "River Quality Assessment:
    Implications of a Protype Project", Science, 9 June 1978, Volume 200,
    pgs. 1113-1118.

2. Krenkel, P.A., and French, R.H., "State of the Art of Modeling Surface
    Water Impoundments", Water Science Technology, 1982.

3. Heany, James P., "Research Needs in Urban Stormwater Pollution", Jour-
    nal of Water Resources Planning and Management, Volume 112, No. 1,
    January 1986.

4. Methodology for River Quality Assessment With Application to the Wil-
    lamette River Basin, Oregon, U.S. Geological Survey, Circular 715-M.

5. Weisskopf, Michael, "Did Water Kill Children in Woburn?", newspaper
    article in the Washington Post dated April 3, 1986, pg. A3.

6. Odum, W.E., and Hawley, Mark E., "The Impacts of Urban Runoff on
    Estuarine Ecosystems", Proceedings of the Engineering Foundation Con-
    ference, Urban Runoff Quality, Its Impacts and Quality Enhancement
    Technology, June 1986.

7. Jenkins, K.D., and Sanders, B.M., "Assessing the Biological Effects of
    Antropogenic Contaminants In Situ", Proceedings of the Engineering
    Foundation Conference, Urban Runoff Quality, Its Impacts and Quality
    Enhancement Technology, June, 1986.

8. Bouwer, H., Groundwater Hydrology, McGraw-Hill, Inc., 1978.

9. Environmental Progress and Challenges: An EPA Perspective, U.S. EPA,
    Office of Management Systems, June 1984.

10. Elemented Concentrations Toxic to Plants, Animals, and Man, Geological
    Survey Bulletin 1466, U.S. Government Printing Office, Washington,
    1979.

11. Beisinger, K.E., et al, "Chronic Effects of Inorganic Organic Mercury
    on Daphnia Magna: Toxicity, Accumulation and Loss", Arch. Environ.
    Contam. Toxicology, Volume 11, 1982.

12. Journal of the Water Pollution Control Federation Annual Literature
    Review Issue, 1982 and 1983 issues, Water Pollution Control Federa-
    tion, Washington, D.C. 20037.

13. Weis, P., and Weis, J.S., "Toxicity of Methylmercury, Mercuric Chlo-
    ride and Lead in Killifish from South Hampton, New York", Environmen-
    tal Research, Volume 28, 1982.

14. Van der Put, I., et al, "Effects of Hexavalent Chromium in Rainbow
    Trout and Prolonged Exposure at two Different pH Levels", Ecotoxicol.
    Environ. Safety, Volume 6, 1982.

15. Miller, T.G., and MacKay, W.C., "Relationship of Secreted Mucus to Copper and Acid Toxicity in Rainbow Trout", Bulletin of Environmental Contaminant Toxicology, Volume 26, 1982.

16. Zamuda, C.D., and Sunda, W.G., "Bioavailability of Dissolved Copper to the American Oyster", Marine Biology, Volume 66, 1982.

17. Walker, H.A., et al, "Comparison of the Incidence of Five Pathological Conditions in Soft Shell Clams from Environments with Various Pollution Histories", Marine Environmental Research, Volume 5, 1981.

18. Doty, R.D., et al, "Suspended Sediment Production from Forested Watersheds on Oahu, Hawaii", Water Resources Bulletin, Volume 17, 1981.

19. Bieri, R.O., et al, Chesapeake Bay Program Technical Studies: A Synthesis, U.S. EPA, Washington, D.C., 1982.

20. Bluzat, R., et al, "Acute Toxicity of Thiram in Gammarus Pulex: Effect of a One Hour Contamination and Degradation of an Aqueous Suspension", Bulletin Environ. Contam. Toxicol., Volume 29, 1982.

21. Trevors, J.T., et al, "Effect of Sequence of Exposure to Chlorophenols in Short-term Bacterial Bioassays", Arch. Environ. Contam. Toxicology, Volume 11, 1982.

22. Hendrix, P.F., et al, "Cadmium in Aquatic Microcosms: Implications for Screening the Ecological Effects of Toxic Substances", Environmental Management, Volume 6, 1982.

23. Attar, E.N., and Maly, E.J., "Acute Toxicity of Cadmium, Zinc and Cadmium-Zinc Mixtures to Daphnia Magna", Arch. Environ. Contam. Toxicology, Volume 11, 1982.

24. Haufmann, R.W., et al, "Aquatic Impacts of Deicing Salts in the Central Sierra Nevada Mountains, California", Water Resources Bulletin, Volume 17, 1981.

25. Forney, D.R., "Effects of Atrazine on Chesapeake Bay Aquatic Plants", M.S. Thesis, School of Agriculture, Department of Botany, Plant Pathology, and Microbiology, Auburn University, 1980.

26. McLease, D.W., and Metcalfe, C.D., "Toxicities of Eight Organochlorine Compounds in Sediments and Sea Water to Crangon Septemspinosa", Bulletin Environmetal Contam. Toxicology, Volume 25, 1980.

27. Wylie, G.D., et al, "Evaluation of the River Die-away Biodegradation Test", Journal Water Pollution Control Federation, Volume 54, 1982.

28. Mehrle, P.M., et al, "Relationship Between Body Contaminants and Bone Development in East Coast Striped Bass", Transactions in the American Fishery Society, Volume 111, 1982.

29. MacKay, D., "Correlation of Bioconcentration Factors", Environmental Science Technology, Volume 16, 1982.

30. Walker, W.W., "A Sensitivity and Error Analysis Framework for Lake Eutrophication Modeling", Water Resources Bulletin, Volume 18, 1982.

31. Mueller, D.K., "Mass Balance Model Estimation of Phosphorus Concentrations in Reservoirs", Water Resources Bulletin, Volume 18, 1982.

32. Mahama, D.S., and Bhagat, S.K., "Performance of Some Empirical Phosphorus Models", Journal Environmental Engineering Division, Proceedings of the American Society of Civil Engineers, Volume 108, 1982.

33. Jewell, T.K., and Adrian, D.D., "Statistical Analysis to Derive Improve Stormwater Quality Models", Journal Water Pollution Control Federation, Volume 54, 1982.

34. Krenkle, P.A., and French, R.H., "State of Art of Modeling Surface Water Quality", Water Science Technology, Volume 14, 1982.

35. Onishee, Y., et al, "Methodology for Overland and Instream Migration and Risk Assessment of Pesticides", EPA-600/382-024, 1982.

36. Hubbard, R.K., et al, "Movement of Diffused Source Pollutants in Small Agricultural Watersheds in the Great Lakes Basin", Journal of Environmental Quality, Volume 11, 1982.

37. Onishee, Y., "Mathematical Transport Modeling for Determination of Effectiveness of Kepone Clean-up Activities in the James River Estuary", National Tech. Information Service CONF-8010123-1, 1980.

38. Viarengo, A., et al, "Accumulation and Detoxification of Copper by the Mussle Mytilus Galloprovincialis: A Study of the Subcellular Distribution in the Digestive Gland Cells", Aquatic Toxicology. Volume 1, 1981.

39. Mason, A.Z., and Nott, J.A., "Role of Intracellular Biomineralized Granules in the Regulation and Detoxification of Metals and Gastropods with Special Reference to the Marine Prosobranch Littorina Littorea", Aquatic Toxicology, Volume 1, 1981.

40. Roch, M., et al, "Hepatic Metallothionein in Rainbow Trout as an Indicator of Metal Pollution in the Campbell River System", Canadian Journal of Fisheries and Aquatic Sciences, Volume 39, 1982.

41. Mason, W.T., "A Rapid Procedure for Assessment of Surface Mining Impacts to Aquatic Life", presented at the 1979 Coal Conference and Expo 5 in Louisville, Kentucky (reprint available from U.S. Fish and Wildlife Service office in Kearneysville, West Virginia).

42. Chadwick, J.W., and Canton, S.P., "Inadequacy of Diversity Indices in Discerning Metal Mine Drainage Effects on a Stream Invertebrate Community", Water, Air and Soil Pollution, Volume 22, 1984.

43. Whipple, W., et al, Stormwater Management in Urbanizing Areas, Prentice Hall, Inc., New Jersey, 1983.

44. Lewis, W.M., et al, Eutrophication and Land Use, Lake Dillon, Colorado, Ecological Studies 46, Springer-Verlag, 1984.

EPA's Perspective of Urban Nonpoint Sources

Dennis N. Athayde*
Carl F. Myers**
Patrick Tobin***

With the passage of the Clean Water Act (CWA) in 1972, there were new requirements for areawide wastewater management and planning for water quality control. Areawide planning is covered under section 208 of the CWA. While it was slow in getting started it was well under way by 1975. Urban runoff was mentioned under section 208 and perhaps because of this, it tended to be considered as a nonpoint source for planning purposes.

From the beginning, section 208 was controversial. In the early years this section sparked much litigation. It was in 1974 that the Agency was first challenged on its point of view that supported the concept of urban runoff being a nonpoint source. If it were a true nonpoint source it would, most likely, not require permitting. The Agency's position was that there are too many discharges and the burden of permitting each would be over-whelming. However, Judge Flannery did not agree with the Agency and stated that administrative convience was not an acceptable argument. The Agency appealed and in 1977 Judge Rosenthal upheld Judge Flannery's ruling stating that while it may be cumbersome and complex, the Agency should use its imagination.

One of the requirements of section 208 was that areawide agencies and States develop water quality control plans. Our initial guidance to these agencies on how to develop these plans was insufficient with respect to nonpoint sources, particularly urban runoff. As a result, most approaches to urban nonpoint sources were not usually fully developed. These plans for urban runoff were reviewed by Headquarters in early fiscal year 1977. Deficiencies were noted and a plan was developed to correct them. From 1978 to 1983 the Agency, in partnership with the U.S. Geological Survey, assisted twenty-eight cities nationwide, to develop urban runoff, water quality control plans.

* Chief, Nonpoint Source Control Section, U.S. Environmental Protection Agency, 401 M Street, SW, Washington, DC 20460

** Chief, Nonpoint Sources Branch, U.S. Environmental Protection Agency, 401 M Street, SW, Washington, DC, 20460

*** Director, Criteria & Standards Division, U.S. Environmental Protection Agency, 401 M Street, SW, Washington, DC 20460

Our guidance on this second round was the opposite of our previous advice. Where we had said collect no new data, we now said collect much data. As a result we began to develop an understanding of water quality problems associated with urban runoff.

Understanding Gained from the NURP

The overall goal of the Nationwide Urban Runoff Program (NURP) was to develop information that would help provide local decision makers, States, EPA, and other interested parties with a rational basis for determining whether or not urban runoff is causing water quality problems and, in the event that it is, for postulating realistic control options and developing water quality management plans, consistent with local needs, that would lead to implementation of least cost solutions. It is also hoped that this information base will be used to help make the best possible policy decision on Federal, State, and local involvement in urban stormwater runoff and its control . Among the many objectives of NURP was the assembly of an appropriate data base and the development of analytical methodologies that would allow us to examine such issues as:

- The quality characteristics of urban runoff, and similarities or differences at different urban locations;

- The extent to which urban runoff is a significant contributor to water quality problems across the nation and

- The performance characteristics and the overall effectiveness and utility of management practices for the control of pollutant loads from urban runoff.

Water quantity problems are relatively easy to identify and describe water quality problems, on the other hand, tend to be more elusive because their definition often involves some subjective considerations, including experiential aspects and expectations of the populace. They are not immediately obvious and are usually less dramatic than, for example, floods. They also tend to vary markedly with locality and geographic regions within the country. Thus, a methodological approach to the determination of water quality problems is essential if one is to consider the relative role of urban runoff as a contributor. An important finding of the work conducted during NURP was to learn to avoid the following simplistic logic train: (a) water quality problems are caused by pollutants, (b) there are pollutants, in urban runoff, therefore, (c) urban runoff causes "problems". The unspoken implication is that a "problem" by definition requires action, and any type of "problem" warrants equally vigorous action. It becomes clear that a more fundamental and more precise definition of a water quality "problem" from urban runoff is necessary. For this purpose, NURP adopted the following three-level definition:

- Impairment or denial of beneficial uses;

- Water quality criterion violation; and

- Local public perception.

The foregoing levels of problem definition provide an essential framework within which to discuss water quality problems associated with urban runoff. However, it is important to understand that when one is dealing at a local level all three elements are typically present. Thus, it is up to the local decision makers, influenced by other levels of support and concern, to carefully weigh each, prior to making a final decision about the existence and extent of a problem and how it is to be defined.

Quality Characteristics

In order to ensure good quality data, we provided guidance on data collection and required a quality assurance and quality control program for the data collection. As a result we feel we have a good substantial data base on urban runoff water quality. We provided guidance and hands-on technical assistance to ensure consistent data. Data that we could use and know that the differences we found in the various cities were due to local conditions and not because of the data collection methods.

The following constituents were adopted as standard pollutants characterizing urban runoff:

$$
\begin{array}{rl}
\text{TSS} & - \text{ Total Suspended Solids} \\
\text{BOD} & - \text{ Biochemical Oxygen Demand} \\
\text{COD} & - \text{ Chemical Oxygen Demand} \\
\text{TP} & - \text{ Total Phosphorus (as P)} \\
\text{SP} & - \text{ Soluble Phosphorus (as P)} \\
\text{TKN} & - \text{ Total Kjeldahl Nitrogen (as N)} \\
\text{NO}_{2+3}\text{-N} & - \text{ Nitrite + Nitrate (as N)}
\end{array}
$$

$$
\begin{array}{rl}
\text{Cu} & - \text{ Total Copper} \\
\text{Pb} & - \text{ Total Lead} \\
\text{Zn} & - \text{ Total Zinc}
\end{array}
$$

The list includes pollutants of general interest which are usually examined in both point and nonpoint source studies and includes representatives of important categories of pollutants--namely solids, oxygen consuming constiutents, nutrients, and heavy metals.

The pollutant concentrations found in urban runoff vary considerably, both during a storm event, as well as from event to event at a given site and from site to site within a given city and across the country. This variability is the natural result of high variations in rainfall intensity and occurrence, geographic features that effect runoff quantity, and so on. Considering this situation, a measure of the magnitude of the urban runoff pollution level and methods for characterizing its variability were needed. The event mean concentration (EMC), defined as the total constituent mass discharge divided by the total runoff volume, was chosen as the primary measure of the pollutant load. The rationale for adopting the EMC for characterizing urban runoff is discussed in the receiving water effects section of this chapter as well as in subsequent chapters. Event mean concentrations were calculated for each event at each site in the accesible data base. If a flow-weighted composite sample was taken, its concentration was used to represent the event mean concentration. Where sequential discrete samples were taken over the hydrograph, the event mean concentration was determined by calculating the area under the loadograph (the curve of concentration times discharge rate over time) and dividing it by the area under the hydrograph (the curve of runoff volume over time). For the purpose of determining event mean concentrations, rainfall events were defined to be separate precipitation events when there was an intervening time period of at least six hours without rain.

A statistical approach was adopted for characterizing the properties of EMCs for standard pollutants. Standard statistical procedures were used to define the probability distribution, central tendency (a mean or median) and spread (standard deviation or coefficient of variation) of EMC data. EMC data for each pollutant from all storms and monitoring sites were compiled in a central data base management system at the National Computer Center. The SAS computer statistical routines and other standard statistical methods were used to explore and characterize the data.

The underlying probability distribution of the EMC data was examined and tested by both visual and statistical methods. With relatively few isolated exceptions, the probability distribution of EMCs at individual sites can be characterized by lognormal distributions. Given this, concise characterization of the variable urban runoff characteristics at each of the sites is defined by only two values, the mean or median and the coefficient of variation (standard deviation divided by mean). Because the underlying distributions are lognormal, the appropriate statistic to employ for comparisons between individual sites or groups of sites is the median value, because it is less influenced by the small number of large values typical of lognormal distributions and, hence, is a more robust measure of central tendency. However, for comparisons with other published data which usually report average values and for certain computations and analyses (e.g., annual mass loads), the mean value is more appropriate.

Several different techniques were used to look at the results. One of the more illuminating was the box plot. The box plot compared the characteristics of all sites within one land use category. The EMC, its 90 percent confidence limits, and the 10, 25, 75, and 90 percent quantities for the sites.

Careful perusal of these box plots leads one to the conclusion that only the open/non-urban land uses category appears to be significantly different overall. Responses of the other land use categories are varied and inconsistent among constituents. While there are no consistent tendencies, there are undeniably some trends.

Thus, regardless of the analytical approach taken, we are forced to conclude that, if land use category effects are present, they are eclipsed by the storm to storm variabilities and that, therefore, land use category is of little general use to aid in predicting urban runoff quality at unmonitored sites or in explaining site to site differences where monitoring data exist.

In Stream Effects

The effects of urban runoff on receiving water quality are very site specific. They depend on the type, size, and hydrology of the water body, the designated beneficial use and the pollutants which affect that use, the urban runoff quality characteristics, and the amount of urban runoff dictated by local rainfall patterns and land use.

One of the products of the NURP was the development of a screening methodology which allows one to estimate in-stream concen-centrations of urban runoff. This analysis technique computes the magnitude and frequency of occurrence of intermittent stream concentrations of pollutants of interest. In addition, if the long term average number of annual storm events is known, this is readily available from the U.S. Weather Service, one can estimate the recurrence intervals for all events. If the two are put together, magnitude and recurrence, one can begin to see the effects of urban runoff over time and be better able to make rational decisions.

Agency Approach For Urban Runoff

Traditionally urban runoff (drainage) has been considered a local matter. We still consider it a local matter, because if anything gets done, it will be local govermnents doing it. Our approach is based on this premis. Urban runoff comes under the Nonpoint Source Program within the Agency.

Quite recently the Agency has taken a renewed interest in nonpoint sources (NPS). Mr. Thomas, our Administrator has said publicly that NPS is a top priority problem. As a result we have been developing strategies on how to deal with it. The CWA is currently up for reauthorization and one of the proposed amendments deals directly with NPS.

Our current program is to continue developing and providing technical assistance to the States, and others. We are developing assessment techniques to aid the States in meeting what we forsee as legislative requirements as a result of the passing of the proposed CWA amendments. We mean specifically those requirements delineated under sec. 319. What we hope to accomplish is that a better understanding of water quality problems from urban runoff is provided to States and others. We feel this is necessary so that States or others may better place the water quality problem in the proper priority and be better able to focus on the most significant problems first.

We feel that much can be done by local governments with individual assistance from, primarily, States but also federal agencies. Currently much work is being done. Some local governmental agencies clearly understand the problems from urban runoff. They have taken it upon themselves to identify the problem, the use impaired, and have designed and implemented the necessary controls after setting up the necessary legal, and institutional infra structure. Two good examples of this are what is being done in Bellevue, Washington, and in the Washington, DC area.

Nonpoint Source Strategy

In 1985 the Association of State and Interstate Water Pollution Control Administrators (ASIWPCA) completed a National assessment on NPS water pollution. This Study reaffirmed that nonpoint pollution is a major remaining water quality problem which will prevent the achievement of established water quality goals, even when applicable point source controls have been fully implemented. The Study reported the following waters were either impaired or threatened by NPS pollution:

- 41 percent of the 404,000 assessed river miles:

- 53 percent of the 15 million assessed lake acres; and

- 28 percent of the 19,000 assessed estuary square miles.

The study also reported NPS impacts on ground water including contamination from agricultural fertilizers and pesticides, septic systems, abandoned mines, and salt storage.

ASIWPCA's Study was based upon a detailed assessment conducted by each of the States, territories and interstate agencies. It represents the first comprehensive, consistent look at the Nation's NPS problems and is a major milestone in our efforts to address this source of water pollution. Other reports, such as State Section 305(b) Water Quality Reports and Regional Environmental Management Reports (EMR's) similarly document the problems caused by NPS pollution.

Given the nature of the problem, significant reductions in nonpoint pollutants will only come by improving the way we all manage our activities on land. America's largest landowner, the Federal government, must also meet its NPS challenges. The Federal government is directly responsible for managing over 720 million acres of land. During FY 1986-1987 a major thrust of EPA's NPS Strategy will be to help the major Federal land-holding agencies address nonpoint problems in areas under their supervision. In addition, we intend to continue to encourage Federal agencies to use their existing outreach and assistance programs to complement State, local and private sector NPS management efforts.

Rather than undertake a new big-money Federal nonpoint program, we believe that we must redirect existing Federal, State, local and private resources to priority nonpoint problems. To help us frame this approach, EPA convened an interagency Nonpoint Source Task Force in 1984. The Task Force recommended a new National policy on NPS pollution to protect surface and ground water. Each Federal agency on the Task Force developed its own nonpoint strategy, which they are now beginning to put into effect. The Task Force strongly supported the idea that States and their localities should play the leading role in the control of nonpoint sources, and that private sector initiatives and cooperation are essential for success.

Coordination and refocusing of existing resources are essential if we are to have a chance at all of coping with this problem. These resources are in fact immense. When you add up the money spent on resource and environmental protection in FY 1985 by the Corps of Engineers, the Soil Conservation Service, and the Forest Service, the Bureau of Land Management, and others it comes to about $10 billion.

Priorities in FY 1986-1987

The Agencywide and Regional NPS Strategies list all the specific activities which we will undertake in FY 1986-1987 to address nonpoint problems. While all of these activities are important, our major emphasis will be in the following three areas:

1. EPA will increase coordination with other Federal agencies to better utilize existing Federal programs to accomplish NPS management objectives.

2. EPA will work with States to incorporate NPS control measures in their water quality programs, where NPS pollution is a major problem in surface and ground water.

3. EPA will intensify it NPS activities and integrate NPS management concerns into all aspects of its programs.

We will continue to maintain the momentum which we have established in the past few years in the NPS area and to continue to work with other agencies to institutionalize management approaches which will lead to substantial NPS environmental results.

Stormwater Permitting

We have had a stormwater permit program since 1976 regulations were promulgated. These regulations underwent minor changes in 1979 and became the Consolidated Regulations of 1980. The Proposed change of November 18, 1982, was directed at industry and stated in effect, that stormwater discharges are conveyances of stormwater contaminated by process wastes, raw materials, toxic and hazardous pollutants, or oil and grease. On September 26, 1984 the Final Rule was published in the Federal Register.

This rule defined a stormwater point source as a conveyance or systems of conveyances channelizing stormwater runoff which: is located in an urbanized area, or discharges from lands or facilities used for industrial or commercial activitites, or is designated by the Director. Application requirements were defined and described two groups of dischargers with separate application requirements. Group I is defined as those sources that are: 1.) Subject to effluent limitations, toxic pollutant standards or new source performance standards, or 2.) located in an industrial plant or its associated area, or 3.) designated by the Director. The requirements were to fill out Form 1 and Form 2c which requires much data collection. Group II refers to any discharger that is not Group I. The requirements are less and is limited to Form 1 plus a narrative description of: 1.) the drainage area, 2.) the receiving water, and 3.) any treatment. The initial deadline for applications was to be April 26, 1985.

The March, 1985 proposed changes offered December 31, 1985 as an extended deadline for Group I and II dischargers and the Agency would solicit comments on whether the deadline should be extended beyond December 31, 1985 for Group II dischargers. While the March proposal made no changes in the scope of coverage, there were proposed changes to the submission requirements. Group I proposed changes would suspend the requirement to submit Form 2c because of alternative data-gathering commitments. Group I would submit Form 1 plus augmented narratives. Also the Agency would solicit comments on whether authority should be provided to EPA to waive data submission requirements for a category of Group I dischargers, if present requirement to submit Form 2c is retained. The definition for an Urbanized Area is proposed to be updated to reflect most current Census Bureau criteria.

These same proposed changes, March 7, 1985, generated 140 comments and questions and the Agency, as a consequence, reproposed. The August 12, 1985 reproposal required municipalities to be the applicant and be held responsible. This was not acceptable, so a new final rule was proposed on August 29, 1985. This rule extends the deadlines for submitting applications for Group I from Dec. 31, 1985 to Dec. 31, 1987 and for Group II from Dec. 31, 1985 to June 30, 1989. In addition sampling requirements were reduced.

We will be using the time from now until 1988 to gain a better understanding of urban stormwater and the need to control it. While we have done some work on urban runoff and have a limited amount of knowledge, we will be looking for help from you and others. We now have an opportunity to develop workable solutions, the rest is up to us.

Bellevue's Urban Storm Water Permit and Program
Pam Bissonnette*

The Bellevue Storm Water Management Utility has been in operation for
over ten years. At its initiation, flooding and erosion control were
its main mission. Today with increasing focus on nonpoint source
water pollution, and extension of the National Pollutant Discharge
Elimination System Permit (NPDES) program to cover urban storm water,
emphasis has shifted to runoff quality, its effects on receiving
waters, and technological controls. Bellevue is to receive a General
NPDES permit in 1986. This paper deals with how the Bellevue Storm
Water Management Utility was created, its current programs, and its
role in water pollution control.

Introduction

To understand how the City of Bellevue expects to respond to the new
urban storm water permit program necessitates an understanding of the
Bellevue Storm and Surface Water (SSW) Utility. The Bellevue SSW
Utility was formed out of a citizen and City commitment to preserve
its network of streams and lakes. It was established in 1974 and
given a mission to manage the storm and surface water system in
Bellevue to maintain a hydrologic balance, to prevent property
damage, and to protect water quality; for the health, safety and
enjoyment of citizens and the preservation and enhancement of
wildlife habitat. The basic concept underlying all policies and
programs concerning storm water management in Bellevue is to use the
natural surface water drainage system to provide for conveyance and
disposal of storm water runoff. The SSW Utility system consists of
an integrated network of pipes and stream channels which form the
conveyance system; and lakes, wetlands, ponds and detention basins
which are the storage facilities for flow equalization and some water
quality control.

In carrying out its charge, the SSW Utility has four major programs:
administration, development regulation, maintenance and operations,
and a capital improvement program. The 1986 operating budget for
funding these programs is $4.3 million. The 1980-1986 capital
improvement budget is $13 million.

The major source of SSW Utility revenue is from a utility service
charge. The rate structure currently is based on contribution of
runoff to the drainage system. For a given storm event, a
relationship exists between the amount of runoff from a property and
land area, and in particular the impervious land area. Since runoff
cannot practically be directly measured for all properties, this

*Director, Storm & Surface Water Utility, City of Bellevue,
P.O. Box 90012, Bellevue, WA 98009

relationship is used to define the rate structure. All properties, including undeveloped and publicly-owned property, participate financially with such a structure since they contribute runoff and benefit from the SSW Utility programs.

Runoff coefficients are the basis of the five rate classifications: undeveloped (up to 0.25), light (0.25-0.4), moderate (0.4-0.5), heavy (0.5-0.75) and very heavy (0.75-1.0). Where runoff controls are provided on a property a commensurate rate reduction is granted.

During the initial five years of the SSW Utility the focus was almost exclusively on runoff volume and velocity, and erosion control. At the same time that the National Urban Runoff Program (NURP) was being initiated the SSW Utility began to shift more attention to the water quality control aspects of its mission. In developing operations and maintenance programs and in designing the $13 million of capital improvement projects, the SSW Utility became aware of the need for more data, particularly in the Pacific Northwest region with its distinctive pattern of weather and land forms, and better information on storm water runoff quality controls. It was with these ends in view that Bellevue requested to become a NURP City.

Bellevue was one of the 27 cities nationwide that participated in the National Urban Runoff Program (NURP). During a six year period extensive monitoring of urban runoff, its sources of pollutant contamination, and its effects on receiving waters was undertaken. Over 200 storm events, and atmospheric and impervious surface pollutant concentrations were monitored. These results were compared to the chemical, physical and biological health of an urban receiving stream, Kelsey Creek. Various management practices were applied such as street sweeping, drainage system maintenance, and detention, and were monitored to evaluate whether these practices had any beneficial water quality effects. We found:

(1) In general, the street surface and drainage system are not the major source of sediment or pollutants to receiving waters.

(2) While intensive street sweeping and drainage system cleaning does remove material from those areas it (a) preferentially removes larger, more inert particles, while storm water runoff removes smaller particles more highly associated with pollutants and (b) produces nonmeasurable effects on the quality of runoff.

(3) The use of on-site detention basins as currently designed had no measurable effect on runoff quality.

(4) Kelsey Creek was seen to suffer more from frequent high flows, stream scour and erosion, sedimentation, and direct dumping of toxic materials than any other causes.

Therefore, management practices targeted on the street surface and structural drainage system, while having some merit, cannot provide a complete solution to urban storm water pollution. An effective control strategy in Bellevue must look beyond the typical public

works and utilities design, operations and maintenance practices to
source controls, in-stream quantity and velocity controls, and even
treatment.

Bellevue's Urban Storm Water Permit Provisions

Shortly after the publication of the NURP results, new rules and
regulations pertaining to the discharge of urban runoff were
promulgated at the federal level. The new regulations basically
applied the National Pollutant Discharge Elimination System (NPDES)
permit requirements to urban storm water. Bellevue made application
for such a permit and has currently a draft which is expected to be
finalized in 1986.

The basic tenants of the permit are:

(1)   Local governments are made accountable for the quality of the
       runoff discharged within their jurisdictions.

(2)   Water quality standards, similar to those for sanitary waste
       water effluent, are to be achieved.

(3)   The initial thrust is to accomplish these standard through
       source control programs and the Utility's operation and
       maintenance program.

(4)   Should source controls and operations and maintenance practices
       be insufficient to achieve water quality standards over a
       reasonable period of time (e.g. five years), then treatment of
       urban runoff may be required.

There are several key issues concerning the urban storm water
permit. First, should the permit be a general permit covering
classes or groups of activities and/or geographic areas, or rather
should there be a permit for every outfall? It would seem obvious
that permitting each of millions of outfalls would be an expensive
administrative nightmare of no certain positive result. In Bellevue
alone there are several thousand such outfalls in an area of only 25
square miles. Bellevue's current draft permit is a single general
permit encompassing all outfalls within our jurisdiction.

Geographic vs. class or group coverage for general permits is also at
issue. The NURP findings were clear that large regional differences
in quality of runoff from the same land use activity can exist due to
local hydrologic conditions. The same is true for control mechanisms
such as street cleaning. Therefore, permitting entire groups without
respect for regional differences would be inconsistent with current
knowledge of urban runoff pollution. A geographic based general
permit such as Bellevue's takes into account regional hydrologic
conditions.

Another key issue is what constitutes a receiving water during a
storm event? Bellevue's draft permit is currently based on a
one-year, six-hour storm. During such an event many of our urban

streams are flowing virtually 100 percent urban runoff. Application
of water quality standards at these locations and times would mean
that pure urban runoff would need to meet the standards, a currently
unattainable objective. We have proposed the following criteria for
determining where and when water quality standards will apply.

(1) Receiving water quality standards shall apply in all drainages
     of greater than or equal to 5 cfs mean annual flow and all
     navigable lakes.

(2) A violation of receiving water quality standards occurs when the
     standards are exceeded during any period in (1) above when (a)
     less than 0.02 inches of rainfall occur during a six-hour
     period, or (b) downstream or beyond the treatment zone per (3)
     below at any time rainfall occurs greater than or equal to 0.02
     inches in a six-hour period but less than or equal to the
     one-year, six-hour rainfall event flow and duration.

(3) The treatment zone is the area from the discharge to the point
     where the baseflow or background of the receiving water would
     dilute by 50 percent or greater the one-year, six-hour storm
     flow delivered by any individual outfall.

These criteria remove bias toward enclosed conduit systems and
recognize the treatment value of detention facilities, wetlands and
other natural treatment mechanisms.

Effluent standards as currently drafted target solids as the most
important factor to control, again based on NURP results. An outfall
is defined as any pipe, conduit, culvert or surface flow delivering
greater than or equal to 5 cfs mean annual flow. For any outfall,
which could be the upper reaches of a small stream, no solids and/or
floatables of greater than or equal to 1/4 inch size fraction shall
be discharged, and no more than 400 lb/ac/yr shall be discharged for
size fractions less than 1/4 inch measured as suspended solids,
excepting loadings from greater than the one-year, six-hour event.
The 400 lb/ac/hr limit was chosen based on the solids delivery from
two, 100-acre, developed and maintained residential areas and a
maintained urban arterial.

Monitoring, its amount and cost has been much debated since
publication of the new federal rules. Bellevue's draft permit
requires sampling at five receiving water sites for water quality
standards compliance and at three representative outfall sites for
compliance with storm water effluent standards. The results of the
definition of receiving water and treatment zone made earlier is to
push the receiving water monitoring sites out to the ends of the
drainage basins into major receiving waters, such as Lk. Washington
and Lk. Sammamish in our case.

Monitoring at the five receiving water sites emphasizes sediment
accumulation and sediment quality rather than water quality. The
three outfall effluent sites include a 100-acre residential basin, an
industrial complex and the central business district. Monitoring at

these outfalls will be the standard flow-weighted composite approach
for the initial six-hours of a storm on a monthly basis throughout
the year. Both water and suspended solids quality will be analyzed
for a number of parameters.

Several special studies are required by the permit as an adjunct to
the routine monitoring program. Similar to other jurisdictions,
records do not now exist identifying each and every storm water
outfall. We are required over a five year period to inventory and
map all storm water drainage systems within the permit area (the
utility's service area boundary). Further, we are required over the
next six years to estimate the mean annual loadings of total solids,
total phosphorus, and total lead for representative land use
classifications: central business district, commercial, industrial,
multi-family residential, single family residential, developed open
space, and undeveloped open space. This will be based initially on
available data to be supplemented by sampling where adequate data
does not exist. The purpose is to estimate total loadings in the
permit area which may influence future permit conditions and control
strategies.

The consequences of violating receiving water quality standards has
not received much attention, yet potentially holds the biggest
challenge for local governments. We have proposed a compliance
philosophy and schedule which emphasizes source controls and
operation and maintenance, and employs treatment as the means of last
resort. For any receiving water or storm water outfall experiencing
significant violation of standards per Figure 1, investigative
monitoring to identify and treat the source(s) of baseflow and/or
storm flow pollution would be required. If a specific source of
violation is identified Bellevue, as permittee, may propose source
control(s) rather than provide outfall treatment. Source control(s)
may be required under the permit if it is determined that no best
available technology exists which is as or more effective than source
control(s). If a specific source of violation is not identified or
if we, the permittee, propose outfall treatment rather than source
control(s) or if we cannot obtain approval of our source control
program, then outfall treatment may be required.

Outfall treatment must use the best available technology and provide
for treatment of all storm flows up to and including that produced by
the one-year, six-hour rainfall event, or the first 3/4 inch of
runoff from a watershed. Standards for treated effluent are:

(1)   85% removal or 50 ppm, whichever is lesser, of suspended solids,
      excepting size fractions greater than 1/4 inch which are
      prohibited from discharge.

(2)   No visible oil sheen present.

(3)   Dissolved oxygen of greater than 5 mg/l but no greater than 110%
      saturation.

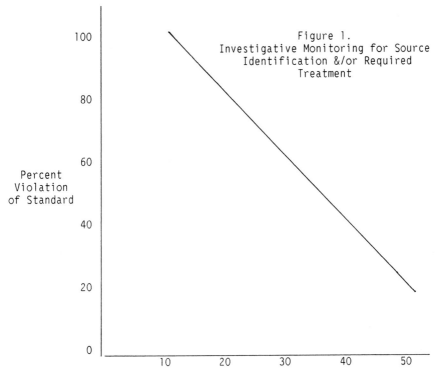

Figure 1.
Investigative Monitoring for Source
Identification &/or Required
Treatment

(4) pH within the range of 6.5 to 8.5.

(5) Fecal coliform less than 50/100 ml.

Because acute pollution events often accompany toxic spills, the
draft permit requires a spill response program and constant response
readiness of trained personnel and equipment. We are also required
to develop and maintain records of the presence and use of toxic and
hazardous materials within the permit area.

In recognition that many non-point sources of pollution contributing
to storm water effluent pollution concentrations and loadings are due
to a lack of public education, and that in many circumstances the
most effective and least costly means of controlling these sources of
pollution is more and better public education, the permit requires
that we develop and sustain a public education program. Such a
program will focus on:

(1) Activities which result in non-point source pollution;

(2) What alternatives exist to causing non-point source pollution;

(3) How to report incidents of non-point pollution; and

(4) The value of good quality surface and groundwater.

Permit Costs and Implementation

The Bellevue permit is expected to be issued shortly and if so, the
following compliance schedule will go into effect:

(1) Submit for review and approval an annual work plan for
     monitoring, maintenance, and enforcement one year from issuance
     of the permit.

(2) Initiate monitoring by January 1, 1987.

(3) Submit a Spill Response Program for approval by January 1, 1987.

(4) Submit a Public Education Program for approval by January 1,
     1987.

(5) Complete the drainage system inventory and mapping and submit by
     December 31, 1990.

(6) Complete the land use classification inventory and loading
     assessment and submit by December 31, 1991.

Because of Bellevue's strong commitment toward maintaining and
enhancing surface water quality, we have anticipated the provisions
of the permit and have already acted to change basic City policies
pertaining to surface and groundwater. Over one hundred separate
policies in the City's Comprehensive Plan have been consolidated to
thirteen related to water quantity, quality, habitat, soil erosion

and sediment control. Specific objectives with time lines and
detailed implementation plans were included and beneficial uses of
receiving water were designated and prioritized. These new policies
direct land use as well as City-wide operational and capital programs
in such a manner as to minimize storm water pollution.

Several tasks are either in progress or remain for the Utility to
accomplish. We are currently revising and upgrading our routine
sampling program (baseflow and storm-related) and instrumenting
stations as required by our permit. We are accomplishing the
sampling and labile parameter monitoring with Utility staff and
contracting for the remaining sample analysis. The same is true for
our investigative monitoring program.

Some increases in our operations program are anticipated in the area
of public detention facility maintenance. While we already have a
program for inspections of private detention system operation and
maintenance, this program needs to be expanded to cover all aspects
of private drainage system discharge.

Design and construction standards must be improved to optimize both
flood control and water quality control.   In a few areas of the
City, new capital improvements are needed to address existing serious
water pollution problems.

The Utility already has a 24-hour, seven day per week Spill Response
Program, and a Public Education Program. Over the past five years,
the Utility has sponsored an Oil Recycling Program through all the
local gas stations. This program has been highly successful and now
operates independently with the Utility providing only publicity.
Last year, the Utility initiated the first Household Hazardous Waste
Pick-up Day. Over 40-55 gallon drums of hazardous materials were
collected from residents and disposed of properly. This event will
be continued at least annually. The Utility also sponsors streamside
workshops and salmon enhancement programs through the school system
and a variety of clubs.

The Utility has been inventorying all elements of the drainage system
and storing the information on the City's Automatic Mapping and
Planning System (AMPS) geo-data base. Such information includes
locations, elevations, conditions, maintenance history and eventually
water quality data. Similarly, the land use inventory data will be
stored in the AMPS geo-data base. The studies to determine
representative loadings from various land uses will be initiated
following receipt of the permit and be likewise stored. This
information, combined with the continuous rainfall and flow records
maintained by the Utility, will be suitable for eventual modeling of
total non-point loadings from the service area.

Permit compliance in its present proposed form will result in new
costs for the Utility as seen in Table 1 of just under $400,000.
Much of this includes one-time set-up costs and capital costs which
are expected to decrease in future years. The total cost of permit
compliance will consume a third of the Utility's program resources.

Bellevue is fortunate in already having a base of programs on which
to build and a dedicated revenue source available for this purpose.
In jurisdictions where these advantageous circumstances do not exist,
the burden of permit compliance likely will be much greater. One
possible course of action to ease this burden would be a federal and
state program granting extensions to deadlines for permit application
and issuance, and even financial incentives, based on progress toward
the creation of drainage utilities. For secure and stable sources of
local funding appear to be the best hope for complying with the new
federal rules and dealing with urban non-point source pollution.

Table 1. Estimated Cost of Compliance with Bellevue's
General Storm Water Permit

Task	Total Cost (1986 $)	Incremental Cost (1986 $)
(1) Permit Monitoring Requirement (Baseflow & Storm)	$ 100,000	$100,000
(2) Investigative Monitoring	$ 50,000	-0-
(3) O & M Program	$ 590,000	$235,000
(4) Private System Inspection/ Enforcement	$ 100,000	$ 50,000
(5) Code & Design Standards Revisions	$ 20,000	-0-
(6) Spill Response	$ 7,000	-0-
(7) Public Education	$ 32,000	-0-
(8) Drainage System Inventory/ Mapping	$ 300,000	-0-
(9) Land Use Loadings Estimation	$ 10,000	$ 10,000
TOTAL	$1,209,000	$395,000

(0584p)

Stormwater Management in Orlando, Florida

by: David W. Zeno[1], Member, ASCE and Carla N. Palmer[2], Associate Member, ASCE

Abstract

Metropolitan Orlando, Florida contains 82 lakes and approximately 200 drainage wells which serve as ultimate outfall for stormwater runoff. The quality of the surface receiving waters has been deteriorating while groundwater has not shown the deleterious effects of drainage wells. Orlando has established ordinances requiring pollution control and hydrograph attenuation in new developments. The City is utilizing best management practices as well as innovative techniques to retrofit systems for pollution control in the built-out neighborhoods. The City has developed a plan to monitor drain wells for water quality and is implementing a lake enhancement program.

This paper discusses administration, costs, ownership, monitoring, possible solutions and results of its stormwater management programs.

Introduction

The control of stormwater for the purpose of improving its quality is a relatively new management objective which is gaining support throughout Florida. The historical emphasis of stormwater management has gradually moved from that of flood control toward water quality control. The City of Orlando emphasizes both objectives in its management of stormwater runoff.

The City of Orlando is located in Orange County, Florida. A location map, Figure 1, is provided to show the City's relative position within the State and the density of lakes within the City limits. There are 82 named lakes within the City. Many of these lakes are the ultimate receiving waters for most of the stormwater runoff in the developed areas. Because there are so many lakes, and people like to live near the water, many neighborhoods are located in land locked basins. The provision of flood control and rapid conveyance of water off the street is a primary consideration in the City's stormwater management objective.

1   David W. Zeno, P.E., City Engineer, City of Orlando, 400 South Orange Avenue, Orlando, Florida 32801

2   Carla N. Palmer, Senior Scientist, Dyer, Riddle, Mills & Precourt, Inc., 1505 East Colonial Drive, Orlando, Florida 32803

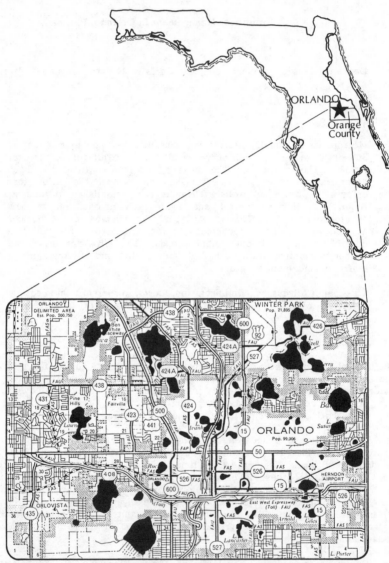

FIGURE 1   LOCATION MAP ORLANDO, FLORIDA

The Central Florida stormwater management challenge is interwoven with hydrological, geological and infrastructural concerns. The area receives 128 - 129 cm (50 - 51 in) of rainfall annually most of which occurs in the summer months. Most of the area is underlain with sandy soils, and in their undeveloped state, provide rapid infiltration for the rainfall. The water that infiltrates into the ground is able to recharge the Floridan aquifer, a limestone formation providing drinking water for nearly all the residents of Central Florida. A few wetland areas, located on poorly drained soils store the water or allow it to run off slowly to lakes and streams. The wet soils are usually underlain with a high water table. Central Florida has a karst topography with sinkholes forming the many lakes in the area. Sinkhole activity continues to create new lakes today. Much of the terrain is relatively flat with elevations averaging 30.5 m (100 feet) above mean sea level.

The rapid development that the City has experienced over the past 25 years has changed the drainage regime of the area. Much of the well drained soils have been covered with impervious materials. The runoff to rainfall ratio ranges from 0.5 to 0.95 in the developed areas. Runoff quantity creates drainage problems, and runoff quality creates lake pollution problems.

The Orlando Urban Storm Water Management (OUSWM) program is a major effort to control the stormwater from a quantity and quality perspective for new developments. The objective of this program is to provide hydrograph attenuation, water pollution control and innovation in stormwater management. The responsibilities of meeting these objectives lie with the developers. OUSWM also encourages retrofitting stormwater management facilities in existing neighborhoods, where the responsibility rests with the City itself.

The quality of the lakes receiving stormwater has been deteriorating steadily over the past several years. In the summer of 1983 the City sponsored a Lake Assessment study (1983). The objective of the study was to determine which lakes were the best candidates for enhancement efforts given the limited amount of money available for the work. While the City is heavily dependent on its lakes to receive stormwater, it is committed to enhancing their water quality in as many ways as possible. As a result of this study, the City is implementing its Lake Enhancement Program.

In some areas of the City stormwater has no outfall to surface water. Stormwater is conveyed ultimately to the aquifer through drainage wells. Drain wells are extremely effective in flood control, and land locked drainage basins in the City are dependent on that fact. The wells are also the most economical method of disposing of stormwater. The consequence of stormwater going to ground may be a detriment to the water supply. The City is currently involved in a monitoring program with the State Department of Environmental Regulation to determine the quality of the runoff water. Recent studies conducted by the U.S. Geological Survey have indicated that there is no apparent degradation of the resource as a result of drain wells.

The Regulation of Stormwater in Florida

Stormwater management is regulated in Florida by two main agencies. The Florida Department of Environmental Regulation (FDER) is the prime agency in stormwater management requiring best management practices (BMPs) be used. Stormwater facilities are required by the FDER to provide retention, or detention with filtration of the runoff from the first 2.54 cm (1.0 in) of rainfall. In the case of drainage basins being less than 40.5 ha (100 ac), stormwater facilities are required to provide retention, or detention with filtration, of the first 1.27 cm (0.5 in) of runoff. The FDER is in the process of delegating stormwater facility permitting to the water management districts in the state. The water management districts have historically been involved with the protection of the resource with respect to water supply and flood controls. The districts are becoming more concerned with surface water supply and its quality. The new regulations coming from the water management districts are more specific with respect to design and performance standards than those of the FDER. Each water management district's stormwater management rules are specific for its jurisdiction or drainage basin causing those municipalities straddling water-shed boundaries to conform to two somewhat different sets of criteria. Stormwater management is regulated on the local level, and home rules may be more stringent than state or district. Orlando is located in Orange County and is subject to the County regulation of stormwater as well.

There is proposed legislation on the State level which if passed will force all local entities to include a stormwater management element in the local governmental comprehensive planning process. The bill as presently written will require local governments to detail the method of funding for any capital improvements regarding stormwater management. It will require local governments to list problem areas needing remedial attention or retrofitting with respect to stormwater's impact on receiving waters.

Stormwater Management Programs of the City of Orlando

The City uses a guide entitled "Orlando Urban Storm Water Management Manual" (OUSWMM) outlining its ordinances for runoff control (1984). OUSWMM addresses urban flooding problems, erosion and sediment control, water quality, and pollution abatement. The manual details design criteria for stormwater management facilities. Table 1 gives a listing of the contents of the OUSWM Manual. The OUSWMM was adopted by the City Council in January 1984.

The City of Orlando recognized the need for a comprehensive approach to stormwater management several years ago in anticipation of the rapid growth to come to the area. It's new stormwater management ordinances require the use of retention/detention systems for all new developments. A retention facility must be designed to retain separately on site either the first 1.27 cm (0.5 in) of runoff or the runoff from the first 2.54 cm (1.0 in) of rainfall, whichever is greater. The rationale behind the control of runoff of the first 2.54 cm (1.0 in) of rainfall stems from the fact that 90% of the storms in Florida have rainfall of less than 2.54 cm (1.0 in) (Wanielista, 1978). Theoretically, a pollution control system designed to handle the runoff from the first 2.54 cm (1.0 in) of rainfall would be able to control 80% to 85% of the pollutant load to the receiving waters. The ordinance does not spell out specifically how this is to be accomplished: the water may be retained in a pond, may flow through an exfiltration system or may be treated in any other way which accomplishes the same results.

The City works with the design engineers of the proposed project in order to accommodate innovative and multiple use systems. For example, a retention pond may be landscaped and shaped to offer a visual amenity to the property; thus keeping new development in line with the philosophy that stormwater facilities do not have to be visually unattractive.

Retention facilities must be designed to allow half the water to percolate, exfiltrate or evaporate within 24 hours after the storm event. All the required retention volume must be drawn down within 72 hours of the storm occurrence. Figure 2 is provided to show the conceptual design for retention/detention facilities.

Urbanization and modification of existing land uses in the City has caused increased volumes, flow rate and pollutant loadings from stormwater runoff, thus contributing to the increase in potential flooding and degradation of receiving waters. Besides off-line retention or its equivalent, the City requires any new development's stormwater facilities to detain on site a sufficient volume of water to attenuate the post development peak runoff to the predevelopment peak runoff. However, in older, built-out neighborhoods the control of stormwater for quality purposes may require retrofitting of all or parts of the conveyance systems. The City is currently investigating problem areas and planning remedial action where necessary and/or feasible. Problems associated with retrofitting have to deal with the inavailability of land for retention or detention, the excavation of existing roadways to replace pipe, the replacement of storm sewer inlets, traffic, and relocation of utilities.

The cost of land in the built-out areas of the City may be prohibitive when compared to the anticipated benefit of pollutant load reduction using a technology that is not yet proven. The cost of retrofitting a storm sewer line can exceed $1.0 million per 1.6 km (1.0 mi) of pipe. There are 254 km (220 mi) of storm sewers within the City of Orlando. The City is investigating the possibility of using park and recreation areas as dual purpose stormwater storage and pollution control facilities. However, there are not enough parks and open areas, nor are they located properly to provide pollution control for the entire system as it presently exists. If stormwater management facilities in built-out areas were upgraded to OUSWMM standards, then theoretically the lakes should show an improvement.

How is Orlando's Stormwater Management Program Administered?

Final development plans and specifications must be submitted with design analysis to the Orlando Bureau of Engineering. The Bureau evaluates the proposed system to ascertain its impact on existing facilities. All plans are reviewed for conformance. Pre-application conferences are encouraged in order to develop a dialog between the Department and the developer's engineers. The Department encourages innovation at these proceedings so that the stormwater management system can become an integral part of the project's amenities, whenever possible. Through the use of gardens, fountains and the like the landscaped areas may be used for recreation as well as pollution control. After conceptual plans are negotiated a final engineering submittal with design analysis is completed and signed by a registered professional engineer. However, additional permits will be required from the water management district in which the project is located, as well as the Florida Department of Environmental Regulation.

The Ownership of Stormwater Management Facilities

Current City policy is in a state of flux with respect to the ownership of stormwater management systems. Should the City own the facility or should the developer own it? The argument on the side of the City's owning the facility postulates that since a stormwater management system generally services

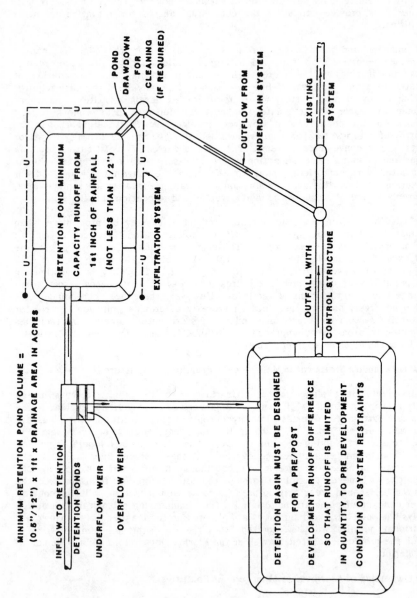

FIGURE 2   DESIGN FOR RETENTION DETENTION FACILITIES

Table 1. Table of Contents of OUSWM Manual:

Design Criteria For Stormwater Management Facilities

Introduction
General
Previous Studies
Outside Agency Coordination
Submittal Procedure
Manual Updating
Appendices

Definition of City-Wide Storm Water Management System
General
Primary Water Control Facilities
Secondary Conveyance Facilities
Tertiary Conveyance Facilities
Retention/Detention Facilities
Flood Prone Areas
Conservation Areas

Hydrology of System Facilities
General
Primary Conveyance Facilities
Secondary Conveyance Facilities
Tertiary Conveyance Facilities
Roadway (Pavement)
Retention/Detention Facility Hydrology
Flow Determination Criteria
Appendices

Hydraulic Design Criteria
General
Roadway (Pavement) Drainage
Storm Sewer Design
Culvert Design
Open Channel Design
Detention Facility Outfall Weir Design
Appendices

Stormwater Pollution Abatement Design Criteria
General
Retention Facilities
Detention Facilities
Water Quality Monitoring
Natural Retention/Detention Areas

Erosion Control
General
Construction
Permanent

public streets of a particular development, the City should acquire it and be responsible for its maintenance. From an operational standpoint the City is the entity that ultimately cares the most about the performance of the facility and should therefore own and maintain it. However, from a practical standpoint it is nearly impossible to access all retention/detention, or exfiltration systems within the City. Many are located at the back end or at the lowest elevation on a project, far removed from the main transportation arteries. To follow along this train of thought, the argument may be made to require developers and/or homeowner associations to maintain the systems. A code enforcement program may be enacted requiring owners to keep stormwater management facilities operational and maintained. However, it is difficult to cite a single entity for code violation in a subdivision with multiple ownership.

The City has accepted the responsibility for maintenance of a number of retention/detention systems. Most of the maintenance done is for aesthetics, such as mowing and sediment removal. The City must have right of access to the facility in order to maintain it. It is difficult to gain access to many of the facilities located at the back of a development totally surrounded by private property. In this case the City has been resistive to accepting the facilities for maintenance.

Cost of the Program

The cost for stormwater management facilities in new developments is borne generally by the developers. The cost varies and is a function of the elaborateness of the system involved.

The cost for maintenance of each system, if borne by the City, may be prohibitive. Work would entail mowing and silt removal. Exfiltration systems would need to be changed out regularly. At this time the City has not developed a policy on who should bear this cost. If the City is made responsible ultimately for the operation and maintenance of these facilities, it will have to look for means of financing this effort.

How Does the City Insure Facilities Are Built In Accordance With The Approved Design?

The City collects an inspection and permit fee with the permit application for the stormwater management system. The facility is inspected, and the system must be approved before the developer is issued a certificate of occupancy. It has been suggested that the developer's registered engineer rather than the City, inspect the system and certify to its conformance with the code. Developer's have voiced the opinion that they would rather the City inspect the facilities, however.

How Does The City Monitor Effectiveness of Stormwater Facilities?

Orlando has no routine process of monitoring stormwater systems. The facilities are examined on the basis of citizen complaints and observation by City inspectors and maintenance crews during their normal work activities. This, of course, does not provide for routine inspection of all systems, particularly private facilities which are often located in remote areas not traversed by City personnel.

It has been suggested that a routine inspection schedule be established utilizing City personnel. However, the sheer number of facilities which would have to be examined during a rainfall event and again 72 hours later make this approach impractical.

The State of Florida is giving cities the rights to establish municipal service taxing units (MSTUs). If the City chooses to accept MSTUs, the maintenance of stormwater systems could be funded through these taxes. Additional manpower, machinery, expertise and administration would be required for this effort.

What Results Have Been Achieved?

It is difficult to document results of the City's stormwater management program. Theoretically, an improvement in lake water quality would prove the systems were doing a good job. However, while it is felt that the current City regulations, as delineated in OUSWMM, are probably the most comprehensive set of guidelines in the State of Florida, it must be pointed out that much of the City had already been developed prior to their promulgation in January, 1984. Very little consideration was given to the quality aspects of stormwater runoff or even the predevelopment/post-development quantity impacts. Much of the damage to the surface waters has been done. Short of a major retrofitting effort on a City-wide basis, the detrimental aspects of those pre-1984 systems will continue to plague the City. On the other hand, development continues and the new regulations appear to be slowing the degradation of our receiving waters which development would be causing.

Perhaps the most important result of the City's program is the new sense of public awareness regarding the impacts of stormwater runoff. The City of Orlando has chosen to publicize its problems associated with runoff and has received a great deal of public support as a result. The development community, while not enamored with the more stringent requirements, have been surprisingly cooperative in attempting to meet the basic intent of the regulations. The public has been cooperative in practicing good stormwater techniques relative to their own activities such as fertilizing, maintaining shoreline vegetation, litter control, etc.

Bouyed by this show of public support, City Council has been generous with stormwater related funding for research, experimental projects and the identification of BMPs for a variety of projects city-wide.

The City is presently involved in planning a research project to monitor existing pollution control facilities for stormwater to ascertain their longevity, efficiency, cost effectiveness, and appropriateness. Some systems work well in the laboratory or immediately after emplacement only to stop working in a short period of time in the field. The City and its consultants will examine those systems which are non-functional to determine the cause. Other systems that have been put into the ground may or may not be working as designed. The research will determine the effectiveness of the BMPs being used. Results of the study will recommend the appropriate use of stormwater management technology based on soil conditions, water table elevation, costs of installation and benefits received.

Possible Solutions to Existing Stormwater Management Problems

The City has investigated the problems and possible solutions regarding stormwater management. A listing of the major problem areas follows:

Problem - Receiving waters in built-out sections of the City are being degraded by stormwater.

Possible Solution - Retrofit existing stormwater facilities to accommodate water quality considerations as well as flood control.

Problem - Retrofitting is expensive.

Possible Solution - Investigate funding alternatives.
*Municipal Service Taxing Units (MSTUs) may be established in neighborhoods which require upgrading of stormwater facilities.
*Stormwater Utilities may be used for capital improvements of stormwater facilities. The City is studying a plan to charge landowners a utility fee based on the amount of impervious area on their property. Owners can have their utility fee reduced by providing on-site retention of stormwater. A beneficial side effect of this program would be the resultant improvement in quality of the runoff, especially in the built-out areas.

Problem - Even with proper funding the land is not available in built-out neighborhoods for retention/detention systems.

Possible Solution - Buy property, raze houses to create needed storage capacity and pollution control on a more regional basis.

Possible Solution - Build treatment facilities beneath the surface in road rights-of-way, medians, etc.

Possible Solution - Use public land as much as possible in providing retention/detention. Possible locations may be City parks, institutional land, rights-of-way.

Problem - Existing private development stormwater management facilities may not be functioning as the designer intended.

Possible Solution - The City is considering using a code enforcement procedure to require owners to properly maintain facilities.

Possible Solution - The City is commissioning research projects to measure efficiencies and appropriateness of pollution control devices and techniques.

Problem - Private developer has left the area, and improperly functioning facility is used by multiple owners.

Possible Solution - City requires perpetual maintenance agreement.

Possible Solution - The City may take over the maintenance of the facility.

Problem - There is not enough manpower to make sure the facilities are operating properly and to visit every single one on a regular basis.

Possible Solution - Wait for complaints from residents to cue maintenance crews to clean out the facility.

Possible Solution - Use innovative funding techniques to pay for a stormwater maintenance program.

The list of problems and possible solutions could grow, but the point to be raised is that the whole process is circular. There is more than one solution to any problem, and one solution may raise more problems. We do not know all the answers and hope that we can generate more questions with the above discussion.

The City's Ongoing Water Quality Programs

In the summer of 1983 the City commissioned a study to ascertain the quality of its 82 lakes and to develop a strategy to enhance those most in need. Two indices were used to rank lakes most in need of enhancement: (1) the Florida Trophic State Index (TSI) conceived by Brezonik (1982) and (2) the Beneficial Use Index conceived by the consulting firm of Dyer, Riddle, Mills & Precourt, Inc. The lakes were sampled for chemical and physical constituents, the water was analyzed, and Brezonik's multivariate regression equations were used to assign each lake its TSI score. A Beneficial Use Field Form (BUFF) was used by investigators to assign the sociological worth to each, or its Beneficial Use Index. Here lakes were judged on their amenities, public access and aesthetic condition. The lakes were further categorized based on their drainage basin to lake surface area ratio, number of stormwater pipes outfalling to the lake and condition of an influencing, upstream lake. All the information was utilized to rank each lake and develop a short list of possible candidates for enhancement (Palmer et al 1984).

This strategy of objectively selecting lakes for enhancement was needed because the City's resources are limited. The City is responsible for maintaining 44 lakes. In the past the City responded to citizen complaints about lakes. The result was that those lakes surrounded by the most vociferous neighborhood associations received the attention. This is not always an accurate indication of relative need for lake enhancement. The results of the study showed those lakes most in need of treatment, and pilot projects were established to begin lake management programs. The City has been implementing the recommendations of the Lake Assessment Study (1983). The City maintains over 22 miles of shorelines and has been involved in a systematic program to replant shorelines with native vegetation. Over the last year the City has expended approximately $75,000 for its revegetation program.

The City has divided its pollution control efforts into three types. A Type I PCD is a simple screening device designed to collect trash and leaves coming from a stormwater outfall to a lake. Over 200 screening devices have been installed. Type II PCDs are those designed to control sediments and their attached pollutants. The City has installed systems with elaborate series of screens to filter sediment, underground exfiltration pipes, and catch basins. Type III pollution control is responsible for removing nutrients from the stormwater. Examples of Type III PCDs include retention basins and exfiltration systems.

City crews conduct routine maintenance of storm inlets and manholes. Street sweeping, especially in March when our oak trees lose their leaves, is an effective tool of pollution control for lakes. The City has a professionally run aquatic plant control program. The City has two airboats equipped for large scale spraying for the control of hydrilla, algae etc.

Some lakes are undergoing aeration treatment. The effectiveness of this program is being monitored. There is definitely a "perceived" benefit acknowledged by the general public.

The City has utilized aluminum sulfate (alum) in an effort to control phosphorus in a pilot lake. The alum was used to bind the dissolved phosphorus and clarify the water. Aquashade (TM) was then used to control recurrence of blue-green algae blooms in the lake. This has proven to be an inexpensive method of lake management. However, this treatment requires continued monitoring and reapplication of the chemicals as a function of the amount of stormwater a lake receives. It would be infeasible to completely reverse the eutrophication process in urban lakes. Therefore, a lake management strategy must be used to control chemical and physical conditions, to plant native aquatic species, to encourage wildlife habitat and thus enhance aesthetic qualities for the populace.

The City relies on drainage wells to remove stormwater in much of its developed area. There are about 200 drain wells within the limits of the City. About one-third of the wells are used for lake level management. Thus, the drain wells prevent lakes from flooding nearby neighborhoods. Another one-third of the wells receive runoff directly from residential areas. With no pretreatment of the stormwater prior to its entering the well. About 28% of the drain wells receive untreated runoff directly from a combination of commercial, industrial and high density types of land uses (Palmer 1984).

The wells discharge the stormwater into the Floridan aquifer, a porous limestone formation from which comes 90% of the drinking water supply. Figure 3 is a conceptual drawing of a drain well. Note that there is an upper as well as lower producing zone. The arrows to the left in the Figure 3 indicate the piezometric surface of the aquifers. Under the conditions shown water could flow through a leaky aquitard from upper to lower Floridan. Most of Orlando's drainage wells are seated in the upper and water supplies for the City are taken from the lower Floridan aquifer. Many supply wells in the County are seated in the upper Floridan, however.

The U.S. Geological Survey published a report by Joel Kimrey in 1978 which stated that water pumped from the Floridan aquifer near drain wells showed no chemical ill effects of the discharge. Biologically, there were higher counts of bacteria found in the ground water near wells than in the area of the control wells. There is a need to know more about the fate of pollutants in the aquifer. There have been no new wells dug by the City or placed in the City since 1968.

The City of Orlando has budgeted $200,000 to date to develop and implement a plan of action to study the chemical and biological makeup of the water entering drainage wells in an effort to satisfy state-wide requirements. The City will be going several steps further than the law requires, however, to investigate the feasibility of closing a well based on criteria of flood control need and basin diversion capabilities. Investigations will be made into the pretreatment of stormwater for pollution control prior to its discharge to

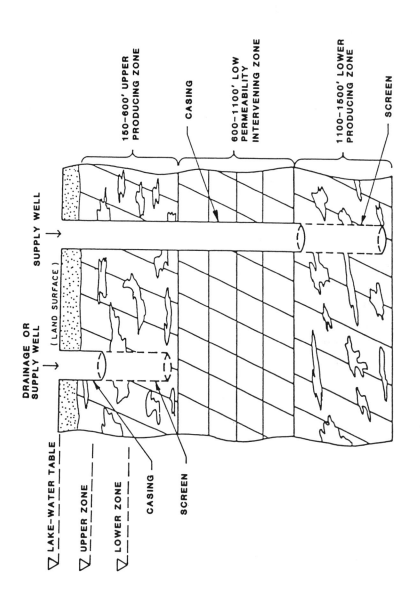

FIGURE 3   CONCEPTUAL DRAWING OF A DRAINWELL

a well. Action will be taken then to pretreat drain well influent for as many sites as possible. This effort is tied to a list of problems concerning land availability in existing neighborhoods. The City will be researching the effectiveness of sediment control inlets and will emplace the best designs into the storm sewer systems draining to wells.

The City of Orlando is committed to the wise use of its water resources. The management of stormwater presents a complex problem given the limited technology available to solve it. The public is conscious of the quality of the receiving waters for runoff because of their recreational and aesthetic amenities to living in Central Florida. The City has made the pledge to stay in the forefront of the application of a comprehensive stormwater management approach to solving the problems unique to the area.

Literature Cited

Brezonik, Patrick. 1982. Development of a Trophic Index Scheme to Rank Florida Lakes. Florida Department of Environmental Regulation.

Kimrey, Joel. 1978. Preliminary Appraisal of the Geohydrological Aspects of Drainage Wells, Orlando Area, Central Florida. USGS Water Resources Investigation 78-37

Orlando Drain Well Monitoring Plan. 1984. Dyer, Riddle, Mills & Precourt, Inc., Carla Palmer, Project Manager

Orlando Lake Enhancement Program, Assessment Study. 1983. Dyer, Riddle, Mills & Precourt, Inc., Carla Palmer, Principal Investigator

Orlando Urban Storm Water Management Manual. 1984. Dyer, Riddle, Mills & Precourt, Inc., Russell Mills, Principal in Charge

Palmer, C.N., M.P.Wanielista, R.L. Mills, G. Nicolson, R. Haven. 1984. A Screening Methodology for the Selection of Urban Lakes Enhancement. In Lake and Reservoir Management. EPA 440/5/84/-001

Wanielista, Martin P. 1978, Stormwater Management. Quality and Quantity. Ann Arbor Science Publishers, Inc. 377 pp.33

Stormwater Regulatory Program in Florida

by: Eric H. Livingston[1]

ABSTRACT

Nonpoint sources, especially urban stormwater, are responsible for
the majority of the pollutant load entering Florida surface waters.
To protect and manage the state's invaluable water resources, the
Florida Department of Environmental Regulation developed a
regulatory program for the control of nonpoint sources. The
Stormwater Rule established a performance standard for the treatment
of stormwater which is based on two properties of stormwater, annual
storm frequency distribution and the first flush of pollutants. The
rule's basic objective is to achieve 80-95 percent removal of
stormwater pollutants before discharge to receiving waters.
Periodic program evaluation has led to rule revisions and proposed
stormwater legislation to enhance the rule's effectiveness. Major
problem areas have included assurances for long term operation and
maintenance of stormwater systems, retrofitting of local government
master systems and enhancement of BMP efficiency to achieve
theoretical levels of pollutant removal. The program's thrust is
evolving to a watershed management concept that strives for
comprehensive stormwater management which emphasizes regional
facilities and more natural BMP's such as wetlands.

INTRODUCTION

Section 208 of the Clean Water Act required states to control
nonpoint sources of pollution generated by agriculture, forestry,
mining, urban, construction and other activities. To accomplish
this objective, the Florida Department of Environmental Regulation
and twelve local designated agencies received millions of dollars in
Section 208 grants to assess the extent of the state's nonpoint
pollution problem and to develop technical and administrative
methods of treatment and control. In Florida, most of the funds
given the designated 208 agencies for nonpoint source assessment
were used for urban stormwater problems, as most of the designated
agencies were located in heavily populated areas. The Department
took responsibility for investigating agriculture and forestry
activities statewide, and developing a management strategy for
controlling nonpoint sources of pollution from those activities.

[a]Presented at the June 22-27, 1986 ASCE Urban Runoff Quality
Seminar held in Henniker, New Hampshire

[1]Environmental Administrator, Nonpoint Source Management Section,
Florida Department of Environmental Regulation, 2600 Blair Stone
Road, Tallahassee, Florida 32301

Stormwater runoff has been recognized for the past decade as a cause of water quality degradation. In Florida, rapid urbanization, with its associated land clearing and paving of pervious areas, has accelerated the problem recently. While some amount of runoff from rainfall is a natural occurrence, the volume and rate of runoff and the accompanying pollutant loads increase as the amount of paved, impervious surfaces increases. Stormwater flowing over roofs, streets, lawns, commercial sites, industrial areas and other permeable and impermeable surfaces transports many pollutants into surface and ground waters. Rain washes sediments from bare soil, motor vehicles' heavy metals, oils and greases deposited on streets and parking lots, nutrients from fertilized lawns and crops, and coliform bacteria from animal wastes into receiving waters.

Recognition of such problems, along with the availability of federal funds, led the Department to begin drafting regulations to control stormwater in the late 1970's. No new legislative initative was undertaken since Florida's existing environmental laws authorized the Department to prevent water quality degradation from pollution sources. The first official state regulation specifically addressing stormwater was adopted in 1979 as part of Chapter 17-4, Florida Administrative Code. Chapter 17-4.248 was the first attempt to control by regulation this source of pollution that, at the time, was not very well understood. Under Chapter 17-4.248 the Department based its decision to order a permit on a determination of the "insignificance" or "significance" of the stormwater discharge. This determination seems reasonable in concept; however, in practice, such a decision can be as variable as the personalities involved. What may appear insignificant to the owner of a shopping center may actually be a significant pollutant load into an already overloaded stream.

In adopting Chapter 17-4.248, the Department intended that the rule would be revised when more detailed information on nonpoint source management became available. About one year after adoption, the Department began reviewing the results of research being conducted under the 208 program. Such research determined that stormwater discharges were responsible for over half of the pollution load entering Florida waters and, in many watersheds, stormwater discharges accounted for all of the pollutant load. In addition, stormwater associated pollution is responsible for:

1. 80 to 95% of the heavy metals loading to Florida surface waters;

2. Virtually all of the sediment deposited in state waters;

3. 450 times the suspended solids going to receiving waters and nine times the load of BOD_5 substances when compared to loads from secondarily treated sewage effluent; and

4. Nutrient loads comparable to those in secondarily treated sewage effluent discharges.

THE RULE MAKING PROCESS

Recognition of the water quality problems caused by nonpoint
sources, especially urban stormwater, led Florida to begin revising
regulations for their control in 1980. The Department had several
major goals in developing a regulatory program. First, the rule
should be easily understood and as unambiguous as possible. Second,
the rule should provide applicants encouragement to use appropriate
stormwater management practices by offering exemptions from
permitting, or general permits. Third, the rule should establish a
clear performance standard of the level of treatment for which to
aim. And fourth, the rule should recognize that stormwater
management involves the coordination of water quality and water
quantity aspects. Therefore, the rule should provide a mechanism
for the Department to delegate stormwater regulatory authority to
water management districts already regulating the flood prevention
aspects of stormwater.

To begin with, the Department established a stormwater task force
with membership from all segments of the regulated and environmental
communities. The rule's development took a little over two years,
required more than 100 meetings between Department staff and the
regulated interests and the dissemination of 29 official rule drafts
for review and comments. As might be expected, the process involved
numerous compromises in developing final rule language which became
effective on February 1, 1982. Since adoption, the rule has been
reviewed regularly to ensure that it remains current with the
rapidly changing stormwater management state-of-the-art and to
correct any problems with its treatment requirements or
administration. The rule was revised in 1983. In more recent
revisions the Department has established performance standards for
incorporating isolated wetlands into comprehensive stormwater
management systems to promote more natural stormwater management
with less intensive operation and maintenance needs. In addition,
these revisions made consistent treatment requirements for point and
nonpoint source discharges and promoted more innovative and
comprehensive stormwater management throughout a watershed.

STORMWATER RULE STANDARDS

The overriding standards of the Stormwater Rule, Chapter 17-25,
Florida Administrative Code, are the water quality standards and
appropriate regulations established in other department rules.
Therefore, an applicant for a stormwater discharge permit must
provide reasonable assurance that stormwater discharges will not
violate state water quality standards. Because of the potential
number of discharge facilities and the difficulties of determining
the impact of any facility on a water body or the latter's
assimilative capacity, the Department decided to establish a rule
based on performance standards.

The performance standard is a technology-based effluent limitation
against which an applicant can measure the proposed treatment
system. If an applicant can demonstrate treatment equivalent to
that provided by the systems described in the performance standard,

then the applicant is presumed to be able to meet the applicable water quality standards. The actual performance standard is the retention or detention with filtration of the runoff from the first one inch (2.54 cm) of rainfall or the first one-half inch (1.27 cm) of runoff, whichever is greater. Projects that meet this performance standard and the rule's other design standards can receive a general permit allowing construction within 30 days after filing a notice. Over 90% of all stormwater facilities are approved with a general permit thus helping an applicant avoid possible delays associated with the review of a full permit application.

TECHNICAL BASIS FOR THE ORIGINAL PERFORMANCE STANDARD

To provide reasonable assurance, the performance standard is built around two properties of stormwater: the annual storm frequency distribution and the "first flush" of pollutants. Based on long term rainfall records, statistical distribution curves have been established that describe the variability in intensity and duration of individual storm events. An average of nearly 90% of all storm events that will occur in any region of Florida during a given year will produce one inch (2.54 cm) of rainfall or less (Anderson, 1980). Also, 75% of the total annual volume of rain will fall in storms of one inch (2.54 cm) or less.

The first flush of pollutants refers to the highest concentration of stormwater runoff pollutants that characteristically occurs during the early part of the storm, with concentrations decreasing as the runoff continues. Concentration peaks and decay functions will vary from site to site depending on land use, the pollutants of interest and the characteristics of the drainage basin.

These two properties of stormwater led to the selection of the first one-half inch (1.27 cm) of runoff as the performance standard for sites less than 100 acres (40 ha) in size. Florida studies indicated that for a variety of land uses the first half-inch (1.27 cm) of runoff, when projected to annual loadings, contained 80 to 95% of the total annual loading of most pollutants (Wanielista, 1977). However, first flush effects generally diminish as the size of the drainage basin increases and as the percent impervious area decreases because of the unequal distribution of rainfall over the watershed and the additive phasing of inflows from numerous smaller drainages in the larger watershed. Florida studies indicated that as the drainage area increases in size above 100 acres (40 ha) the annual pollutant load contained in the first one-half inch (1.27 cm) of runoff drops below 80% due to the diminishing effects of first flush in stormwater from larger watersheds (Wanielista, 1979). As a consequence, the performance standards for projects larger than 100 acres (40 ha) is the treatment of the runoff from the first one inch (2.54 cm) of rainfall.

Stormwater treatment is generally accomplished either through retention or detention with filtration. Retention, by definition, requires the diversion of the prescribed amount of stormwater to a separate treatment area with no subsequent discharge of the diverted water to surface receiving waters. Pollutants are removed during retention principally by preventing discharge of polluted water using percolation through soil and settling as the treatment mechanisms. Therefore, retention results in nearly total treatment of the diverted water. Detention facilities are typically on-line systems where all of the stormwater from a site passes through the treatment pond and is subsequently discharged to surface waters. The Stormwater Rule requires that discharges from detention ponds be passed through a suitable filter material, typically two feet (60 cm) of natural soil or mixtures of sand, soil and gravel, to remove pollutants. The resultant treatment removes suspended materials and that fraction of the dissolved pollutants in stormwater that are found in association with particulate materials.

An applicant can also use other best management practices, alone or in combination, that provide equivalent treatment. However, these stormwater management systems must be permitted by other than a general permit.

STORMWATER PROGRAM EVALUATION AND EVOLUTION

Since the adoption of the Stormwater Rule in 1982, the Department periodically has reviewed its implementation with respect to meeting the rule's water quality objectives and staying current with the very dynamic stormwater management technology. The evaluation process has included review of permits issued by water management districts which have been delegated stormwater permitting; field inspections of constructed systems; water quality monitoring of permitted systems; Department sponsored investigations of BMP effectiveness; and regular discussions with the regulated community and other state and local agencies. These evaluations led to revisions of the Stormwater Rule's design and performance standard in 1983 and 1985; the legislative authorization to use certain isolated wetlands for stormwater management in 1984; and a comprehensive stormwater legislative initiative in 1986.

The major problem areas that have arisen since the Stormwater Rule's implementation, and which are areas for future rule revisions and legislation include:

1.   Assuring the long term operation and maintenance of stormwater management systems. Since stormwater management systems are designed to provide water quality and flood protection benefits for the life of a project, it is imperative to develop an institutional means by which to assure system operation and function. Presently, property owner associations typically are identified during permitting as the operation/maintenance entity yet they typically do not have the administrative, legal, financial or technical capabilities to do the job. The proposed stormwater legislation would require local governments to either accept stormwater systems for operation/ maintenance or perform annual inspections and pursue code enforcement for those systems in need of maintenance.

2. The actual field efficiency of BMP's versus the theoretical
    efficiencies that were used to establish the rule's performance
    standards. The basic objective of the rule is to achieve
    80-95% pollution removal on an annual basis, yet some BMP's,
    especially filtration mechanisms, are much less efficient. A
    comprehensive research program is now underway to verify
    removal effectiveness of systems permitted and constructed
    under the rule.

3. The design, construction and maintenance of filtration systems
    which are typically used in areas with flat terrain and high
    water tables. Besides the problems of maintenance, filter
    systems have also presented a design and operation problem.
    Many filter designs simply do not provide sufficient hydraulic
    head for them to function in many parts of Florida. Just as
    retention systems will not function properly and are prohibited
    except in locations with highly permeable soils, side bank
    filtration systems probably should also be prohibited in many
    areas of the state. However, since these areas typically have
    high water tables and tight soils thus prohibiting retention
    systems also, an effective alternative to filtration that can
    receive a general permit needs to be established.

    The Department has initiated actions to establish a general
    permit for wet detention systems to achieve this objective.
    However, many design variables such as residence time, shape,
    depth, inflow/outflow patterns, percentage of vegetated
    littoral zone and pollutant removal effectiveness of littoral
    zone aquatic plants must be determined. We hope that current
    research and a review of existing information will allow us to
    develop a general permit for wet detention systems by this
    fall.

4. The grandfathering of existing stormwater systems, especially
    local government master systems, which were built only for
    flood control purposes during the "dig it, ditch it and drain
    it" era. The retrofitting of existing systems that are causing
    water quality degradation is a major objective of the proposed
    stormwater legislation. The selected approach is to prioritize
    watersheds based on their ambient water quality and existing
    stormwater discharge loadings, target the worst problem areas
    for BMP implementation and systematically address these areas
    over a 25 year period. Redevelopment projects would also be
    required to include on-site stormwater management systems
    unless the local government had established a master stormwater
    plan that provided for stormwater treatment by regional
    facilities.

5. The promotion of a piecemeal approach to stormwater management
    which relies upon individual on-site stormwater management
    (CDM, 1985). A major concern with this approach is that the
    combined effects of individual randomly located detention
    basins can increase downstream peak flows and cause channel
    scouring. A second concern is the lack of integration between

the water quality and water quality aspects of stormwater
management. In addition, the proliferation of numerous small
on-site systems increases the opportunities for system failure
from a lack of maintenance and increases the difficulty of
enforcing operation and maintenance requirements.

For several years we have promoted a watershed management
approach. Such an approach can provide for comprehensive water
resources management that incorporates appropriate controls for
point and nonpoint sources. By looking at an entire watershed,
opportunities exist for point-nonpoint trade offs,
implementation of master stormwater management systems that
include on-site and regional facilities and improved land use
planning which recognizes the importance of floodplains and
other natural stormwater management areas and sets these areas
aside to serve their natural functions.

6.   The lack of coordination between state, regional and local
       governments with stormwater management responsibilities. The
       proposed stormwater legislation seeks to enhance
       intergovernmental coordination by requiring local governments
       to establish master stormwater management plans which
       are integrated into regional plans implemented by the water
       management districts. The legislation hopefully will also
       establish a minimum flood protection level (i.e., 25 year
       storm) which will form the basis for the local and regional
       master plans and end the difficult problem of varying levels of
       flood protection established by different local governments
       within the same watershed.

ADMINISTRATION OF THE STORMWATER RULE

Under the Florida Water Resources Act of 1972, the Department of
Environmental Regulation, a water quality agency, serves as the
umbrella administering agency delegating authority to five regional
water management districts whose primary functions historically have
been related to water quantity management. Therefore, a second
objective in developing the Stormwater Rule was to coordinate the
water qualtiy considerations of the Department's stormwater permits
with the water quantity aspects of the Districts' surface water
management permits. Consequently, the Department delegated
stormwater quality permitting to the South Florida Water Management
District in 1982, to the Southwest Florida Water Management District
in 1984 and to the Suwannee River and St. Johns River Water
Management Districts in April 1986. These districts have the
resources to administer and have requested delegation of the
program.

These two aspects of the stormwater program have allowed the
Department to administer it with an extremely small work force.
State revenues fund six engineers in our district offices around the
State to process stormwater applications and review management
plans. However, they also have responsibility for other permitting
programs and for inspecting stormwater facilities for compliance. A

Section 205(j) grant from EPA funds the six-person Nonpoint Source Management Section located in the Department's Tallahassee headquarters. This staff provides technical assistance to the stormwater engineers and to local governments in establishing or improving their existing nonpoint source control programs. The Section is also responsible for nonpoint source water quality management planning activities and public education programs, coordinating the nonregulatory agriculture and silviculture nonpoint source control programs, coordinating the onsite wastewater treatment program, managing nonpoint research programs, and developing revisions to the Stormwater Rule.

CONCLUSION

Florida's stormwater management program has provided important water quality protection benefits during its first few years, especially given the tremendous rate of growth and development that has occurred since the regulatory program was implemented in 1982. Program evaluation has identified problem areas and fostered rule revisions and legislation to enhance the efficacy of the Stormwater Rule. During the next few years emphasis will shift to comprehensive stormwater management throughout a watershed and the use of isolated wetlands and multipurpose wet detention regional facilities to provide for more natural stormwater management with lower operation and maintenance costs.

ACKNOWLEDGEMENTS

I wish to thank Mimi Drew for her review and constructive comments on the draft manuscript and Alisa Gregory for typing the draft and final manuscripts.

APPENDIX I. - REFERENCES

Anderson, D.E. (1980). "Evaluation of Swale Design", thesis presented to the College of Engineering, University of Central Florida, Orlando, Florida, in partial fulfillment of the requirements for the degree of Master of Science.

Camp, Dresser and McKee, Inc. (1985). "An Assessment of Stormwater Management Programs". Final report submitted to the Florida Department of Environmental Regulation.

Wanielista, M.P. (1977). "Manual of Stormwater Management Practices". Final report submitted to the East Central Florida Regional Planning Council.

Wanielista, M.P. (1979). Stormwater Management Quantity and Quality. Ann Arbor Science, Ann Arbor, MI.

Commentary on Papers on Institutional Issues

L. Scott Tucker*

The objective of this review is to comment on the four papers presented during this session and to highlight institutional issues about which I am particularly concerned. Institutional issues are critical in terms of successfully implementing a technically oriented program or any program for that matter. What exactly are institutional issues? They represent the management side of the equation as compared to the technical side that this conference has addressed thus far. Given the technical basis and justification, one must then outline a program of implementation if that is what the decision makers decide to do. Institutional issues include defining the objectives, developing a program of implementation, adopting laws, promulgating regulations, defining and agreeing upon who should do what and to whom, financing the program of implementation, monitoring the effectiveness of the program, maintaining facilities constructed as a result of the program, and modifying the program of implementation as experience is gained.

The four papers presented in this session deal with the implementation of programs at the three levels of government; i.e. local, state and federal. Local levels of government represent the most varied of situations. There are 945 cities with a population of over 25,000, and 3,049 counties in the United States. In addition there are councils of governments, water and sanitation districts, and drainage and flood control districts. All of these local governments have different problems, different responsibilities, varying degrees of ability to pay, varying degrees of expertise, different priorities, and different authorities. Their interests, approaches, concerns, and knowledge, about stormwater quality problems vary immensely. The states represent a lower number, 50, but the variance between them may be as great. There are states, albeit very few, that have aggressive stormwater management programs. Florida and Maryland are two such states. There are many other states that have no programs at all.

Then there is the federal level. Programs passed by Congress through such laws as the Clean Water Act (CWA) mean federal agencies must be involved. The Clean Water Act has spawned several programs including the Section 404 permit program and the National Pollution Discharge Elimination System (NPDES) program. These programs have become institutional problems because they work from the top down. The federal government decides what should be done, then they promulgate

*   Executive Director, Urban Drainage and Flood Control District, 2480 West 26th Avenue, Suite 156B, Denver, CO   80211

regulations, then they try to implement them. States and local
governments try to react, comply, resist, or whatever.

The focus of this conference is on urban runoff quality, the focus
of this session on institutional issues, and the four papers direct
their attention to this combination.

Local Level

There are relatively few comprehensive stormwater management
programs at the local level. However, local governments commonly deal
with storm drainage systems and stormwater detention is a common
requirement. The two papers presenting the local viewpoint are
therefore exceptions rather than the rule. They represent programs that
are innovative and unusual. One is for Bellevue, Washington and the
other is for Orlando, Florida.

Bellevue, Washington. Bellevue, Washington was one of the first
cities to create a Stormwater Management Utility which has been in
operation for over ten years. The organization is called the Bellevue
Storm and Surface Water (SSW) Utility. At its initiation, flooding and
erosion were the main problems, but today its focus is shifting to
non-point water pollution with the extension of the NPDES permit program
to municipal separate storm sewer systems. Bellevue's program is
summarized in the paper titled "Bellevue's Urban Storm Water Permit and
Program," by Pam Bissonnette.

The Bellevue experience is important because it demonstrates how
local governments, can and will solve problems if they are the ones to
identify them. In this case the SSW Utility was formed out of a citizen
and City commitment to preserve its network of streams and lakes. It
was established in 1974 and given a mission to manage the storm and
surface water system in Bellevue to maintain a hydrologic balance, to
prevent property damage, and to protect water quality; for the health,
safety and enjoyment of citizens; and the preservation and enhancement
of wildlife habitat. The underlying precept is to use the natural
surface water drainage system to provide for conveyance and disposal of
stormwater runoff.

Bellevue has the institutional framework through the SSW Utility
for implementing a stormwater management program. What came first,
however, was the commitment of the City to a comprehensive program.

With that commitment and with the Utility as the institutional
framework a comprehensive program has been developed. Their program has
four major elements: administration, regulation, maintenance and
operations, and a capital improvement program.

Money is always a necessary ingredient for a successful program.
The major source of revenue for the utility is from a service charge
based on contribution of runoff to the drainage system. All properties,
including undeveloped and publicly owned property pay the service
charge.

Initially the focus of the Utility was on runoff quantity problems (volume, velocity and erosion). Because of the Utility participation in the National Urban Runoff Program (NURP), however, they began to shift more attention to the water quality control aspects of its mission. The NURP study helped Bellevue to identify their stormwater related water quality problems and to develop a program to address those problems.

In addition to NURP the National Pollutants Discharge Elimination System (NPDES) permit requirements for municipal separate storm sewers has had an impact on the Bellevue program. Here Bellevue is ahead of most all if not all other cities in the United States in that they are negotiating a NPDES permit with the State of Washington. The NPDES permit requirements is a whole issue in and of itself and is also discussed later in the "Federal Level" section. The critical point to be made is that Bellevue because of its institutional arrangement is able to respond in a positive manner to a national program (NPDES) that is in my opinion fatally flawed.

The basic tenants of the Bellevue permit program are:

(1) Local governments are made accountable for the quality of the runoff discharged within their jurisdiction.
(2) Water quality standards, similar to those for sanitary waste water effluent, are to be achieved.
(3) The initial thrust is to accomplish these standards through source control programs and the Utility's operation and maintenance program.
(4) Should source controls and operation and maintenance practice be insufficient to achieve water quality standards over a reasonable period of time (e.g. five years). Then treatment of urban runoff may be required.

When Bellevue receives its NPDES permit from the State it will be a general permit for all stormwater outfalls within the City. The State of Washington has the authority to issue general permits which other states may not have. This is a critical point because issuance of a general permit will avoid the needs to obtain an individual permit for every outfall of which there are several thousand within the 25 square miles of Bellevue.

As a part of the permit requirement, Bellevue proposed criteria for determining where and when water quality standards will apply. The draft permit will require sampling at five receiving water sites for water quality standards compliance and at the three representative outfall sites for compliance with stormwater effluent standards. Bellevue has been able to reduce the monitoring requirements to what they feel is a reasonable level.

Again, Bellevue is way ahead of everyone else. Final regulations still have not been promulgated by EPA regarding stormwater NPDES permits, but Bellevue is about to receive theirs from the State of Washington.

Bellevue's permit would presumably serve as a prototype for other cities in Washington. The point is repeated, however, that Bellevue is the exception, and I do not know of another city that has received or is about to receive a NPDES permit for all of their stormwater discharges. Also, try to imagine every other city and county in the United States implementing such programs; a seemingly impossible task. Bellevue is to be commended.

Orlando, Florida. Orlando has developed a stormwater management program called the OUSWM program (Orlando Urban Storm Water Management). The program has been developed within the existing city institutional structure and is coordinated by the City Engineer through the Orlando Bureau of Engineering. The OUSWM program is a relatively recent commitment that came together in a total program in January 1984 when the City adopted the "Orlando Urban Storm Water Management Manual" (OUSWMM). The manual addresses urban flooding problems, erosion and sediment control, water quality, and pollution abatement. The OUSWM program is a major effort by the City to control stormwater from a quantity and quality perspective for new developments. It is the objective of the program to provide hydrograph attenuation, water pollution control, and innovation in stormwater management. The responsibilities of meeting these objectives lie with developers, but the program also encourages retrofitting stormwater management facilities in existing neighborhoods where responsibility rests with the City.

The State of Florida has adopted aggressive stormwater management rules that have placed requirements at the local level. The State's program is summarized more completely in the next section. The state of Florida is unique in its stormwater management requirements, and this has provided for the development of stormwater management programs at the local level that respond to the State's rules. As a quick summary from a local perspective stormwater management is regulated in Florida by two main agencies; the Florida Department of Environmental Regulation (FDER) and regional water management districts. The FDER is the prime agency and they require that best management practices (BMP's) be used in all new developments. The FDER requires retention, or detention with filtration. The FDER is in the process of delegating stormwater facility permitting to regional water management districts. The new regulations coming from the regional water management districts are more specific with respect to design and performance standards than those of the FDER. Orlando, and presumably other Florida cities, therefore, seem to be responding to both a local recognition of stormwater problems as well as state mandated programs.

Even with a strong state and regional stormwater program, local governments are still the primary focus of activity. In Orlando development plans are submitted with design analysis to the Bureau of Engineering. The Bureau evaluates the plans, works with the developer and when satisfied issues permits. A key point, however, is that the developer is not through at this time, and additional permits must be obtained from the regional water management district and the FDER.

The problem of who should own stormwater management systems, which is common to other local governments, is a concern in Orlando as well. The City is in a state of flux as to whether the City should own the facility or if the developer should in some way retain responsibility.

The City recognizes that they are the entity that ultimately cares the most about the performance of the systems. However, from a practical standpoint it is nearly impossible for them to access all retention/detention or exfiltration systems in the City. The City has accepted the responsibility for maintenance of a number of retention/detention systems where access can be provided. They remain resistive, however, to accept facilities for maintenance where access is difficult such as when facilities are located at the back of a development totally surrounded by private property.

Orlando does not have a revenue that is collected for the purpose of stormwater management activities such as is the case in Bellevue. Some local governments have levied fees for drainage purposes but such fees are still the exception rather than the rule. Financing is such a critical element of effective stormwater management programs, that the trend will be for more and more local governments to assess drainage fees of one type or another.

In Orlando the cost for stormwater management facilities in new developments is borne generally by developers. Zeno and Palmer note in their paper that the cost for maintenance of each facility, if borne by the City, may be prohibitive. Work would entail mowing and silt removal, and exfiltration systems would need to be changed regularly. At this time the City has not developed a policy on who should bear the cost of operation and maintenance, and if the City is to assume O & M responsibility then a means for financing will have to be developed.

The importance of financing and a dedicated revenue source is illustrated by this rather typical dilemma. Requirements for detention/retentions systems are placed on developers, but no sure way of maintaining the facilities is in place. If a long term effective maintenance program is not developed then most of the detention/retention facilities will fall into a state of disrepair over a period of time and eventually become ineffective and will be burdens on the community.

Orlando does charge a fee for permit application for stormwater management systems. These fees are applied toward the cost permit application review, facility inspection, and issuance of a certificate of occupancy.

Zeno and Palmer make the point that Orlando has no routine process of monitoring stormwater systems. Facilities are examined only in response to citizen complaints and observation by City personnel during normal work activities. This does not provide for routine inspection of all facilities. They note that the sheer number of facilities which would have to be examined during a rainfall event and again 72 hours later would make it impractical to use city personnel.

The State of Florida is giving cities the authority to establish municipal service taxing units(MSTU). The City could use this authority to raise revenue for stormwater facility maintenance. The bureaucracy would have to be established to handle it, however, which would include manpower, machinery, expertise, and administration.

It is difficult to document the results of Orlando's program. Much of the City was developed prior to the adoption of the OUSWMM, but the new regulations appear to be slowing the degradation of the receiving waters. The program has developed a new sense of public awareness and support regarding the impacts of stormwater runoff. The City Council in turn has supported stormwater related funding for research, experimental projects, and the identification of BMP's for a variety of projects citywide.

Orlando has a general commitment to water quality problems that may impact their many lakes. This has provided the motivation for a locally defined program to enhance the quality of its 82 lakes through a variety of efforts. Meeting state requirements has provided the incentive to develop and implement a plan of action to study the chemical and biological makeup of the water entering drainage wells.

Orlando has a comprehensive and aggressive stormwater management program. The program is partly driven by state requirements and partly by locally identified problems. A dedicated revenue source is not available as of this time, however, and this will limit the program as stormwater issues compete for City funds with police and fire protection, parks, potholes, etc.

State Level

There are relatively few comprehensive stormwater management programs at the state level. The same observation was made with regard to the local level. This can be expected since local levels of government derive their authority from state governments, and interest at the state level is reflected at the local level. An exception is the State of Florida that has an aggressive stormwater water management program which is addressed in the paper by Eric Livingston entitled "Urban Stormwater Management in Florida: An Evolving Regulatory Program."

A key point which has been made before and is made again is that state and local governments will act to address a problem when they decide it is in their best interest to do so. At the state and local level program costs have to be carefully considered compared to program benefits and weighed against other needs, because they are close to the citizen's pocket book. State legislatures, county commissioners, and city councils must appropriate money for the programs they impose. Therefore, a program is not implemented unless there is true need and unless the program can be sold to the local citizens.

Unfortunately this is not true at the Federal level. Laws are passed placing burdensome requirements on state or local governments, but Congress many times makes no fiscal linkage with their action. Florida has determined that non-point sources, especially urban stormwater, are responsible for the majority of the pollutant load entering Florida surface waters. The freshwater resource is very important to Florida so they adopted a regulatory program for the control of urban non-point sources. What is good for Florida, however, is not necessarily what is good for every state. Urban Stormwater is not the primary source of pollution of surface waters in other states and similar regulatory programs would not make sense in all other states. From an institutional perspective it is important that problems be identified and solved at the level of government that is paying the bill, and not forced from the Federal level down such as is the case with the NPDES program. States and local governments cannot solve all problems and they must allocate their finite resources to the problems they feel are the most important to their citizens. Florida's program is a good program because they want to do it, and not because the Federal government is making them do it.

Because of recognition by Florida of the water quality problem caused by non-point sources, they decided to develop a regulatory program. This was possible under existing legislation because Florida's existing environmental laws authorized the Department of Environmental Regulation (FDER) to prevent water quality degradation from pollution sources. The situation in other states is different so enabling legislation may or may not be necessary, may or may not be complicated, and may or may not be possible.

The major goals in developing the Florida regulatory program were, first, to have the rules as understandable and unambiguous as possible. Second, the rules should provide applicants encouragement to use appropriate stormwater management practices by offering exemptions from permitting through general permits. Third, the rule should establish a clear performance standard of the level of treatment for which to aim. And fourth, the rules should recognize that stormwater management involves the coordination of water quality and water quantity aspects. From an institutional point of view, Florida was able to take advantage of regional water management districts that were in existence and already were regulating the quantity aspects of stormwater.

Another important decision the FDER made was to establish a stormwater task force and involve all segments of the regulated and environmental communities. The rules development took a little over two years, required more than 100 meetings between FDER staff and the regulated interests, and the dissemination of 29 official rule drafts for review and comment. The rule has been regularly reviewed and revised since adoption to keep it up to date and to correct problems. Involvement of a wide spectrum of interests and a process for changing are important ingredients to a sound program.

Because of the potential number of discharge facilities and the difficulties of determining the impact of any facility on a water body or the latter's assimilative capacity, the FDER decided to establish rules based on performance standards. The actual performance standard is the retention or detention with filtration of the runoff from the first one inch (2.54 cm) of rainfall or the first one-half inch (1.27 cm) of runoff whichever is greater. Projects that meet the performance standard can receive a general permit allowing construction to start 30 days after filing a notice. Over 90% of all stormwater facilities are approved with a general permit which points to the value of the general permit concept.

Florida's program, at least prior to the 1986 legislative session, required a permit for new construction only. Proposed legislation, however, is addressing existing stormwater systems, and if and how they should be handled. Retrofitting detention or retention systems is particularly difficult because of the cost. Florida is considering a program that will target the worst problem areas for BMP implementation and systematically address these areas over a 25 year period. Redevelopment projects would also be required to include on-site stormwater management plans.

One of the major problem areas that has arisen is assuring long term operation and maintenance of the detention and retention systems. This problem was also identified in the Orlando paper, and is a problem that has been continuously identified by local public works people in connection with randomly placed developer constructed detention facilities. Changes being considered are to require local governments to either accept stormwater systems for operation/maintenance or perform annual inspections and pursue code enforcement for those systems in need of maintenance. A potential institutional conflict may exist between the state and local governments, because this requirement could be expensive to implement by the local governments. The old issue of how to pay for mandated programs surfaces again.

The FDER has also noted a lack of coordination between state, regional and local governments with stormwater management responsibilities. The FDER is supporting legislation that would require local governments to establish master stormwater management plans which are integrated into regional plans implemented by the regional water management districts. Again, the conflict of how much it costs and who pays for plan development may be an issue.

Federal Level

Programs addressing municipal separate storm sewer discharges have been addressed at the Federal level by EPA through the Nonpoint Sources Branch of the Criteria and Standards Division. The approach to the problem from the responsible Federal agency's point of view, EPA, is presented in Athayde's paper titled "Urban Nonpoint Sources, The Environmental Protection Agency Point of View." For all intents and purposes EPA has considered urban runoff as a non-point source of pollution. This makes sense and tracks logically with the nature of the problem and certainly the basic driving source of urban runoff which is rainfall, an obvious non-point source.

Unfortunately, EPA's logical approach does not track with the Clean Water Act (CWA), PL92-500, originally passed in 1972, and court decisions that have been made since its adoption. Basically the courts through suits brought by environmental special interest groups have held that just because there are too many storm sewer discharges to effectively "permit" them that is not an excuse for not doing it anyway. Translated, the court is saying that do it regardless, even if it does not make sense, because that is the law. These court decisions have forced EPA to think of municipal separate storm sewers as point sources of pollution and develop permitting systems pursuant to the NPDES program. The EPA is trying to adapt the NPDES program, which was originally designed for process sources, to municipal separate storm sewers. Professionals familiar with the problem know that it will be practically impossible to have individual permits based on effluent standards for every storm sewer in America. EPA knows this well but is being forced by the perfidities of the system to apply the NPDES permit program to municipal separate storm sewers.

The EPA after adoption of the Clean Water Act in 1972 did not place a high priority on separate storm sewer systems. From an institutional resource allocation point of view this made sense. They concentrated enforcement on Section 402 of the Act, which required all point sources of pollution to obtain NPDES permits, on industrial or process point discharges and publicly owned wastewater treatment plans.

After the litigated issues were decided in 1977 in favor of the plantiff and against EPA, EPA had to begin developing a strategy for "non-point" point sources. From 1978 to 1983 EPA in partnership with the U.S. Geological Survey assisted 28 cities nationwide to evaluate urban runoff quality problems and to evaluate control technologies. The overall goal of the Nationwide Urban Runoff Program (NURP) was to develop information that would help provide local decision makers, states, EPA, and other interested parties with the information needed to define the extent of the problem and to decide what to do about it. It was also hoped that the information base could be used to make sound policy decisions on federal, state, and local involvement in urban stormwater runoff quality and its control.

The federal institutional framework is still struggling with what to do about urban runoff. The law says to get permits which infers eventual treatment if necessary for every separate municipal discharge in the U.S. The federal agency in charge of implementing the law, EPA, is at a loss as how to proceed because of the inherent weakness of what is required in the law. The environmental special interest groups are poised on the side lines ready to file more law suits against EPA or local governments if they feel the program is not heading in what they consider is the right direction. Local governments have finally realized that while this flailing is taking place at the federal level, that they are the ones who will be most directly impacted. The cost to local governments would be enormous if treatment of stormwater is required; the cost will be enormous just to get permits for every urban storm sewer discharge.

The NURP project found that pollutant concentrations in urban runoff vary considerably, both during a storm event, from event to event at a given site, and from site to site within a given city and across the country. It also found that the effects of urban runoff on receiving water quality are very site specific. They depend on the type, size, and hydrology of the water body, the designated beneficial use and the pollutants which affect that use, the urban runoff quality characteristics, and the amount of urban runoff dictated by local rainfall patterns and land use. The importance of these findings is that urban runoff may be a problem, but it is not necessarily a problem, and also that effluent or end-of-pipe standards are not appropriate for stormwater. Storm events are of relatively short duration and their impact on the receiving water may be an issue for only a short period of time. Wet weather standards are needed.

Athayde notes in his paper that urban runoff has traditionally been considered by EPA as a local matter. The Agency "still considers it a local matter because if anything gets done, it will be local governments doing it. Our approach is based on this premise. Urban runoff comes under the Nonpoint Source Program within the Agency." While EPA may be saying this, the fact is that stormwater programs will be forced on state and local governments by EPA. Where states and local governments have decided for themselves to address stormwater quality, they will be ahead of the federal juggernaut. However, for the large majority of states and local governments the NPDES permit requirement will be an unwelcomed and unneeded burden. It does not appear that any federal funding will accompany the permit requirements and local governments will be considered as violators until they obtain permits.

The EPA strategy and NPDES requirements seem in some ways to be at cross purposes. Athayde noted that rather than undertake a new big money Federal non-point program, EPA believes that existing Federal, state, local, and private resources must be redirected to priority non-point problems. This approach is logical. However, the impact of the current NPDES permit requirements will be to concentrate all resources on the paperwork of preparing and processing millions of permits. Local governments on balance cannot afford to spend scarce and limited resources preparing permits and then additional resources doing whatever EPA requires them to do to get the permit. Also, urban stormwater runoff is considered by EPA as a non-point source (NPS) problem and Agencywide strategies are developed as a part of their NPS strategy. At the same time, the NPDES program is a point source program whose strategies are different than those for NPS problems. Consequently, EPA's thinking and strategy development processes are in terms of NPS "appropriate technology", but the Agency is headed toward a massive regulatory program based on point source problems.

Summary

The most important point to make in summary is that local and state governments can, will, and do solve pollution problems attributed to urban stormwater runoff if they perceive it as a high priority concern. Bellevue is an excellent example of a City making a commitment to stormwater management. Orlando is another example and there are other cities throughout the U.S. that have also taken positive steps on their own to address urban stormwater quality problems. It is noted, however, that this is the exception and not the rule at this point in time.

From an institutional perspective, stormwater quality management must be addressed at the local level. Also, local governments must be allowed to make the decision as to how much of their resources should be committed to stormwater quality management. Congress is blind to this concept at this time and is treating local governments with storm sewers as polluters and violators. Congress puts a municipality with a storm sewer in the same category as the discharger of a processed waste product. The Federal government can and should provide technical assistance and guidance, but their current approach is to apply the stick approach with no carrot; do it or else. Amendments are needed to the CWA that will recognize urban stormwater as a non-point source of pollution, and that will direct EPA to develop programs and strategies based on the nature of problems.

The states are in the middle somewhere. Municipalities are technically extensions of the states, but most states are reluctant to provide much in the way of guidance and leadership in the area of stormwater management. They consider it a local problem too. There are notable exceptions, however, including Florida, Vermont, Maryland, and California. But there are 46 other states with varying degrees of interest and understanding in stormwater quality problems.

Discussion of Session 5: Institutional Issues

I.   "Urban Nonpoint Sources - The EPA Point of View: (Speaker: Dennis Athayde)

Questions and Answers

1)   Q: if non-point source pollution control is a state problem, why is EPA driving the permit program so hard?

     A: its the law.

2)   Q: were ASWIPCA samples just urban?

     A: no.

3)   Q: if §319 is passed, will cities be able to get grants for treating stormwater?

     A: it will be State money, and consequently, it will be used for demonstration projects at the State's discretion.

4)   Q: how does EPA evaluate State programs such as Vermont's?

     A: gather data.

5)   Q: Comment: Stafford is the biggest obstacle to "retreats" in PL 92-500.

II. "Drainage Program Implementation by Drainage Utility" (Speaker: Pam Bissonnett)

Questions generally focused on the charges associated with the utility and the problems associated with selling such a program in a high tax district. Pam noted that Bellevue is a very affluent community and can therefore afford to be very environmentally conscientious.

III. "Stormwater Management and Regulation in Florida" (Speaker: Eric Livingston)

Questions and Answers

1)   Q: what are the boundaries of the districts?

     A: they are political boundaries.

2)   Q: when do detention ponds become water quality problems?

     A: detention ponds not considered state waters.

3)   Q: what about quantitative impacts of water quality
          measures?

     A: needs to be researched; Florida doesn't utilize models.

VI. "Development of Urban Runoff Program in Orlando, Florida"
     (Speakers: Carla Palmer and David Zeno)

     Points made during Question and Answer period:

     1)   don't treat if nature will do the job for free.

     2)   alum program costs $3,000/yr.

     3)   sediment traps should be used upstream of exfiltration
          systems.

     4)   life expectancy of exfiltration systems has yet to be
          determined.

Infiltration as a Stormwater Management Component

H. Earl Shaver*

This paper discusses the implementation of infiltration
practices in Maryland. The benefits of infiltration are briefly
discussed along with the regulatory background. Standards and
Specifications for Infiltration Practices have been developed and
provide a framework for proper design and construction.
Feasibility tests are presented along with appropriate design
methodologies. Experiences with implementation in Maryland are
discussed along with additional related research activities.
Some conclusions are also presented based on the efforts underway
at this time.

Introduction

Infiltration practices in Maryland are essential to the
stormwater management program as necessitated by State
legislation that was enacted in 1982. Prior to that date,
infiltration practices were used only at various locations, and
their effectiveness was seldom monitored. One essential element
of the 1982 State law required the Department of Natural
Resources to promulgate rules and regulations that establish
criteria and procedures for stormwater management in Maryland.
The rules and regulations had to indicate that the primary goal
of the State and local programs is to maintain after development,
as nearly as possible, the predevelopment runoff
characteristics. This requirement of the law effectively
mandates the control of the peak discharge rate, water quality,
and runoff volume and thus, the use of infiltration practices.

Benefits of Infiltration

The regulations require consideration of infiltration
practices on each proposed development because of the benefits
that they provide. These benefits include groundwater recharge,
low stream flow augmentation, water quality enhancement, and
reduction in the total runoff volume. Each of these benefits
help to negate the adverse environmental impacts resulting

*Department of Natural Resources, Water Resources Administration,
Sediment and Stormwater Division, Tawes State Office Building,
Annapolis, Maryland 21401.

from development and land use changes. The growing concerns
expressed by environmental groups over the decline in our aquatic
resources also prompted the use of infiltration practices to
mitigate environmental damages. The multiple benefits make these
stormwater management measures suitable for meeting the intent
and goals of maintaining the predevelopment runoff
characteristics.

Standards and Specifications

There was early recognition that design guidance needed to be
provided to consultants and regulatory agencies if infiltration
practices were to be utilized on a widespread basis. To that end
the Department developed the "Standards and Specifications for
Infiltration Practices" document which was the initial
comprehensive design document needed for the use of infiltration
practices for urban runoff management.

The purpose of the Standards and Specifications was to
establish minimum criteria for the design, review, approval,
construction, and maintenance of infiltration practices on land
being developed. The practices detailed in the document include
the following:

1. Infiltration Basin
2. Infiltration Trench
3. Dry Well
4. Porous Asphalt Pavement
5. Vegetated Swales with Check Dams
6. Vegetative Filter

To effectively design an infiltration practice, the following
site information is necessary: the textural character of the
soil horizons and/or strata units within the subsoil profile; the
location of seasonal high groundwater table; and the depth to
bedrock.

A number of feasibility tests can be performed to determine
if an infiltration practice may be constructed on a specific site
and the areal extent that it may be applied. These feasibility
tests include:

1. Soil textural classes with minimum
   infiltration rates that permit adequate
   percolation of stored runoff.

2. Maximum allowable ponding or storage
   time within the structure.

3. Available depth between the bottom of
   the infiltration practice and the
   seasonal high groundwater table or depth
   to bedrock.

4.   The topographic character of the site
      including the slope, nature of the soil
      (natural or fill), and proximity of
      building foundations and water supply
      wells.

Based on the soil textural classes and the corresponding
infiltration rates, a restriction is established to eliminate
unsuitable soil conditions. Soil textures with minimum
infiltration rates of 0.17 inches per hour or less are not
suitable for usage with infiltration practices. These unsuitable
soils include soil textures that have at least a 30 percent clay
content, making them susceptible to frost heaving and possible
structural instability, in addition to having a poor capacity to
percolate runoff.

The feasibility criteria for using infiltration practices may
also be based upon the concept of a maximum allowable ponding
time (Tp) for surface storage or a maximum allowable storage time
(Ts) within a subsurface stone aggregate reservoir. The maximum
allowable time will vary depending upon the storage mechanism of
each practice which governs the available storage volume within
the structure. The established maximum ponding and storage time
is a 72 hour period in which runoff within the structure should
be completely drained, with the exception of vegetative swales
which has a maximum ponding of 24 hours.

The maximum allowable time frame in conjunction with the
minimum infiltration rate (f) of the soil will dictate the
maximum allowable design depth (d_{max}) of the structure. The
maximum depth of an infiltration basin and a vegetated swale may
be defined as:

$$d_{max} = fTp \quad (1)$$

The maximum depth of an infiltration trench, dry well, and porous
asphalt pavement subbase will depend upon the void ratio (Vr) of
the aggregate reservoir and may be defined as:

$$d_{max} = \frac{fTs}{Vr} \quad (2)$$

The maximum allowable design depths for various soil textures and
ponding or storage times are given in Table 1 for the criteria in
equations 1 and 2. The portion of the table that is shaded
represents soil infiltration rates that are unsuitable (i.e.,
less than 0.17 inches per hour).

An additional feasibility criterion is the distance between
the bottom of the infiltration structure and the elevation of the
seasonal high groundwater table. This distance is important in
preventing the filling of the aggregate reservoir due to the rise
of the water table, rendering the structure ineffective. The

Table 1. Maximum Allowable Depths (Inches) of Storage For Two Criteria, Selected Maximum Ponding or Storage Times (Tp or Ts), and Minimum Infiltration Rates (Inches/Hour)

Criterion	Tp or Ts (hrs)	Soil Texture / f (inches/hour)										
		Sand	Loamy Sand	Sandy Loam	Loam	Silt Loam	Sandy Clay Loam	Clay Loam	Silty Clay Loam	Sandy Clay	Silty Clay	Clay
		8.27	2.41	1.02	0.52	0.27	0.17	0.09	0.06	0.05	0.04	0.02
f(Tp)	24	198	58	24	13	6	4	2	1	1	1	0
	48	397	116	49	25	13	8	4	3	2	2	1
	72	595	174	73	37	19	12	6	4	4	3	1
f(Ts)/Vr	24	496	145	61	31	16	10	5	4	3	2	1
(Vr=0.4)	48	992	290	122	62	32	20	11	7	6	5	2
	72	1489	434	183	93	49	31	16	11	9	7	4

(Hatched cells in the f(Tp) section — Sandy Clay Loam through Clay — denote unfeasible solutions.)

Note: Tp = Maximum allowable ponding time
Ts = Maximum allowable storage time
Vr = Void ratio
▨ = Values that are unfeasible solutions

Environmental Protection Agency criteria for onsite wastewater
treatment and disposal systems specifies that a 2 to 4 foot
distance should be provided between the bottom of the waste
disposal system and the water table or bedrock (EPA, 1980).
Thus, it is also recommended that infiltration structures be
located only in areas where the bottom of the structure will be
at least 2 to 4 feet above the seasonally high groundwater table
and/or bedrock.

The topographic conditions of the site, including the slope,
nature of the soil (natural or fill), and the proximity of
building foundations and water supply wells represent feasibility
factors that need to be examined prior to incorporating
infiltration structures on specific sites. If local health
authorities document existing problems regarding water supply
well pollution, infiltration shall not be utilized.

The maximum allowable slope will vary for each particular
practice and may restrict the use of infiltration practices on
steep slopes. The use of porous asphalt pavement and vegetated
swales, for example, requires a relatively level or gently
sloping area not in excess of 5 percent (20h:1v). All other
infiltration practices shall be located in areas where the slope
does not exceed 20 percent (5h:1v). The application of
infiltration practices on a steep slope increases the chance of
downstream water seepage from the subgrade and reduces the amount
of runoff which infiltrates into the soil.

Developments with a sloping and rolling topography often
require the use of extensive cut and fill operations. The use of
infiltration practices on fill material is not recommended due to
the possibility of creating an unstable subgrade. Fill areas can
be very susceptible to slope failure due to slippage along the
interface of the in-situ and fill material. This condition could
be aggravated if the fill material is on a slope and is allowed
to become saturated by using infiltration practices.

Building foundations should be at least 10 feet up gradient
from infiltration practices to prevent the possibility of
flooding basements. Additionally, infiltration practices
receiving runoff from commercial or industrial impervious parking
areas shall be located a minimum of 100 feet from any water
supply well. Other criteria included in the standards and
specifications are runoff filtering, spillway combinations,
vegetation, scheduling, excavation, sediment control during
construction, and maintenance.

The standards and specifications also present the design
methodologies for the sizing infiltration practices. The design
procedures are based on the Soil Conservation Service
methodologies for controlling the increases in discharge rates
either by storing the increased runoff depth due to impervious
land use or by reducing the contributing area by capturing the

entire runoff depth of a selected design storm. The stormwater
management policies in Maryland require the peak discharge rates
for a 2- and 10-year storm event (2-year only for the Eastern
Shore) to be unchanged after development. However, if the
increase in peak discharge cannot be managed due to limiting
constraints (i.e., maximum allowable depth), the infiltration
practice can be designed to capture the first flush of runoff.
The first flush is recommended to be 0.5 inches of runoff per
impervious area and capturing this volume will result in removal
of many of the waterborne pollutants.

There are a number of other factors that may limit the
practicality of infiltration practices on a specific site. Sites
having extremely high proportions of impervious surfaces and
sediment loads may require maintenance so frequently making the
usage impractical. Clogging of the soil pores will occur with
reconstruction of the practice the only maintenance alternative.
Another concern with maintenance that may limit the use of
infiltration is areas that may be subject to wind erosion.

Implementation in Maryland

Rules and regulations specifying the minimum content of local
stormwater management ordinances were promulgated in July, 1983.
These regulations apply to development of land for residential,
commercial, industrial, and institutional use, but do not apply
to agricultural land management practices. In addition to the
peak discharge criteria, exemptions, and minimum program
elements, the regulations contain a preferential list of
practices. The ranking of the practices on this list is
determined by the water quality benefits associated with each
practice with infiltration the preferred method.

Each local ordinance must require that stormwater management
plan be developed using stormwater management practices according
to the following order of preference:

1. Infiltration of runoff on-site;

2. Flow attenuation by use of open
   vegetative swales and natural
   depressions;

3. Stormwater retention (wet pond)
   structures; and

4. Stormwater detention (dry pond)
   structures.

Infiltration practices shall be used to reduce volume increases
to the extent possible as determined in accordance with
infiltration standards and specifications. A combination of
successive practices may be used to achieve the applicable

minimum peak discharge control requirements. Justification shall
be provided by the person developing land for rejecting each
practice based on site conditions.

The stormwater legislation required that local ordinances be
implemented by July 1, 1984, and contain the minimum criteria
established in the State regulations. Nine counties out of a
total of 23 counties had existing stormwater management programs
which pre-dated the State regulations, but all nine had to make
significant programmatic changes to comply with State
requirements. All of the existing local programs were directed
at controlling the quantity and rate of runoff with little or no
regard for the quality of runoff. The remaining 14 counties had
no previous stormwater management experience and a model
ordinance was prepared by the Department for approval and
implementation at the local level. Every county in Maryland now
has an approved stormwater management program in effect.

Obviously, implementation can only be effective if adequate
staffing is provided at the local level for plan review and
inspection. To facilitate the local efforts, the State provides
approximately $1.7 million per year to the local governments to
hire and fund plan reviewer and inspector positions. This is a
small allocation of funds on a statewide level, but it has
significant impact on overall program implementation. The
funding availability has conveyed the commitment by the State to
the stormwater management program and those jurisdictions
receiving funding are trying to properly implement stormwater
management at the local level.

The use of infiltration throughout the State has proceeded in
a relatively cautious manner. There have been several concerns
expressed regarding the use of infiltration for a number of
reasons:

1.   The pollution of groundwater through
      the entry of runoff into soil
      subgrade. Most existing literature
      indicates that the metals bind up very
      quickly with soil particles but
      additional research is needed.

2.   Premature failure of infiltration
      practices due to clogging of the
      surface filter cloth, or soil-stone
      interface. The prevention of sediment
      entry into the infiltration practice is
      imperative. Significant problems have
      been encountered during the site
      construction time period.

3.   Maintenance of these practices may be
      neglected or difficult to accomplish.

There have been problems in the use of infiltration to date.
Two primary problems encountered are poor construction techniques
and a lack of sediment control protection of the structure before
stabilization of contributory drainage areas has been
accomplished. Significant storage capacity is lost in the
reservoir before the infiltration practice is placed into use if
stringent sediment control is not implemented and maintained
until the entire contributory drainage area has been stabilized.
The surface layer of porous asphalt paving is prone to clogging
unless vacuuming is accomplished on a frequent periodic
schedule. The frequency of maintenance will obviously depend on
the amount of traffic movement at a specific site, but vacuum
sweeping is recommended at least four times per year. Another
major concern with the use of porous paving is the application of
road salts and its movement through the soil column to
groundwater. Little documentation exists regarding the effects
of road salts on groundwater.

The need for training and education of all individuals
involved with stormwater management is becoming increasingly
apparent, partiacularly with the use of infiltration practices.
Consultants, plan reviewers, inspectors, developers, contractors,
and the general public should have a greater understanding and
acceptance of the need for stormwater management and why proper
design and implementation are so important. Test procedures to
accurately identify the soils need to be established and required
for each infiltration practice installation. Initial planning
can be based on soils maps but on-site testing must be conducted
to verify soil suitability. To some degree the engineering
community resists change, and there has been a significant change
toward water quality control of stormwater management in
Maryland. As a result, the engineering community must also
redirect their aproach regarding the development of a management
plan to receive either local or State approval.

The lack of pertinent experience by plan reviewers and
inspectors is a problem because the program is still relatively
new. In many jurisdictions, plan reviewers need more experience
in hydrologic/hydraulic modelling and design review.

Inspectors are frequently unsure of how a practice should be
constructed or what a practice should look like in the field.
Significant effort in education and training needs to be
performed if the stormwater management program is to be
successfully implemented.

Research Efforts in Maryland

A three year joint agency study is currently underway with
the United States Geologic Survey to monitor the groundwater

impacts of infiltration practices. Monitoring will be
accomplished on five sites where infiltration practices have been
constructed. Two of these sites will be located on piedmont type
soils, two sites will be located on sites in the coastal plain,
and one additional site in the coastal plain will have porous
asphalt paving. Site selection is almost completed at this time
and well monitoring will commence this summer. Criteria will be
developed through this project that establishes a minimum
distance to the groundwater table to prevent potentially adverse
pollution impacts from infiltration practices.

A recently completed project involved quantifying the amount
of runoff that should be infiltrated to achieve significant water
quality benefits. Infiltration practices alone are generally not
capable of achieving peak discharge control, due to the large
increases in the runoff volume associated with urban
development. Approximately 90% of all annual rainfall events in
the State of Maryland are less than one inch and the "first
flush" of runoff from impervious surfaces transports large
pollutant loadings. Criteria was developed which recommends that
infiltration of the first 1/2 inch of runoff from impervious
surfaces should be provided for water quality benefits. This
minimum infiltration requirement in conjunction with other peak
control techniques will provide a good overall plan for site
control. In addition to the water quality benefits, there are
also significant benefits to stream baseflow enhancement by
maintaining a minimum level of infiltration. A stream which once
had perennial flow before watershed development often becomes
only intermittent as groundwater levels are lowered. This change
in streamflow character would cause a significant loss to
biologic diversity. Infiltration is one of the few tools that
may allow for maintenance of stream baseflow after watershed
development.

Another document recently completed is an Inspector's Manual
for Inspection and Maintenance of Infiltration Practices. Proper
construction and subsequent maintenance is so important and the
inspector is the individual whose actions provide guidance and
control during these phases. The Maintenance is a much more
critical issue for infiltration practices than for stormwater
detention practices. The major reason for cleanout requirements
is that sediment, suspended organic matter, oil/grease, and
debris accumulate in the small soil pores on the surface of the
practice, and may reduce or prevent infiltration. In comparison,
the same materials that can clog the soil surface of an
infiltration practice are typically removed through settling
within the detention basin's storage reservoir or entirely passed
through the outlet structure of the basin. For this reason, a
major objective of the inspector's manual is to emphasize that
infiltration practices, and upstream sediment and oil/grease
traps require much more frequent inspection and maintenance than

conventional detention basins. Local inspection programs have to
be restructured or expanded to accommodate these additional
maintenance needs.

Several other projects related to infiltration research are
also being accomplished at this time. Soil testing procedures
that will accurately indicate site suitability for infiltration
practices is being developed. A number of testing procedures
currently exist, but accuracy of these procedures needs to be
compared and assessed to determine infiltration suitability.
Another project evaluates qualitative differences in filter
mediums such as geotextile or sand filters for pretreatment of
runoff before entry of the runoff into the aggregate reservoir.
A commercial site in Maryland on which porous paving has been
installed has a surface layer that has become clogged. There is
no mechanism for the entry of surface water into the underlying
six feet of stone reservoir. A number of storm drain inlets will
be installed on the parking lot each having a different filtering
mechanism to remove particulates and transfer the runoff to the
reservoir base. These inlets will be evaluated over time to
evaluate their relative performance for proposed expanded use in
the future.

There are several other research projects underway at this
time which also are related to stormwater management. Criteria
is being developed related to the creation of shallow marsh
systems for urban stormwater control. The nutrient uptake,
wildlife benefits, and overall water quality benefits make the
future use of this practice very promising. Another project
being pursued is the consideration of the maximum discharge that
may be released from a stormwater management basin to protect
downstream channels from erosion. There is a growing concern
that the release of a two-year predevelopment peak discharge
after site development may not adequately protect downstream
channels due to the duration of flow and additional work done on
the channel boundaries.

Conclusions

The widespread use of infiltration practices in Maryland is
only a recent occurence. Implementation has not gone as well as
expected to date. This is primarily due to a lack of
understanding for the need of carefully designed plans and
construction techniques of these practices. Plans have been
designed and approved that will not function properly due to the
poor location of the practices on a given site or where the soils
are not appropriate. Thought has to be put into the design of
these practices for them to work properly in the field.

The other serious problem is that the prevention of sediment
entry into the practice cannot be overstated and has to be
repeated. These practices are not like detention basins and are

very prone to clogging or sealing due to sediment entry.
Stringent sediment control must be applied during construction
and maintained to allow for proper performance.

All of these items can be addressed in some degree through
education and training. Several individuals within the
Department have been allocated to develop training programs for
developers, builders, consultants, and regulators. Slide and
audio-visual programs are now being developed to address this
problem. Until these practices can be installed properly, we
will not be able to evaulate long term effectiveness and specific
maintenance requirements.

Continued maintenance presents another stage in the evolution
of these practices. Maintenance responsibility is generally
transferred to the property owner or homeowners association, and
is obviously not an adequate solution as experience has
indicated. In fact, a major consideration for using regional
stormwater management over specific on-site control is the
maintenance issue. Stormwater management provides public
benefits and is a State mandated program, so it is logical that
maintenance should be a public responsibility. The lack of
proper maintenance can effect everyone if declining performance
becomes a widespread problem.
    Proper implementation of stormwater management requires a
combination of strategies to be really effective. On-site
controls, in conjunction with regional practices would provide
the best overall blend for watershed protection, and in the case
of Maryland, protection of the Chesapeake Bay. A maintenance
infrastructure must be created and funded for both on-site and
regional practices. These practices are being built now, and
construction represents only the beginning of our
responsibilities related to stormwater control.

We are at the bottom of a staircase with one foot on the
first step. As our knowledge grows and the program evolves we
will climb the staircase, but we have to be careful and not
attempt to climb too quickly. The stormwater problem is not a
simple one and does not lend itself to simple solutions.

Effectiveness of Erosion Control

Byron N. Lord*

Abstract

Erosion control in the urban environment is addressed from the perspective of the mechanisms of erosion. The primary cause of erosion in urban areas is flowing water. Measures are identified to reduce the energy of falling rain and thereby reduce the soil displacement. Techniques and materials to hold soil particles in place are discussed as well as methods to reduce the volume and velocity of flow to reduce or prevent soil scour. The consequences of urban soil erosion are reviewed. Effectiveness is a function of local conditions, early and effective implementation of anti-scour preventive measures, and comprehensive stormwater management.

*Supervisory Environmental Engineer, Office of Engineering and Highway Operations Research and Development, Federal Highway Administration, 6300 Georgetown Pike, McLean, Virginia 22101.

The dictionary defines the process of erosion: "to diminish or destroy by degrees; to cause to deteriorate or disappear as if by eating or wearing away." Obviously, since matter can neither be created nor destroyed, erosion is merely the process of the transportation of matter. Further with regard to transport, Newton's first law of gravity states: "Every body persists in its state of rest, or of uniform motion in a straight line, unless it is compelled to change that state by forces impressed on it."

Erosion control can be viewed as a war. The battlefield is the soil and the battle is lost when the soil particles begin to move. From the beginning of time, man has struggled to overcome the forces of nature. Erosion is simply the result of nature's struggle to fulfill the laws of gravity.

Since the first raindrop formed, its fall out of the atmosphere on its journey to the seas, the process of erosion has been underway. Great mountains have been transformed into rich and fertile plains through the forces of wind and water. The birthplaces of civilization were founded on the fertile sediment floodplains of the world's rivers.

Early man watched the rain wash his top soil and crops away. When the topsoil was gone, he moved on to new fields. Over time, he discovered ways to prevent the rapid loss of his fields, as evidenced by terraces throughout the world to slow the flow of water and reduce erosion.

In North America, evidence exists of early Indian efforts to stop erosion. Later in 1769, George Washington was experimenting with ways to protect the fields at Mount Vernon from erosion. Patrick Henry, the author of "Give me Liberty or Give Me Death," after the revolution stated "since the achievment of independence, he is the greatest patriot who stops the most gullies."

Historically, the focus of erosion control has related to agricultural efforts. This is easy to understand because when the soil was gone, so was a farmer's livelihood. It is only in the last several generations that we have looked beyond farming to controlling erosion from other activities. Road building was one of the first non-farming activities to attempt to control erosion. Since about the 1900, the Bureau of Road Inquiry of the Department of Agriculture, now the Federal Highway Administration, was investigating ways to control erosion. Research is still underway looking for more effective and less costly measures. At the Federal

level, it is only since the 1972 Federal Water Pollution Control
Act, "Public Law 92-500," that erosion control in the urban environment became a national priority.

Although a significant difference exists between erosion control
for agriculture and the control needed, or used, in the urban
environment, the results of the erosion are similar.

1. Creation of unsightly rills, gullies, ditches, etc.

2. Loss of structural support due to undercutting and in collapse
   of buildings, walls, etc.

3. Deposition of sediment into lakes and streams.

4. Destruction of terrestrial and aquatic ecosystems.

5. Clogged storm sewers, ditches, catch basins, etc.

Although the principal cause of erosion in the urban environment
is the action of water, there are two primary mechanisms at work in
erosion (soil particle movement): the energy in falling raindrops,
and the scour of flowing water. The process of erosion control
focuses on the elimination or the ameliorization of these two
mechanisms.

It is probably appropriate to draw a distinction between the
control of erosion and control of sediments by again using the
analogy of a battlefield. Erosion control is akin to holding your
position in the face of the onslaught of the enemy's advance.
Sediment control can be viewed as attempting to halt the enemy's
advance after he has overrun your position and taken prisoners.
Perhaps this analogy will also help to give insight into the
effectiveness of erosion control. The focus of this paper is to
emphasize the effectiveness of specific erosion control measures.
However, a broader perspective is essential in the context of urban
nonpoint water pollution. If erosion is prevented from occurring,
soil is not lost and sediment is not produced. Thus the costs
involved in trapping or removing sediments are not incurred.
Simarilarily, the damages caused from the sediment or loss of soil
do not occur. Hence, damaged areas do not have to be restored,
repaired or abandoned. Erosion control is somewhat like the horse
shoe nail that was missing and resulted in the loss of a shoe, a
horse, a knight, a skirmish, a battle, a war and, utimately, the
kingdom.

As discussed earlier, erosion is a naturally-occurring process
which has been ongoing since time began. The purpose of erosion
control is not to change nature, but to reduce the rate as much as
practical and to prevent the causing conditions which enhance the
rate of erosion.

The principal sources of erosion in urban areas are industrial, commercial, and residential growth and development. Erosion increases as a result of soil disturbance due to construction, loss of vegetative cover and increases in runoff volumes and velocities due to reductions of pervious areas.

The key to effective erosion control is in understanding the causes of erosion and in implementing control measures as early as possible. From past experiences it is evident that an effective control program must be incorporated into the plan for growth and development in urban areas. In light of the explosive growth which has been experienced by many cities it is apparent this plan should be in place to direct the growth and to minimize the erosion. Effective stormwater management is a critical element in the control of urban erosion. To some, this may seem like putting the cart in front of the horse; everyone knows erosion control is just one part of stormwater management. The point to be made is that these activities go hand in hand, as will be seen as we look more closely at the techniques of controlling erosion.

There has been significant research into the subject of erosion controls. So much so that it is almost overwhelming when one undertakes a synthesis paper on the topic. However, there are common threads which run through most of the work. The effective-ness of specific measures varies greatly with local conditions (soil, climate, topography, construction quality, etc.). Cost information, including cost effectiveness, is extremely sparse and is frequently difficult to separate out.

Techniques to control erosion can be looked at from several perspectives, however, in keeping with the theme of promoting an understanding, the mechanisms of erosion may be categorized as:

o Reduction or absorption of falling raindrop energy
o Holding soil particles more firmly in place.
o Reduction of runoff volume.
o Reduction of runoff velocity.

Erosion control measures can be management, vegetative, physical, chemical, or design (including structural).

Depending on the area's rainfall, intensity can be severe and the ability for it to dislodge soil can be significant. If bare soil is subjected to falling droplets, it is not long before erosion begins. This is a problem which is common during nearly all construction activities. Management options to reduce soil loss include (1) the timing of construction to coincide with the dry season (if wind erosion is not severe); (2) soil stabilization, or covers; (3) the early establishment of vegetative cover; and (4) controlling the amount of area exposed at any given time. Proper exercise of these options through proper construction scheduling can be very cost effective.

Erosion control techniques to reduce falling raindrop energy may

be temporary or permanent. Paving or establishment of a
sound vegetative cover will provide long term mitigation. However,
paving may create future erosion. The use of mulches and mats of
varying materials (wood, paper, rocks, grids, etc.) may be
temporary or permanent. But, temporary soil cover is essential
during the early phases of vegetation establishment. Sod is a
very effective, instant vegetative cover which protects against
falling rain and scour. It is frequently used as a ditch and
swale liner.

The selection of plant material is highly dependent on local
factors. However, several basic threads exist between all sites.
Vegetation must be compatible with existing soil and moisture
conditions. In many locations, successful establishment of
vegetative cover may be as difficult as control of erosion.
Maintenance of vegetation is another important consideration.
Care should be taken to select vegetative material which is
compatible with the intended land use. Wherever possible native
species or adapted native species should be given preference over
introduced species.

Establishment and maintenance of selected plant material are
important to the success of a vegetative erosion control program.
Proper preparation of the soil including physical preparation,
chemical conditioning and irrigation may be critical to vegetation
success. Vegetation should be established as soon as possible.

Mulching is essential on most critical areas and slopes.
Mulches of organic material such as straw, hay or chips, are the
most popular methods for temporary erosion control prior to
vegetation establishment. Mulch is used to protect the seed from
excessive erosion prior to germination until the vegetation is
firmly established. Mulch should provide a favorable environment
for seed germination and establishment. Mulches also serve to hold
moisture and reduce evaporation to enhance vegetative growth.
Mulches may also be used prior to seeding or planting to protect
soils from severe erosion.

For longer term application, mulches of non-organic,
non-biodegradable materials, including fiberglass and various
plastic mats normally are effective. They protect seedbeds during
germination and early plant development, as well as providing
extended long-term reinforcement and anchoring of vegetation.
These materials include netting, meshes, and loose stringy products
which become securely enmeshed in the vegetation at and below the
surface in the rootmat.

More permanent forms of nonvegetative erosion control
are required when vegetation alone can not withstand
severe erosion forces or when it is not possible to
establish vegetation because of extremely poor soil or
climatic conditions, excessive traffic and other
factors. These measures include riprapping, paving,
fabric liners and grade control.

Erosion control fabrics can be used as an alternative to portland cement or asphalt concrete paving and rock riprap. This allows the establishment and maintenance of vegetation where nonvegetative stabilization is undesirable or aesthetically unpleasing. Erosion control fabrics are also used in conjunction with riprap and other liners to prevent loss of fines. Current applications of fabrics are limited to critical areas because of high installation costs. However, fabrics have been highly effective when used for silt fences and filter barriers.

Measures to more firmly hold soil particles in place include chemical soil stabilizers and vegetation. For the most part, use of chemicals for preventing erosion has been less successful than other measures. Chemical soil stabilizers are designed to coat and penetrate the soil surface and to bind soil particles together. Normally they are used to protect bare slopes, which are not exposed to traffic, from erosion prior or during establishment of vegetation. Chemical stabilizers may be used in lieu of, or in conjunction with, temporary mulches. Chemical stabilizers can be applied only to finely prepared surfaces. It is recommended prior to use that they be tested on small representative plots. As a general rule chemical stabilizers do not provide protection for as long a period of time as organic mulches. The roots of healthy vegetation, however, are excellent soil stabilizers. Chemical tacks have been effective in stabilizing mulches providing temporary cover while vegetation is being established.

Another subgroup of soil stabilizers is the on-site sediment control measures. Technically, these are not forms of erosion control, yet they represent a critical part of any construction erosion control program. The primary objective for use of these measures is to limit the travel of the soil during the period where in-place erosion control is not possible. These include filters, berms, brush, bales, fabrics, rock, etc. and the traps, small sediment basins, and dams. The advent of engineering fabrics has significantly improved on-site sediment management. An essential aspect of effective on-site sediment control is maintenance. All too frequently a measure is never cleaned out, repaired, or replaced after installation. A sound management program should include inspection and maintenance for all erosion control measures, both temporary and permanent.

Silt fences are composed of a synthetic filter fabric attached on a wire-support fence to slow water flow and filter sediments before they enter a stream or waterway. The silt fence is designed generally for conditions where only sheet or overland flow is expected.

Normally, they should not exceed 3 feet or the height at which they pond sufficient water to cause failure of the supporting fence. Fabrics should be continuous; where joints are essential, they should occur at support (posts) with sufficient overlap and proper sealing. Silt fences should be "keyed" into the soil to prevent undercutting or short circuiting. An important factor in the design and implementation of silt fencing is the concept of onsite control. Travel distance and flow buildup should be minimized. Silt fences must be inspected periodically for damage, and excessive accumulation. Sediment deposits should be removed when they exceed one half the height of the barrier.

Variations of the silt fence include other forms of filters such as brush and bales. These are barriers placed to impede the flow of surface runoff and to stop the transport of sediment, mulch or other surface protection. Normally they are used on moderate slopes for sheet flow or at the top of steep slopes. They are not as effective as fabric in trapping sediment. Both are susceptible to undercutting and short circuiting. Bales also have the additional problem of joints. Like fabric, both must be anchored in place to resist the forces of flowing water. Fabrics may be used in conjunction with bales to improve efficiency. However, bales may be more costly than fencing. Inspection and proper maintenance are again essential for proper operations.

Filter berms constructed out of any porous material which can be established in rows, banks, or mounds can also be utilized to reduce the energy of flowing water and to trap sediment. They are used around drain inlets, along the toes of small slopes, and adjacent down hill properties. Proper inspection and cleaning is essential to effective operation. The efficiency of these devices is generally low and their use should be confined to minimum transport distances and low velocity uses.

Sediment traps are small sediment basins. They include catch basins, small ponds, dammed ditches, check dams, etc. Their primary purpose is to hold the sediment-laden water for a sufficient period to allow sediment removal by sedimentation, settling. These are not to be confused with the sediment basin which is quite large and is designed to receive runoff from large areas. On-site sediment control is intended as just that "on-site." The accumulation of flow from large areas is beyond their scope. In general, most sediment traps are relatively ineffective. Conditions which improve their efficiency are very low flows and maximum holding times. Frequently a sediment trap may be effective for one runoff event. However, the next event will result in

the scour and removal of trapped sediment. It is obvious
frequent cleanout of sediment traps is required to obtain
optimum efficiency.

On-site design measures to reduce runoff volume include
infiltration basins, artificial and natural wetlands,
wide-flat vegetated swales, flow spreading, flow diversion
(cut-off ditches, down drains, etc.) and retention basins.
Infiltration basins and wetlands are measures which may
compensate for losses in pervious area. Properly designed
and operated, they are highly effective in reducing runoff
volume. Normally, both of these measures are beyond the
scope of on-site protection and are considered stormwater
management. Stormwater management is one of the more
effective ways to reduce the volume and velocity of flow
and to minimize scour. It can be effected by improving
the in-place infiltration or by minimizing the area of
imperviousness so as to eliminate or reduce peak discharges. It is beyond the scope of this paper to attempt
to discuss stormwater management, other than to
re-emphasize it is an essential component of urban erosion
control.

The objective of all these measures is to reduce the
amount of water leaving a site. Obviously reduced volumes
of runoff have a reduced capacity for eroding soil and
transporting sediment. Measures to reduce runoff volume
need to be a keystone in urban design and mitigation to
minimize and prevent erosion. Unfortunately, by its basic
nature, urban development tends to increase runoff by
reducing pervious area.

Diversion ditches are constructed at the top of cut
slopes to collect water from adjacent areas and to divert
it around the cut. They may also be used to intercept the
flow of water and convey it past unstable or highly
erodable areas. Materials to construct diversion
ditches will vary upon the slope of the ditch and the
magnitude of the flow. They may range from sod to steel or
concrete pipe. Diversion ditches may be temporary or
permament measures.

Retention basins are designed to hold major volumes of
water for extended periods. They are very efficient in
reducing runoff volumes as well as for removing sediment.
However, normally they also are beyond the scope of on-site
measures.

Reduction of flow velocity is frequently accomplished
with a reduction in volume. It is the velocity component
which is frequently responsible for erosion. Once again,
vegetation is an effective control measure providing a
roughness element to reduce the velocity of flow as well
as a protective cover and binding for the soil. However,

there are maximum velocities for which vegetation (grass)
is ineffective and erosion will take place.

Wide-flat vegetated channels, swales, reduce the
velocity of water by spreading out the flow. The vegetation serves as a further method of flow reduction by
increasing channel roughness. This increases the time for
infiltration to take place. The vegetation serves not only
to protect the channel from erosion but also as a trap to
catch sediment. Level spreaders may be installed in
channels to spread the channel flow to sheet flow, again
reducing velocity and increasing infiltration. These
devices may be a simple berm or terrance which collects
flow, levels it out and allows it to pass along over a
significantly increased area. It is important the surface
of level spreaders be protected from erosion.

Design measures to reduce velocity include: dams and flow-checks of
varying materials (rocks, logs, bales, etc.); structures; slope
flattening by earthwork; retaining walls, breast walls, etc.;
terracing; serration of slopes and the previously discussed
measures for reducing the flow volume.

The key to an effective erosion control program, whether for a
project or for an urban area, is comprehensive implementation.
This includes development of guidelines and regulations, inspection
and enforcement, promotion and training at the contractor,citizen,
community, country, State and county levels. Effective erosion
control must be tailored to the local area and conditions. It
must be part of a comprehensive program of urban stormwater
management and it must be a commitment of all those affected.

Runoff Controls in Wisconsin's Priority Watersheds

Robert Pitt*

Wisconsin's Priority Watershed Program

Wisconsin officials recognized years ago that fishable and swimmable waters would not be reached in many areas without an aggressive program for controlling urban and rural nonpoint sources of pollution (Konrad, et al., 1985). In 1978, the Wisconsin Legislature created the Wisconsin Nonpoint Source Water Pollution Abatement Program (nonpoint source program) as part of the Wisconsin Department of Natural Resources (WDNR) to improve and protect water resources threatened by nonpoint pollution in priority areas throughout the state. The nonpoint source program is a water quality program, with application of land management practices restricted to critical nonpoint pollution sources. The program is also implemented on a watershed basis, focusing the financial and technical resources needed to achieve an adequate level of pollution control on critical watersheds. Of the state's 330 watersheds, 130 (mostly located in the southern part of Wisconsin) will likely require comprehensive management activities to control nonpoint pollutants. A 25 year plan was developed in 1982 which would require the start-up of about eight or nine new watersheds per year by 1990. Since 1979, 29 priority watersheds have had pollution control activities started.

The mechanism for achieving control of critical nonpoint pollution sources is the voluntary installation of land management practices by landowners or operators, including municipalities. State cost share funds are available to eligible participants to help pay for installing approved pollution control practices. Cost share rates generally vary from 50 to 70 percent of the total cost. Structural urban runoff control practices usually have moderate to high effectiveness, moderate capital costs, but low private on-site benefits and low relationships to customary operating practices. They are therefore usually cost shared at the maximum 70 percent rate. State appropriations for the Wisconsin nonpoint source control program for the fiscal years 1979 through 1985 have totalled nearly $24 million, with less than 20 percent of this amount for state and local administration of the program and the remainder for cost sharing of control practices.

* Environmental Engineer, Nonpoint Source and Land Management Section, Wisconsin Department of Natural Resources, P.O. Box 7921, Madison, Wisconsin 53707

Counties, cities, and villages within each priority watershed implement the projects by providing project administration, technical assistance, and educational services. The state provides financial suppport needed by these local agencies to carry out their management responsibilities and for the cost sharing of the control practices, besides providing technical guidance and preparing the watershed plans. The watershed plans are prepared by the state with cooperation and reviews by local government agencies. They contain detailed analyses of the water resources objectives (existing and desired beneficial uses including the problems and threats to these uses), the critical sources of problem pollutants, and the control practices that can be applied within each watershed. The plans also include implementation schedules and budgets to meet the pollution reduction objectives.

Each plan requires one year to prepare, including the necessary fieldwork. Various field inventory activities are needed to prepare the plans, including aquatic biology and habitat surveys to identify existing and potential fishery uses, streambank surveys to identify the nature and magnitude of streambank erosion problems and to help design needed controls, field and barnyard surveys to supply information needed to estimate and rank their pollution potentials and to design farm control practices, and urban surveys needed to evaulate urban runoff pollution potential and its control.

After the plan is prepared and approved, a sign-up period of three years exists when cost share agreements can be prepared with eligible landowners. The practices must then be installed within a five year period.

Evaluation monitoring is now included as an important part of the newer priority watershed projects to measure the actual receiving water benefits of the installed practices. Although participation in the state funded program is voluntary, substantial pollutant load reductions (50 to 70 percent, depending on the pollutant and its source) have been achieved (Konrad, et al., 1985).

Most of the priority watershed projects with finished plans have been in rural areas and have therefore stressed agricultural nonpoint pollution. Three completed plans (Sixmile and Pheasant Branch Creeks in Dane County, the Root River in Racine, Waukesha, and Milwaukee Counties, and the Oconomowac River in Waukesha and Washington Counties) have included important urban components. The urban practices eligible for cost sharing identified in these three plans have included streambank protection, detention basins, and infiltration devices for existing urbanized areas. Construction site erosion controls are also usually required as a condition for a grant agreement in an urban area, but they are not eligible for state cost sharing.

A law was passed by the Wisconsin Legislature (1983 WI Act 416) that authorizes the Wisconsin Department of Natural Resources to develop five new priority watershed plans in

the heavily urbanized Milwaukee and Menomonee River Basins.
This law also requires the WDNR to prepare a state
construction site erosion control and stormwater runoff
control plan and model ordinance. The model ordinance will
be followed by all state agency construction and will be
used as a model for local adoption. The plan, currently in
draft form, also contains a comprehensive "manual of
practice" (Pitt 1986) that describes runoff control options
and guidelines for their design.

The Wisconsin nonpoint source program is therefore
becoming more heavily involved in urban runoff controls.
About $3 million of state cost sharing money has already
been allocated to controlling urban runoff in the three
watershed plans containing urban elements. At least $10 to
$15 million of state money will be used in the Milwaukee
projects, while another $10 to $15 million will be needed in
new urban projects that will begin in the next two or three
years. It is estimated that about $3 to $5 million per year
will be used by the nonpoint source program over the next 20
years in controlling urban runoff. The development of
efficient urban inventory and analysis procedures has
therefore become a high priority item in the nonpoint source
program. Extensive use of previous urban runoff research
results, the development of a source oriented urban runoff
model, and monitoring special urban runoff control
demonstration projects have all been recently used in the
nonpoint source program. Actual watershed assessment
monitoring activities will also be used over the years to
modify the tools currently being used to evaluate urban
runoff problems and to design needed controls.

Use of Available Urban Runoff Information and the
Development of Needed Analysis and Design Tools

Wisconsin is fortunate in that several major urban
runoff research projects have been conducted in the
Milwaukee area. A five year project conducted by the
Wisconsin Department of Natural Resources, sponsored by the
International Joint Commission and the U.S. Environmental
Protection Agency, began in 1973 to investigate urban runoff
characteristics at several locations in the Menomonee River
watershed in the Milwaukee metropolitan area (Bannerman, et
al., 1979). One of the U.S. EPA's 28 Nationwide Urban Runoff
Program (NURP) projects was also conducted in the Milwaukee
area by the WDNR over four years beginning in 1979
(Bannerman, et al. 1983). This local NURP project
investigated sources of urban runoff pollutants from several
land uses and the effects of street cleaning as an urban
runoff control measure. The U.S. Department of
Transportation (Gupta, et al., 1981) also has conducted
significant portions of highway runoff research projects and
the U.S. EPA (Field and Tafuri 1977) has investigated the
effects of different urban runoff and combined sewer
overflow controls in the Milwaukee area.

These studies have provided substantial information concerning urban runoff characteristics, potential receiving water effects of urban runoff, sources of urban runoff pollutants, and the effects of selected urban runoff controls for Milwaukee conditions. Many urban runoff projects conducted elsewhere, especially the NURP projects (EPA 1983), have also been very useful, especially in developing design procedures and specifications for urban runoff controls.

As mentioned previously, the WDNR is required to develop a state plan and model ordinance for the control of construction site erosion control and urban stormwater runoff. This plan (currently in draft form) includes a manual of practice that contains comprehensive discussions of performance expectations, recommended design features, design procedures tailored for specific Wisconsin urban runoff conditions, and design specifications for many control practices, most based on actual monitoring experience. The manual of practice also contains example design problems stressing the multiple water quality and flood control benefits of many of the practices. Besides the specific Wisconsin urban runoff projects listed above, several hundred other urban runoff studies conducted elsewhere were also reviewed in the development of the manual of practice.

Because relatively few urban runoff controls have been monitored in Wisconsin, a local demonstration project program was started as part of the nonpoint source program. Several urban runoff control practices (stressing infiltration devices and wet detention basins) are being constructed during early phases of urban priority watershed projects. These demonstration projects stress appropriate design, installation, and maintenance procedures, and are being monitored to documment construction and maintenance costs and control effectiveness. They will also be used as examples for display.

The model ordinance was developed using the Milwaukee monitoring data and literature information as summarized in the manual of practice. The ordinance contains specific construction site erosion control practices required for different sizes of construction projects. Stormwater criteria are also contained in the ordinance, but are mostly based on performance specifications in order to give the site developer flexibilty in selecting controls. Specific requirements are also given in the ordinance for certain developments, such as industrial areas or shopping centers. The manual of practice contains the required design procedures to allow different control programs to be evaluated.

A source oriented urban runoff model (Source Loading and Management Model, or SLAMM), is also being developed through partial funding of the Ontario Ministry of the Environment and the WDNR (Pitt 1984 and 1985). This model estimates urban runoff contributions from many individual source areas, depending on land use, development practices, and the presence of source area and outfall controls, based on the information contained in the manual of practice. It is being used in the development of the watershed plans and in evaluating alternative control program designs for specific watershed conditions.

Finally, it must be stressed that the manual of practice, the model ordinance, and SLAMM will be evaluated and modified as necessary based on future watershed project evaluation and demonstration project monitoring activities.

Urban Runoff Pollutant Sources

Urban runoff is comprised of many separate components that are combined at the discharge location before entering the receiving water. It may be adequate to consider the combined outfall conditions alone when evaluating the long-term, area-wide effects of many separate outfall discharges to a receiving water. However, if better predictions of outfall characteristics or source area controls are needed, then the separate components must be recognized (Pitt 1984).

Figure 1 is a schematic diagram showing the many component sources for an idealized residential and light industrial area. This diagram shows three major sets of components: impervious areas, pervious areas, and drainage system components. The drainage system captures sheetflows from many sources and begins at the roof gutters and downspouts. If these are discharged onto a paved area that in turn drains to the road gutter and storm drain inlet, such as (a) on Figure 1, they are considered "directly connected" to the storm drain system. Some roof drains are connected to the household sanitary sewer connectors and would not contribute to the storm drain flows. This practice is currently discouraged and many cities are actively disconnecting roof drains from the sanitary system. If the roof drains are discharged to pervious areas (b), much of their runoff flows would infiltrate and not contribute to the overland flow. There are also several types of roadside drainage components: paved or concrete gutters (e), sealed (paved) ditches (c), and grass swale ditches (d). Overland flow and street runoff enter these roadside drainages which direct the flows to drainage inlets. Some inlets may be over catchbasins (g1) that have more sediment accumulation potential than simple inlets. Catchbasins or inlets are also typically located in large paved areas (g2). Man-holes (h) are usually located in intersections where several connectors from close inlets are collected, and the flows drop to the storm sewerage (i). The storm sewerage then discharges to the receiving water (k) through an outfall (j).

The various source areas all contribute different amounts of flows and pollutants, depending on their specific characteristics. Impervious areas (shown as upper-case letters on Figure 1), such as paved parking lots, streets,

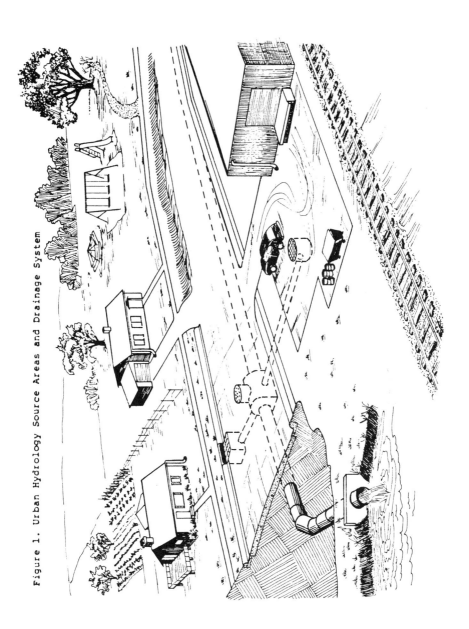

Figure 1. Urban Hydrology Source Areas and Drainage System

Figure 1. Urban Hydrology Source Areas and Drainage System (Cont.)

Impervious Areas
    A) Paved parking lot
    B) Footpath
    C) Road
    E) Driveway
    G) Sidewalk
    H) Rooftop
       H1) Residential composition shingle
       H2) Industrial tar and gravel
       H3) Residential tar and gravel

Pervious Areas
    1) Unpaved parking and storage areas
    2) Bare ground
    3) Grass
    4) Gardens
    5) Driveways
    7) Road shoulders
    8) Park dirt foot path
    9) Railroad right-of-way
    10) Soil near treated wood

Drainage System
    a) Connected roof drain
    b) Disconnected roof drain
    c) Seaded drainage ditch
    d) Grass swale drainage ditch
    e) Road gutter
    f) Roof trough
    g) Catchbasin
    h) Man-hole
    i) Sewerage
    j) Outfall
    k) Receiving water

driveways, roofs, and sidewalks, may contribute most of the
runoff materials during small rains. Pervious areas (shown
as numbers on Figure 1), such as gardens, lawns, bare
ground, unpaved parking areas and driveways, and undeveloped
areas, become important contributors of runoff flow and
pollutants for larger rains. The relative importance of the
sources is a function of their areas, their pollutant
washoff potentials and pollutant delivery, and the rain
characteristics. The outfall discharge is therefore made up
of different source area contribution mixtures, depending on
drainage area and the specific rain characteristics. Source
area control effectivenesses are also highly site and rain
specific.

Pollutant depositions and removals for the different
source areas are shown on Figure 2. Unconnected ("upland")
sources, such as rooftops and paved areas draining to
pervious areas, unpaved parking areas, driveways, streets,
undeveloped land, landscaped ground, and bare ground, are
affected by atmospheric deposition sources, and specific
activities carried out in those areas. If unpaved lots are
used for equipment or material storage, the soil can become
contaminated by spills and debris. Undeveloped land
remaining relatively unspoiled by activities can contribute
solids, organics, and nutrients if eroded. During rains,
runoff originates from pervious areas only during relatively
large events (after soil infiltration and surface storage,
or ponding, capacities are exceeded). The washoff of debris
and soil is dependent on the energy of the rain and the
properties of the material. Pollutants are removed from
these areas by winds, litter pickup, or other clean-up
activities. The flows and pollutants from these areas will
directly enter the drainage system, or, more likely, will
affect impervious areas that are directly connected to the
drainage system. Paved area sources include on-site
particulate storage that cannot be removed by usual
processes (rain, winds, street cleaning, etc.). Atmospheric
deposition, deposition from activities on these surfaces
(auto traffic, material storage, etc.) and the erosion
material from the upland unconnected areas are the major
sources of pollutants to the directly connected impervious
areas. The runoff from these connected areas enter the storm
drainage system, where sedimentation, or sewerage cleaning
may affect the ultimate discharges to the outfall. In-stream
physical, biological, and chemical processes affect the
pollutants after they are discharged.

It is important to know when the different source areas
become "active". If pervious source areas are not
contributing flows or pollutants, then the prediction of
urban runoff conditions is much simplified. The mechanisms
of washoff and delivery yields of flows and pollutants from
paved areas is much better known than from pervious urban
areas. In many cases, pervious areas are not active except
for rains greater than about five or ten mm. For small
rains, almost all flows and pollutants originate from

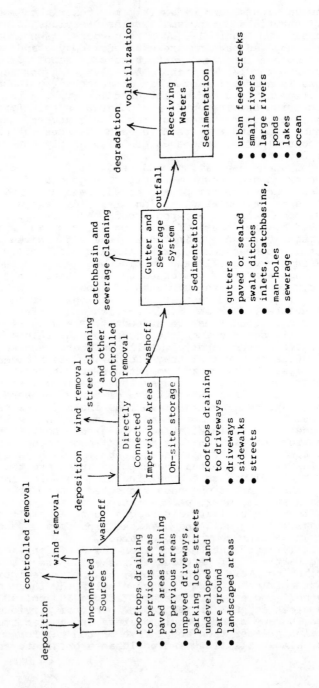

Figure 2.   Pollutant Depositions and Removals at Source Areas

impervious surfaces. In the upper mid-west, most rains are
less than ten mm in depth. However, these small events
generate only about 20 percent of the total annual runoff
volume. If the number of events exceeding a criteria are of
importance (such as for bacteria standards), then the small
rains are of most concern, because most of the runoff events
are associated with small rains. If annual discharges are of
most importance (such as for long-term effects), then the
larger rains are more important, because the large rains
produce most of the annual runoff volume. The specific
source areas that are of importance for these different
conditions varies widely, and modeling procedures that are
sensitive to source contributions as a function of rain
characteristics are needed.

Individual source area contributions can be modeled by
assuming the mass balance relationship (Pitt 1984):

$$L = \sum_{i=1}^{n} (A_i Q_i P_i W_i D_i)$$

for n total source areas
    where L is the total discharge of a specific
            particulate pollutant at the outfall
        A is the area of the source in the
            drainage basin
        Q is the total quantity of source area
            limited particulates (per unit area)
        P is the pollutant strength of the source
            area particulates
        W is the washoff fraction of the source
            area particulates
    and D is the delivery yield of the washed-off
            source area particulates to the outfall.

The Q parameter is applicable for particulate source limited
areas, but it is not applicable for non-source limited
discharges (such as from most pervious areas). The washoff
of particulates (expressed by the W parameter) from
impervious areas is usually source limited by armoring and
the lack of particulates that can be removed by rains.
Washoff of particulates from pervious areas is usually
controlled only by rain characteristics. The delivery of
pollutants to the outfall (reflected in the D parameter) is
determined by specific drainage characteristics and
controls. Source area controls (such as street and parking
area cleaning and erosion controls) can be used to reduce
the availability of particulates for washoff. Other controls
(such as grass swales and on-site infiltration trenches)
reduce pollutant delivery through infiltration of runoff
flows and associated pollutants. Overland flow across turf
areas (grass filter strips) reduce pollutant delivery
through infiltration and sedimentation.

The Source Loading and Management Model (SLAMM) was
prepared based on these source contribution relationships to

determine the relative contributions of different pollutants
from many source areas (such as industrial parking areas,
residential streets, commercial roofs, etc.). SLAMM also
evaluates the effects of various controls in reducing the
flow and pollutant contributions from the source areas and
from the complete drainage. Figure 3 is an example of a
SLAMM evaluation of total runoff volume source contributions
for a medium density residential area, and Figure 4 is a
similar example showing source area lead contributions for a
strip commercial area. These figures summarize the variable
importance of different source areas as a function of rain
volume. As an example, Figure 3 shows how pervious areas
contribute little runoff volumes during small rains, but
become more important during large rains. Knowing the
distrubution of flow and pollutant sources for different
rains is necessary when evaluating the effectiveness of
different source area controls for different families of
rains.

Summary of Source Area Control Performance

    One of the main functions of the Source Loading and
Management Model (SLAMM) is to predict the effectiveness of
various stormwater runoff source area, sewerage, and outfall
controls, while the Manual of Practice for the Control of
Construction Site Erosion and Stormwater Runoff Control
extensively documments performance expectations and design
standards based on many urban runoff research studies.
    Tables 1 and 2 summarize the performance of many
control measures for reducing runoff flow volumes and lead
discharges for a mixed residential/commercial area and for a
light/medium industrial area in Toronto (Pitt and McLean
1986). These tables are based on extensive land surveys and
outfall and source area monitoring conducted during 1984 and
1985. Almost 100 rains, 50 snowmelts, 200 source area
sheetflows, and 50 dry weather flow periods were monitored
in these two catchments. In addition, special washoff tests
and source area particulate sampling were also conducted.
This data was used in conjunction with extensive literature
information concerning the effects of many source area and
outfall urban runoff controls and the SLAMM model to obtain
estimates of the performance of these controls in the study
areas.
    These tables show the estimated control performances
for individual control practices that may reduce pollutant
or flow discharges by at least ten percent for any one flow
period. Most analyses of urban runoff controls only address
warm weather stormwater runoff. During this Toronto study,
dry weather flows (especially for many metals in the
industrial area) and snowmelt runoff were found to be very
important urban runoff pollutant sources. Based on actual
measurements of almost all of the annual flows and pollutant
discharges and as shown on Table 2, only about 30 percent of
the annual urban runoff flows occurred in the light/medium

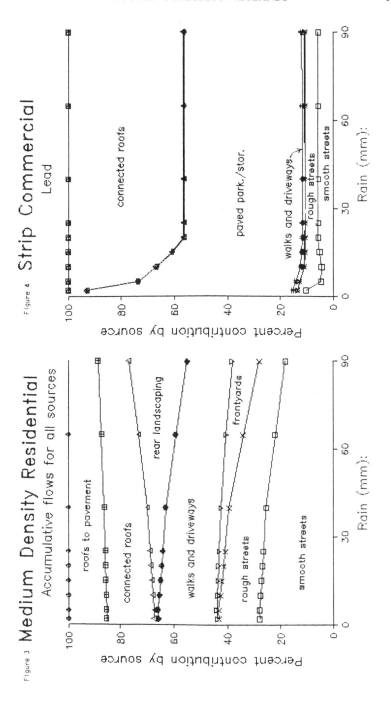

Figure 4 Strip Commercial
Lead

Figure 3 Medium Density Residential
Accumulative flows for all sources

Table 1 APPROXIMATE CONTROL EFFECTIVENESS FOR MEDIUM DENSITY RESIDENTIAL AREAS

Controls Applicable for Residential Areas	Flow					Lead				
	warm		cold		weighted total annual	warm		cold		weighted total annual
	base-flow	storm-water	base-flow	melt-water		base-flow	storm-water	base-flow	melt-water	
Street cleaning on smooth streets										
one or more passes/week	0	0	0	0	0	0	25	0	0	5
one pass/two weeks	0	0	0	0	0	0	23	0	0	5
one pass/month	0	0	0	0	0	0	20	0	0	4
one pass/two months	0	0	0	0	0	0	16	0	0	3
one pass/three months	0	0	0	0	0	0	13	0	0	3
Street cleaning on rough streets										
one or more passes/week	0	0	0	0	0	0	15	0	0	3
one pass/two weeks	0	0	0	0	0	0	12	0	0	2
one pass/month	0	0	0	0	0	0	10	0	0	2
one pass/two months	0	0	0	0	0	0	7	0	0	1
one pass/three months	0	0	0	0	0	0	6	0	0	1
Sidewalks										
total infiltration	0	0	0	0	0	0	0	0	0	0
Driveways										
total infiltration	0	16	0	4	4	0	35	0	9	14
Walkways										
total infiltration	0	0	0	0	0	0	0	0	0	0
Connected roofs										
total infiltration	0	18	0	5	5	0	17	0	4	7
redirect from pavement to lawns	0	14	0	4	4	0	14	0	4	6
Catchbasins										
clean twice per year	0	0	0	0	0	0	8	0	8	8
Roadside drainage systems										
grass swales	0	90	0	13	20	0	90	0	13	28
perforated drainage system	0	90	0	23	23	0	90	0	23	36
Main storm drain lines										
perforated pipe	90	90	90	90	90	90	90	90	90	90
Outfall wet detention basin										
0.8% of contributing resid. area	0	0	0	0	0	80	80	80	80	80
0.3% of contributing resid. area	0	0	0	0	0	60	60	60	60	60
% mass contrib. during period:	30%	17	20	33	100	0	20	0	80	100

Table 2 ESTIMATED CONTROL EFFECTIVENESS FOR LIGHT INDUSTRIAL AREAS

Controls Applicable for Light Industrial Areas	Flow					Lead				
	warm		cold		weighted total annual	warm		cold		weighted total annual
	base-flow	storm-water	base-flow	melt-water		base-flow	storm-water	base-flow	melt water	
Driveways										
total infiltration	0	0	0	0	0	0	0	0	0	0
Paved parking areas										
total infiltration	0	29	0	15	11	0	70	0	35	54
small wet detention basins	0	0	0	0	0	0	42	0	42	42
large wet detention basins	0	0	0	0	0	0	56	0	56	56
Connected roofs										
total infiltration	0	54	0	27	20	0	0	0	0	0
small wet detention basins	0	0	0	0	0	0	0	0	0	0
large wet detention basins	0	0	0	0	0	0	0	0	0	0
Catchbasins										
clean twice per year	0	0	0	0	0	0	8	0	8	8
Roadside drainage system										
grass swales	0	45	0	7	14	0	45	0	7	27
perforated drainage system	0	45	0	23	17	0	45	0	23	35
Main storm drain lines										
perforated pipes	45	45	45	45	45	45	45	45	45	45
Outfall wet detention basin										
2% of contrib. indus. area	0	0	0	0	0	80	80	80	80	80
0.8% of contrib. indus. area	0	0	0	0	0	60	60	60	60	60
% mass contrib. during period:	42%	29	13	16	100	0	53	0	47	100

industrial area during warm weather rain storms, while warm
and cold weather baseflows contributed more than half of the
annual runoff volume. In the residential area, less than 20
percent of the annual urban runoff flows occurred during the
warm weather rain storms. The breakdown of pollutant
discharges for different runoff periods varied greatly, but
in all cases, dry weather flows and snowmelt runoff were
found to be significant polluting flows. The ability of
control measures to reduce flows and pollutant discharges
during these other periods must therefore also be
considered.

Few of the source area stormwater controls (such as
street cleaning and roof or parking area runoff
infiltration) can be expected to significantly reduce the
runoff volume or pollutant discharges during dry weather.
The dry weather flow and pollutant sources were all subsurface in the two areas extensively studied in Toronto. In
some Milwaukee industrial areas, however, dry weather flows
were observed in roadside grass swales. These swales would
significantly reduce these dry weather flows and pollutant
discharges. Because industrial dry weather flows have been
found to be heavily contaminated with soluble heavy metals,
these swales may be contributing to groundwater
contamination. The heavy metals in industrial stormwater
runoff are mostly in particulate forms, reducing their
groundwater contamination potential.

Source area infiltration would only work during frozen
ground conditions in infiltration trenches having surface
grates. Paved parking and storage area infiltration trenches
can therefore be expected to work during snowmelt periods,
as surface grates would be needed above the recommended
grease and oil traps (assuming the grates are kept clear).
Well designed outfall wet detention basins are expected to
perform well in controlling all urban runoff particulate
pollutants, irrespective of the runoff period. The best
control for dry weather pollutants would be to find and
disconnect the inappropriate sources (such as industrial
floor drains, process waters, illegal waste dumping,
accidental spills, and sanitary sewage connections),
instead of trying to justify potential groundwater
contamination by infiltration.

Selection of Controls

SLAMM also allows combinations of source area and
outfall controls to be evaluated for complex drainage areas.
In order to help select the most appropriate control
program, as much information concerning the benefits and
problems associated with each complete control program is
needed. The Manual of Practice discusses each individual
control in detail and is very important when final selection
of project locations and designs are made. A multi-objective
decision analysis procedure should also be used when
selecting the appropriate control program. In order to use a

decision analysis procedure, the objectives of concern must
be identified and the ability of each alternative control
program to meet each objective must be known. Cost
considerations, including both initial capital cost and
operation and maintenence cost, are the most obvious
objectives, after control performance. Other considerations
that may affect the selection of a control program include
political feasibility, recreation benefits, aesthetics,
safety, nuisance potential, labor intensity, etc. The Manual
of Practice summarizes many of these considerations for the
different controls, including how specific design
specifications can be used to minimize the adverse
characteristics of the control options. This example only
addresses the important cost and performance information.

    a) Control Options Analysed.

    Ten different control programs were evaluated using
SLAMM, made up of various combinations of source area and
outfall control practices for a typical large mixed land use
area. These ten programs were:

    1) Increased street cleaning (to one or more passes per
       week in residential and commercial areas and one pass
       every two weeks in industrial and open space areas)
    2) Increased street cleaning (as above) and catchbasin
       cleaning (to twice per year)
    3) Large wet detention basins (capable of 95% suspended
       solids control) serving 25 percent of the drainage area
    4) Increased street cleaning and large wet detention
       basins
    5) Infiltration of runoff from half of the residential
       roofs currently draining to pavement and infiltration
       of runoff from half of the high rise residential,
       commercial, and industrial roofs and paved parking
       areas.
    6) Increased street cleaning and partial infiltration
    7) Increased street and catchbasin cleaning and partial
       infiltration.
    8) Partial infiltration and large wet detention basins.
    9) Increased street cleaning, partial infiltration, and
       large wet detention basins.
    10) Increased street and catchbasin cleaning, partial
       infiltration, and some large wet detention basins.

    The above control programs are for retro-fitting in
existing areas and assume that not all areas would be
suitable. As an example, it is very difficult to locate wet
detention ponds in existing areas and not all large parking
areas or roofs would be located in areas having soils
suitable for infiltration. It was also assumed that
replacing curb and gutter systems with grass swales would
not be feasible and are therefore not considered.

b) Costs of Alternative Control Programs.

Capital costs are annualized assuming 9-1/2 percent
interest over 20 years.
Street cleaning costs are estimated to be about $50 per
curb-km cleaned. This cost estimate includes all associated
street cleaning program costs, including equipment
amortization, equipment operating expenses, equipment
repairs, labor, overhead and debris disposal. The total
increased street cleaning cost for this control alternative
is estimated to be about $60 per hectare per year.
Catchbasin cleaning costs are estimated to be about $50
per catchbasin cleaned. This cost estimate also includes all
associated catchbasin cleaning program costs. The increased
catchbasin cleaning effort is estimated to cost about $210
per hectare per year.
Infiltration program costs are divided into two parts:
redirecting residential roofs draining onto pavement, and
infiltrating large paved parking areas and roofs in high
rise, commercial and industrial areas. A per-house cost of
about $125 is assumed, resulting in a total cost for this
infiltration component of about $9 per hectare per year. It
is estimated that infiltration trenches capable of completly
infiltrating most rains cost about $40,000 per hectare of
paved area or roof. Assuming that only half of the areas
would be suitable for infiltration, these infiltration costs
would be about $320 per hectare per year. Total infiltration
program costs would therefore be about $330 per hectare per
year. Annual maintenance would be minimal, but the life of
these infiltration devices may be limited (to about 20
years?) before reconstruction may be needed.
Initial construction costs of large wet detention
basins capable of removing about 90 percent of the
particulate residue in runoff from all land uses are
expected to be about $200,000 per hectare of pond surface.
About one percent of a mixed land use area should be used
for wet detention ponds. Total construction costs for these
wet detention basins is therefore estimated to be about $60
per hectare per year. Annual maintenance costs are estimated
to be about four percent of the initial construction cost,
or about $22 per hectare per year.
These unit area annualized costs ($ per hectare per
year, assuming 9-1/2% interest over 20 years) are summarized
below:

1) Increased street cleaning: $60.
2) Increased street and catchbasin cleaning: $270.
3) Some large wet detention basins: $80.
4) Increased street cleaning and some large wet detention
   basins: $140.
5) Partial infiltration of runoff from residential
   roofs and from high rise residential, commercial, and
   industrial roofs and paved parking areas: $330.
6) Increased street cleaning and partial infiltration:

$390.
7) Increased street and catchbasin cleaning and partial
   infiltration: $600.
8) Partial infiltration and some large wet detention
   basins: $410.
9) Increased street cleaning, partial infiltration, and
   some large wet detention basins: $460.
10) Increased street and catchbasin cleaning, partial
    infiltration, and some large wet detention basins:
    $680.

    c) Stormwater Runoff Control Cost-Effectiveness
Evaluation.

    Figures 5 through 8 graphically present selected data
plots showing unit removal costs verses maximum percent
pollutant reductions (only for stormwater runoff) available
for the ten alternatives. Plots are only shown for
particulate residue, phosphorus, fecal coliforms, and lead.
These four plots demonstrate the variety of cost-
effectiveness relationships that can be obtained for
different constituents. This variety can make it difficult
to select a control program to achieve all the objectives.
An effective control program will most likely require
several component individual control practices, with the
specific control applications varying for different drainage
areas, depending on many factors including different land
uses, different land development practices, and different
control objectives.
    Six "clusters" of removal effectiveness verses cost
groups are shown on Figure 5 for particulate residue. Only
three are "cost- effective". Program #2 (increased street
and catchbasin cleaning) may remove a maximum of about 13
percent of the particulate residue, but at a cost of almost
$13 per kg. Two other programs (#3 - detention basins, and
#4 - street cleaning and large detention basins) can remove
much more particulate residue (up to about about 26 percent)
at much lower costs ($2 to $3 per kg). Therefore, program #2
cannot be justified for this situation. Similar observations
can be made concerning programs #5 and #6, which are much
more costly than programs #3 and #4 for similar maximum
particulate residue removals. Program #7 (street and
catchbasin cleaning plus infiltration) is also much more
expensive than programs #8 (infilt. and detention) and #9
(street cleaning, infiltration and detention) and has a
lower particulate residue removal potential. Program #10
(street and catchbasin cleaning, infiltration, and
detention) includes all of the individual elements,
resulting in the highest cost and the greatest particulate
residue removal potential.
    The three cost-effective clusters for stormwater runoff
particulate residue control are therefore programs #3 and #4
at $2 to $3 per kg particulate residue removed with a
potential maximum control of 26 percent, programs #8 and #9

Figure 5 **Unit Removal Costs for Control Programs**
Suspended Solids

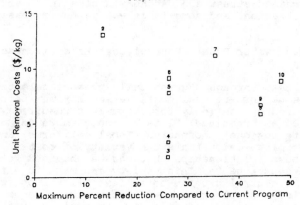

Figure 6 **Unit Removal Costs for Control Programs**
Phosphorus

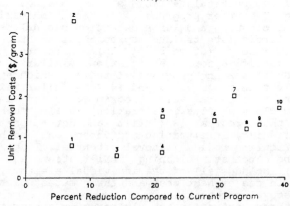

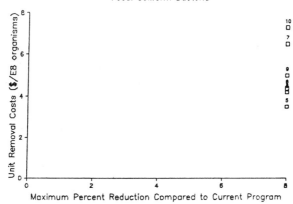

Figure 7 Unit Removal Costs for Control Programs
Fecal Coliform Bacteria

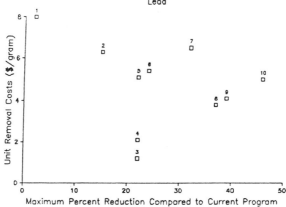

Figure 8 Unit Removal Costs for Control Programs
Lead

at about $6 per kg with a amximum control potential of about
44 percent, and program #10 at about $9 per kg with a
maximum contro potential of about 47 percent. Unless the
extra level of control was needed, it would be hard to
justify program #10 (everything). The most reasonable
programs are probably either #8 or #9, depending on other
objectives and other runoff period analyses.

When similar plots for total Kjeldahl nitrogen,
phosphorus, chemical oxygen demand, copper, and zinc are
evaluated, it is clear that program #8 (infiltration and
detention) allows much more pollutant removals to be
obtained at a relatively low unit cost as compared to the
other control programs. If flow, total residue, filterable
residue, fecal coliform bacteria, and pseudomonas aeruginosa
are the most important constituents, then program #5
(infiltration alone) is the most cost-effective solution.
The most general recommended control program for stormwater
runoff is therefore program #8 (infiltration and wet
detention).

Control Measure Performance for Different Land Uses.

The effects of the different source area controls on
outfall runoff water quality and flow varies greatly for
different areas because of the variety of sizes of the
different source areas and development practices. As a gross
example, parking lots and roofs contribute almost all of the
stormwater runoff and pollutants from shopping centers, but
very little of the stormwater runoff and pollutants from low
density residential areas. The outfall control
effectivenesses of the different source area controls
therefore also varies greatly for different land uses.

Land use alone, however, may not be an adequate method
to categorize different areas when examining urban runoff
quality and control effectiveness. Analyses of about 100
separate areas in Toronto (Pitt 1985) showed that the major
factors affecting urban runoff and its' control could be
adequately defined by using both land use and age of
development. Similar analyses are currently being conducted
in Milwaukee for about 300 different areas, with the
preliminary conclusions being similar to those found in
Toronto. As an example, the major factors affecting
stormwater runoff quality and quantity in most residential
areas was found to be the presence of grass swales or curb
and gutter drainages and if roof runoff was directly
connected to the storm drainage system, or allowed to
infiltrate into pervious areas. Many older residential areas
in the Milwaukee area have grass swales and disconnected
roofs, while many newer residential areas are required to
have concrete curb and gutters and connected roofs. About 12
to 18 categories reflecting different land uses and ages
were found to be adequate to describe urban runoff for major
portions of these two large cities.

The following paragraphs summarize typical urban runoff
control recommendations for different land uses in the upper
mid-west, as determined through many analyses using SLAMM
for typical Wisconsin conditions. Because of different
development practices in similar land uses and problems
during other runoff periods, as described above, the
following is therefore only a general discussion. Specific
control programs need to vary reflecting the specific
receiving water use objectives, other considerations (such
as cost, flood control, recreation use, etc.) and land
development practices.

a) Residential Land Uses

Street cleaning in most residential areas may cause
significant outfall reductions in phosphorus, fecal
coliforms, and to a lesser extent, lead, compared to no
cleaning. When compared to typical infrequent current street
cleaning efforts, relatively minor further improvements may
occur. It is therefore difficult to justify increasing
street cleaning beyond about one pass every month or every
two weeks in most residential areas. Spring cleanup and fall
leaf removal are expected to be very important (for all land
uses) and should be encouraged.

If roof runoff is not currently directed towards
pervious areas (away from building foundations, walkways and
driveways), then an infiltration retro-fitting program can
be very cost effective. High rise apartments have large
paved parking areas and suitable infiltration of the
associated flows would significantly reduce many pollutant
and flow discharges.

The most practical runoff control for lower use areas
is grass swales instead of curb and gutter systems. These
have been shown in monitoring programs to be as much as 90
percent effective during warm weather in reducing flows and
pollutant yields. If grass swales currently exist in an
area, changing to curb and gutters should be strongly
discouraged. Groundwater contamination from grass swale
infiltration in residential areas is not expected to be
important.

b) Institutional Land Uses

Street cleaning in school and hospital institutional
areas produce about the same effects as in most residential
areas: important reductions of a few constituents compared
to doing nothing, but very little improvement beyond
relatively infrequent cleaning. Again, spring cleanup and
fall leaf removal is expected to be important.

These areas have large parking lots and connected
roofs. Suitable retro-fitting to encourage infiltration of
the flows from these areas (and from the paved playgrounds
at schools) would produce significant reductions in runoff
volume and for most pollutants. Grass swales are also

applicable for institutional land uses and can be very
effective during warm weather.

c) Commercial Land Uses

Again, street cleaning at low levels of effort in strip
commercial and office park areas is important, but increases
beyond about once per week (typical current effort) may not
be worthwhile.
Paved parking and roof runoff infiltration are the most
effective source area control options for all commercial
areas. Pretreatment of water before infiltrated may be
necessary to reduce groundwater contamination potential.
Grit chambers with oil and grease traps should be the
minimum pretreatment required. Shopping centers may be best
treated with wet detention basins to significantly reduce
groundwater contamination potential as compared to large
parking area runoff infiltration.

d) Industrial Land Uses

Some street cleaning increases in industrial areas may
be needed. Typical industrial area street cleaning
frequencies (next to nothing) should be increased to at
least once per month.
Infiltration of paved parking and storage area runoff
and roof runoff would be very significant, but would require
pretreatment for most source areas to prevent groundwater
contamination. Because of the potential problem of heavily
contaminated dry weather flows from industrial areas, wet
detention basins at the outfalls of industrial parks is
strongly encouraged. This will produce some attenuation of
both wet and dry weather pollutant discharges, but more
importantly, it will offer an opportunity to control spills
that enter the storm drainage system. Grass swale drainages
occur in many industrial areas but may pose a threat to the
groundwater because of the heavily contaminated runoff
flows.

e) Open Space Land Uses

Open space areas are relatively unimportant flow and
pollutant sources. However, important erosion losses can
occur from bare ground or steep hills, especially if near
the storm drainage system. Careful evaluations of erosion
potential should be made for open space areas, especially if
undergoing development. Minimum levels of street cleaning is
also necessary for these areas (especially spring cleanup if
road deicing materials were used), along with effective
infiltration of paved parking areas. Few roofs are expected
in these areas, but any roof drains should be directed to
the available large expanses of landscaped areas. Grass
swales are quite common in open space areas and are very
effective controls during warm weather.

References

Bannerman, R., J.G. Konrad, D. Becker, G.V. Simsiman, G. Chesters, J. Goodrich-Mahoney, and S. Abrams. "The IJC Menomonee River Watershed Study", U.S. Environmental Protection Agency, EPA-905/4-79-029-C, Chicago, Ill., 1979.

Bannerman, R., K. Baun, M, Bohn, P.E. Hughes, and D.A. Graczyk. "Evaluation of Urban Nonpoint Source Pollution Management in Milwaukee County, Wisconsin", U.S. Environmental Protection Agency, PB 84-114164, Chicago, Ill., 1983.

Environmental Protection Agency (U.S.). "Results of the Nationwide Urban Runoff Program", Water Planning Division, PB 84-185552, Washington, D.C., 1983.

Field, R. and A.N. Tafuri. "Urban Runoff Pollution Control Technology Overview", U.S. Environmental Protection Agency, EPA-600/2-77-047, Cincinnati, Ohio, 1977.

Gupta, M.K., R.W. Agnew, and N.P. Kobriger. "Constituents of Highway Runoff", Volume one of a six volume series, Federal Highway Administration, U.S. Department of Transportation, FHWA/RD-81/042, Washington, D.C., 1981.

Konrad, J.G., J.S. Baumann, and S.E. Bergquist. "Nonpoint Pollution Control: The Wisconsin Experience", Journal of Soil and Water Conservation, Volume 40, Number 1, January-February 1985.

Pitt, R. "Small Storm Urban Flow and Particulate Washoff Contributions to Outfall Toxic Pollutant Discharges", Dissertation proposal submitted to the Civil and Environmental Engineering Department, University of Wisconsin, Madison, 1984.

Pitt, R. "Toronto/Source Loading and Management Model - Sensitivity Analysis", Ontario Ministry of the Environment, Toronto, Ontario, 1985.

Pitt, R. "Manual of Practice for the Design of Construction Site Erosion and Stormwater Runoff Controls", Wisconsin Department of Natural Resources, Madison, Wisconsin, 1986.

Pitt, R. and J. McLean. "Humber River Pilot Watershed Project", Ontario Ministry of the Environment, Toronto, Ontario, 1986.

Best Management Practices Overview

Martin P. Wanielista*, MASCE and Yousef A. Yousef*, MASCE

INTRODUCTION

In the general list of best management practices for stormwater
control, many practices are currently being used. On-line retention and
detention ponds are used frequently and their importance warrants a
complete section within this publication. However, there are other best
management practices which are frequently used and will be addressed
here:

It is the purpose of this paper to summarize efficiencies and design
considerations related to:
1. Off-line Retention (Infiltration) Systems
2. Vegetated Swales (with and without berms)
3. Other practices such as street cleaning, catch basin cleaning,
    roof and parking lot infiltration, and erosion control.

DEFINITIONS

The term best management practice refers to that practice which is
used for a given set of conditions, which are: land use, groundwater/
soils, topography, and local cost. The practice achieves satisfactory
water quality and quantity enhancement at a minimum cost. Thus the
practice is cost effective or among those practices achieving desired
efficiencies, the least cost alternative is chosen.

Stormwater management practices have been classified by many people
for clarity in identification and conversation. Unfortunately,
confusion still exists as to which practice one is referencing when
identified. Thus, within this paper, the following practices are
defined:

1. On-line retention/detention - structures in which runoff is stored
    for disposal primarily to surface waters and to a lesser extent by
    evaporation, and infiltration.
2. Off-line retention - structures which include diversion and infil-
    tration basins in which the first flush volume of runoff is disposed
    primarily by infiltration but also by evaporation, with no surface
    discharge from the infiltration basin.
3. Street cleaning - cleaning of street surfaces by both vacuum and
    brush machines to dispose of some materials before removal with
    runoff waters.

*Professors of Engineering, College of Engineering, University of
Central Florida, Orlando, FL   32816.

4. Catchbasin cleaning - mechanisms to dispose of materials stored in the bottom of a catch basin before the materials are removed by runoff waters.
5. Erosion control - vegetation, chemicals or structures that prevent soil disposal from a site.
6. Roof and parking lot infiltration - a specific application of off-line retention to dispose of the first volume of runoff primarily by infiltration.

In a recent survey of over 800 State and County stormwater facility records in Florida, approximately 50 percent of the facilities used in low-water table areas relied primarily on off-line retention. While in high water table areas characteristic of South Florida and coastal regions, over 70 percent of the facilities relied primarily on on-line detention/retention systems. Catchbasin cleaning and street cleaning were not used, parking lot infiltration basins were.

OFF-LINE RETENTION (INFILTRATION) BASINS

Off-line retention systems are designed to divert the first flush of runoff waters for infiltration. There is no direct surface water discharge of the diverted waters. The infiltration system is located above or below ground.

The infiltration rate and watershed areas with runoff volumes must be estimated. Shaver (1986) presented data on minimum infiltration rates for various soil conditions. He also stated that approximately 90% of all annual rainfall events in Maryland have less than one inch volume. This compares with data reported in the State of Florida (Anderson, 1982). Rainfall frequency distribution work for the New England area also produced similar rainfall frequency distributions on storm volume (Wanielista, 1982). These rainfall frequency results are shown in Figures 1 thru 4. Figures 1 and 3 indicate that about 90% of the storms have a volume of rainfall less than or equal to one inch. Figures 2 and 4 indicate that over 80% of the runoff volume can be diverted if the runoff from the first inch of rainfall is disposed of by diversion for infiltration. These Figures assume that all rainfall goes to runoff. Of course, the runoff volume is usually a fraction of the rainfall volume. If an off-line retention pond were able to prevent discharge of the runoff from the first inch of rainfall, Wanielista (1979) estimated an average annual removal efficiency of about 80-90% for all chemical constituents and solids in runoff waters. In Florida at least 60 percent of the yearly runoff waters also would be prevented from direct discharge to surface waters when off-line retention is used.

Average annual removal efficiency is calculated considering the annual mass of chemicals and solids available for discharge and the annual mass diverted for infiltration. Thus for each storm, storm efficiencies will vary from 100% for runoff volumes less than diversion design volume to lower efficiencies for higher runoff volumes. Using a simulation model dependent on 20 years of rainfall data and 16 measured storm event runoff quantities and qualities, Wanielista (1977) developed cumulative frequency distributions for storm related efficiencies. The results are shown in Table 1. If one were able to design the

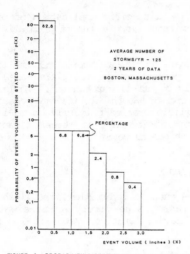

FIGURE 1   PROBABILITY DISTRIBUTION OF PRECIPITATION
           VOLUME FOR BOSTON DURING THE
           PERIOD 1979-1980

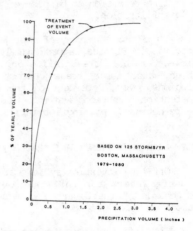

FIGURE 2   PERCENTAGE OF YEARLY RAINFALL PRODUCED
           BY STORMS EQUAL TO OR LESS THAN STATED
           EVENT VOLUME

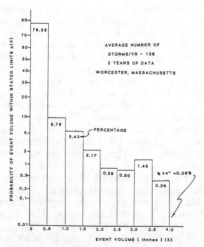

FIGURE 3   PROBABILITY DISTRIBUTION OF PRECIPITATION
           VOLUME FOR WORCESTER DURING THE
           PERIOD 1979-1980

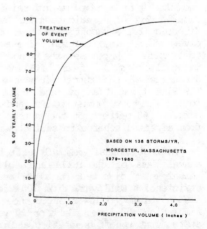

FIGURE 4   PERCENTAGE OF YEARLY RAINFALL PRODUCED
           BY STORMS EQUAL TO OR LESS THAN STATED
           EVENT VOLUME

infiltration pond to treat the first 0.64 cm (.25 in) of runoff, from Table 1, one can expect 100% efficiency for 66.4% of the storms and the efficiency can be expected to be greater than 72% for 97.3% of the storms. These results are for a very small area (4.6 acres) which exhibits a first flush effect. Here, first flush is defined as a majority of the mass of pollutants included in the first runoff waters.

TABLE 1 Cumulative Frequency Distributions on Efficiencies per Storm Event as a Function of Storage Volume Area = 4.6 Ac, 85% Impervious, T_c = 20 min

Average* Efficiency	Volume of Storage centimeters (inches)			
	0.25 (0.1)	0.64 (0.25)	1.27 (0.5)	2.54 (1.0)
100	35.4	66.4	92.9	99.0
>96	42.5	74.3	97.3	100.0
>92	46.0	77.9	97.4	
>88	47.8	81.4	98.2	
>84	50.4	90.3	100.0	
>80	56.6	92.9		
>76	61.1	96.3		
>72	66.4	97.3		
>68	72.6	98.2		
>64	82.3	100.0		
>60	94.7			
>56	100.0			

*Average Efficiency is the average removal of BOD_5, SS, N, and P over a twenty year period. Average number of rainfall events producing runoff per year are 116.

The State of Florida (Livingston, 1985) has adopted the criteria for treating the runoff from the first inch of rainfall using off- line retention. The volume of retention is calculated using the average rational coefficient of runoff and the contributing area, or

$$Vol = cPA/12 \qquad (1)$$

where   Vol = volume of off-line retention, Ac-Ft (1 Ac-ft=1233m^3)
              c = rational runoff coefficient, dimensionless
              P = rainfall volume, one inch
              A = watershed area, acres
             12 = inches/foot

Suggested values for the rational coefficient are shown in Table 2.

TABLE 2   Runoff Coefficients for Off-line Retention Volume
          (also rational formula)

Type of Drainage Area	Runoff Coefficient (General Range)
Commercial:	
Downtown areas	0.70-0.95
Neighborhood areas	0.50-0.70
Residential:	
Single-family areas	0.30-0.50
Multi-units, detached	0.40-0.60
Multi-units, attached	0.60-0.75
Suburban	0.25-0.40
Apartment dwelling areas	0.50-0.70
Industrial:	
Light areas	0.50-0.80
Heavy areas	0.60-0.90
Parks, cemeteries	0.10-0.25
Playgrounds	0.20-0.40
Railroad yard areas	0.20-0.40
Unimproved areas	0.10-0.30
Lawns:	
Sandy soil, flat, 2%	0.05-0.10
Sandy soil, average, 2-7%	0.10-0.15
Sandy soil, steep, 7%	0.15-0.20
Heavy soil, flat, 2%	0.13-0.17
Heavy soil, average 2-7%	0.18-0.22
Heavy soil, steep, >7%	0.25-0.35
Streets:	
Asphaltic	0.70-0.95
Concrete	0.80-0.95
Brick	0.70-0.85
Drives and walks	0.75-0.85
Roofs	0.75-0.95

(from ASCE, 1960)

VEGETATED SWALES

A vegetated swale is one which both infiltrates and transports
runoff waters. Measures to retain soil particles in the swales include
chemical soil stabilizers and vegetation. Vegetation within the swales
are very effective (Lord, 1986). Immdeiately after construction,
erosion can be lessened by a vegetative area within the swale.   The
swale is designed based on runoff volume, a projected infiltration rate,
and wetted swale area. Avellaneda (1985) conducted 20 hydrologic
studies of vegetative swales. The swales had a water table at least one
foot below the bottom during dry conditions. Infiltration rates were
measured from the actual field experiments and a minimum rate of about
5-7.5 cm/hr (2-3 in/hr) was reported. Laboratory permeabilities and
field double ring infiltrometer measurements over-estimated actual
rates. For the same swales, the double ring infiltrometer estimated

infiltration rates of 12.5-50 cm/hr (5-20 in/hr). The soils beneath the swales were primarily sandy in texture with a liquid limit of between 15-25. By a mass balance of runoff waters and infiltration waters, the following equation for a triangular shaped cross-sectional area was developed to estimate the length of the swale necessary to infiltrate the runoff waters:

$$L = \frac{K \, Q^{5/8} \, S^{3/16}}{n^{3/8} \, i} \qquad (2)$$

where   L = length of swale (m)
         K = constant which is a function of side slope parameter
             Z (1 vertical/Z horizontal) (see Table 3)
         Q = average runoff flow rate (m^3/s)
         S = longitudinal slope (m/m)
         n = Mannings roughness coefficient (for overland flow)
         i = infiltration rate (cm/hr)

Another equation was developed for a trapezoidal cross-sectional shape.

TABLE 3   Constant (K) for Design Equation for Trinagular Shape

Z (Side Slope) (1 vertical/Z horizontal)	K (US UNITS)	K (SI UNITS)
1	10,516	75,552
2	9,600	68,971
3	8,446	60,680
4	7,514	53,984
5	6,784	48,740
6	6,203	44,565
7	5,730	41,167
8	5,337	38,344
9	5,006	35,966
10	4,722	33,925

For most residential, commercial and highway watersheds, the length of swales necessary to percolate the runoff waters was found to be excessive or at least twice the distance available. Thus some type of swale block (berm) or on-line detention/retention may be more helpful. Pitt (1986) indicated the most cost effective solution for the reduction of runoff volume, residual solids, and bacteria was infiltration, and control of chemical constituents, such as, Kjeldahl nitrogen, chemical oxygen demand, copper and zinc should be accomplished by infiltration plus detention. He was working with an assumed watershed land use and thus the results are not generally transferable to other watershed conditions. Nevertheless, this result is similar to that of Yousef, et al. (1985) who recommends that swale blocks should be considered to reduce further the chemical constituents and runoff volumes.

Using as a design criteria, the runoff volume from 7.5 centimeters (3 inches) of rainfall and storage of non-infiltrated runoff, Wanielista et. al. (1986) has developed swale block designs for highway applications. In Florida, about 92% of yearly rainfall volume is contained in all storms less than or equal to 3 inches. Basically, the swale block volume can be calculated for a fixed length of swale and swale geometry using:

Volume of Runoff - Volume of Infiltrate = Swale Block Volume

$$Q(\Delta t) - Q_I(\Delta t) = \text{Vol of Swale}$$

$$Q(\Delta t) - \left[\frac{L\, n^{3/8}\, i}{K\, S^{3/16}}\right]^{8/5} \quad (\Delta t) = \text{Swale Volume} \tag{3}$$

where Q_I = average infiltration rate (m^3/s)

Δt = runoff hydrograph time (sec)

EXAMPLE PROBLEM - VEGETATED SWALE

Consider as an example, a swale section along Interstate 4 near Orlando, Florida. The parameters of equation (3) are:

$n = 0.05$
$S = 0.0279$
$Q_I = .0023\ m^3/s$ (0.08 cfs) for $\Delta t = 100$ min
$i = 7.5$ cm/hr (3.0 in/hr)
$Z = 7$

a) First, what swale length would be necessary to percolate all the waters? (using equation 2)

$$L = \frac{41,167(0.0023)^{5/8}(.0279)^{3/16}}{(.05)^{3/8}(7.5)} = 193 \text{ meters}$$

b) Only 76 meters (250 feet) were available, thus how much storage volume is necessary? (using equation 3)

$$(.0023)(60)(100) - \left[\frac{(76)(.05)^{3/8}(7.5)}{41,167(.0279)^{3/16}}\right]^{8/5} \quad 60(100) = \text{Volume}$$

and Volume of Storage = 11.4 cubic meters

Thus, volume in the swale must be available to contain the runoff waters. In highway designs for high speed situations, safety must be considered, thus a maximum depth of water equal to 0.5 meters (about 1.5 feet) and flow line slopes on the berms of 1 vertical/20 horizontal are recommended. Along lower speed highways or in some residential/commercial urban settings, steeper flow line berm slopes (1 on 6) are acceptable.

OTHER MANAGEMENT PRACTICES

Pitt (1986) discussed other source controls and presented some cost and efficiency data based on about 100 rain events during 1984 and 1985. These included street cleaning on smooth surfaces, street cleaning on rough surfaces, catchbasin cleaning, vegetative swales, and infiltration of roofs, walkways, and driveways. Lord (1986) presented other data for vegetative swales to prevent erosion. Lead from residential areas can be reduced by street cleaning during warm weather times (no snow) by up to 25% with one or more street cleanings per week. Rough streets reduce this effectiveness to about 15 percent. Total infiltration of driveway runoff waters can result in up to 35 percent reduction. Catchbasin effectiveness is only reported to be 8 percent (Pitt, 1986).

The efficiencies reported by Pitt (1986) are some of the first data useful for comparative purposes. In some heavy developed areas without infiltration potential or land for surface ponding, one must consider street cleaning, catchbasin cleaning, and runoff flow rate reduction in combined sewer systems. These may be the only economical alternatives. Street and underground storage with flow rate attenuation may be an acceptable alternative when treatment systems are not overloaded or treatment plant efficiencies are significantly reduced. These must be addressed on a site-by-site basis. The computer program SLAMM (Pitt, 1986) should be helpful in determining cost effective alternatives. As in the use of any computer aided decision making model, input data on efficiencies must be carefully examined to increase the credibility of results. The quantity of actual storm related data used by Pitt appears to produce credible results, especially for the local areas in Wisconsin.

CONCLUSIONS

Off-line retention, swales, and other management practices should be part of the many alternatives available for stormwater quality and quantity control. Diversion of the first flush of runoff waters for disposal by means of infiltration can obtain high efficiencies at competitive cost. The diversion can be used both as a source (parking lot, roof drains, etc.) control and as a watershed control. The design of swales to achieve quality control equal to that of off-line retention should consider berming to retain runoff waters not infiltrated during flow through conditions.

All the management practices of this paper have application for stormwater quality control. Some of the runoff volume associated with large volume (design) storms also will be controlled. Attenuation of peak flows should not be expected with off-line retention. Swales with or without berms will attenuate peak flows. The design criteria and average annual efficiencies reported here should be of use.

REFERENCES

1. American Society of Civil Engineers, "Design Manual for Storm Drainage", New York, 1960.

2. Anderson, D.E. 1982. "Evaluation of Swale Design". Master's Thesis, University of Central Florida, Orlando, Florida.

3. Livingston, E. 1985. "The Stormwater Rule: Past, Present and Future". Stormwater Management: An Update, Edited by Wanielista, M.P., Orlando, Florida, July 15.

4. Lord, B.N. 1986. "Effectiveness of Erosion Control". Urban Runoff Technology, Engineering Foundation Conference, New England College, New Hampshire, June.

5. Pitt, R. 1986. "The Incorporation of Urban Source Area Controls in Wisconsin's Priority Watershed Projects". Urban Runoff Technology, Engineering Foundation Conference, New England College, New Hampshire, June.

6. Shaver, H.E. 1986. "Infiltration as a Stormwater Management Component". Urban Runoff Technology, Engineering Foundation Conference, New England College, New Hampshire, June.

7. Wanielista, M.P. 1977. "Quality Considerations in the Design of Holding Ponds", in Stormwater Retention/Detention Basins Seminar, edited by Yousef A. Yousef, University of Central Florida, Orlando, Florida, August.

8. Wanielista, M.P. 1979. Stormwater Management: Quality and Quantity". Ann Arbor Science Publishers, Ann Arbor Michigan.

9. Wanielista, M.P. 1982. Lake Cochituate Restoration. Report to State Department of Environmental Quality Engineering. State of Massachusetts.

10. Wanielista, M.P., Yousef, Y.A., Van DeGraaff, L., and S. Rehmann-Kuo. 1986. "Best Management Practices for Highway Runoff Erosion and Sediment Control". Report submitted to Florida Department of Transportation, Tallahassee, Florida, July.

11. Yousef, Y.A., Wanielista, M.P., Harper, H.H., Pearce, D.B., and Tolbert, R.D. 1985. "Removal of Highway Contaminants by Roadside Swales". Final Report FL-ER-30-85, Submitted to Florida Department of Transportation, Tallahassee, Florida, July.

Effectiveness of Extended Detention Ponds

T. J. Grizzard, M.ASCE, C. W. Randall, M.ASCE
B. L. Weand, and K. L. Ellis[*]

Abstract

Field and laboratory studies of the performance of detention
facilities for the removal of selected pollutants from urban
stormwater were conducted. The laboratory studies consisted
of the measurement of pollutant concentration reductions as
a result of quiescent settling of stormwater in plexiglass
columns. The studies were carried out for stormwaters of
low, moderate, and high initial suspended solids. Measurements were also made of particle size distribution changes
during the settling studies. A full scale detention pond
was also retrofitted with a restricted release structure to
increase the residence time of the average stormwater event.
Long term measurements were made of pond inflow and outflow
pollutant loads, and efficiencies of removal determined.
Comparisons of laboratory and field data showed comparable
results, and provide a basis for the selection of design
parameters for full-scale facilities.

Introduction

The practice of detaining urban stormwater flows for the
purposes of flood and stream bank erosion control has been
in use in the United States for over three decades. The
approach to the design of such facilities has usually been
based on determining the storage volume required for a
post-development design storm in order to restrict downstream discharges to the pre-development rate. At the
site level, this type of peak-shaving practice may be
generally shown to have achieved its hydrologic goals.

In recent years, largely as a result of the recognition of
the great pollution potential of urban stormwaters (2,7),
detention ponds have received new attention as a type of

[*]Respectively,
Director, Occoquan Watershed Monitoring Laboratory,
9408 Prince William St., Manassas, VA 22110
Lunsford Professor of Civil Engineering, Virginia Tech,
Department of Civil Engineering, Blacksburg, VA 24061
Assoc. Director, Occoquan Watershed Monitoring Laboratory,
9408 Prince William St., Manassas, VA 22110
Environmental Engineer, Presearch, Inc., Arlington, VA

structural control measure which offers some promise in the
reduction of receiving water pollutant loads. In the early
1980's, the U. S. Environmental Protection Agency sponsored
the Nationwide Urban Runoff Program (NURP) as a means of
obtaining comprehensive data on the evaluation and control
of pollution from urban stormwater. During the program, a
large number of urban stormwater pollution control measures,
generally known as Best Management Practices (BMP's), were
studied to determine their performance relative to the
removal of undesirable substances from stormwater. A wide
range of structural and non-structural practices were
investigated at 29 project sites across the United States.
Several projects focused on the performance of conventional
and modified stormwater detention ponds in attempts to
assess the applicability of the practices in the multi-
purpose role of managing urban stormwater quantity and
quality. In an era of declining funds for the management of
environmental pollution, the extension of the scope of an
existing practice such as stormwater detention to achieve
water quality management goals has been seen as offering the
dual attraction of cost-effective implementation, and ready
acceptance by local governments.

The reduction of flow velocities in peak-shaving detention
basins is a natural consequence of the hydraulic function of
the facilities in reducing downstream flow rates. Reduction
of flow velocity, in turn, may be seen to encourage the
separation of suspended solids, and any associated pollutants, from the liquid phase prior to release from the
facility. The theoretical efficiency of removal of such
dilute suspensions of solids under quiescent flow conditions
may be seen to be a function of the surface overflow rate,
which is equal to the discrete settling velocity of the
smallest size particle removed (11). To the extent that
non-quiescent flow and other basin problems, such as
short-circuiting, exist in a given facility, the expected
removal efficiency of suspended solids may be adversely
affected. On the other hand, Randall, et al. (8) observed
that the actual solids separation processes in the sedimentation of urban stormwaters consist of a combination of
discrete (Type I) and flocculent (Type II) settling. The
natural process of agglomeration of smaller particles into
larger ones having higher settling velocities implies that
detention time increases may raise the removal efficiency of
small particles by a higher factor than would be expected
with Type I settling only. As it has also been shown that
many stormwater-borne pollutants are initially associated
with, or may sorb to, smaller particle sizes (9) this observation has heightened importance.

Because of the mixture of settling processes, the great
variability of pollutant associations, and the uncertain
effects of full scale basin effects such as turbulence and
short-circuiting, it is currently difficult to make accurate
a priori predictions of the efficiency of extended detention

basins in removing most water pollutants. It is the purpose
of this investigation to examine performance data from a
full scale study of a detention pond, and to compare it to
observations of separation processes under controlled
conditions in the laboratory.

Methods

Prototype Extended Detention Pond. The prototype pond was a
facility selected for study and modified to achieve extended
detention times during the Metropolitan Washington Urban
Runoff Program (4). The pond was located in Montgomery
County, Maryland, and had physical characteristics as follow
(5):

> Land Use: Townhouse/Garden Apartments
> Drainage Area: 34.4 acres
> Impervious cover: 19.2 percent
> Land slope: 4.7 percent
> Pond NPS Storage: 38,000 ft^3

The pond was originally designed as a conventional peak-
shaving stormwater detention pond, but was modified for the
study to achieve longer storage times. Modification
consisted of installing a 36-inch diameter corrugated metal
riser in a vertical position, and sealing it to the 24-inch
outlet pipe already in place. The riser was perforated with
0.5-inch holes which were designed to give the pond a
top-of-riser drawdown time of 40 hours. This release rate
was selected to correspond to a 24 hour drawdown for an
event of moderate size. The riser crest was left open in
order to provide the original design release rate for
stormwater events larger than the modified NPS storage pool.
Examinations of the runoff records from the site (1), and
Post-modification inspections of the facility during runoff
events, showed the actual release rates to be substantially
higher than the design values. This was ultimately
determined to be caused by a leak in the vicinity of the
joint between the riser and the outlet pipe. The defect
caused the average detention time to decrease to about 25
percent of the design value (5). The performance of the
pond in removing pollutants from site stormwater may
therefore be assumed to be somewhat less efficient than what
would have been observed if the design detention times had
been achieved. This deficiency, while unfortunate from the
standpoint of original study objectives, nevertheless made
it possible to conduct an interesting analysis of the
applicability of moderate extensions of pond detention time.

The pond site was instrumented with primary flow control
structures at both the outlet and the principal inlet.
Bubbler-type flowmeters were used to sense static head, and
to perform a conversion to instantaneous values of
discharge. Automatic samplers were installed at both
locations, and were controlled by the flowmeters in order to

collect flow-weighted composite samples during all runoff
events. Pond efficiences were determined by comparison of
inflow and outflow unit area loadings (1).

Laboratory Settling Column Studies. Partially because of
the operational problems experienced with the modified
prototype facility, it was decided to conduct a series of
laboratory-scale settling column studies on the removal of
of pollutants carried by urban stormwater. Large volume
stormwater samples were collected from commercial shopping
center catchments on seven occasions, and employed in a
series of long-term settling column tests. The site
drainage areas ranged from 23 to 54.7 acres, and averaged 90
percent directly connected impervious surface. The samples
were collected and transported to the laboratory in acid-
washed polyethylene carboys. The carboys were agitated to
insure good mixing, and a sample withdrawn to initially
characterize the stormwater. The remaining sample, again
with agitation, was placed in settling columns five feet
deep and 6 inches inside diameter. The columns were
equipped with sample ports at depth intervals of one foot.
Samples were withdrawn at intervals of 2, 6, 12, 24, and 48
hours.

Laboratory Methods. Samples from both the prototype pond
and the settling columns were analyzed at the Occoquan
Watershed Monitoring Laboratory of the Virginia Tech
Department of Civil Engineering. Measurements of residue
(TSS and VSS), and Chemical Oxygen Demand (COD) were made
according to protocols in Standard Methods (12). Nitrogen
and phosphorus determinations were made using a Technicon
AutoAnalyzer II (13) system operated according to applicable
EPA methodologies (3). Trace metals determinations were
made by atomic absorption spectroscopy according to EPA
methods (3), as were measurements of total organic carbon
(TOC). Particle size distributions were determined with a
Model PC-320 HIAC particle size analyzer.

Results

Prototype Extended Detention Pond. A total of 47 inflow
storm events, and 33 outflow storm events were monitored at
the prototype pond facility. Pollutant removal efficiencies
for the pond were determined by calculating the median unit
area loading rate reductions between the inflow and outflow
stations, as described in the field study report (1). The
median event mean concentration (EMC) of selected pollutants
in the influent stormwater is shown in Table 1.

Settling Column Studies. The seven storm events sampled
were observed to fall into ranges of initial total suspended
solids (TSS) which were characterized as low, moderate, and
high. The median initial concentration data for all ranges
are also shown in Table 1. A complete data listing has been
provided by Randall et al (8).

Table 1. Minimum, Maximum, and Median Concentrations of all
          Pollutants in Laboratory and Field Study.

	TSS	COD	TP	TKN	OX-N	TZN	TPB
	<----------------- mg/L ----------------->						
Low TSS Columns							
Minimum	15	6.8	0.14	2.12	0.06	0.302	-
Median	35	-	0.19	3.65	2.14		-
Maximum	38	82	0.83	4.5	2.26	0.368	-
Mod. TSS Columns							
Minimum	100	50	0.25	1.26	0.04	0.112	0.127
Median	155	87	0.45	1.27	0.74	0.160	0.144
Maximum	215	138	0.48	2.35	0.77	0.172	0.370
High TSS Column							
Minimum							
Median	721	908	0.82	4.25	0.04	0.692	0.913
Maximum							
Field Study							
Minimum	5	8	0.10	0.71	0.10	0.020	ND
Median	42	21	0.30	1.65	0.68	0.075	ND
Maximum	238	100	1.55	4.19	2.42	0.245	0.360

Particulate Surface Area

The total surface area of a suspension may be taken as an
indicator of the available sites for surface phenomena such
as coagulation/flocculation, physisorption, chemisorption,
and precipitation to occur. The total particulate surface
area of each of the samples collected for the column studies
was estimated by assuming the particles to spherical in
shape, and calculating an area using the geometric mean
diameter of each size range:

$$\text{Total Area} = 3.1416(N)(D1)(D2)$$

where,

N = number of particles in size range
$D1,D2$ = smallest and largest diameters in
range, respectively

Figure 1 shows the relationship of surface area percentage to
particle size for each of the initial TSS ranges of the
collected samples. As may be seen, the distribution of area
is skewed to the smaller particle sizes, although not as
greatly as the skew previously reported for particle counts
(8). In any case, however, it may be seen that all initial
TSS ranges had the dominant surface area in particles of
sizes less than 60 um. The skew to the smaller particles
was even more pronounced in the moderate and high initial

TSS data, with pronounced peaks in the percent of total
surface area occurring in particle size ranges less than 40
um. If particulate surface is used as an indirect measure
of the size associations of other suspended pollutants in
the stormwater, it may be seen that this distribution is in
substantial agreement with the previous work of Sartor and
Boyd (9).

The reduction of median total particulate surface area as a
function of settling time for all three initial TSS ranges
is shown in Figure 2. The moderate to high initial TSS
samples displayed a rapid decrease in total surface area in
the first 2-hour settling period, followed by a declining
rate of reduction out to 12 hours, at which point the rate
of decrease displayed a further decline. The high initial
rate of reduction may be reasoned to be a function of a
combination of natural flocculation and the rapid settling
of larger particles. The low initial TSS data displayed
relatively low rates of surface area reduction throughout
most of the experiment.

Suspended Solids

Figure 3 shows the results of TSS removals at various time
intervals for the settling column studies, and for the
median performance of the prototype detention pond. For
purposes of comparison, it may be seen from Table 1 that the
range of influent TSS concentrations to the prototype pond
overlapped the ranges of low and moderate TSS column study
samples. The settling column test results show that for the
low range, removals approached 30 percent within two hours
and remained static out to the 24-hour mark, at which point
increased removals occurred until a level of approximately
80 percent was reached at the 48-hour mark. The delayed
increase in the low TSS settling may have been due to
natural flocculation of the dilute suspensions almost 24
hours into the tests. By contrast, the moderate to high TSS
storms achieved rather high initial removals, reaching
80 to 90 percent of the total removal by the 6-hour mark.
The median percent removal of TSS by the prototype pond was
slightly over 60 percent, which fell between the performance
of the low and moderate TSS column studies for the period up
to 24 hours of settling. The pond average detention time of
approximately 6 hours would tend to lend credence to the
comparability of the column and full scale performance data.

Chemical Oxygen Demand

The results of the settling column and full scale pond
studies for the removal of COD are shown in Figure 4. No
6-hour or 12-hour settling data were available for COD
removal calculations. As with TSS, the distribution of the
COD EMC data for the field study approximates that of the
low to moderate TSS column study samples, as may be seen in

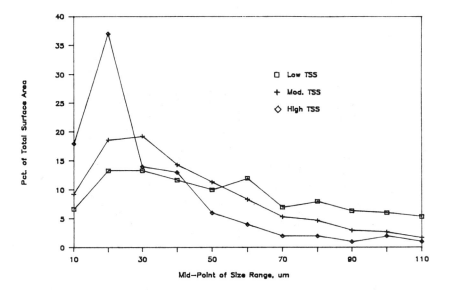

Figure 1. Distribution of Median Surface Area with Particle
           Size for Settling Column Samples.

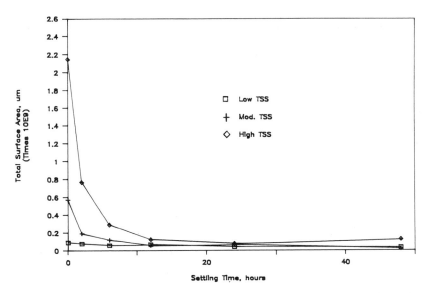

Figure 2. Reduction of Median Surface Area as a Function of
           Settling Time for Column Studies.

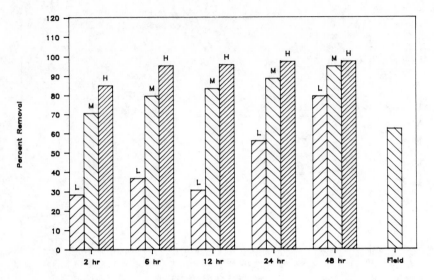

Figure 3. Median Settling Column and Prototype Pond Removals of
          Total Suspended Solids.

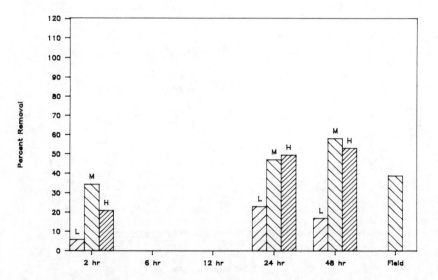

Figure 4. Median Settling Column and Prototype Pond Removals of
          Chemical Oxygen Demand.

Table 1. At the 24-hour mark, it may be seen that the
median field study removals fell between those for the low
and moderate TSS column studies. It should also be noted
from Figure 4 that after the 24-hour mark, no appreciable
increase in median COD removal was observed in any of the
column studies, indicating that the fraction associated with
settleable matter, or degradable in a 24-hour period had
already been removed.

Phosphorus

Figure 5 depicts the results of the settling column and full
scale pond studies for the removal of total phosphorus (TP).
Examination of the phosphorus data in Table 1 shows that the
range of the TP EMC data from the field study closely
approximate that of the low TSS column study data, but that
the median values are closer to those of the moderate TSS
data set. The settling column TP removals for the moderate
and high TSS samples are in the range of 60 to 70 percent,
with a substantial fraction of the total removal being
obtained in the first 12 hours of settling. By contrast,
the low TSS column data show only modest removals of
phosphorus out to the 12-hour mark. Between 12 and 24 hours
of settling, however, the removal of TP approximately
doubled, suggesting that the mechanism was related to
delayed settling of very small particles. Even though
substantial quantities of very small particles were present
in the moderate and high TSS samples, their removal earlier
in the settling process may have been enhanced by natural
flocculation in the higher solids systems. The indicated
median TP removal from the field study is comparable to that
obtained at the 6-hour mark in the low TSS column study. It
should be noted that the median influent EMC value for TSS
in the field study was quite low (42 mg/L), and comparable
to that for the low TSS column data. The results of the
settling column study indicate that the pond performance
with respect to TP removal would have been substantially
enhanced by a longer average detention time.

Nitrogen

TKN. The results of the settling column and full scale pond
studies for total Kjeldahl nitrogen (TKN) are shown in
Figure 6. It is of interest to note that for all initial
TSS ranges except the lowest, most of the ultimate TKN
removal was attained in the first two hours of settling.
The range of the field study influent TKN EMC data
was most similar to that for the low TSS column studies,
while the median value most closely resembled that of the
moderate TSS column studies. As was the case with TSS and
COD, the observed removal of TKN in the prototype pond was
between that achieved in the low and moderate TSS column
studies after 6 hours of settling.

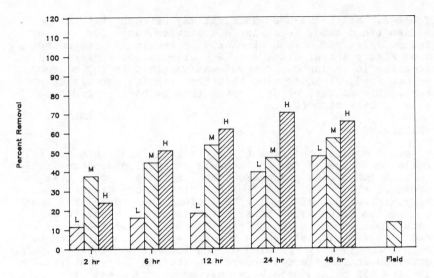

Figure 5.   Median Settling Column and Prototype Pond Removals of
            Total Phosphorus.

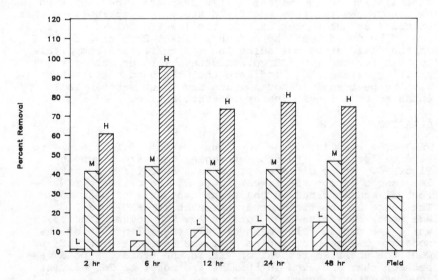

Figure 6.   Median Settling Column and Prototype Pond Removals of
            Total Kjeldahl Nitrogen.

Oxidized Nitrogen. The data for removal of oxidized
nitrogen forms (OX-N = nitrite + nitrate) are shown in
Figure 7. Because nitrate and nitrite are anions, they
have little affinity for the negatively charged surfaces
generally present in urban stormwater as a result of soil
erosion. As would be expected, then, the data show no trend
towards increasing removal with settling time. In fact, the
data sets for all laboratory studies and the field investigation serve as a good demonstration of the inapplicability
of extended stormwater detention in removing oxidized forms
of nitrogen. Should this be desirable, other methods such
as continuous pool retention ponds should be considered.

<u>Metals</u>

Figures 8 and 9 depict the results of the settling column
and full scale pond studies in the removal of zinc and lead,
respectively. The quality of the removals observed in
the higher TSS studies were in in approximate proportion to
the affinity of the two trace metals for suspended matter.
Lead removals on the order of 60 to 70 percent were observed
in the moderate to high TSS column studies in the first two
hours, with steady increases to values approaching 80 to 90
percent at 24 hours. The removal of zinc in the high TSS
studies was also characterized by reaching a large fraction
of the ultimate removal in the first two hours of settling.
In the low initial TSS studies, no lead removal data were

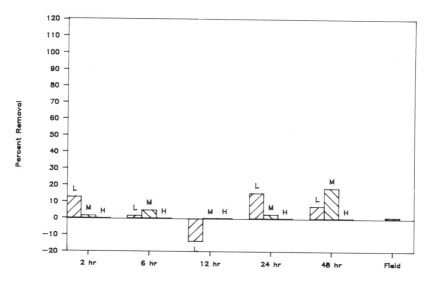

Figure 7.   Median Settling Column and Prototype Pond Removals of
            Oxidized Nitrogen.

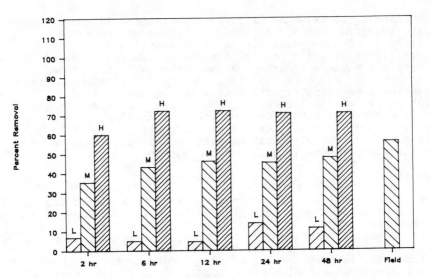

Figure 8.   Median Settling Column and Prototype Pond Removals of
            Total Zinc.

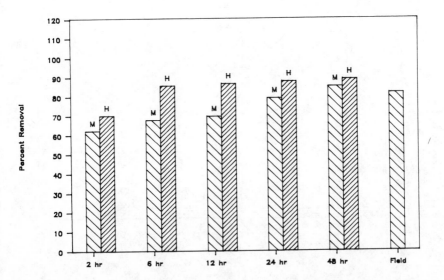

Figure 9.   Median Settling Column and Prototype Pond Removals of
            Total Lead.

available, but for zinc the median removals were quite low,
reaching less than 15 percent at 24 hours, as shown in
Figure 8. The poor quality of the removal was most likely
related to the high initial zinc concentrations, and the low
available surface area for sorption afforded by the low
solids concentrations. The concentrations of zinc and lead
in the stormwater of the field study catchment were
generally much lower, and therefore not comparable to those
observed in the settling column study samples. For the
events monitored, however, the median removals of zinc and
lead in the pond were approximately 60 and 80 percent,
respectively.

Particle Size - Pollutant Relationships

The data presented in the previous section   suggest
a relationship between the reduction of surface area in
stormwater solids and the observed removal of a number of
pollutants from suspension. In order to determine if this
was in fact the case, a stepwise regression was conducted on
the column settling data sets. The data were segregated
according to the initial TSS groupings (low, moderate, and
high), and each pollutant reduction evaluated as the
dependent variable in a series of models which included
change in particulate surface area in from one to three size
intervals as the independent variables. The STEPWISE
procedure of the Statistical Analysis System was used for
the computations (10). The procedure examines all relevant
models, and selects the best representation. Table 2
contains the results of the analysis. The independent
variables are listed in order of overall importance to the
regression model. For the high initial TSS grouping (from a
storm of 721 mg/L TSS), it may be observed that the removals
of TP, TKN, Zn, and Pb were all strongly correlated with
reduction of surface area in the size ranges with midpoints
of 30, 40, 40, and 40 micrometers, respectively. The
results were somewhat less conclusive for the storms of
moderate initial TSS. For each of the four constituents
cited above, the correlation coefficients were all below
0.80, and three independent variables were required for the
model. For the storms in the low initial TSS grouping, the
same observation may be made, as the coefficients were lower
still, and multiple size ranges were required for the
models.

The data from the high initial TSS models, however, may be
useful in confirming a target particle size for use in the
design of extended detention facilities. Examination of
Table 2 shows that the the size ranges which are most
closely related to the removal of total P, TKN, zinc, and
lead are from 25 to 45 micrometers. Of course, a basin
design based upon that size range would result in a theoretical removal efficiency of 100 percent for any larger
particles of a similar specific gravity. Using a Type I
settling analysis with water at 20 c, and a particle

specific gravity of 2.65, the following calculations may be
made for discrete particle settling velocities in quiescent
basins:

Particle Diameter (um)	Settling Velocity (m/day)
25	0.3
30	2.0
40	2.9
45	4.0

Using the above target settling velocities, it would be
possible to design a basin nonpoint storage pool overflow
rate which would be compatible with complete removal of
particles in the selected size range. In order to assure
that defects in basin geometry or unanticipated turbulence
do not unduly affect the removal of particles from suspension or resuspend previously removed particles, the overflow
rates shown above should be adjusted by some design factor
of safety.

Pond design should further account for the need for relatively rapid drawdown of the nonpoint pollution management
pool storage so that it might be available for capture of
subsequent runoff events, particularly the small to moderate
size events that characterize most of the stormwater runoff
in the course of a year. A study of urban runoff systems
conducted by the Northern Virginia Planning District
Commission (NVPDC) has examined the hydrology of the
national capital region, and has proposed storage volumes
for various levels of site imperviousness which represent a
trade-off between optimum volume stored and the desire to
achieve an average pool drawdown time of 24 hours (6). The
pond storage and release for the prototype examined in this
study were taken from these recommendations. An examination
of the storage recommendations in the NVPDC study shows that
a good linear relationship exists between recommended pond
NPS pool volume and site imperviousness, as follows:

NPS Storage Pool (ft.^{3}) = 29.87(% impervious) - 16.00

The above recommendation is based upon a brim-full drawdown
time of 40 hours for the NPS storage pool, which corresponds
to an average drawdown time of 24 hours on an annual basis.
The observed data show that the performance of the full-
scale prototype facility generally corresponded quite well
to that of the low to moderate TSS column studies in the 6
to 12 hour settling time periods. Because the actual median
detention time of the basin was determined to be in the
range of 6 hours, this is quite encouraging with respect to
the anticipation that a properly operating basin will
achieve removals similar to those of the settling columns at
the 24 hour mark.

Table 2. Correlation of Concentration Reductions
with particulate surface area reduction.

Parameter	TSS Grouping	Multiple Corr. Coeff.	Significant Particle Sizes in Model, um
Total P	Low	0.52	25-35, 55-65, 65-75
	Moderate	0.69	25-35, 55-65, 95-105
	High	0.97	25-35
TKN	Low	-	no significant corr.
	Moderate	0.78	105-115, 25-35, 35-45
	High	0.99	35-45
Total Zn	Low	0.37	45-55, 15-25
	Moderate	0.35	105-115, 95-105, 75-85
	High	0.99	35-45
Total Pb	Low	-	-
	Moderate	0.88	75-85, 35-45, 55-65
	High	0.99	35-45

References

1. Department of Civil Engineering, Virginia Tech, Final Report - MWCOG NURP, 1983, 299 pp.
2. Field, R., "Urban Runoff Receiving Water Impacts: Program Overview and Research Needs," Proceedings, Second International Conference on Urban Storm Drainage, pp. 246-255, University of Illinois, 1982.
3. Methods for Chemical Analysis of Water and Wastes, U. S. Environmental Protection Agency, 625/6-74-003, 1971.
4. Metro. Washington Council of Governments, Final Report - Washington, D.C. Area Urban Runoff Project, 1983, 158 pp
5. Northern Virginia Planning District Commission, Washington Metropolitan Urban Runoff Demonstration Project, 1983, 101 pp.
6. Northern Virginia Planning District Commission, Guidebook for Screening Urban Nonpoint Pollution Management Strategies, 1979, 121 pp.
7. Randall, C. W., et al., "The Significance of Stormwater Runoff in an Urbanizing Watershed," Progress in Water Technology, Vol. 9, pp. 547-562, (1976).
8. Randall, C.W., et al, "Urban Runoff Pollutant Removal By Sedimentation," Proceedings, Conference on Stormwater Detention Facilities, pp. 205-219, ASCE, NY, NY, 1982.
9. Sartor, J. D., and G. B. Boyd, "Water Pollution Aspects of Street Surface Contaminants," EPA-600/2-77-047, U.S. Environmental Protection Agency, Washington, D.C., 1977.
10. SAS Inst. Inc. Statistical Analysis System, Cary, N.C.
11. Sedimentation Engineering, ASCE, New York, NY, 1975.
12. Standard Methods for the Examination of Water and Wastewater, 15th Edition, APHA, 1980.
13. Technicon Industrial Systems, Tarrytown, NY, 1978.

DESIGN AND EFFECTIVENESS OF URBAN RETENTION BASINS

Yousef, Y.A.*, MASCE; Wanielista, M.P.*, MASCE
and Harper, H.H.*

ABSTRACT

Retention basins are recommended by practicing engineers and regulatory agencies for stormwater management in new land developments. They may require considerable space which limits their use in densely urbanized areas with expensive land and property values. Practicing engineers very often emphasize flow attenuation and flood control with pollution control as a side effect, but regulators emphasize both functions. Design considerations which enhance the performance of these ponds for pollution control should be fully developed and enforced.

Effectiveness of these basins and removal mechanisms of pollutants detected in urban stormwater have rarely been documented. This paper summarizes existing design considerations and removal efficiencies of selected pollutants in retention systems.

INTRODUCTION

Retention basins include on-line and off-line percolation ponds, infiltration and exfiltration systems (underground perforated pipes), vegetated swales, marsh land and other systems utilized for urban stormwater management. These basins are classified as off-line systems if there is no direct discharge to surface water and on-line systems if there is a potential for direct discharge. In other words, stormwater is diverted, stored and gradually removed by infiltration, evaporation and/or evapotranspiration within a specified period of time. On-line and off-line retention basins are built to increase abstraction and infiltration within the watershed and reduce peak discharge, and lessen potential pollutants in urban runoff.

Urban runoff contributes pollution loadings of nutrients and toxic substances such as heavy metals, oils and greases to receiving water bodies (Sartor et al., 1972; Wanielista, et al., 1981). Recent studies completed by the Nationwide Urban Runoff Program (NURP, 1983) concluded that heavy metals especially Cu, Pb and Zn were by far the most prevalent priority pollutant constituents in urban runoff. Copper appeared to be the most toxic of the three metals to aquatic life in some areas of the country. Nutrients were also detected in concentrations sufficient to produce accelerated eutrophication in lakes

*University of Central Florida, Department of Civil Engineering and Environmental Sciences, P.O. Box 25,000, Orlando, FL 32816.

and severely limit their recreational uses. However, organic priority pollutants were infrequently detected and at lower concentrations than the heavy metals.

Urban runoff characteristics are difficult to predict and considerable variability is exhibited both within a single event as well as between events. Intensity, duration, and frequency of storm events as well as antecedent dry periods and existing land use are significant parameters affecting runoff characteristics. Extensive studies on characterization of highway runoff at Maitland overpass and Interstate 4 located north of Orlando, Florida showed that lead, zinc and copper were the most common vehicle related heavy metals in ratios of 4.70:1.91:1.0, respectively for total concentrations, and ratios of 0.85:1.04:1.00, respectively, for dissolved species. Together these three metals accounted for approximately 91 percent of the dissolved heavy metals and 94 percent of the total metal concentrations analyzed (Pb, Zn, Cu, Ni, Cr, Cd) (Harper, 1985).

On-line retention requires containment of water for a long period (days-weeks) of time while detention basins hold water for short periods of time (hours-days) (Wanielista and Yousef, 1981). Other researchers in urban hydrology may differentiate between retention and detention based on shorter residence time which is the length of time stormwater runoff is held inside the basin. Retention basins with a fairly long residence time, concentrate most of the metals and phosphorus in the bottom sediments and the nitrogen is reduced by nitrification/denitrification processes (Yousef, et al., 1984; Jacobsen, et al., 1984). As a result, detention basins may be less effective for enhancement of the effluent water quality than retention basins. However wet retention/detention basins which maintain permenant pools have greater performance capabilities than dry basins which detain portions of flow from larger storms for a limited period of time (Sullivan and Schueler, 1985). Dual-purpose basins are conventional dry basins with modified outlet structures which significantly extend detention time. They appear to provide effective reductions in urban runoff loads. When basins are adequately sized, removals in excess of 90 percent for TSS and total Pb can be obtained. Pollutants with relatively high soluble fractions in urban runoff show lower reductions, approximately 65% for total P, 50% for BOD, COD, TKN, Cu and Zn (NURP, 1983).

Retention/detention basins, if designed adequately, remove suspended and dissolved pollutants by sedimentation, physical and chemical interactions and biological processes. Design features that promote these processes should effectively enhance the overall performance of these basins. Discussion of existing design considerations and effectiveness of retention basins for removal of nutrients and selected heavy metals will follow.

DESIGN CONSIDERATIONS

Retention basins are generally open excavated or natural depressions of varying size and depth loacted in excess land areas, green space of developments and/or recreational sites. The alternatives to open retention systems may include diversion to underground exfiltration tanks within road right-of-way. Whether retention basins are off-line

or on-line with controlled discharge to surface water, they are designed
to store a selected volume of runoff for a specified period of time with
a pre-determined bleed-down rate or infiltration rate. The State of
Florida Administrative Code (FAC) Chapter 17-25 (Cox, 1985) and the
State of Maryland Standards and Specifications for Infiltration
(February, 1984) specify draining of runoff water within a period of 72
hours following a storm event.

The soil and/or controlled release rates from retention basins must
have the capacity to drain off stored water between storm events. This
is particularly suitable in areas with deep sandy soil or in areas in
which impermeable lenses protect underlying groundwater. The bleed down
rates are based on water storage capacity and minimum infiltration rates
for the surrounding soils as shown in Table 1. The effective water
storage capacity of a soil is the void space available for water
storage. The minimum infiltration rates during saturated conditions can
be simulated in the field using double ring infiltrometers.
Relationships between infiltration rates by static double ring
infiltrometers and dynamic flow conditions have been initiated. These
infiltration rates were estimated for on-line swale systems with sandy,
sandy loam, and loamy sand soils. The estimates were based on a
materials balance of swale input and swale output waters. Minimum rates
of about 2-3 in/hr were noted for the swales, while the double ring
infiltrometer results were about 5-20 in/hr for the same sites
(Avellaneda, 1985). The soil texture specified in Table 1 is based on
the U.S. Department of Agricultural Soil texture triangle. It is
realized that minimum infiltration rates measured in the field may be
reduced by continuous deposition of fine and colloidal particles and/or
oil and grease films transported with runoff waters. Therefore
maintainance procedures are essential and should not be ignored.
Currently there is no or very little regional information on changes in
infiltrtion rates with operational time of retention systems.
Wanielista (1978) for the Orlando Area 208 program reported on infiltration rates and the variability with time associated with off-line retention ponds that were operating for up to 8 years. In sandy soil,
initial infiltration rates were greater than 10 in/hour. However
infiltration rates useful for design would be the limiting infiltration
rates which occur most of the time. These rates were approximately one
inch/hour for sandy and sandy loam soils.

The volume of storage required and the maximum permitted release
rates are based on the general concept that requires peak discharges for
a selected return period(s) to be unchanged after development. The
difference in runoff volume, between predevelopment and after development, should be stored temporarily. The FAC prescribes that "retention"
must be provided for the runoff resulting from 1.0 inch of rainfall; or,
for areas less than 100 acres, retention must be provided for 0.5 inch
of runoff. The FAC defines retention as an off-line system. These
regulations also require that retention in the form of on-line swales be
designed to percolate 80% of the runoff resulting from a 3-yr/1-hr
rainfall event and that a combination of retention practices provide for
the percolation of 100% of the runoff resulting from a 3-yr/1-hr
rainfall event. The rainfall volume associated with this return period
is assumed to be about 3" by most regulatory engineers in Florida.

TABLE 1 Hydrologic Soil Properties Suitable for
Retention Basins
(After Rawls, Brankensick and Saxton, 1982)

Soil Texture Class	Effective Water Capacity (in. of water/ in. of Soil)	Minimum Infiltration Rate	
		inches/hr	cm/hr
Sand	0.35	8.27	21
Loamy Sand	0.31	2.41	6.1
Sandy Loam	0.25	1.02	2.6
Loam	0.19	0.52	1.2

Similarly the State of Maryland requires design storm events with 2 and 10 year return periods with precipitation volumes of 3 and 5 inches/24 hours, respectively. These design storms are higher than those used in the State of Florida. The retained volume based on the pre-selected design storm event is constantly revised. Eventually it should reflect the desired pollutant removal efficiencies.

On-line retention systems may be designed with water depth varying between less than one foot (0.3 m) to more than 12 feet (3.66 m). For systems which maintain a permanent pool of water, shallow ponds with depth less than 4-6 feet (1.22-1.83 m) are desirable to promote aerobic environments and enhance water quality improvement. Also the bottom of the retention facilities should be above the mean high water table elevation by a minimum distance of 2-4 feet (0.61-1.22 m). This is consistent with recommended standards for land spreading and on-site wastewater treatment and disposal systems (EPA, 1980).

EFFECTIVENESS OF RETENTION PONDS

On-line stormwater retention ponds which may also be classified as wet ponds provide temporary storage for runoff waters and also have a permanent pool of water throughout the year. They have the potential to be very effective in removing pollutants borne in urban runoff (Sullivan and Schueler, 1985). The NURP study (1983) suggests that their performance should be expected to improve as the overflow rate ($Q_{R/A}$ = mean flow rate divided by basin surface area) decreases and as the volume ratio (V_B/V_R = basin volume divided by mean runoff volume) increases. Poor performance was found to occur in a basin with an average overflow rate during the mean storm of about six times the median settling velocity of 1.5 ft/hr (0.46 m/hr). Reductions in percent overall mass load for nine wet detention basins were less than 91, 69, 69, 79, 71, 60, 80, 66, 71, 95, and 71 for TSS, BOD, COD, TP, soluble P, TKN, NO_{2+3}, T Cu, T Pb and T Zn, respectively (NURP, 1983).

Luzkow and others (1981) reported the effectiveness of a pond in Michigan receiving runoff from a 66.7 acre residential, commercial and parkland in Michigan. Dead storage volume of the pond was 233,000 ft^3 (6594 m^3), live storage was 310,000 ft^3 (8778 m^3), and residence time was estimated to range from one to several days. Suspended solids removal was greater than 50% for 11 of the 14 monitored storms. Total phosphorus removals were greater than 50% for 8 of the 14 storms, and total kjeldahl nitrogen removal was greater than 80 percent for 6 of the 7 monitored storms.

Retention through wetlands was studied by Scherger and Davis (1982). The wetland dead storage was 630,000 ft^3 (17829 m^3) and live storage was 2,620,000 ft^3 (74146 m^3) receiving stormwater from 1200 acres of mixed residential, parkland, and agricultural land uses. Total phosphorus removal ranged from 40 to 60%, and nitrogen removal was 20 to 30%. Nigrogen was removed in the summer and released in the winter.

Nine storm events were sampled during an eighteen month period to evaluate the retention/detention pond system in Timbercreek development, Boca Raton, Florida. Timbercreek is a 122 acre single family residential development. The drainage system consists of grassed swales, catch basins, stormsewers and 7.9 acres of interconnected lakes. The treatment efficiency averaged greater than 80% for OP and NOX of the loading removed from the system. Total suspended solids had 64%, total phosphate 60% and total nitrogen 15% efficiency (Cullum, 1985).

Researchers have attempted to predict the pollution removal efficiencies based on settleability of various sized particulates transported with runoff water. Whipple and Hunter (1981) concluded that detention of runoff in an undisturbed environment with a water depth of 6 feet for 32 hours resulted in removal of substantial quantities of the common pollutants associated with urban runoff. Therefore, technology is emerging which will help estimate constituent removal rates through sedimentation based on relationships to be developed between suspended solids particle size to constituent concentration (Ben Urbonas, 1984).

It appears that retention ponds with dead storage throughout the year could be effective in removal of urban pollution constituents if designed for a long mean residence time (days-weeks) and a depth limited to six feet. The removal mechanisms include sedimentation, chemical interactions and biological processes. Removal efficiencies of retention ponds receiving highway runoff located in Orange County, Florida at Maitland Interchange and Interstate 4 and near Disney World will be discussed.

STUDY SITE

The site selected for this investigation is the Maitland Interchange on Interstate 4. This interchange, located north of the city of Orlando, Florida, was constructed in 1976 (see Figure 1). Three ponds are interconnected by way of large culverts so that when the northeastern pond (A) exceeds the design level it can discharge to the northwestern pond (B). The northwestern pond has the capability to discharge to the southwestern pond (referred to hereafter as the West

Pond) when design elevations are exceeded. However, since the volume of
both Pond A and Pond B are quite large relative to their receiving
watersheds, it is anticipated that a discharge from Ponds A or B to the
West Pond would only occur as a result of an extreme rainfall event.
Therefore, under normal conditions, the only input into the West Pond is
by way of a 45 cm concrete culvert which drains much of the Maitland
Boulevard overpass. Discharge from the West Pond travels to Lake Lucien
through a large culvert. A flashboard riser system regulates the water
level in the West Pond, and a discharge rarely occurs to Lake Lucien.
Because of the well-defined nature of both the inputs and outputs to the
West Pond, this system was chosen for investigation.

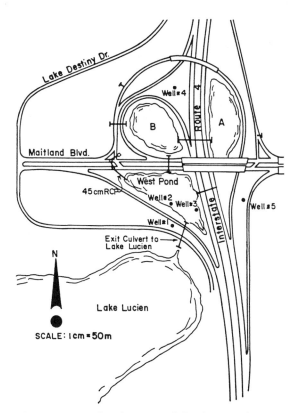

FIGURE 1   Study Site at Maitland Interchange

The West Pond has an approximate surface area of 1.3 ha, and average
depth of 1.5m, and a total drainage area of 19.8 ha. The pond maintains
a large standing crop of filamentous algae, particularly Chara,
virtually year round. Because of the shallow water depth and large
amount of algal production, the pond waters remain in a well-oxygenated
state. The sediment material is predominately sand which is covered by
a thin 1 cm layer of organic matter.

Field investigations conducted during 1982-1984 at the West Pond were divided into the following tasks: 1) determination of the quantity of pollutants entering the West Pond by way of stormwater runoff; 2) determination of the average water quality parameters in the retention basin water; 3) assessment of the accumulation of nutrients and heavy metals in the sediments of the pond: and 4) monitoring of heavy metal concentrations in groundwaters beneath the retention basin.

RAINFALL-RUNOFF-RETENTION POND WATERS

Five sets of water samples were collected in duplicate, filtered in the field, and analyzed in the laboratory. Each set included composite samples of rainfall, runoff and water samples from retention ponds at Maitland Interchange and I-4, Orlando, Florida. The results were averaged and presented in Table 2. Dissolved solids, alkalinity, and total hardness in the Maitland Pond water were higher than the same parameters in runoff water, presumably due to their concentration by evaporation of the pond water.

TABLE 2 Changes in Selected Water Quality Parameters by
Retention at Maitland Interchange and Interstate-4
North Orlando, Florida (milligrams/liter)

Parameter	Rainfall		Runoff		Retention Pond	
	$\bar{x}$	σ_x	$\bar{x}$	σ_x	$\bar{x}$	σ_x
pH (lab)	5.2	0.7	6.9	0.2	6.8	0.2
Dissolved Solids	9.8	2.1	75.9	39.9	113.3	10.4
Alk ($CaCO_3$)	1.0	1.0	44.4	16.2	50.4	9.5
$SO_4^=$	2.7	1.4	11.9	10.2	26.2	5.5
Cl	1.6	0.7	2.9	1.5	5.1	1.0
TN as N	0.66	0.50	0.79	0.18	0.51	0.16
NH_4-N	0.11	0.10	0.09	0.07	0.04	0.02
NO_3-N	0.31	0.26	0.33	0.26	0.15	0.26
TP as P	0.02	0.0	0.05	0.01	0.01	0.0
OP as P	0.01	0.0	0.03	0.02	0.0	0.0
Ca^{++}	1.6	1.0	27.0	28.3	20.5	3.4
Mg^{++}	0.2	0.1	1.17	1.34	4.5	0.4
Na^+	2.2	2.6	2.9	2.3	5.6	0.9
K^+	0.5	0.4	1.7	1.6	4.3	1.6
SiO_2	0.1	0.1	1.9	1.4	1.2	1.2
Humic Acids	1	0.5	5	4	4	2

It was interesting to notice that the average total nitrogen (TN) and total phosphorus (TP) concentrations in Maitland Pond Water were lower than those in rainfall and runoff waters. Inorganic nitrogen was the major nitrogen fraction in rainwater and organic nitrogen was the major fraction in pond water. The average inorganic nitrogen and total phosphorus concentrations in Maitland pond water did not exceed 30% of the average concentrations in highway runoff water. The pond appears to be very efficient in the removal of inorganic nitrogen and phosphorus species from highway runoff water. The same conclusions were reached during a detailed analysis of the pond by Hvitved-Jacobsen et al (1984).

REMOVAL EFFICIENCIES

A more detailed analysis was completed to investigate the effectiveness of the pond. The average water quality concentrations in stormwater runoff and the West Pond is shown in Table 3. Removal of particulate metals averaged 95.1, 96.2, and 77 percent for Pb, Zn and Cu respectively, while removal of dissolved fractions averaged 54.5, 88.3, and 49.7 percent respectively. Similarly dissolved phosphorus, ammonia nitrogen and nitrite/nitrate removals averaged 90.1, 81.6, and 86.5 resepctively. Particulate phosphorus and organic nitrogen removals were poor as indicated in Table 3. Water quality parameters for pond water such as chlorophyll a, dissolved oxygen, BOD and turbidity indicate a well-aerated pond of high water clarity.

TABLE 3 Water Quality Parameters in Highway Runoff and Retention Pond Waters at Maitland and I-4

Parameter	Runoff			Pond			Percent Removal In Pond*
	N	$\bar{x}$ (ug/L)	σ_x	N	$\bar{x}$ (ug/L)	σ_x	
Lead (Pb)							
Dissolved	150	33.0	40.2	30	15	8.5	54.5
Particulate	150	148		30	7.2		95.1
Zinc (Zn)							
Dissolved	150	40.0	42.6	30	4.7	2.6	88.3
Particulate	150	33.9		30	1.3		96.2
Copper (Cu)							
Dissolved	150	28.6	24.7	30	14.4	0.5	49.7
Particulate	150	10.0		30	2.3		77.0
Phosphorus (P)							
Dissolved	121	42.5	47.6	40	4.2	3.5	90.1
Particulate	121	31.7		40	28.4		11.4
Nitrogen (N)							
Organic	55	928	895	40	826	491	11.0
$NH_3 + NH_4^+$	108	176	341	40	34.1	37.3	81.6
$NO_2^- + NO_3^-$	111	295	326	40	39.8	33.5	86.5

*based on concentration

Hvitved-Jacobsen et al. (1984) concluded that 99% of the total input
of phosphorus during 7 years had accumulated in the bottom sediments and
85-90% of the total nitrogen had been removed probably by nitrification-
denitrification (Figure 2).   Also it is interesting to notice that
concentrations of phosphorus in the bottom sediments of the ponds
investigated near Orlando, Florida were higher than concentrations of
total nitrogen (Figure 3).   Apparently there is a continuous
accumulation of phosphorus in the sediments and a loss of nitrogen by
denitrifiction (Yousef et al., 1984).

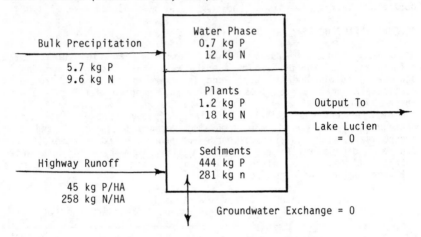

FIGURE 2   Nutrient Balance for the West Pond at
            Maitland Interchange and I-4

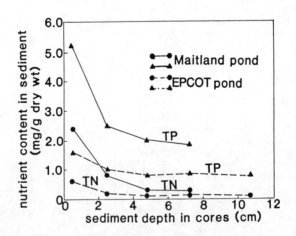

FIGURE 3   Average Phosphorus and Nitrogen Content in the
            Sediments of Retention Ponds Receiving Highway Runoff

FATE OF HEAVY METALS

The pond was found to be very effective in removal of heavy metal inputs from highway runoff. Particulate species were removed to a larger degree than dissolved species and appear to concentrate in the top layer of the sediments (Table 4). Heavy metal concentrations in the top one centimeter of the Maitland pond suggest that upon entering, the majority of particulate metals settle out quickly and are deposited near the point of input. This tendancy was most obvious for Pb and Zn which peaked in sediment concentrations at a distance of only 15 m from the inlet followed by a rapid decline with increasing distance. Cu did not appear to exhibit pronounced peaks in sediment concentrations, but seemed to settle out over a larger flow path length. However most of the metals were retained in the pond sediments within a distance 60-90 m from the stormwater inlet. Designs should provide physical configurations where the flow velocity is minimized and the distance from the pond inlet to the discharge point is maximized. The possibility of short circuiting and hydraulically dead zones should be avoided.

TABLE 4   Average Metal Concentrations in Bottom Sediments from Maitland Pond

Metal	Concentration (ug/g Dry Weight)				
	0-1 cm	1-3.5 cm	3.5-6 cm	6-8.5 cm	8.5-13 cm
Pb	112.7	37.6	24.5	17.0	13.5
Zn	45.4	10.7	6.5	4.6	3.2
Cu	19.1	9.4	7.5	5.1	4.2

The vertical distribution of metal concentrations through the sediment cores (Table 4) shows a rapid decline following an exponential decay. The majority of metal species are attenuated in the top 5-10 cm of sediments. After eight years of operation, most metals associated with sediments have remained in the top 10 cm. Experiments were conducted to examine the potential release of heavy metals in the pond sediments back to solution. Speciation and redox experiments concluded that Cu and Zn are stable and exist in relatively immobile association with Fe/Mn oxides and organic matter. Pb is held to a large degree in a strong exchangeable association. Changes in redox potential from strongly oxidized to strongly reduced conditions did not appear to affect the release of metals from the sediments under current pH values of 7.5-8.5 (Harper, 1985).

IMPACT ON GROUNDWATER

Multiport groundwater monitoring wells were installed to depths 6 m at five locations in the Maitland Interchange in retention pond, swale and control areas. Groundwater samples were collected on a monthly basis for 16 months from five sample ports on each monitoring well. Average concentrations in these wells are presented in Table 5. In general, mean concentrations of all heavy metals measured except copper, were greater beneath the pond than within the pond. Also Pb, Zn and Cu concentrations beneath the pond were lower than concentrations beneath dry swale areas. The control area did not receive highway runoff and the underlying groundwater concentrations were found to be the lowest among locations tested. It is believed that slower infiltration rates combined with increased mean residence time in the wet area favor retention of metals in the sediments. There is no evidence to indicate that metals concentrated in the sediments are migrating, and it is very unlikely in this case that a pollution hazard exists to nearby surface or groundwater.

TABLE 5   Concentrations in Monitoring Wells at Maitland
          Interchange Drainage Basin

Metal	Average Concentration (ug/l)		
	Beneath West Pond	Beneath Dry Swales	Control
Pb	18.3	28.2	12.8
Zn	19.8	27.4	20.6
Cu	12.6	14.6	10.8

CONCLUSION AND RECOMMENDATIONS

There are generally used for stormwater management two types of retention ponds, namely off-line and on-line ponds. Off-line ponds are designed in Florida primarily for pollution control. Current criteria specifies an off-line pond must have the volume to store the runoff from the first one inch of rainfall, provided the pond will permit infiltration of all waters within 72 hours.

Classification of on-line retention ponds among practitioners is arbitrary, based on mean residence time. However the most effective ponds for pollution control are those designed with permanent water pool, relatively long mean residence time (days-weeks) and shallow depth (4-6 ft or 1.32-1.83 m). These ponds could be designed to effectively remove nutrients (N and P) and heavy metals (Pb, Zn, Cu). These systems should be evaluated based on their frequency of overflow discharges to adjacent surface waters. There may be a limited use of these systems because of the cost and available land. Therefore an urgent need exists to optimize their effectiveness.

Other forms of retention basins are used to treat urban runoff but are less effective or not adequately studied. For example marsh land and wetland systems may be effective in removal of heavy metals but less effective in removal of nutrients. Systems to be designed for nutrient removal should avoid stagnant conditions which promote anaerobic environments. Similarly dry swales may remove heavy metals but they are very poor in removing nutrients. Also, there exists the possibility of contaminating groundwater beneath dry swales.

Maintenance procedures have to be developed based on the magnitude of organic debris to be deposited to the bottom of retention basins. Probably restoration procedures every 10-15 years may be required. A well-oxygenated pond with minimum organic debris appears to provide the environment for improved removal efficiencies of nutrients and selected heavy metals.

APPENDIX 1 - References

1. Avellaneda, Eduardo, "Hydrologic Design of Swales", Thesis, University of Central Florida, December 1985.

2. Cox, John H. "Overview of BMP's and Urban Stormwater Management" in proceedings of Stormwater Management "An Update" edited by M.P. Wanielista and Y.A. Yousef, University of Central Florida at Orlando, pp. 237-246 (July 15, 1985).

3. Cullum, Michael G. "Stormwater Runoff Analysis at a Single Family Residential Site" in proceedings of Stormwater Management "An Update" edited by M.P. Wanielista and Y.A. Yousef, University of Central Florida at Orlando, Publication #85-1, pp. 247-256, (July 15, 1985).

4. Harper, H.H. Ph.D. Dissertation, University of Central Florida, Fall 1985.

5. Hvitved-Jacobsen, T., Yousef, Y.A., Wanielista, M.P. and Pearce, D.B. "Fate of Phosphorus and Nitrogen in Ponds Receiving Highway Runoff", published in The Science of the Total Environment, Elsevier Science Publishers B.V., Amsterdam-Printed in the Netherlands, Vol. 33, pp. 259-270, (1984).

6. Luzkow, S.M., Scherger, D.A. and Davis, J.A. "Effectiveness of Two In-line Urban Stormwater Best Management Practices", International Symposium on Urban Hydrology, Hydraulics and Sediment Control, University of Kentucky, Lexington, Kentucky, pp. 193-206, (July 27-30, 1981).

7. Maryland Department of Natural Resources, Stormwater Management Divison, "Maryland Standards and Specifications for Stormwater Management Infiltration Practices", pp 2-19, February 1984.

8. Rawls, W.J., D.L. Brakensiek, and K.E. Saxton, "Estimation of Soil Properties", Transactions of the American Society of Agricultural Engineers, Vol. 25, No. 5, pp 1316-1320, 1982.

9. Sartor, J.D. and Boyd, G.B. <u>Water Pollution Aspects of Street Surface Contaminants</u>, U.S. Environmental Protection Agency Report #EPA-R2-72-081, (1972).

10. Scherger, D.A. and Davis, J.A. "Control of Stormwater Runoff Pollutant Loads by a Wetland and Retention Basin", International Symposium on Urban Hydrology, Hydraulics, and Sediment Control, University of Kentucky, Lexington, Kentucky, pp. 109-123, (July 27-29, 1982).

11. Sullivan, M.P. and Schueler, T.R. "Simulation of Stormwater and Water Quality Attributes of Ponds with HSPF" published in Proceedings of Stormwater and Water quality Model Users Group Meeting April 12-13, 1984, EPA-600/9-85-003, January 1985.

12. U.S. Environmental Protection Agency, "Design Manual: Onsite Wastewater Treatment and Disposal Systems", Office of Water Program Operations, U.S. EPA 20460, October 1980.

13. U.S. Environmental Protection Agency, "Final Report of the Nationwide Urban Runoff Program" prepared by Water Planning Division, WH 554, Washington, D.C. (1983).

14. Urbonas, Ben, "Report on 1982 Engineering Foundation Conference on Stormwater Retention Facilities", Proceedings of the Third International Conference on Urban Storm Drainage, Goteborg, Sweden, June 4-8, 1984, pp. 743-748.

15. Wanielista, M.P. "Stormwater Management - Quantity and Quality", Ann Arbor Science Publishers Inc., 1978.

16. Wanielista, M.P., Yousef, Y.A., Golding, B.L., and Cassagnol, C.L. "Stormwater Management Manual", for Florida Department of Environmental Regulation, (1981).

17. Whipple, W. Jr and Hunter, J.V. "Settleability of Urban Runoff Pollution", Journal of Water Pollution Control Federation, Vol 53 No. 12, pp. 1726-1731, December 1981.

18. Yousef, Y.A.; T. Hvitved-Jacobsen; M.P. Wanielista; and R.D. Tolbert. "Nutrient Interactions in Retention/Detention Ponds Receiving Highway Runoff", presented at the 51st Annual Conference for Water Pollution Control Federation, October 1-4, 1984, New Orleans, Louisiana.

19. Yousef, Y.A.; M.P. Wanielista; H.H. Harper; D.B. Pearce; and R.D. Tolbert. <u>Best Management Practices - Removal of Highway Contaminants by Roadside Swales</u>, final report submitted to Florida Department of Transportation, Contract No. 99700-7292 (1984).

REGIONAL BMP MASTER PLANS

John P. Hartigan, M. ASCE*

Introduction

The majority of local stormwater management programs implemented during the past two decades have relied upon onsite runoff control facilities financed and constructed by land developers in accordance with local performance standards. Consequently, when urban nonpoint pollution management programs were spawned by the 208 planning programs in the 1970's, it was understandable that most local programs relied upon the use of onsite best management practices (BMPs) to achieve water quality management objectives. The popular approach is to modify traditional detention storage designs for peak flow control to achieve enhanced solids settling (1) or additional biological and physical/chemical processes for pollution removal (2).

In recent years, the reliability of an onsite control or "piecemeal" approach to peak runoff management has been called into question. Assessments of piecemeal approaches with stormwater models have led several investigators to conclude that the random placement of stormwater detention facilities in a watershed may result in little or no reduction of peak flow in downstream sections of the watershed, and may sometimes even aggravate flood hazards (3,4,5,6,7,8,9). These studies have concluded that stormwater detention facilities must be strategically located within an urban watershed in order to achieve significant peak flow control in downstream areas. For example, Bonuccelli et al. (3) found stormwater detention facilities in the Four Mile Run watershed of northern Virginia were most effective at achieving downstream flood protection when located in the central and upper central sections of the watershed. Similar conclusions about locational differences in detention effectiveness were reached by Duru (5) and Traver and Chadderton (9) based upon stormwater modeling studies. Some investigators have documented the capital and O&M cost-savings which can be achieved by strategically locating regional stormwater detention facilities (6,10), while others have developed optimization models for locating and sizing regional detention facilities based upon system constraints such as total costs and peak flow control (11,12,13).

Although the piecemeal approach to BMP implementation is widely used throughout the U.S. today, many of the same arguments for strategically locating peak runoff controls in a watershed also apply to nonpoint pollution controls. One of the first areas to recognize the viability of regional BMP facilities is the State of New Jersey

---

*Associate, Camp Dresser & McKee, 7630 Little River Turnpike, Suite 500, Annandale, VA 22003.

where the use of strategically located "master" detention basins
serving areas of up to 200 acres each is considered to be an acceptable nonpoint pollution management technique. The regional BMP
approach is also achieving growing acceptance in southeastern Virginia
where nonpoint pollution management plans to protect water supply
reservoirs have recently been formulated (2,14).

This paper summarizes some important considerations and procedures
for developing comprehensive nonpoint pollution management plans
relying upon regional facilities. The advantages and disadvantages of
piecemeal and comprehensive approaches to nonpoint pollution management are discussed. Procedures for developing a comprehensive
regional BMP master plan are outlined.

Comparison of Piecemeal and Regional BMP Approaches

In comparison with the regional BMP approach, the major advantages
of the piecemeal approach are ease of implementation and reduced
administrative costs. Unlike the regional BMP approach which requires
the local government to carry out advanced planning and the design,
financing, and construction of regional facilities, the piecemeal
approach delegates most responsibilities to the land developer. The
onsite BMPs are planned, designed, financed and constructed for each
development site by the individual land developers to conform with
general performance standards promulgated by the local government.
The local government is typically only responsible for reviewing each
facility design to ensure conformance with design requirements and for
inspecting the facility upon completion of construction. Maintenance
responsibility is typically assigned to the property owner (e.g.,
homeowner's association).

Because the developer assumes most responsibilities for BMP
implementation, the piecemeal approach can be implemented by a local
government at little additional increase in administrative costs,
particularly if an onsite control program for peak runoff management
is already in effect. By comparison, there are greater "front-end"
costs for a regional program, including the costs of advanced planning
studies to site and design regional BMPs and the financing requirements associated with constructing these facilities in advance of
future urban development.

Under the regional BMP approach, a single BMP facility is strategically located to simultaneously control nonpoint pollution loadings
from multiple development projects. The maximum drainage area of
regional BMPs is typically restricted to a few hundred acres so that
the facilities do not have to be permitted under state dam safety
regulations and to minimize the length of unprotected stream channels
upstream of each BMP. Each regional BMP facility must be programmed
and constructed by the local government prior to the start of major
urban development in its drainage area. The total capital costs for
each BMP facility can be recovered by "fee-in-lieu-of" contributions
by the individual developers in the watershed or by other financing
mechanisms. For example, the pro-rata cost-share formula for each BMP
facility might be based upon the proportion of total imperviousness
within the respective land development projects that the BMP serves.

In comparison with the piecemeal approach, the major advantages of the regional BMP approach are as follows:

(1) Reduction in Maintenance Costs: Surveys conducted during the EPA NURP studies (15) indicate that average annual O&M costs for detention basin BMPs are about 3%-5% of the base construction cost. Since there will be fewer BMP facilities to maintain, the annual cost of local government maintenance programs are significantly lower. For example, Hartigan and Quasebarth (2) documented savings in average annual maintenance costs of $20,000 to $45,000 per sq mi of development for a regional BMP plan for a watershed in southeastern Virginia. Moreover, since a large watershedwide BMP facility can be designed to facilitate maintenance activities, annual maintenance costs are further reduced in comparison with onsite BMP facilities. Examples of design features that are typically only feasible at large watershedwide facilities to reduce maintenance costs include: improved access roads that facilitate the movement of equipment and work crews onto the site (by comparison, onsite detention facilities often adjoin residential backyards); additional storage capacity to permit an increase in the time interval between facility clean-out operations; and onsite containment areas for sediment and debris removed during clean-out.

(2) Reduction in Capital Costs for BMP Facilities: The use of a single stormwater detention facility to control runoff from 5 to 20 development sites within a 100- to 200-acre subwatershed permits the local government to take advantage of economies-of-scale in designing and constructing the regional BMP facility. In other words, the total capital cost (e.g., construction, land acquisition, engineering design) of several small onsite detention basins is greater than the cost of a single detention basin which provides the same total storage volume. For example, a regional BMP plan for a 6 sq mi urbanizing watershed in southeastern Virginia documented up to a 60% reduction in capital costs in comparison with an onsite BMP approach (2). If reductions in land consumption were taken into consideration, the total cost savings associated with the regional approach would be even higher.

(3) Increase in Land Development Opportunities: Placement of a single BMP facility at the mouth of a 100- to 200-acre subwatershed requires less consumption of buildable land than the piecemeal approach. Besides requiring less acreage for ponding because of economies-of-scale, the regional BMP approach typically relies upon existing floodplain areas for a considerable amount of the required surface area. As a result, the regional BMP approach can permit an increase in the number of residential lots that can be developed in a watershed and a corresponding increase in a local government's tax base.

(4) Increased Opportunities for Recreational Uses: Because they are larger detention facilities, are typically located in floodplains, and can be designed to provide sufficient access, regional BMP facilities are better suited to recreational uses than typical onsite BMPs.

(5) <u>Opportunity to Manage Nonpoint Pollution Impacts of Existing Development</u>: Some existing urban development will typically be located within the watersheds of regional BMP facilities. Thus, the regional approach offers opportunities to retrofit some percentage of urban development with nonpoint pollution controls in a cost-effective manner.

(6) <u>Improved Peak Flow Control</u>: Regional BMPs can be designed as multipurpose facilities which achieve peak flow control as well as nonpoint pollution management. For example, sufficient storage capacity can be provided above the permanent pool of a wet detention basin to achieve a peak-shaving performance standard for a single design storm or mutliple design storms (e.g., 25- and 2-year). Because they can be strategically located within a watershed, these multipurpose regional facilities can be sited to ensure more reliable peak flow control than randomly located onsite controls.

Land developers typically recognize that economies-of-scale available at a single regional BMP facility should produce lower capital costs in comparison with several onsite BMP facilities. The regional BMP approach would also eliminate the need for a developer to provide more than one onsite BMP facility for development sites that do not have a single runoff outlet. Finally, land developers tend to prefer the watershedwide approach because it eliminates the need to set aside acreage for an onsite BMP facility, and therefore could permit an increase in the buildable acreage within the development site.

The major disadvantages of the regional BMP approach include the following: local governments must perform advance planning studies to locate and develop preliminary designs for regional BMP facilities; local governments must finance, design, and construct the regional BMP facilities before the majority of future urban development occurs, with reimbursement by developers over a build-out period that can be 5-20 years in duration; and, in some cases, local governments may be required to carry out extraordinary maintenance activities for regional BMPs which are perceived by the public to be primarily recreational facilities that merit water quality protection.

Development of Regional BMP Master Plan

The cornerstone of the regional BMP approach is a facility master plan which addresses BMP siting requirements, facility design criteria, water quality benefits, and financing requirements. Key issues are summarized below.

<u>Facility Siting</u>. Important issues to be considered in strategically locating regional BMPs include the following: type of BMP; drainage area restrictions; whether the BMPs should control existing land use as well as future land use; locational constraints related to water quality management and peak runoff control; and land availability.

<u>Type of BMP</u>: The first step in the planning process is to select the type(s) of BMPs to be applied in different study areas. Unlike

detention basin BMPs, the feasibility of infiltration BMPs is heavily dependent upon the physical features of the study area. For example, infiltration BMPs are typically unsuitable for areas with a seasonally high water table and/or relatively low soil permeability (16). Further, the only infiltration BMP which is suitable for relatively large drainage areas is the infiltration basin which is typically limited to a 50-acre drainage area. Thus, drainage area constraints tend to limit the feasibility of basing a regional BMP plan on infiltration measures. For purposes of this paper, it is assumed that regional BMP facilities will be limited to wet detention basins.

In order to perform facility planning evaluations, the approximate storage requirements of each regional BMP must be known. For planning purposes, the storage requirements of the wet detention basin BMP may be based upon the permanent pool criteria presented in this paper plus any peak flow control storage. Permanent pool storage factors for each land use category can be multiplied by the fraction of the BMP drainage area in each land use to calculate the total required storage. Similar storage factors can be developed for calculations of the temporary detention storage required for peak runoff control.

Drainage Area Restrictions: A concern that is often raised about regional stormwater management facilities is that areas upstream of each facility are not protected from streambank erosion and flooding. These concerns are also applicable to regional BMP's, since they are likely to be multipurpose facilities which achieve peak runoff control as well as water quality management benefits. In order to minimize the amount of unprotected upstream area and also achieve significant cost-savings due to economies-of-scale, the maximum drainage area of a regional BMP facility should be on the order of a few hundred acres. Average imperviousness in the watershed will influence the maximum permissable drainage area, with highly impervious areas requiring a lower maximum value and vice versa. If there are still significant concerns about peak runoff impacts upstream of the regional BMP despite the drainage area restriction, channel improvements and onsite runoff controls might also be considered for unprotected areas.

Another constraint on regional BMP drainage areas is that relatively high storage volumes may result in dam heights which require permits under the state's dam safety program. In most areas, a drainage area of a few hundred acres will not fall under the purview of dam safety regulations.

Control of Existing Land Use: An important factor in siting regional BMP's is whether nonpoint pollution loadings from both existing and future land use patterns must be controlled. Traditionally, peak runoff management requirements have been restricted to new development, with the costs of required control measures assumed by developers and passed onto the eventual property owners. These peak runoff requirements typically are based on a performance standard which limits postdevelopment peak flow from a specified design storm to the predevelopment level. The tendency to restrict runoff control requirements to new development reflects the emphasis of early stormwater management programs on easily administered approaches and nondegradation performance standards.

Regional BMP's provide an opportunity to retrofit existing urban development with nonpoint pollution controls. By strategically locating regional facilities, they can be used to control nonpoint pollution from existing urban or agricultural land uses as well as new urban development. Land availability may influence the feasibility of using regional BMP's to control existing urban development as well as proposed development, since acceptable BMP sites are likely to be in shorter supply within built-up areas. Likewise, the location of the regional BMP facility and the resulting level of control of existing development may be influenced by the mechanism selected to finance the facility. Under traditional financing mechanisms (e.g., "fee-in-lieu-of" program), local governments may only be permitted to recover BMP capital costs from new development projects. Consequently, BMP retrofit projects are likely to be more attractive if the financing mechanism involves a user-charge system (e.g., stormwater utility) which applies to existing development as well as new development.

Locational Constraints--Water Quality Management: The locational differences in urban nonpoint pollution impacts should be considered when siting regional BMP's. The nonpoint pollution impacts of runoff are likely to be positively related to the hydraulic residence time of the downstream receiving water body. In other words, more significant water quality impacts are likely to occur if the downstream receiving water is a reservoir, embayment, or estuary than if it is a stream or river system. Reservoirs, embayments and estuaries will typically exhibit relatively high residence times in comparison with the same lengths of free-flowing streams and rivers. The higher residence times can result in algal growth and dissolved oxygen impacts follow-ing the return to quiescent conditions after the rainstrom, as well as the undesirable buildup of nutrients and toxicants. By comparison, the discharge of urban nonpoint pollution into stream or river systems may not produce adverse impacts due to conditions such as higher flow velocities, shorter residence times, greater reaeration, and higher turbidity levels, although elevated concentrations of heavy metals may contravene aquatic life criteria for a few hours during many rain-storms.

Therefore, an important criterion for regional BMP siting is the hydraulic residence time of downstream receiving waters. Areas which are upstream from reservoirs, embayments, or estuaries may warrant more extensive coverage of regional BMP's than areas which will only impact stream or river systems. Likewise, the section of the receiving water which is directly impacted by urban nonpoint pollution discharges should be considered in evaluating the required coverage of regional BMP's. For reservoirs, the water quality in the vicinity of the dam is often more critical than water quality in the headwaters since water supply intakes tend to be located at or near the dam and nonpoint pollutant transport through the upper end of the reservoir generally results in some pollution removal. Therefore, more extensive coverage of regional BMP's will often be warranted for drainage areas which discharge directly into the lower end of a reservoir. For embayments and estuaries, drainage areas discharging directly to the lower end of the tidal system may be less critical than areas which discharge into the headwaters. This is because tidal exchanges can result in nonpoint pollution discharges near the mouth of the embayment or estuary being significantly diluted and rapidly flushed out of the system into adjoining estuarine or ocean waters, where water quality impacts may not be significant. By comparison, nonpoint pollution discharges into the headwaters of embayments and estuaries may encounter poor tidal flushing and significant hydraulic residence times, with severe water quality problems a possible result.

For streams and river systems, urban nonpoint pollution impacts are likely to be greatest where small stream gradients result in relatively low flow velocities and the ratio of urbanized drainage area to rural drainage area is relatively high. However, regional BMP's could certainly be warranted for other circumstances such as the protection of a rural stream from nonpoint pollution discharges originating in an urbanized tributary area.

Another locational factor which should be considered in siting regional BMP's is the distribution of beneficial uses within the receiving water. Drainage areas which discharge into receiving water segments exhibiting more critical beneficial uses may warrant more extensive coverage of regional BMP's.

Locational Constraints--Peak Runoff Control: Where feasible, regional BMP's should be designed as multipurpose facilities which achieve both peak-shaving and water quality management benefits. For example, a typical performance standard might be for the regional wet detention basin to maintain both the 25-year and 2-year peak flows for ultimate development conditions at the levels associated with an un-developed watershed. The performance standard for the 25-year design storm would address downstream flooding impacts, while the performance standard for the 2-year design storm would address streambank erosion impacts.

In order to maximize the peak-shaving benefits of the regional BMP system, locational differences in peak runoff control benefits should be considered during the facility siting evaluation. Preferably, the regional BMP master plan should be developed at the same time as a peak runoff control master plan, so that both water quality management and peak-shaving requirements can be considered in a single evalu-ation. Such an analysis should be based upon sensitivity studies with a hydraulic model, such as SWMM/EXTRAN (17), which can simulate water-shedwide impacts of the elongated hydrograph recession limbs associ-ated with the BMP outflow. Individual BMP sites and combinations thereof should be iteratively deleted from the hydraulic model for evaluations of the downstream attenuation of peak-shaving benefits. Any BMP sites that exhibit either significant downstream reductions in peak-shaving benefits or higher downstream peak flows than undeveloped conditions are potentially undesirable and should be flagged for further analyses. These additional analyses might include moving the regional BMP to an upstream or downstream location which should also be screened with the watershedwide hydraulic model to ensure adequate peak-shaving benefits. If alternate BMP locations cannot produce satisfactory peak-shaving benefits, the BMP site in question should be designated a single-purpose facility (i.e., nonpoint pollution management only) and consideration should be given to either relying upon onsite peak-shaving controls for the facility drainage area or

substituting additional peak-shaving storage capacity at another
regional BMP site.

If a peak-shaving master plan is not available and it is not
feasible to concurrently develop master plans for peak-shaving and
nonpoint pollution management, the evaluation should at least consider
general guidelines reported in the literature. For example, previous
studies (3,5,9) have shown that peak-shaving facilities tend to be
least effective if located near the mouth of a watershed and most
effective if located in the middle sections of the watershed. Travel
time contours can be developed to help apply some of the general
locational guidelines available in the literature.

Land Availability: An important constraint is the availability of
suitable land areas for regional BMP facilities. One of the initial
steps in facility siting is to identify potential BMP locations which
have the following characteristics: appropriate drainage area (e.g.,
a few hundred acres); a sufficient amount of proposed and/or existing
urban development within the drainage area; design pool elevations
which will not impact upstream structures, roads, or other facilities;
and sufficient acreage for access roads for inspection and maintenance
activities. Following this initial screening and an evaluation of
the locational constraints discussed above, the preliminary design
phase should consider geological and geotechnical constraints at each
regional BMP site as well as impacts on utilities and required
mitigation measures.

Multipurpose facilities will have greater land requirements than
BMP's designed to achieve water quality management benefits only.
Therefore, land availability constraints may prevent the inclusion of
peak-shaving storage capacity at some regional BMP sites. Where
feasible, the regional facilities should be integrated into existing
or proposed public parkland, since many local governments concentrate
park facilities in stream valley areas which are also suitable for
regional BMP's. It may be advisable to include a landscape architect
on the facility siting team in order to maximize multi-use opportunities. The integration of the nonpoint pollution control facility into
public park areas can enhance political support for the regional BMP
master plan, since these facilities will be perceived as achieving
recreational benefits as well as stormwater management objectives.
However, this multi-use facility approach has some disadvantages. The
public may perceive the regional BMP as a recreational resource which
merits more frequent maintenance than necessary for nonpoint pollution
control and perhaps the placement of upstream control measures to
protect water quality within the BMP's permanent pool. To help avoid
such misconceptions that can lead to additional maintenance and construction costs, it is important that the BMP master plan emphasize
that the primary objective of the regional facilities is nonpoint
pollution control, not recreational uses or aesthetics. It is also
advisable to require that the deed of sale for any property in the
drainage area of the regional BMP include a statement regarding the
primary purpose of the stormwater control facility.

Facility Design Criteria

Since the use of relatively large drainage areas tends to preclude the use of infiltration BMP's, the typical design criteria presented herein covers wet detention basins only. The recent EPA Nationwide Urban Runoff Program (NURP) studies demonstrated that wet detention basins exhibit some of the highest pollutant removal efficiencies of any BMP, particularly in comparison with dry detention basins (15).

Pollutant Removal Mechanisms. A wet detention basin consists of a permanent pool and an overlying zone of temporary storage to accommodate increases in the depth of water resulting from runoff and typically to achieve peak-shaving performance standards. Dry detention basins can only rely upon sedimentation processes which will reduce suspended solids and suspended pollutant loadings. Wet detention basins can take advantage of the following physical, chemical, and biological processes within the permanent storage pool to achieve significant removal of dissolved as well as suspended pollutants (2,18): uptake of nutrients by algae and rooted aquatic plants growing around the edge of the permanent pool; adsorption of nutrients and heavy metals onto bottom sediments; biological oxidation of organic materials; and sedimentation of suspended solids and attached pollutants. Aerobic conditions at the bottom of the permanent pool will maximize the uptake of phosphorus and heavy metals by bottom sediments and minimize pollutant release from the sediments into the water column (18). Since permanent pools that exhibit thermal stratification are likely to exhibit anaerobic bottom waters during the summer months, relatively shallow permanent pools that maximize vertical mixing are preferable to relatively deep basins.

During storm events, urban runoff can replace "treated" waters which were detained within the permanent pool after the previous storm, making the storage capacity of the permanent pool an important design criterion. The larger the permanent pool storage volume in comparison with design runoff conditions (e.g., first 0.5 inch of runoff), the lower the outflow of urban runoff inflows and the higher the retention and treatment between rainstorms.

Approaches to Developing Design Criteria. Two different approaches have typically been used to formulate design criteria for wet detention basins. One approach relies upon solids settling theory and assumes that all pollutant removal within the BMP is due to sedimentation (19). The other approach views the wet detention basin as a lake achieving a controlled level of eutrophication, in an attempt to account for biological and physical/chemical processes that have been documented for these facilities (2,20). Both approaches suggest that pollutant removal efficiency should be positively related to hydraulic residence time.

The solids settling theory approach relies upon rainfall/runoff statistics, settling velocities for assumed particle size distributions and the assumed percentage of pollutant mass attached to sediment in order to calculate suspended pollutant removal for specified overflow rates. Separate efficiency calculations for dynamic

conditions during storm events and for quiescent conditions following
storm events are weighted to determine a long-term average pollutant
removal rate. The method is applied to runoff and loading statistics
at NURP BMP sites to demonstrate that it provides a reasonable
estimate of long-term average efficiencies (19). The method appears
to be most appropriate for handling suspended solids and constituents
such as lead which tend to appear primarily in suspended form, since
sedimentation should be the dominant pollutant removal process.
However, it would appear to be less appropriate for the evaluation of
nutrient removal efficiencies since monitoring data at several NURP
BMP sites (Westleigh, Burke, Traver, Swift Run, Waverly Hills)
indicate that the majority of total P and/or total N mass removal was
in the form of dissolved P and dissolved N. This suggests that
sedimentation theory alone does not account for the most important
nutrient removal mechanisms in wet detention basin BMP's. The same
suggestion applies to other constituents, such as zinc, which exhibit
a significant dissolved fraction in urban runoff.

The controlled level of eutrophication approach is an attempt to
account for biological and physical/chemical processes in addition to
sedimentation. It provides a less quantified approach to setting
design criteria than solid settling theory, since the pollutant
removal mechanisms are more complex and less clearly defined. The
basis of the design method is that runoff waters should be detained
within the permanent pool long enough to produce adequate levels of
nutrient uptake by algae and wetland vegetation, but that the
hydraulic residence time should not be so long that it induces
stagnant conditions and significant thermal stratification. Likewise,
this method relies upon guidelines for the bathymetry and
configuration of the permanent pool which attempt to minimize the risk
of short-circuiting and anaerobic bottom waters. Hydraulic residence
times that are sufficient for significant nutrient uptake by algae and
wetland vegetation should also be quite adequate for other mechanisms
such as BOD decay and adsorption of nutrients and metals onto bottom
sediments.

Specific design criteria based upon the controlled level of
eutrophication approach are summarized below.

Permanent Pool Storage Volume. Since the major biological
mechanisms (e.g., algal uptake) for pollutant removal in a wet
detention basin are essentially lake eutrophication processes,
eutrophication modeling theory can be used to adequately size the
permanent pool. For example, input/output eutrophication models
specify that the average hydraulic residence time (T) should be at
least 2 weeks, in order to ensure that the models adequately
approximate biological processes within a reservoir (21). A "T" of 2
weeks is considered to be the minimum duration that ensures adequate
opportunity for algal growth. By comparison, two of the more
effective wet detention basins (Burke and Westleigh) monitored during
the Metropolitan Washington, D.C. NURP study exhibit a "T" of 3 to 4
weeks (computed by dividing the permanent pool storage volume by the
average annual runoff) while most of the NURP sites which achieved
relatively low nutrient removal rates exhibited "T" values of only a
few days. While enhanced sedimentation is likely to result from the

use of a "T" which is much greater than two weeks, such a BMP facility would have a greater risk of thermal stratification and anaerobic bottom waters. As a result there would be increased risk of short-circuiting and significant export of nutrients from bottom sediments subjected to anaerobic conditions. Consequently, it is advisable to maintain the average residence time at the lowest level which can ensure adequate nutrient uptake.

In order to determine the permanent pool storage capacity which achieves the desired "T" (e.g., 2 weeks), the annual runoff volume should be calculated for the BMP drainage area using continous simulation techniques or statistical analyses. Since flows during non-storm periods will affect the residence time in the prototype, baseflow and interflow contributions should be included in the calculation. Annual runoff volumes calculated for each land use category should be weighted according to the build-out land use pattern to determine the total inflow from the drainage area of the regional BMP. Runoff volumes from undeveloped areas should be included in the calculations since these flows affect the residence time within the permanent pool. The required permanent pool storage volume is calculated by multiplying the annual runoff volume by "T" in units of "years" (e.g., 0.0385 yrs for 2 weeks). For example, based on an example from southeastern Virginia and a "T" of 2 weeks, a permanent pool storage volume of 0.9 inches would be required to control a drainage area producing a total annual runoff of 23.3 inches/yr, 120 acres of single family development (25 inches/yr annual runoff), 20 acres of commercial development (41 inches/yr), and 60 acres of undeveloped land (14 inches/yr).

Depth of Permanent Pool. Mean depth of the permanent pool is calculated by dividing the storage by the surface area. The mean depth should be low enough to minimize the risk of thermal stratification, but high enough to ensure that algal blooms are not excessive. The prevention of significant thermal stratification will help minimize short-circuiting and maintain the aerobic bottom waters that should maximize sediment uptake and minimize sediment releases. A mean depth of about 1 to 3 m should be capable of maintaining an acceptable environment within the permanent pool. The mean depths of the more effective wet detention basins monitored by the NURP study typically fall within this range as do the recommendations of recent Florida monitoring studies of retention basins (18).

The maximum depth of the permanent pool should be set at a level which minimizes the risk of thermal stratification. Based upon typical thermal profiles for different impoundment sizes and geographical regions (22), a maximum depth of no greater than 4 to 6 m should be acceptable for most regions assuming a "T" of 2 weeks.

Length:Width Ratio. Since it is generally not an important factor in achieving flooding/erosion control performance standards, length:width ratios are rarely considered in the design of peak-shaving detention basins. However, relatively high length:width ratios can help maximize plug flow conditions to minimize short-circuiting, enhance sedimentation, and also help prevent vertical stratification within the permanent pool. A minimum

length:width ratio of 3:1 is probably a reasonable planning goal for
the permanent pools of wet detention basins. In addition, the
location of the outlet structure within the basins should maximize
travel time from the inlet to the outlet.

Side Slopes Along the Shoreline. The slope of the littoral zone
around the perimeter of the permanent pool should be gradual enough to
promote the growth of wetland vegetation along the shoreline. Side
slopes no steeper than 4:1 (horizontal:vertical) are recommended. The
side slopes should also be topsoiled, nurtured or planted from 2 ft
below to 1 ft above the permanent pool control elevation to promote
vegetative growth. Wetland vegetation will not only improve the
aesthetic qualitites of the detention facility, but they will also
help minimize the proliferation of free-floating algae. The nutrient
uptake achieved by wetland vegetation will help keep the algae concentrations in check by limiting the amount of nutrients available for
phytoplankton.

Assessment of Water Quality Benefits

The regional BMP master plan should define the estimated water
quality benefits of the recommended facility plan. This assessment
should consider not only the nonpoint pollution loading reductions
achieved by the BMP plan but also the water quality benefits in
downstream receiving waters. Average long-term efficiencies monitored
at NURP BMP testing sites can be used to approximate removal rates for
critical pollutants (15). For wet detention basins sized according to
the criteria recommended herein, typical efficiencies are on the order
of 40%-80% for total P, 30%-60% for total N, 80%-95% for lead, and
40%-70% for zinc.

Approximations of water quality benefits can be based upon either
desktop or computer-based models. Desktop methods include input/
output models of lakes (21), estuary box models (22), and
probabilistic methodologies for free-flowing streams (15).
Computer-based methods include the use of continuous simulation
techniques (23) for analyses of reservoirs and streams and
steady-state modeling techniques for estuaries (24). Water quality
benefits should be discussed in terms of beneficial use attainability.

Financing Requirements

The regional BMP master plan should identify the financing
mechanism to implement the facility plan. In order to be effective,
the regional BMP's must be constructed in advance of major new
development in each drainage area. Traditonally, regional
peak-shaving facilities have been funded through one or more of the
following mechanisms: general obligation bonds, land development
fees, and special districts. Land development fees, also known as
"fee-in-lieu-of" contributions, became quite popular in the early
1980's the failings of piecemeal stormwater management programs became
more evident (6). Under this approach, each developer is assessed a
fee which covers a pro-rata share of the capital costs for an offsite
runoff control measure. The pro-rata fee can be based upon a number
of factors including impervious acreage, land use, or each site's

contribution to the total nonpoint pollution load or total peak flow
from the drainage area. If the "fee-in-lieu-of" approach is selected
for the study area, the regional BMP master plan should present the
cost-share formulas. Separate cost-share formulas can be developed
for each BMP or major watershed, if it is not feasible to establish a
single formula for the entire study area.

Under the "fee-in-lieu-of" program, the cost-share formula is
typically restricted to new urban development, even though existing
development may be served by the regional BMP. Further, the
"fee-in-lieu-of" program can usually only cover construction costs,
meaning that maintenance costs must be assumed by the local
government. These disadvantages can be overcome by designating
stormwater management as a "utility," much like sanitary sewers, gas,
and electricity are considered as public utilities. Under the
stormwater utility approach, property owners within a jurisdiction are
assessed a monthly user-charge which can cover both capital and O&M
costs for stormwater management. User-charges are related to each
parcel's stormwater contribution in excess of that contributed in its
natural state. Thus, existing development can share in the costs of
stormwater and nonpoint pollution management in proportion to its
contribution to the problem. A review of fee structures in use or
being considered by local stormwater utilities around the U.S.
indicates that the typical monthly base rate in the range of
$1.00-$4.00 per single family dwelling unit, with charges for more
impervious land uses often based upon the relationship to single
family residential imperviousness. In addition, some stormwater
utilities also rely upon a "new construction fee" (e.g., $500 per
dwelling unit) which is related to the "fee-in-lieu-of" charge for
runoff control facilities designed exclusively for new urban
development. The financing of capital projects is accomplished with a
combination of bonds and revenue from the utility fees. With the
broad revenue base that is available under the stormwater utility
approach, the use of revenue bonds to fund the construction of
stormwater management controls becomes a more viable option.

In summary, the stormwater utility provides a continuing funding
source for both capital and operating costs without impacting a local
government's general fund. The end result is that local public works
departments will have an adequate revenue source to construct more
cost-effective regional facilities and to carry out maintenance
activities. The establishment of local stormwater utilities is a
concept which has achieved growing popularity in the western United
States during the past decade and is now starting to catch on in the
southeast. Camp Dresser & McKee recently developed implementation
plans for stormwater utilities which will serve two cities in Florida
(Tallahassee and Tampa) beginning in 1987. Given the focus of the
State's stormwater management regulations, stormwater utilities in
Florida will be designed to achieve nonpoint pollution management as
well as peak-shaving benefits.

References

1. Whipple, W., "Dual-Purpose Detention Basins," Journal of the Water Resources Planning and Management Division, ASCE, Vol. 105, No. WR2, September 1979, pp. 403-412.

2. Hartigan, J.P. and T.F. Quasebarth, "Urban Nonpoint Pollution Management for Water Supply Protection: Regional vs. Onsite BMP Plans," Proceedings of Twelfth International Symposium on Urban Hydrology, Hydraulics, and Sediment Control, University of Kentucky, Lexington, Kentucky, 1985, pp. 121-130.

3. Bonuccelli, H.A., J.P. Hartigan, and D.J. Biggers, "Urban Runoff Management in a Multijurisdictional Watershed," Proceedings of Second International Conference on Urban Storm Drainage: Volume II, B.C. Yen, ed., Department of Civil Engineering, University of Illinois, Urbana, Illinois, June 1982, pp. 431-440.

4. McCuen, R.H., "Downstream Effects of Stormwater Management Basins," Journal of Hydraulics Division, ASCE, Vol. 105, No. HY11, November 1979, pp. 1343-1356.

5. Duru, J.O., "On-Site Detention: A Stormwater Management or Mismanagement Technique?" Proceedings of International Symposium on Urban Hydrology, Hydraulics and Sediment Control, University of Kentucky, Lexington, Kentucky, 1981, pp. 297-302.

6. Berg, V.H. and L.H. Williams, "Institutional Arrangements-- Stormwater Management," Proceedings of the Conference on Storm- water Detention Facilities, De Groot, W., ed., American Society of Civil Engineers, New York, New York, 1982, pp. 392-400.

7. Abt, S.R. and N.S. Grigg, "An Approximate Method for Sizing Detention Reservoirs," Water Resources Bulletin, Vol. 14, No. 4, August 1978, pp. 956-961.

8. Amandes, C.B. and P.B. Bedient, "Stormwater Detention in Developing Watersheds," Journal of Environmental Engineering Division, ASCE, Vol. 106, No. EE2, April 1980, pp. 403-419.

9. Traver, R.G. and R.A. Chadderton, "The Downstream Effects of Storm Water Detention Basins," Proceedings of International Symposium on Urban Hydrology, Hydraulics and Sediment Control, University of Kentucky, Lexington, Kentucky, 1983, pp. 455-460.

10. Hartigan, J.P., "Watershed-wide Approach Significantly Reduces Local Stormwater Management Costs," Public Works, Vol. 114, No. 12, December 1983, pp. 34-37.

11. Dendrou, S.A., et al., "Optimal Planning for Urban Storm Drainage Systems," Journal of Water Resources Planning and Management Division, ASCE, Vol. 104, No. WR1, November 1978, pp. 17-33.

12. Mays, L.W. and P.B. Bedient, "Model for Optimal Size and Location of Detention," Journal of Water Resources Planning and Management Division, ASCE, Vol. 108, No. WR3, October 1982, pp. 270-285.

13. Bennett, M.S. and L.W. Mays, "Optimal Design of Detention and Drainage Channel Systems," Journal of Water Resources Planning and Management Div., ASCE, Vol. 111, No. 1, January 1985, pp. 99-112.

14. Camp Dresser & McKee, "Reservoir Water Quality Protection Study," prepared for Department of Public Utilities, Newport News, Virginia, November 1985.

15. U.S. Environmental Protection Agency, "Results of the Nationwide Urban Runoff Program: Volume I: Final Report," Water Planning Division, Washington, D.C., December 1983.

16. Maryland Water Resources Administration, "Standards and Specifications for Infiltration Practices," Maryland Department of Natural Resources, Annapolis, Maryland, February 1984.

17. Camp Dresser & McKee Inc., "Stormwater Management Model User's Manual Version III: Addendum I EXTRAN," Municipal Environmental Research Laboratory, U.S. Environmental Protection Agency, Cincinnati, Ohio, November 1981.

18. Yousef, Y.A., et al., "Fate of Pollutants in Retention/Detention Ponds," Stormwater Management: An Update, Publication #85-1, University of Central Florida, Environmental Systems Engineering Institute, July 1985, pp. 259-275.

19. Driscoll, Eugene D., "Performance of Detention Basins for Control of Urban Runoff Quality," prepared for 1983 International Symposium on Urban Hydrology, Hydraulics and Sediment Control, University of Kentucky, 1983.

20. Camp Dresser & McKee Inc., "Use of Stormwater Infiltration Practices for Water Quality Management: Minimum Criteria and Planning Guidelines," prepared for Maryland Water Resources Administration, Annapolis, Maryland, July 1985.

21. Rast, W., R. Jones, and G.F. Lee, "Predictive Capability of U.S. OECD Phosphorus Loading-Eutrophication Response Models," Journal of Water Pollution Control Federation, Vol. 55, No. 7, July 1983, pp. 990-1003.

22. Mills, W.B., et al., "Water Quality Assessment: A Screening Procedure for Toxic and Conventional Pollutants," EPA-600/6-82-004, USEPA, Environmental Research Laboratory, Athens, Georgia, 1982.

23. Hartigan, J.P., et al., "Post-Audit of Lake Model Used for NPS Management," Journal of Environmental Engineering Division, ASCE, Vol. 109, No. 6, December 1983, pp. 1354-1370.

24. Hanson, S.A. and J.P. Hartigan, "Development of Flows and Loads for Steady-State Estuary Models: Tampa Bay Case Study," Proceedings of Stormwater and Water Quality Model Users Group Meeting, EPA-600/9-85-003, USEPA, Environmental Research Laboratory, Athens, Georgia, 1985.

Cost of Urban Runoff Quality Controls

Cameron Wiegand, Thomas Schueler, Wendy Chittenden, Debra Jellick[1]

Abstract

Concerns about water quality impacts of urban runoff have prompted local governments in the Washington, D.C. metropolitan area to encourage or require the construction of multi-purpose urban BMPs which have greater pollutant removal capabilities in addition to achieving stormwater control. This paper attempts to provide guidance in the evaluation, selection and planning of various BMPs by comparing their costs and cost-effectiveness, in terms of pollutant removal capabilities. Using available BMP cost estimates, regression relationships between construction costs and storage volume are developed for a variety of BMP types, and shown to provide a reasonable means for predicting BMP construction costs. Routine and non-routine maintenance needs and associated costs for typical BMPs are explored. Estimates of the initial and project life costs of urban BMPs are made based upon relationships identified between design storage, construction costs and estimated maintenance requirements. These estimates are utilized to compare the cost effectiveness, in nutrient removal of different types and sizes of BMP facilities. Examination of nine hypothetical land use/drainage area scenarios indicates that extended detention dry ponds represent the most cost-effective BMP for most applications. Wet ponds and infiltration basins are found to be cost effective when applied to larger drainage areas. The results further indicate that the incremental costs of multi-purpose BMPs, over conventional "dry" stormwater management ponds, vary substantially, and decrease as drainage area and impervious area increase. In addition to pollutant removal capabilities, the paper discusses other, non-economic factors which play a role in BMP selection. Recreational and aesthetic amenities associated with multi-purpose BMPs, notably wet ponds, are identified as important considerations in the process of planning and selecting urban BMPs.

INTRODUCTION

Stormwater management requirements have been in place in the Washington, D.C. metropolitan area for nearly fifteen years. Traditionally, local stormwater management strategies have been oriented towards shaving the peak discharge associated with the design storm, and have relied almost exclusively on the conventional detention or "dry" pond. Concerns about the water quality impacts of urban runoff in recent years have prompted many local jurisdictions to require consideration of alternative urban best management practices, or BMPs, which have a greater capacity to remove pollutants in addition to achieving stormwater control. These BMPs, which include wet ponds, extended detention dry ponds (X-D), infiltration trenches, infiltration basins and porous pavement, vary considerably in cost, physical suitability and pollutant removal capability (9). This paper examines comparative construction and maintenance costs of BMP alternatives as well as their relative cost-effectiveness in removing nutrients.

---

[1]Chief of Water Resources, Environmental Engineer, Environmental Planner, and Research Technician, respectively, Metropolitan Washington Council of Governments, Washington D.C.

The paper first describes the derivation of a series of quantitative relationships between BMP storage volume and construction costs. Next, typical operation and maintenance (O&M) costs associated with alternative BMPs are identified, and best estimates of their costs are provided. Comparative costs of alternative BMPs are then evaluated under nine hypothetical development scenarios, and predictive total cost relationships are combined with nutrient loading and removal estimates to arrive at an approximation of BMP cost-effectiveness. Finally, conclusions are drawn as to the possible implications of economic and other considerations in developing effective nonpoint source management strategies.

COMPARATIVE BMP CONSTRUCTION COSTS

An objective of the current study was to compare BMP cost and volume of storage relationships based on actual BMP construction costs, with those developed by the Metropolitan Washington Council of Governments (MWCOG) in 1983 (5). In the earlier study, BMP cost/volume relationships were derived from construction costs which were estimated through the application of standardized unit costs to the construction components of 31 local, representative ponds (26 dry, 5 wet). The present study utilized estimates of construction costs of urban BMPs drawn from a survey of engineering estimates and construction bids for 65 facilities built in the Washington metropolitan area since 1982. These cost estimates were felt to provide the best available approximation of actual BMP construction costs. The predictive cost equations developed from this data were compared to the 1983 cost equation with respect to their applicability for: a) actual, as-built BMPs, b) newer urban BMP designs, c) larger BMPs (in excess of 100,000 cu ft (2,800m³)), and d) local differences in engineering requirements and design.[2]

As in previous studies (5,12), log-transformed BMP cost and storage volume data were analyzed for the purpose of developing a predictive relationship. As shown in Figure 1, the storage volumes of many BMPs fell into rather restricted volumetric ranges. For example, all of the infiltration trenches and most of the underground detention facilities had storage volumes of less than 10,000 cu ft (280 m³) while all of the wet ponds had capacities in excess of 100,000 cu ft (2,800 m³). Only dry ponds were found over the entire range of storage volumes. Given these natural biases in the data set, regression results for different BMP types should be considered applicable for structures with volumes similar to those used in the analysis.

Individual regression equations relating BMP costs with storage volumes were developed for infiltration trenches, underground detention facilities, wet ponds, dry and extended detention dry ponds, and all ponds (wet, dry and extended detention). Results (where C=construction costs in dollars and Vs=volume of storage in cubic feet) are presented in Table 1.

---

[2]Adjustments to 1985 dollars were made using the Engineering News Record, Baltimore Construction Index.

Figure 1 - Distribution of BMPs by Construction Cost and Volume
of Storage

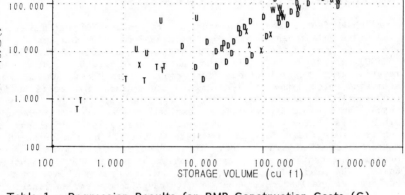

Table 1 - Regression Results for BMP Construction Costs (C)
as a Function of Storage Volume (Vs)*

BMP TYPE (N)	N	EQUATION	ADJ R^2	APPLICABLE VOLUME RANGES
All Ponds	53	$C=6.11\ Vs^{0.752}$	$R^2=0.80$	Vs>10,000 cu ft
Wet Ponds	13	$C=33.99\ Vs^{0.644}$	$R^2=0.76$	Vs>100,000 cu ft
Dry Ponds w/ X-D	40	$C=10.71\ Vs^{0.694}$	$R^2=0.73$	Vs>10,000 cu ft
Infilt Trench	7	$C=26.55\ Vs^{0.634}$	$R^2=0.93$	Vs<10,000 cu ft
Underground Det	5	$C=29.25\ Vs^{0.816}$	$R^2=0.91$	Vs<100,000 cu ft

*Note: Storage Volumes for each BMP type are defined as follows:

Wet Ponds- Stormwater volume to the top of the emergency spillway plus
the permanent pool volume.
Dry Ponds- Calculated total stormwater volume for the maximum design
event frequency.
Infiltration Trench- Stormwater volume of void space for the maximum
design event frequency.
Underground Detention- Stormwater volume of detention facility for the
maximum design event frequency.

Regression results for all BMP types indicated a significant relationship between volume of storage and construction costs. Correlation coefficients for the various equations ranged from a high of 0.93 for infiltration trenches to a low of 0.73 for dry and extended detention dry ponds. The limited number of cost estimates available on infiltration trenches and underground detention facilities suggests that the predictive ability of these particular equations may be somewhat more limited. Nonetheless, it seems reasonable to conclude that the cost of constructing underground detention facilities, in comparison with the other types of BMPs, is notably higher. Further, underground detention facilities appear to have only slight economies of scale. Such results might be expected given the extensive engineering requirements of underground detention BMPs. Infiltration trenches, on the other hand, appear to have moderate costs when small storage volumes are controlled. However, the lack of large volume infiltration structures in the Washington metropolitan area suggests that trenches may rapidly become uneconomical or physically infeasible when larger storage volumes are required.

A plot of the wet pond, dry pond and "all pond" regression equations illustrates the strong relationship between storage volume and construction costs (Figure 2). However, there is a high degree of variability in the data, which probably reflects the site specific nature of each cost estimate used in the analysis. Differences in site topography, engineering design and material requirements, for example, can cause substantial variation in construction costs.

The regression equations predict somewhat higher costs for wet than dry ponds. Conversely, the slope of the wet pond equation is slightly less than that of the dry pond, suggesting that greater economies of scale may exist for large volume wet ponds. Despite observed differences in the wet and dry pond equations, in view of the variability in the data, the "all pond" equation, probably provides the most representative means of estimating pond BMP construction costs.

The updated "all pond" equation was compared with the original 1983 MWCOG pond cost equation (after adjustment to 1985 dollars) and was found to have a significantly higher slope (0.752 versus 0.51 for the 1983 equation) (Figure 3). This difference in slopes suggests that economies of scale associated with building larger ponds are somewhat less than originally estimated. However, the lower intercept shown in the updated equation may signify that start-up costs associated with pond construction are less than previously indicated. It is important to note that while the two equations predict significantly different costs at the extremes of storage volume, they predict very similar costs over the 20,000 to 200,000 cu ft (560 to 5,600 m^3) range of storage volumes, which is most representative of the BMPs being constructed in the Washington region. The disparity between the two equations beyond pond storage volumes of 200,000 cu ft, probably reflects the fact that very few large ponds were included in the 1983 study (only 3 ponds in excess of 200,000 cu ft), whereas the current study included 20 such ponds. The updated cost equation is, therefore, thought to be more reliable as a predictive tool for BMP ponds over a larger range of storage volumes.

Figure 2 - Wet Pond, Dry Pond and "All Pond" Cost Equations

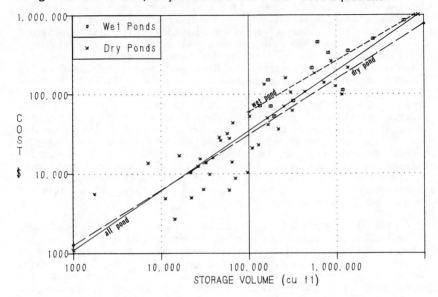

Figure 3 - Comparison of "All Pond" Equation with the 1983 Cost
      Equation (5) *

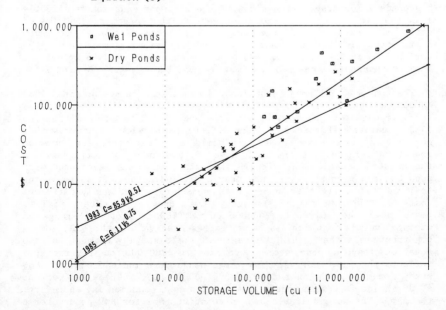

*1983 Cost Equation adjusted to 1985 dollars.

An examination of component costs for various types of BMPs provides
further insight into why BMP costs differ. The component costs for
four types of BMPs were analyzed based on 35 structures for which
itemized cost data was available. Figure 4 reveals that earth-work
(cut and fill, clear and grub) constitutes the largest component of wet
pond construction costs. Dry ponds, by contrast, typically have
proportionally lower earth-work costs, and higher costs for
inlet/outlet works. The higher earth-moving costs depicted for wet
ponds appears to reflect higher excavation requirements. A comparison
of excavation (cut and fill), in cubic feet, with pond storage volume
(cu ft) indicated that the wet ponds, on average, required 60% more
excavation than dry ponds of comparable volume. This may, in part,
explain why wet pond construction costs are often higher than for dry
ponds. The analysis suggests that efficient use of natural topography
in conjunction with embankment construction is usually sufficient to
meet the storage volume requirements for most dry pond applications.
On the other hand, substantial additional excavation is often needed to
create a suitable depth and surface area for the permanent pool of a
wet pond.

**Figure 4 - BMP Component Costs as a Percentage of Total
Construction Costs**

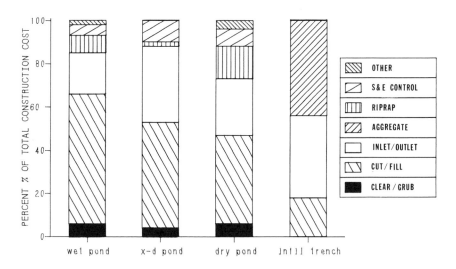

In summary, the BMP regression equations in Table 1 offer a means
for estimating the capital costs associated with the construction of a
given type of BMP facility, of a known storage volume. However, use of
these equations should be tempered by the knowledge that actual BMP
construction costs vary significantly with site conditions, material
prices, and local design requirements. With these caveats in mind, the
cost equations can be most appropriately and usefully applied in
preliminary planning comparisons of alternative stormwater management
investments.

OPERATING AND MAINTAINING URBAN BMPs

Regular inspection and maintenance programs are essential if BMP structures are to function properly and safely over their design life. However, after large initial investments are made in BMP construction, subsequent responsibilities for facility maintenance are often not clearly delineated. As a result, many stormwater management programs have historically lacked sufficient resources to permit much more than ad hoc and cosmetic approaches to BMP maintenance which, in the long run, prove ineffective. As an example, a recent study of dry ponds constructed in several rapidly urbanizing Maryland counties (3) indicated that only a quarter of the structures were functioning as they were originally designed, while about half were suffering from clogged outlets and/or other standing water problems. Successful O&M programs involve a commitment to both routine and non-routine tasks.

Routine O&M Activities and Costs

Typical O&M requirements involve a number of preventive and corrective tasks including periodic site inspections, grass mowing, litter and debris removal, bank stabilization and the maintenance of site vegetation for erosion control (3,4,5). Table 2 compares the general nature of O&M activities and problems for six BMPs.

As a result of the poorly developed nature of BMP maintenance programs, consistent and comparable data on the actual costs of O&M programs are scarce. However, a survey of six local and national agencies having organized stormwater management O&M programs suggested that routine annual O&M costs can be roughly approximated for pond BMPs as 2 to 3 percent of the base construction cost (5).

Non-Routine Sediment Removal Costs

If a BMP is effective at removing pollutants, it will eventually accumulate enough sediment to significantly reduce stormwater storage capacity and aesthetic values. The best available estimate is that approximately one percent of the BMPs 2-year design storm storage will be lost annually (5). Smaller stabilized urban watersheds will lose capacity at a lower rate, while larger watersheds with unprotected stream channels or ongoing construction fill in more rapidly (8). In the Washington area, sediment removal, from pond BMPs, is generally carried out once every ten to twenty years (5).

The one-time costs for sediment removal can be staggering. For example, sediment removal costs in excess of $100,000 are not uncommon for larger wet ponds. A review of six recent private pond dredging projects in suburban Virginia indicated that dredging costs ranged from $6.25 to $22.40 per cubic yard ($8.17 to $29.28/m^3) (mean $14.15/cu yd or $18.50/m^3). The observed variability in sediment removal costs is due to differences in the size and accessibility of the BMP, the proximity of a suitable disposal site and the method used to remove and transport sediment. Costs for small ponds (Vs < 100,000 cu ft) typically range from $5-10/cu yd ($6-13/m^3) since sediment can usually be mechanically removed with a front-end loader after the basin is de-watered.

Table 2 - Summary of BMP Maintenance Requirements

DRY POND:
Grass on pond bottom must be mowed at least twice per year to prevent woody
plant growth and up to 14 times per year for landscaping appearances. Storms
during growing season may keep pond bottom marshy, contributing to permanent
loss of bottom vegetation, increasing erosion potential and interfering with
scheduling and performance of mowing operations. Simple outlet structures,
built at the low end of the pond embankment, clog easily and require frequent
inspection and debris removal to assure proper operation. Trash accumulates
quickly and is visible, resulting in more frequent need for debris removal.
Sediment removal by mechanical means.

EXTENDED DETENTION DRY POND:
Maintenance activities similar to dry ponds. Longer detention times may keep
bottom in permanent marshy condition in growing season and impede opportunities for mowing and debris removal. Use of perforated riser outlets with a
stone filter jacket aids in the prevention of outlet clogging problems which
occur more frequently because of small orifice size. Sediment removal by mechanical means.

WET POND:
Mowing operations limited to side slope maintenance. Use of side slopes of 3
or 4:1 or greater facilitates mowing. Repairs to riser require dewatering of
ponds. Floatable trash may accumulate and require boat access to remove. Algae growth may occur in summer periods. Planting of cattails and other vegetation along shoreline aids in nutrient uptake and may help to reduce algae
growth. Such vegetation also provides attractive habitat wildlife, which can
help in the control of mosquitos. Sediment accumulation can be mitigated by
use of sediment forebays at primary inlets and through additional storage
within permanent pool area. Dragline or hydraulic dredging required for sediment removal in larger ponds.

INFILTRATION TRENCH:
Subject to clogging by sediment, oil, grease, grit, and other debris. Performance and longevity of structures not well documented. Consequently a monitoring observation well is required and should be monitored on quarterly
basis and after every large storm. Sediment buildup in the top foot of stone
aggregates near the surface inlet should also be monitored at same frequency
as observation well. After the first year of observation, monitoring frequencies may be reduced, depending on structure performance and sediment
accumulation rates. Sediment deposits should not be allowed to build up to a
point where infiltration rates into trenches are reduced.

INFILTRATION BASIN:
As with trenches, maintenance needs and schedules are not well documented.
Side slope mowing recommended two times per year (June and Sept.). On a vegetated basin floor, well established turf should grow through sediment deposits
and prevent the formation of an impermeable layer. On a non-vegetated basin
floor, sediment removal and tilling should be done once each year (preferable
in June-Sept. period) to restore infiltration capacity.

POROUS PAVEMENT (ASPHALT):
Surface must be cleaned quarterly to avoid having pavement pores becoming
clogged by fine material and oils and grease which bind dirt. Cleaning should
be done by a vacuum cleaning street sweeper followed by high pressure water
washing of the pavement (approximately 4 times/year). Vacuum cleaning alone
is ineffective. In periods of snow and ice, abrasive materials should not be
used for traction as they can clog pavement pores. Pothole maintenance is
most economically accomplished by using normal asphalt patching, and drilling
1/4 inch holes/sq ft through the base course to retain infiltration capacity.

Larger ponds normally require the use of a drag-line or hydraulic dredge. Additional costs are incurred in transporting dredged sediments to a suitable on-site disposal area, and in the grading and reclamation of the disposal area after the dredging is completed. Thus, for larger ponds, sediment removal costs are typically on the order of $15-20/cu yd ($20-26/m³). Off-site hauling of dredged sediments may increase costs by an average of $5-10/cu yd (or even more if a tipping fee is levied).

Several steps can be taken early in the BMP design process to reduce the magnitude of sediment removal costs. First, since excavation costs during construction are much less expensive than dredging ($3.00/cu yd versus $14.15/cu yd), it is economical to allow for excess capacity in the pond design, particularly near the inlet and outlet where sediment tends to accumulate. Second, disposal areas should be reserved at the development site to minimize the cost of transporting dredged sediments. Third, clear right-of-way access to the structure should be provided to prevent damage to lawns, sidewalks and utilities by heavy equipment during dredging operations. Finally, local governments and homeowners associations must plan and budget for sediment removal early to ensure that sufficient funds are available. For planning purposes, it has been estimated that the annualized cost of sediment removal will average 1 to 2 percent of BMP base construction cost (5).

Total O&M Costs

Based on the preceding discussion, total annual O&M costs for both routine activities and sediment removal were estimated to range from 3 to 5% of base construction costs for pond BMPs. No cost data was available to evaluate the expected total O&M costs for infiltration BMPs, due to the lack of long-term experience with these structures in the Washington metropolitan area. For this paper, it was assumed that total annual O&M costs for infiltration BMPs are roughly comparable to pond BMPs.

COMPARATIVE BMP COSTS AND COST-EFFECTIVENESS

For a comparative assessment of typical BMP costs, the runoff storage requirements for nine hypothetical land development scenarios were evaluated. These scenarios included a single family residential development (2 dwelling units per acre (DU/acre) - 25% impervious), a townhouse development (8 DU/acre - 65% impervious), and a commercial shopping center (85% impervious). Each development case was evaluated under three drainage area conditions: 1, 10, and 25 acre watersheds (0.4, 4.1 and 10.1 hectares). The TR-55 tabular method (11) was used to estimate the increase in post-development peak discharge and runoff volume associated with the 2-year design storm at each site. Curve numbers (CN) of 70, 85 and 92 were assumed for the single-family residential, townhouse and commercial developments respectively. All sites were assumed to have soils and slopes typical of the Atlantic piedmont ("B" hydrologic soil group and 3-5% slopes).

The stormwater management criteria for all sites was to maintain the increase in post-development peak discharge (pond BMPs) or upland runoff volume (infiltration BMPs) to pre-development levels (defined as meadow, CN 58), for the 2-year design storm. The required runoff storage volume (Vs) to be controlled by BMPs at each site was determined by either the short-cut routing method (pond BMPs) or current Maryland design standards for infiltration BMPs (4). For some BMPs, additional storage volume was included (e.g., for the permanent pool of a wet pond). The equations and assumptions used to estimate BMP costs for each development scenario are specified in Table 3.

Comparative BMP Costs

Total BMP costs (TCC) for each hypothetical development scenario were calculated as TCC = (Cb+Cc)+OMpv; where Cb= base construction cost, Cc= construction related contingencies and, OMpv= present value of twenty years of annual O&M payments.[3] Base construction costs were multiplied by 0.25 to account for contingency costs involved in planning, designing and overseeing construction of a BMP. The present value of each BMP's annual O&M cost (Table 3) was determined assuming an 8% discount rate and a twenty year project life. Finally, the equivalent annual payment (Ap) needed to finance the total BMP cost (TCC) was calculated.[4]

While dry ponds generally represent the least cost alternative for managing stormwater runoff, they are ineffective as water quality BMPs (6,10). Therefore, results of the comparative cost analysis have been expressed, for each BMP option, as the incremental annual cost beyond that incurred for installing and operating a dry pond at the same site. Results are shown in Table 4.

As can be seen, modifying a dry pond for extended detention represents the least cost water quality BMP option at most sites. Infiltration basins are also relatively inexpensive, particularly when applied in more intensive development situations. Infiltration trenches and porous pavement with extra runoff storage are the most expensive water quality BMPs. Porous pavement applications without extra storage appear to be economically attractive, but may not always be physically feasible. Wet ponds typically have intermediate incremental costs. Nearly all of the BMPs examined exhibited significant economies of scale, that is, it is normally less expensive to construct and maintain a BMP on a larger watershed than a smaller one.

---

[3]All costs are expressed in 1985 dollars. Differential land costs were assumed to be zero, since BMPs within Washington area jurisdictions are usually located in dedicated open space.
[4]Annual payment calculations are expressed in 1985 dollars and assume a twenty year note and an 8% interest rate.

Table 3 - Methods Used to Estimate Total BMP Costs

BMP TYPE	CONSTRUCTION COST (Cb)	CONTINGENCY COST (Cc)	ANNUAL O&M	COMMENTS
Dry Pond	$6.11Vs^{0.75}$	0.25Cb	0.05Cb	"All Pond" Equation Used (Table 1).
Wet Pond	$6.11Vs^{0.75}$	0.25Cb	0.05Cb	"All Pond" equation used. Storage volume includes runoff storage needed to control each land use/drainage area scenario plus additional storage to provide for a permanent "wet" pool. This additional storage requirement was assumed to be equivalent to 0.5 inches (1.27 cm) of runoff from the controlled drainage area.
Extended Detention	$6.11Vs^{0.75}$	0.25Cb	0.05Cb	"All Pond" equation used with an extra 10% of storage volume for extended detention of runoff. The 10% extra volume represents the mean storage volume increment required to convert nine dry ponds to extended detention ponds (5).
Infiltration Basin	$3.05Vs^{0.75}$	0.25Cb	0.10Cb	Construction cost equation derived from the "All Pond" equation by factoring out 50% of costs for assumed outlet and riser structures. O&M costs adjusted to account for more frequent mowing and sediment removal.
Infiltration Trench	$26.55Vs^{0.63}$	0.25Cb	$286/acre ($706/ha) of trench and grass buffer	Infiltration Trench equation used (Table 1) may underpredict costs for a trench of >10,000 cu ft (280 m) of void space. O&M for debris removal and mowing of grass buffer.
Porous Pavement (without extra storage)[1]	Incremental cost over conventional pavement	0.35Cb	$0.003/ sq ft ($0.032/ m)	Incremental costs include: higher unit cost of porous over conventional asphalt, extra filter cloth and test wells. Extra contingency costs for site surveys, soil testing and obtaining asphalt. O&M represents commercial rate for vacuuming 4 times/year.
Porous Pavement (with extra storage)[2]	As above, plus cost of extra storage for runoff control	0.35Cb	$0.003/ sq ft ($0.032/ m)	Depth of extra aggregate base course computed (4). Extra costs include additional excavation and course stone fill.

1. Assumes extensive application of porous pavement over 60% of total site area. Runoff storage provided by the normal depth of base aggregate found under conventional pavement plus soil infiltration.

2. Assumes only 15-40% of site area paved. Additional base aggregate depth provided to meet storage requirement.

Table 4 - Comparative Costs of Constructing and Maintaining BMPs*

DEVELOP-MENT SCENARIO	Dry Pond Annual Payment	Extended Detention $ (%)	Wet Pond $ (%)	Infiltration Basin $ (%)	Infiltration Trench $ (%)	Porous Pavement w/out Extra Storage $ (%)	Porous Pavement w/ Extra Storage $ (%)
Single-Family Residential							
1 acre	151	17 (11)	237 (157)	119 (79)	403 (267)	0 (0)	463 (307)
10 acre	1005	76 (8)	1290 (128)	513 (51)	1617 (161)	301 (30)	5189 (516)
25 acre	2292	177 (8)	2497 (109)	425 (19)	3436 (150)	765 (33)	13200 (576)
Townhouse Residential							
1 acre	327	36 (11)	201 (62)	187 (57)	669 (205)	0 (0)	689 (211)
10 acre	2176	165 (8)	1084 (50)	527 (24)	3117 (143)	1083 (50)	7981 (367)
25 acre	4699	348 (7)	2114 (45)	677 (14)	5535 (118)	3427 (73)	20002 (426)
Commercial Shopping Ctr							
1 acre	422	47 (11)	189 (45)	185 (44)	839 (199)	0 (0)	762 (181)
10 acre	3162	234 (7)	888 (28)	251 (8)	3427 (108)	1093 (35)	8680 (275)
25 acre	6696	496 (7)	1839 (27)	90 (1)	6364 (95)	3943 (59)	20308 (303)

*Note: Costs and percentages shown reflect the incremental annual costs of each BMP over dry pond costs.

Comparative Cost-Effectiveness of BMPs for Nutrient Removal

A primary objective in applying water quality BMPs in the Washington area has been to reduce nutrient loadings introduced into receiving waters from urban runoff sources. Since earlier studies have shown considerable variation in terms of nutrient removal efficiency among urban BMPs (5,10), it is useful to calculate their relative cost-effectiveness in nutrient removal. The cost-effectiveness of BMP structures for each of the hypothetical development scenarios was evaluated using a three-step procedure. First, the annual total phosphorus (TP) and total nitrogen (TN) loads from each of the development sites were determined using a nutrient load estimation technique derived from extensive small urban watershed monitoring (8). Second, estimates of average BMP pollutant removal rates (6) were developed and applied to calculate annual nutrient removal from each BMP. Finally, nutrient load reductions (in pounds) achieved by each BMP were divided by the respective annual payment to measure BMP cost effectiveness, in dollars expended per pound removed per year ($/lb/yr).

Results of the BMP cost-effectiveness analysis are presented in Table 5. Blanks in the table represent situations where a particular BMP cannot be realistically applied due to specific site constraints, such as excessive land consumption or insufficient watershed area. (A complete discussion of these "infeasible situations" is described in (9)). Because of the inherent uncertainty associated with each phase of the analysis (i.e., prediction of BMP costs, loadings and pollutant removal capabilities), the cost-effectiveness calculations presented here should be viewed in relative, rather than absolute, terms.

Table 5 - Cost Effectiveness of Urban BMPs in Nutrient Removal

DEVELOPMENT SCENARIO	Ponds X-D[1]	Wet[2]	Infiltration Basin[3]	Trench[3]	Porous Pavement[3] No Extra Storage	With Extra Storage
Incremental Cost, $/lb/yr - TOTAL PHOSPHORUS removed						
(SI Conversion Factors: 1 acre=0.4 ha; $1.00/lb=$2.21/kg)						
Single-Family Residential						
1 acre	-	-	225	760	-	-
10 acre	25	315	96	305	-	-
25 acre	24	242	32	219	-	
Townhouse Residential						
1 acre	-	-	128	458	-	468
10 acre	21	96	36	213	-	546
25 acre	17	74	19	123	-	566
Commercial Shopping Ctr						
1 acre	-	-	89	412	2	68
10 acre	20	55	12	166	53	19
25 acre	17	46	6	123	76	92
Incremental Cost, $/lb/yr - TOTAL NITROGEN removed						
(SI Conversion Factors: 1 acre=0.4 ha; $1.00/lb=$2.21/kg)						
Single-Family Residential						
1 acre	-	-	32	110	-	-
10 acre	6	81	14	44	-	-
25 acre	6	62	5	38	-	
Townhouse Residential						
1 acre	-	-	19	66	-	68
10 acre	5	24	5	51	-	79
25 acre	4	19	3	22	-	82
Commercial Shopping Ctr						
1 acre	-	-	13	59	0	54
10 acre	5	14	1	24	8	61
25 acre	4	12	1	18	11	57

[1]Assumes 50% removal TP, 30% removal TN (field results, MWCOG, 1983).
[2]Assumes 70% removal TP, 40% removal TN (field results, MWCOG, 1983).
[3]Assumes 90% removal TP and TN (high removal due to lack of outlet).

IMPLICATIONS FOR NONPOINT SOURCE MANAGEMENT STRATEGIES

The analysis of BMP costs with respect to pollutant removal effectiveness (Table 5) provides some useful guidance in setting nonpoint source pollution priorities. Results indicate that extended detention ponds are the most cost effective BMP for controlling nutrients. This suggests that nutrient loadings can be economically reduced not only by constructing new extended detention ponds, but also through retrofitting existing dry ponds to increase detention times. Wet ponds and infiltration basins are also shown to be cost-effective options in larger, more intensively developed sites. Unfortunately, BMPs appear to be far less cost-effective when applied to sites of less than ten acres. A possible exception to this would be applications of porous pavement (without extra storage) on commercial sites.

The reduced cost-effectiveness of BMPs for smaller development sites implies that successful nonpoint source control strategies should probably focus on the control of larger drainage areas (25 acres or greater). This has become increasingly recognized in the Washington area, where there is a growing trend toward the use of larger "off-site" BMPs which may control several developments, and take advantage of the economies of scale in construction and maintenance associated with fewer and larger structures controlling drainage areas of up to 400 acres.

The cost-effectiveness analysis indicates that the use of infiltration trenches and intensive porous pavement BMPs with extra runoff storage are not very economical approaches either for nutrient control or peak discharge reduction. In the case of these BMPs, it is probably more efficient to use undersized versions for water quality control, in combination with less expensive structures, such as dry ponds, to reduce peak runoff.

NON-ECONOMIC FACTORS IN BMP SELECTION

The preceding discussion has examined BMPs solely in terms of their relative costs and pollutant removal capabilities. In many cases, carefully designed and landscaped BMPs can provide other enhancements to the urban environment. Some of these amenities include aesthetics, recreation, wildlife and waterfowl habitat, enhanced downstream channel protection, and groundwater recharge. While it is difficult to assign a dollar value to such amenities, recent resident surveys indicate that BMPs which provide them are highly regarded, and often result in real monetary assets such as higher property values (1,2). These same surveys have indicated that wet ponds, when properly designed and maintained, are the BMP option most preferred by residents. The importance now being placed on the types of amenities provided by wet ponds, in combination with their relatively low annual costs per dwelling unit (5), has led to a policy trend in some Washington area jurisdictions to encourage or require their implementation. A recent survey of regional patterns in stormwater management programs (7) indicated that the percentage of wet ponds and other multi-purpose BMPs constructed in the Washington region has increased from 14% of total structures in 1982 to over 30% by 1984.

Summary

Based on the analysis of costs and cost-effectiveness of various urban BMPs discussed within this paper, some general conclusions can be drawn. First, although somewhat variable, BMP construction costs can be reasonably explained by a regression model in which base construction costs are a function of storage volume. The resulting regression equations can, in turn, be used to generate planning level estimates of comparative BMP construction costs. Second, the incremental costs of building a multi-purpose water quality BMP, in lieu of the conventional stormwater management dry pond, vary with land use and watershed size. In general, structures serving larger drainage areas are more cost-effective. Finally, economic factors, while important, are often not the only consideration in urban BMP selection. Other factors such as pollutant removal capability, and aesthetic and recreational values are becoming more important factors in the selection of stormwater management BMPs.

References

1. Adams, L.W., L.E. Dove and D.L., "Public Attitudes Toward Urban Wetlands for Stormwater Control and Wildlife Enhancement", *Wildlife Society Bulletin,* 12(3), 1984, pp. 299-303.

2. Baxter, E.H., G. Mulamoottil and D. Gregor, "A Study of Residential Stormwater Impoundments: Perceptions and Policy Implications", *Water Resources Bulletin,* 21(1), 1985, pp.83-88.

3. Geis, A.C., J.F. Tassone and R.M. Toedler, "Implications of Shallow Ponds as Stormwater Management Basins", Patuxent Wildlife Research Center Report, U.S. Fish and Wildlife Service, 1985, 10 pp.

4. Maryland Department of Natural Resources, "Standards and Specifications for Infiltration Practices", Stormwater Managment Division, Water Resources Administration, 1984, 180 pp.

5. Metropolitan Washington Council of Governments, "An Evaluation of the Costs of Stormwater Pond Construction and Maintenance", Report to the U.S. EPA, Nationwide Urban Runoff Program, 1983, 98 pp.

6. _____, "Urban Runoff in the Washington Metropolitan Area: Final Report Washington, D.C., U.S. EPA, Nationwide Urban Runoff Program, 1983, 98 pp.

7. _____, "Potomac River Water Quality 1984: Conditions and Trends in Metropolitan Washington", Metropolitan Washington Water Resources Planning Board, 1985, 110 pp.

8. _____, "Handbook for Screening Urban BMPs for Water Quality Control, Metropolitan Washington Water Resources Planning Board, (In Press).

9. Schueler, T.R., R. Magill, M.P. Sullivan and C. Wiegand, "Comparative Pollutant Removal Capability, Economics and Physical Suitability of Urban Best Managment Practices in the Washington Metropolitan Area", in *Proceedings of Nonpoint Pollution Abatement Symposium,* Marquette University, Milwaukee, WI, April 1985.

10. United States Environmental Protection Agency, "Results of the Nationwide Urban Runoff Program, Volume I: Final Report to Congress", Water Planning Division, Washington, D.C., 1983.

11. United States Soil Conservation Service, "Urban Hydrology for Small Watersheds", U.S. Department of Agriculture, Technical Release No. 55, 1975.

12. United States Soil Conservation Service, "Stormwater Management Cost Study", Final Report to Maryland National Capital Park and Planning Commission, Hyattsville, Md., 1977.

Detention and Retention Controls for Urban Runoff

Eugene D. Driscoll, M. ASCE *

INTRODUCTION

It is interesting to recall that less than ten years ago, discussions of Best
Management Practices (BMP's) would frequently involve lengthy lists of
practices and devices that had a theoretical potential to control pollutant
discharges from urban stormwater runoff. There was little in the way of
quantification of the reductions that might be achieved, with the notable
exception of a few structural approaches that were studied under the
sponsorship of EPA's Storm and Combined Sewer group (Field). However,
most of these techniques were adaptations of devices for the control of
Combined Sewer Overflows, and generally have not found acceptance for
urban runoff applications. Other attempts at quantifying performance were
restricted to inference based on quite different applications, for example the
efficiency of a sedimentation basin treating domestic sewage.

Consistent with the qualitative orientation, which reflects the relevant
data that was then available, there appears to have been little consideration
given to the significance of the reductions that could be accomplished by a
particular BMP, relative to the overall pollutant load in runoff from an
area. Every pound of pollutant removed was striking a blow for the
environment and a step in the right direction. Cost information was
rudimentary or non-existent. In fact, much of the euphoria at having
discovered the BMP approach, was based on the assumption that costs would
be trivial.

I indulge in these dramatic simplifications because they are not far off
the mark, and they help to dramatize the very substantial progress that has
been made. Contrast the situation described with the content of the four
papers that have been presented in this session. Progress has been real and
it has been fairly dramatic. We are still a long way from knowing all we
need to know, but we have acquired a sound practical basis for designing
systems to control pollutant discharges from urban areas.

* Senior Consultant, Woodward Clyde Consultants, 101 Manito Avenue,
Oakland, New Jersey 07436

A significant share of the credit for the advances that have been made in our ability to "engineer" effective control systems for stormwater runoff must be given to EPA. The Nationwide Urban Runoff Program (NURP) which they conceived, organized and supported produced a substantial advance in the base of pertinent data needed to support decisions, and it provided important support and enhancement for the activities of specific agencies that had begun to address the urban runoff issue. Each of the papers in this session reflect excellent individual contributions to different aspects of the control issue. I believe the authors would agree that the NURP program has contributed importantly to their effort, either through direct support or through the information it made available.

We should recognize however, that EPA's attention has been absorbed by other issues, and support for additional urban runoff activities is not to be expected, at least to any significant extent. The role that this forum has served so usefully in the past, becomes even more important looking ahead. It is probably the best, and might become the only practical vehicle for coordinating and consolidating the substantive information developed from a wide variety of individual sources. We should consider whether there are things that might be done in addition to the convocation of this forum on a regular basis. Some thoughts on this will be presented later.

The papers presented in this session address what are, in my opinion, the two most effective of the broadly applicable techniques for control of urban runoff. They are:

1. RETENTION DEVICES - The operating principle is the interception and capture of runoff, preventing its direct release to surface waters. The most common mechanism by which captured runoff is diverted is by infiltration. Performance efficiency is measured by the fraction of total runoff that is prevented from discharging to a surface water body.

2. DETENTION DEVICES - Virtually all runoff that enters the device is ultimately discharged to surface waters. Performance efficiency is measured by the reduction in pollutant concentrations, and hence mass loads that result from physical (sedimentation) or other (biological) processes that are given a chance to operate during the residence time that runoff is detained in its passage through the basin.

The terminology used reflects one that I believe to be widely accepted. It is not universal, as indicated by differences in nomenclature applied to specific systems in todays papers. There are, in addition to the fundamental control approach, variations and special distinctions based on either design details or the dominant mechanism by which pollutant removal is accomplished. Although a careful reading provides a clear picture of how each of the systems described operates, it may be useful for this group to sponsor the development of a standardized terminology to enhance effective communication in future exchanges.

OBSERVATIONS

There is a value in looking at the same data and information from different points of view. I have done so for certain aspects of each of the papers. This in no way challenges the analyses performed, or the author's interpretations. What it does do is provide an opportunity to extract additional useful information by examining a data set from a different perspective.

COST

The only substantive comment I have on the material presented by Wiegand and his associates at the Metropolitan Washington COG is the observation that they provide the best (and prossibly only extant) comprehensive data and analysis of cost factors for urban runoff controls. It seems reasonable to anticipate that this work will serve as the benchmark against which future refinements and additions will be based.

SETTLING COLUMN TESTS

Testing urban runoff by the settling column procedure used to develop the information presented by Grizzard and Randall is a very useful and relatively inexpensive technique. It provides important information about the characteristics of runoff that are useful in a general sense as well as having a direct application for the evaluation of control devices whose principal removal mechanism is sedimentation.

The NURP studies collectively produced settling column results from about 50 runoff samples, but only TSS was measured in these tests. Grizzard and Randall provide an important extension by measuring the settling characteristics of additional pollutants of interest. The practice of conducting settling column tests and monitoring removal rates for all pollutants of concern, should be encouraged. Because of the variability of stormwater runoff, confidence in conclusions and inferences requires a large number of tests. An effective way of accumulating an adequate data base is to be able to consolidate the results from a number of different independent studies. This in turn, requires that independent studies adhere to a set of common ground rules for test procedures and data reporting. This group might wish to consider an activity that encourages the development of such a set of guidelines.

There is an additional way to process the basic data produced by a column test. It provides a different perspective, and when taken together with that of the authors, considerably increases the information content of their data set. FIGURE 1 illustrates the basic settling column procedure, and

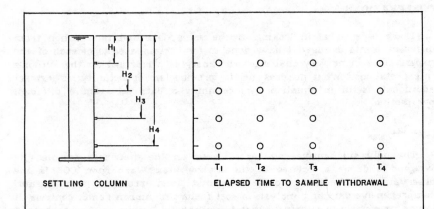

SETTLING COLUMN   ELAPSED TIME TO SAMPLE WITHDRAWAL

O = DATA POINT – RECORD % REMOVED BASED ON OBSERVED
VS. INITIAL CONCENTRATION

SETTLING VELOCITY (V_S) FOR THAT REMOVAL FRACTION IS DETERMINED
FROM THE CORRESPONDING SAMPLE DEPTH (H) AND TIME (T)

$$V_S = H/T$$

OBSERVED % REMOVED REFLECTS THE FRACTION WITH VELOCITIES
EQUAL OR GREATER THAN COMPUTED V_S

A PROBABILITY PLOT OF RESULTS
FROM ALL SAMPLES DISCRIBES THE
DISTRIBUTION OF PARTICLE SETTLING
VELOCITY IN THE SAMPLE.

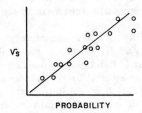

FIGURE 1   SETTLING COLUMN TESTS

the manipulation of the observations to produce information on particle settling velocities.

Sample ports at different depths are simultaneously monitored at a sequence of elapsed times. Pollutant concentrations in each sample are expressed as a percent of the initial concentration, which represents the percent removed via sedimentation at each location and time. Further, each sample withdrawn reflects a specific settling velocity. For example, the 1 hour sample at the 2 foot port, and the 2 hour sample at the 4 foot port, both correspond to a settling velocity of 2 ft per hr. If the observed concentrations in these samples reflect a 50% reduction in the initial condition, then it may be concluded that 50% of the particles associated with this pollutant have settling velocities that are equal to or greater than 2 feet per hour.

Urban runoff carries a wide range of particle sizes and hence settling velocities. When all of the column data is analyzed this way and plotted on probability paper we can develop an estimate of the probability distribution of particle settling velocities (and by inference sizes) in the particular sample. FIGURE 2 shows a crude estimate of the distribution of settling velocities of TSS in the samples analyzed by the authors. It is crude because removal efficiencies were scaled from the bar charts that were presented, and assumed to represent samples drawn at a settling depth 3.5 ft below the surface. The low (L), medium (M), and high (H) initial solids sample sets are shown, and compared with the NURP distribution (dashed line) which represents the average from about 50 tests. Individual samples in the NURP data set showed differences comparable to that shown by the H, L, and M lines.

For the pollutants other than TSS, there is both a particulate and a soluble fraction to the measured total concentration. Again as an initial crude estimate, it was assumed that 48 hours of quiescent settling removed about 95% of the particulate forms of these other pollutants. This permits the efficiency based on the total concentration present – to be converted to a removal efficiency for the fraction subject to removal by sedimentation. The settling velocity distributions of the authors "M" samples for TSS, Lead, Zinc and Phosphorus are shown by FIGURE 3, again compared with the NURP TSS data. Allowing for the fact that the plots are based not on the actual data, but rather on a fairly crude approximation of the details, it still seems valid to conclude that the particulate fractions of heavy metals and phosphorus behave very much like TSS in terms of settling characteristics.

SEDIMENT ACCUMULATION AND DETENTION BASIN DESIGN

The settling column data for urban runoff indicate that a large fraction of TSS and other pollutants removed by sedimentation, will settle out very rapidly. As a general approximation, on the order of 50 or 60% of the particulates have settling velocities that exceed 1 or 2 feet per hour.

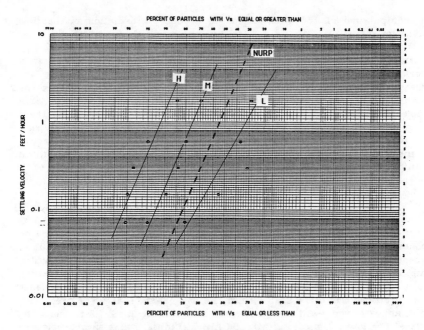

FIGURE 2   DISTRIBUTION OF SETTLING VELOCITIES FOR TSS

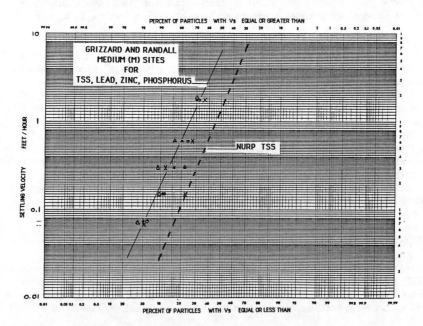

FIGURE 3   SETTLING VELOCITIES OF OTHER POLLUTANTS

This is consistent with Yousef's observation that "a majority of the particulate metals settle out quickly and are deposited near the point of input". His observation is in turn confirmed by independent data from one of the NURP basins (Lake Ellyn, IL), that also examined sediment accumulation patterns in detail.

Consider the foregoing information in context with Wiegand's observation that "the one-time costs for sediment removal can be staggering". . . even though carried out only once every 10 to 20 years. The evidence suggests that there should be significant practical and economic value to the development of a basin design that has a two stage operation with the following features.

1. A relatively small inlet section with size and design features that will permit capture of the easily separated particulate fraction, and convenient and economic removal of accumulated sediment. More frequent cleaning will be required, but there will be a practical benefit if this activity becomes a semi-routine element of a maintenance program. The likelihood of long term maintainence of effectiveness should be enhanced if sediment removal can be converted from a 20 year event with staggering cost and difficulty.

2. A final section that provides the bulk of the storage volume determined by applicable local criteria. The effective life of these larger, more costly to dredge sections should be extended substantially.

The practical feasibility of this concept needs further thought, but it has a direct analogy in the use of grit chambers in sewage treatment plants as treatment devices that process influent to the primary sedimentation basins.

DETENTION BASIN SIZE

Hartigan suggests that detention basins be sized to provide sufficient volume for an average residence time of two weeks. The principal basis for this size selection is the enhanced reduction in soluble nutrients it is expected to provide. The concept is rational, and the suggested size is reasonable, based on the available performance data. We should, however not lose sight of the fact that data are still quite limited. More cost-effective refinements may well be possible as additional data become available for analysis. Both cost considerations and added flexibility for siting in the type of regional system he discusses, argues for continuing efforts to improve our ability to size devices on a sound technical basis.

There are a number of other "sizing rules" in use that, unlike Hartigan's, have a questionable rational basis. These empirical designs are understandable given the need to establish simple ground rules for on-site basins where the opportunity for case by case evaluation is not feasible. However, as additional understanding of size-performance relationships is developed from an expanding data base, it will be desireable to periodically evaluate and revise such standard rules. Certainly, in the type of regional system suggested by Hartigan, which presumes a site specific engineered system, flexibility in sizing individual basins should be allowed.

We have accumulated good documentation that relatively large basins provide high levels of pollutant removal. However, I submit that we also need to improve our understanding of the relationship between size and performance. The NURP study was fortunate in having a data base that represented the performance of detention basins covering a very wide range of relative sizes. A methodology for predicting performance, calibrated against the data from nine basins, provides the relationship shown by Figure 4. It can be considered to be a reasonable estimate of the removal efficiency for TSS, and for the particulate fractions of other pollutants. For the larger basin sizes at the right end of the scale, biological removals of soluble nutrients can also be expected.

The availability of a general size-performance relationship provides a basis for decisions where site constraints exist, or where a network of basins is being considered in a regional scheme. It also makes clear the effect of regional rainfall patterns on basin size required to achieve a given level of performance. The performance levels indicated are compatible with those suggested in Hartigan's paper, which primarily reflects the fact that both drew on the same data set. The translation of the basin in his sizing example, is shown by the circle overplotted on the graph.

MISCELLANEOUS OBSERVATIONS CONCERNING DETENTION BASINS

One sidelight of the analysis performed to develop the relationship shown by Figure 4, provides useful design information. For the basins that are large enough to produce significant removals, the dominant fraction of the total removal results from quiescent settling during the intervals between storms. Basin geometry appears to be much less important than it would be for sedimentation under constant dynamic conditions in a flow-through basin. This indication tends to be confirmed by results from one of the NURP basins (Waverly Hills, Lansing MI), which was a circular basin with inlet and outlet closely spaced. Despite the poor configuration, this basin had an efficiency similar to others of the same relative size.

This observation is not intended to suggest that favorable basin geometry be ignored during design stages, but rather to suggest that it is apparently not a critical design factor for relatively large basins. Where design flexibility or cost would be adversely affected to a significant degree by use of an ideal geometry, the suggestion is that compromises may be made without significant effect on performance.

A final observation on the topic of detention basins that is relevant to the

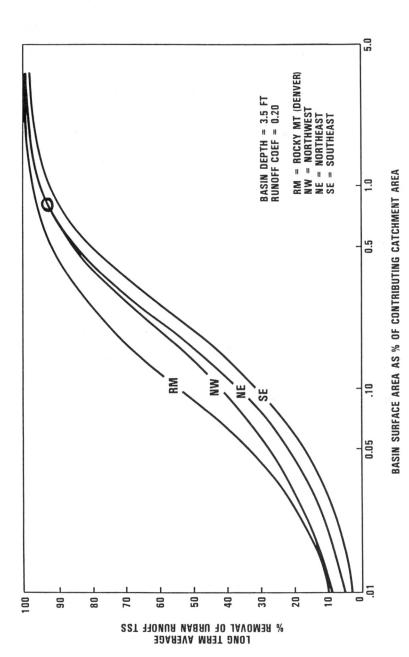

BASIN SURFACE AREA AS % OF CONTRIBUTING CATCHMENT AREA

BASIN DEPTH = 3.5 FT
RUNOFF COEF = 0.20

RM = ROCKY MT (DENVER)
NW = NORTHWEST
NE = NORTHEAST
SE = SOUTHEAST

LONG TERM AVERAGE
% REMOVAL OF URBAN RUNOFF TSS

FIGURE 4. DETENTION BASINS SIZE PERFORMANCE RELATIONSHIP

design of monitoring programs and interpretation of data, for studies designed to assess performance, may be in order. It was a subject of discussion during the NURP program. For basins that are large enough to achieve significant levels of removal by sedimentation and associated biological processes, the detention volume is many times larger than the volume of runoff produced by the mean storm, and 60 to 70 percent of all storms produce volumes smaller than the mean storm volume. Hartigan's criteria, for example, results in a basin volume that is 4 times the mean storm runoff volume. The final pond studied by Yousef is estimated to have a volume 15 to 20 times the mean runoff event.

This means that it takes a significant number of subsequent storm events to displace the runoff introduced into the basin by a particular storm. The outflow during an event is therefore unrelated to what is entering during a particular event, and treating inlet and outlet data as a paired set makes no sense. A broader framework for interpreting this type data is required.

RETENTION BASINS

The very comprehensive study described in Yousef's paper provides a wealth of useful information covering several different facets of the overall issue of stormwater runoff control.

The primary function of the ponds at the Maitland interchange is to operate as a retention system, to capture runoff and prevent its direct discharge to adjacent Lake Lucien. Captured stormwater is "diverted" by subsurface percolation and evaporation. Based on his observation that "a discharge rarely occurs to Lake Lucien", the system achieves its design objective with a high degree of efficiency, quite independently of the concentration reductions in heavy metals and nutrients.

Nevertheless, the Maitland system should be recognized to be not at all typical of retention/recharge systems commonly applied for runoff control. Most typical systems are designed to drain out fairly rapidly, and be dry a fairly high percentage of the time. These natural "resting periods" are analogous to the operating practice for land application of sewage, considered necessary to maintain soil permeability. One NURP project (Long Island, NY), monitored a number of the 2000 odd recharge basins in their study area. The sandy soil provides high infiltration rates, such that the basins rarely have standing water for any length of time. Many of these basins have been in service for 20 years or more, without any particular maintenance required to maintain permeability. Figure 5 shows the size-performance relationship for recharge devices developed for the NURP study. Capture efficiency depends on both the permeability of the soil and on the detention storage available.

The high water table, and possibly low infiltration rates at Maitland results in a permanent pool of water in the basins, and therefore its

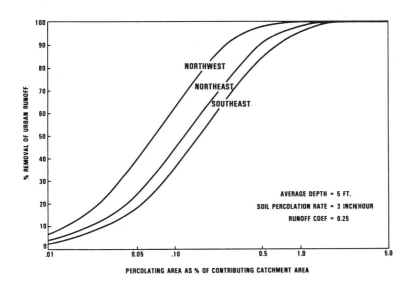

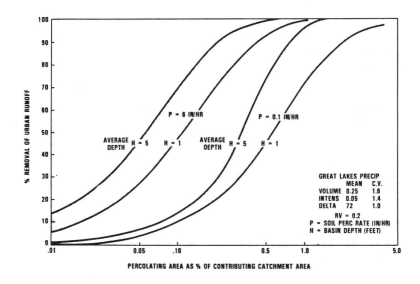

FIGURE 5. RETENTION BASINS   SIZE PERFORMANCE RELATIONSHIP

performance is not related to the general relationship shown. The results do indicate that retention systems which are non-typical, and have less than ideal site conditions, can be designed to produce high levels of control.

The evidence presented that heavy metals, perhaps the principal toxic pollutants of concern in urban runoff, are effectively trapped in soil at relatively shallow layers, is an important finding, and consistent with similar observations by two of the NURP studies (Long Island, NY and Fresno, CA). Still unresolved is the issue of eventual saturation and breakthrough of pollutants, however such concerns do not appear to represent an immediate threat. The basins studied in both Long Island and in Fresno had been in service for two decades or longer. Still, it would be wise to remain aware of this issue, and to encourage some necessarily long term monitoring programs to deal with this area of uncertainty.

The concentration data in the standing pond water do not relate directly to either the potential for ground water contamination, or to the performance capabilities of a typical retention/recharge system. They do however provide useful information on the removal of pollutants in wet ponds due to sedimentation and biological action. In this regard, the observed reductions in heavy metals, and in soluble nutrients is fairly consistent with other performance results presented in this session. Yousef's data is appreciably more detailed than that previously available, and highlights several interesting aspects.

1. The very long residence and active algal growth removes 80 to 90% of the soluble nutrients.

2. The poor (11%) apparent removal of particulate nutrients can be explained by the algal activity. These particulate forms represent the N and P tied up in algal cells, and not the particulate forms that entered with the runoff. This is an important factor. It will be useful to develop the data and evaluation procedures that will ultimately permit us to optimize basin design for net removal, to strike a balance between removal by algal activity and release with algal cells. Bigger may not always be better.

3. For heavy metals, the high removal of particulate forms is expected. What is not clear is the reason for the quite high (more than 50%) for the soluble forms.

CONCLUSIONS AND RECOMMENDATIONS

There is an active national interest in the control of pollutant discharges from urban runoff. Detention and Retention devices and systems probably provide the most effective practical approaches for doing so. Although we have progressed to the point where we can design effective systems, additional effort is required to move design considerations further from the principally empirical basis that now prevails, toward a more scientific engineered basis.

Considerably more information and understanding can be extracted when results from a number of different control devices can be examined, analyzed and compared, than when inferences must be drawn from a single data set.

EPA should probably no longer be relied on to play a very active role in coordinating and organizing pertinent results from various sources. However, local agencies and the academic and engineering communities, will in all probability continue to address the subject, and hopefully focus on the outstanding technical issues.

This forum has played an important role over the past decade, in fostering the exchange of information on urban hydrology. It may be appropriate for it to consider adding the following detailed items to its overall scope of activities. This could be either by an ad hoc group drawn from this gathering, or by referring the issues to some existing ASCE committee.

1. Standardize the nomenclature, principally as an aid to communication.

2. Encourage the use of settling column tests, and suggest standardized procedures for testing procedure and the reporting of basic data.

3. Provide guidance on appropriate technical data to be obtained in a study and a reporting format that will maximize its ability to be consolidated with and independently compared to results from independent studies.

4. Encourage further studies and papers on cost factors, particularly the sediment removal aspect. Provide criteria for terminology and standardized factors (e.g., interest rate, amortization period) to use in reports to facilitate comparisons between different sources.

5. Encourage the initiation of appropriate studies to address the issue of long term migration of pollutants to groundwater from percolating systems.

6. Encourage the presentation of some papers that deal with systems that do not provide outstanding performance, preferably those with marginal results. These will improve our understanding and appreciation of the important design issues to a much greater extent than an exclusive diet of successful designs.

Workshops on Research and Future Activities Needs

Thomas O. Barnwell, Jr., M. ASCE [1]

D. Earl Jones, F. ASCE [2]

Introduction

On the last night of the conference, participants met in small groups to discuss needs for future research and professional activities in urban stormwater quality. During the conference, a questionnaire listing proposed topical areas was given to participants, along with instructions to indicate their first three preferences and to propose additional discussion areas. The questionnaires were collected and participants were assigned to workgroups according to their wishes. Each workgroup met for approximately 3 hours and prepared a report that was discussed by all participants on the final day.

The topic of each workgroup is given in Table 1 and their written reports are attached. Individual workgroup reports should be read in their entirety to appreciate each group's concerns. This paper is an attempt to summarize the workgroup reports and to draw from them some common recommendations for the engineering and scientific community.

Table 1. List of Workgroup Topics

1. Pollution Sources and Receiving Water Impacts
2. Modeling and Data Management
3. Institutional Issues
4. NPDES Permits and Data Requirements
5. Control Technology (Two Groups)

Workgroup on Pollution Sources and Receiving Water Impacts

The workgroup on pollution sources and receiving water impacts identified several research needs for evaluating impacts of stormwater. One major need is development, refinement and standardization of tools and techniques to assist in identifying, evaluating and communicating impacts of stormwater. Particular needs include methods to determine when a beneficial use is impaired or threatened and to evaluate the capacity of a receiving water to assimilate stormwater

---

1. Civil Engineer, U S Environmental Protection Agency, Athens, GA.

2. Chief Engineer, U S Department of Housing and Urban Development, Washington, DC.

discharges. This would include methods for evaluation of chemical and biological water quality and measures of habitat adequacy. Other research needs include disposal of residuals from stormwater pollution control facilities and impacts of control measures on groundwater.

A general need is a better understanding of causative bio-geochemical agents that impair beneficial uses. Stormwater events are episodic and shortlived and it was thought that the basic environmental sciences are lacking in understanding the impacts of these events. Specific needs include a better understanding of sediment-water interactions, a method for identifying problem-causing forms of pollutants, and techniques for identifying sublethal stress in biota.

The workgroup recommended establishment of a national clearinghouse for collection and distribution of information related to all aspects of stormwater management, ranging from Manuals of Practice to ordinances and case law related to stormwater. In this workgroup, as in several others, there was a perception that much valuable information exists at the state and local level but there is, at present, no mechanism to communicate this information.

Workgroup on Modeling and Data Management

The workgroup on modeling and data management thought that an objective of modeling should be the ability to model water quality with the same accuracy as one can measure it. The group thought that this was now possible for quantity models.

The group recommended that existing data should be assembled and made available to researchers for further analysis. There was a perception that much greater understanding can be gained from study of these data. Another recommendation was to develop methods to estimate modeling uncertainty quantitatively and incorporate these methods into stormwater quality models. The ability to determine how good models are is a prerequisite to determining whether we have good models.

There is also a perception that there is still much that we do not understand and that we must assess what we don't know in order to proceed intelligently. A procedure is discussed that would postulate and examine processes affecting urban water quality in detail. A suggested framework in which to implement this methodology is an urban watershed similar to the Hubbard Brook experimental watershed, which examined the impacts of forestry practices.

Development of a chemical processes model of urban runoff that includes chemical speciation, kinetics and transformations, particularly of processes at the sediment-water interface, was recommended. This model must be able to make use of existing data bases and should improve our ability to properly interpret existing data.

Improved modeling procedures also were recommended, especially methods to help proceed intelligently through an analysis, using both simple and complex models in concert with technologies such as expert systems and sensitivity and error analysis. These systems should include procedures to identify optimum data requirements. It was thought that regression models can be improved by designing models with better functional forms that include more causal parameters as independent variables.

Several activities to promote technology transfer were recommended by this workgroup. Professional societies should promote access to existing data bases. New data collection activities should follow United States Geological Survey (USGS) guidelines for quality control and reporting format and should use USGS standards for archiving. The USGS should be encouraged to add acceptable processed data to their data base. Training should be provided in the use of models and data on microcomputers and simpler, "user-friendly" ways to approach complex models and data bases should be promoted through the development of pre- and post-processors.

Workgroup on Institutional Issues

Discussion centered around recommended research in institutional issues and activities that would promote better understanding of urban stormwater runoff issues, particularly related to local, regional and state governments. The activities recommended by the workgroup focus on integrating activity at local, regional, and state levels and in the private sector.

The workgroup strongly encouraged EPA to seek out local government and professional participation in the regulation development process for NPDES storm sewer permits.

The group sees the need for a single repository of information on various important aspects of urban stormwater runoff. Examples of information categories are listed in the workgroup report.

Workshops to strengthen urban runoff elements of state implementation programs were seen as a valid activity of regional EPA offices, actively supported by professional organizations. In particular, education and certificate training programs related to Best Management Practices (BMPs) for urban stormwater are needed for local government staffs, the engineering community, and the development/construction community. ASCE, APWA and other appropriate organizations should continue sponsoring programs, activities, and conferences on urban stormwater quantity and quality. These professional activities should be concurrent and supportive of official federal or state activities in the urban stormwater area.

Two research needs were identified by the work group. Research is needed into costs for installation and/or construction, maintenance and operation, monitoring and compliance of urban stormwater BMPs. Research is also needed into institutional frameworks in which state responsibility for water quality and local government responsibility for land use decisions can be integrated. For example, Florida's objective is delegating quality and quantity permitting to the local level. Program criteria need to be established to allow this delegation of authority.

Workgroup on NPDES Permits and Data Requirements

The September 26, 1984 <u>Federal Register</u> regulations require all municipalities with a population over 2,500 within the 366 urbanized areas of the United States (US) to obtain National Pollutant Discharge Elimination System (NPDES) stormwater permits. The workgroup discussed issues arising from this regulation.

A significant issue that has yet to be resolved is exactly who is to be the permittee. To ease the regulatory burden, EPA is considering the issuance of general permits that would not require a permit for each discharge point. In this case, the permittee may range from a shopping center to a municipality to a regional government to a state government. Indeed there is the possibility of a general permit for <u>all</u> shopping centers. Many issues arise from this general permit including responsibility for financing, sampling and enforcement. The work group attempted to identify these issues.

The workgroup believed that objectives for the permit process should be established with certain minimally acceptable scientific and engineering underpinnings. For example, the objectives should include protection of beneficial use of the nation's waterways, protection of groundwater users who may be affected by the permitted flow and associated controls, and consideration of variability of weather, geomorphology, land use mixes and positionings, and perceptions of aesthetic values in different communities.

The workgroup discussed several criteria for a permit, including criteria for variability of rainfall, criteria for definition of a storm event, criteria for violation of a permit, and criteria for definition of "natural water quality." Research needs evolving from these criteria include research on the state-of-the-receiving waters and the effects that stormwater may have on them, including establishment of standards by which stormwater quality can be judged.

There is a need for development of criteria for definition of a storm that will violate water quality standards as this will likely be the basis for design of pollution control facilities. There is a need for criteria for what constitutes violation of a permit and for what constitutes adequate and reasonable data collection requirements for a permit. The group speculated that the National Urban Runoff Study (NURP) data will be taken to be representative of "average" stormwater and will be the basis for comparison of monitoring data for permit compliance purposes. Based on this speculation, the group recommended that monitoring data should be collected by some institution and that institution should continually update the "national average."

Workgroup on Control Technology No. 1

The workgroup based its recommendations on the principle that nonpoint pollution will be decreased by practices that increase infiltration rates, absorption, reaction rate and subsequent sediment deposition or biological consumption, or that decrease desorption, erosion or initial concentration of chemicals in rainfall, on surfaces, or in the top layer of soil. Several areas were suggested as worthy of further investigation, including source controls, BMP effectiveness, and structural and nonstructural controls.

Research is needed into the potential for source control measures such as modification of automobile and highway materials and practices that reduce undesirable pollutants such as metals and wood perservatives. Additional work is needed to improve infiltration techniques that lose effectiveness because of clogging, such as in porous pavement, and in the chemical treatment of stormwater. Structural controls that need further work include in-line filters, evaluation of outlet control structures, swirl concentrators, plate separators, presettling filtration, and backwash of filters and filter cloth. The effect of depth on wet pond performance bears investigation, as does the use of wetlands and trees for stormwater pollution control.

Several activities were considered worthy of consideration, including "Public Awareness" campaigns to reduce dumping and littering, a clearinghouse for information exchange (perhaps as an EPA function), regional workshops for technology transfer, and development of design manuals for BMPs.

Workgroup on Control Technology No. 2

The second workgroup on control technology restricted its scope to engineered systems for mitigation of nonpoint source pollution. Non-structural measures such as zoning or public education were excluded from consideration. The group believes that the state-of-the-art in control technology is much better than the state-of-the-practice and only a small portion of what is known is being used.

In commenting on the state-of-the-art, pollutants were categorized as solids, nutrients, or toxics. The group believed that solids control was achivable with source controls, retention, and "dry" and "wet" retention; that nutrients can be controlled with detention and that wetlands are a promising technology; and that toxics can be controlled with retention and infiltration/exfiltration. Work needs to be done on controlling nutrients and toxics with other technologies. However, controls can proceed with existing technologies if necessary. It was observed that almost all state-of-the-art control technology requires little or no use of electro-mechanical devices.

Research needs for improving the state-of-the-art were identified in several areas, including field performance of some technologies, development of performance criteria for commonly used material such as filter cloth, documentation of technology failures, life-time costs of control technologies, and the life-time performance and total system impacts of nonpoint source pollution control.

Other recommended activities deal with transferring knowledge about state-of-the-art technologies to practitioners. These recommendations include encouraging engineering colleges to introduce students to urban stormwater management, and encouraging engineers to include other disciplines such as chemistry and biology on design teams.

And the group recommended convening an Engineering Foundation Conference on Design, Construction and Operation Criteria for Urban Stormwater Management Facilities in 2 years. The thrust of this conference should be the presentation of design, construction, and operation criteria based on actual experience.

Conclusions and Recommendations

Several common themes emerged from the workgroup discussions.

There was much discussion about the impacts of pollutants in urban runoff. It was thought that these impacts tend to be subtle and long-term rather than immediate and obvious, and that the general public and environmental managers do not perceive urban runoff as a problem for this reason. The impact of heavy metals seemed to be a particular concern.

There was also a general consensus that the study of urban runoff should not end with the NURP program. Several groups proposed an intensive, long-term study on the order of the Hubbard Brook experimental forested watershed. Such a study should include side-by-side comparisons of disturbed and "natural" drainage basins and focus on fundamental processes in the urban environment including urban pollutant sources, fate and transport, effects, and control technology.

Perhaps the most commonly expressed need was for the transfer of technology from the researcher to the practitioner. Recommendations to help satisfy this need take several forms, including some type of clearinghouse for information and educational programs on urban stormwater quality

Closely related to this need for a clearinghouse was a recommendation to continue conferences such as this to promote professional exchange in the area. Indeed, it was decided at the end of the conference to implement the recommendation of the Workgroup on Control Technology No. 2 and begin planning for an Engineering Foundation Conference on Design, Construction and Operation Criteria for Urban Stormwater Management Facilities in two years.

Disclaimer

This report was prepared by the authors in their capacities as members of the American Society of Civil Engineer's Urban Water Resources Research Council. While both authors are employed by agencies of the United States Government, the opinions and recommendations in this report should in no way be considered to reflect an official position of either the U S Environmental Protection Agency or the U S Department of Housing and Urban Development.

Attachment

Workgroup Reports

Workgroup on Pollution Sources and Receiving Water Impacts

Jonathan Jones, Chairman
Alan Johnson, Reporter
Carla Palmer
Pat Davies
Bill Odum
Nancy Driver
Bill Walker
Tim Miller
Mike Revitt
Bryan Ellis
Bob Pitt
Bob Bastian
Zdnek Novak

Basic Research needs on Evaluating Impacts of Stormwater

A) Development, refinement and standardization of tools and techniques
that will assist in:

- Identifying and evaluating impacts of pollutants/physical factors
related to stormwater.

- Conveying message to policy makers and public what constitutes a
"problem" and, conversely, identify when a "problem" is corrected.

Specifics -

a. Problem Identification - when is a beneficial use impaired or
threatened?

b. Data interpretation methods - what does the data mean once we
have it (such as organics and metals)

c. Simplified methodology to evaluate assimilative capacities of
various receiving waters: what are appropriate discharges to
urban receiving waters?

d. Extent of problem on local/regional levels - how do we account
for regional differences in hydrology, soils, instream habitat?
What are various outlooks on the issue?

e. Fate of pollutants - effects on groundwater; residual management
from stormwater control devices.

B) Methods and data that are appropriate for various beneficial uses
that will aid in identifying causative bio-geo-chemical agents that
are impairing a desired beneficial use.

Specifics -

a. Better understand sediment/water interactions.

b. Development of appropriate analytical methods for problem pollutants - i.e. what form of the pollutant is causing the problem?

c. Techniques for measuring/identifying sublethal stress in biota.

C) Uniform Approaches to detect trends in the quality and quantity of
instream habitat. These approaches would be used to :

a. Evaluate present and future impacts.

b. Assist in location of control facilities (i.e. regional type
facilities).

D) Need for further advances in basic environmental sciences as
related to stormwater, especially the frequent, small storm event.

Specifics -

a. Impacts and fates of pollutants in different receiving waters
such as groundwater and coastal waters.

b. Physical processes of sediment transport

c. Pollutant origin and transport through entire watershed system.

d. Data on storm characteristics as influenced by seasonal
meteorological events including: 1) warm/cold weather events;
and 2) base flows.

e. Contributions and characteristics of pollutant loads for various
land uses (e.g. industrial areas).

E) Need for establishment of a national clearing house for collection
and distribution of national and international information related
to all aspects of stormwater management (in particular quality
aspects). This information could include:

- Manuals of practice on stormwater quality, regulatory ordinances
and laws.

- Various court decisions and case law related to stormwater

- Educational materials

- Upcoming conferences, short courses and other educational
materials.

- Case histories (both successes and failures)

- Rehabilitation and enhancement methods

- Listing of professionals and their area of expertise.

Ed Herricks, who could not attend the work group meeting,
submitted a separate report:

I would like to submit a few comments and suggestions for
research needs directed to both specific and general issues associated
with water quality and urban runoff.

Short Term Effects Testing

There is little doubt in my mind that short term effects testing is necessary to meet the challenge of regulations which are on the horizon. Every effort should be made to avoid the use of existing water quality criteria for the development of permit limitations. Some explanation is necessary!

As you well know, the existing criteria follow a history built on presumptive applicability. Although some efforts have been made toward site specific criteria development, the focus of existing regulations seems to be water quality based toxics control. One of the major issues in the existing criteria/permit arena is selection of appropriate time-concentration relationships (e.g. what is an acceptable 24 hr average or long term average.)

This group should recognize that urban runoff events are episodic - concentration variability is going to be the norm in any runoff monitoring. My reasoning follows that direct application of existing water quality criteria will result in incalculable differences. Limits are likely to be extremely stringent because conservatism and application factors will produce safety factors on the order of 1000 or so. The environment will be protected but the difficulties faced by urban stormwater runoff managers will be monumental.

I would suggest the following:

1) Develop a laboratory research program (short-term toxicity test emphasis) which carefully evaluates episodic exposure of receiving system organisms to contaminants expected in urban runoff. If carefully performed with some tests providing expected ambient exposures it should be possible to adequately address initial concerns for environmental protection from these tests.

2) Encourage the development of "mechanism" analysis (i.e. Jenkins et. al., this conference) as a means of assessing environmental effects. Note that I used the term environmental here! Jenkins' proposed approach is not really a chemical specific analysis procedure (although it could be), it is a promising approach to dealing with true environmental effects starting with the mechanism of effect at the subcellular level and working upward.

3) As the Jenkins' approach tends to work up the biological hierarchy, a corresponding approach should be directed to working down the hierarchy. This approach will not be as clean as the mechanistic approach (you might take note of EPA's efforts to correlate field effects with laboratory testing) but it should be undertaken. My suggestion would be identification of several long term monitoring sites and carefully develop a program of analysis of these sites. The long term monitoring would meet my requirement for a focus on environmental analysis and mitigation planning nationwide.

Long Term Effects Testing

There has been a common concern expressed by participants about environmental effects. That concern is that we know so little about possible effects (even short term) that we are taking real risks with long term exposure, etc.

I feel this needs to be attacked head on. I have forgotten which speaker said what we need is not a $100 million program for 5 years but a $2 million program for 50 years. My response to analysis of NURP analyses is that it provides us the opportunity to ask the right questions now. We should begin the process of answering those questions. Where innovative techniques are being tried, a 5 or 10 year monitoring program should be established to evaluate effectiveness.

Let me digress for a moment. Natural systems are very resilient. Biologists are now developing tools to measure that resiliency, but its importance is not in short term effects analysis, it is the foundation for long term effects analysis. If we don't follow up on the studies we have done, we will still be speculating 10 or 50 years from now about probable long term effects. If we initiate a long term monitoring program for several sites, including a carefully developed sampling program for physical, chemical and biological parameters we will improve both our question answering and question asking capabilities.

Thus as a major recommendation/research need issue I suggest this conference strongly recommend that an effective, long term monitoring program be developed for urban runoff.

First, the implementation of this long term monitoring program should reflect regional differences in climate and receiving system condition and build on strong existing programs of analysis. For example, it has been very clear at this conference that things are different in Florida and Maryland and Wisconsin and Washington. Several regional centers should be established to reflect these differences and the monitoring effort focused on these centers. Second, it is essential that the proper questions be asked in the development of these programs. The proper questions are well defined and lead to data collection which is responsive to the questions while still being cost effective. Lastly, the regional programs should be coordinated and reviewed regularly. (Although not perfect, NSF's LTER program might serve as a model for what might be done.)

<u>Workgroup on Modeling and Data Management</u>

Wayne Huber, Chairman
Mow-soung Cheng
Mike Collins
Mike Terstriep
Jerry Marsalek
Marshall Jennings

The workgroup first listed the objectives of modeling urban runoff water quality: a) Protection of receiving waters; b) Public health; c) Water supply and water reuse; d) Effects on quantity controls, e.g., sedimentation and erosion. The workgroup felt that one should be able to model water quality with the same accuracy as measurements - stating that this was now possible for quantity models.

RESEARCH NEEDS:

A) Analyze existing data!

The existing data needs to be assembled and made available to researchers.

B) Uncertainty Analysis

Develop methods to estimate modeling uncertainty quantitatively, e.g., first-order error analysis, and incorporate these methods into models.

C) What don't we know?

We must assess what we don't know in order to proceed intelligently. A suggested procedure is to:

a) Identify unquantified micro- and macro- scale processes potentially affecting urban stormwater quality, for example:

Dry weather processes	Wet weather processes
atmospheric deposition	rainfall quality
traffic-related	washoff
pavement	erosion, sedimentation
autos	time and spatial scales
traffic counts	
wind effects	Transport
construction	
erosion	sediment transport
canopy, vegetation	routing
particle size and composition	transformations
absorption	
time and spatial scales	

b) Postulate mechanisms associated with each process.

c) Collect data to test postulates.

d) Incorporate mechanisms into models.

A suggested framework in which to implement this methodology is to establish an urban experimental watershed similar to Hubbard Brook.

D) <u>Chemical process modeling</u>

Develop a chemical processes model of urban runoff, including
chemical speciation, kinetics and transformations, particularly of
processes at the sediment-water interface. In developing this
model, we must be able to make use of existing data! For example,
we should be able to distinguish total vs. dissolved metals.

E) <u>Improve modeling procedures</u>

Develop methods to help an analyst proceed intelligently through an
analysis, using both simple and complex models in concert with
technologies such as Expert Systems and sensitivity and error
analysis in model pre- and post- processors. These systems should
also identify data requirements and indicate data to be measured.

F) <u>Regression modeling</u>

Design simpler models with better functional forms, including more
causal parameters as independent variables.

<u>ACTIVITIES (Technology Transfer)</u>

A) <u>Existing Urban Runoff Data</u>

Access to existing data bases should be advertised and promoted by
professional societies. The USGS-sampled NURP site data is available now and the remaining sites will be available through the
Illinois State Water Survey soon. In addition, a report and
magnetic tape of other urban runoff data is available from the
University of Florida. The group recommended that individual site
data be made available on 5-1/4" floppy diskette. Good
cooperation from USGS was noted by the group.

B) <u>New Urban Runoff Data</u>

New data collection activities should follow USGS guidelines for
quality control and formats and use USGS standards for archiving.
USGS should add acceptable and processed data to their data base to
the limit of their resources.

C) <u>Training</u>

Training should be provided in the use of models and data on microcomputers.

D) <u>Access to models</u>

Simpler, "user-friendly" ways to approach complex models should be
promoted through the development of pre-processors.

Workgroup on Institutional Issues

Scott Tucker, Chairman
Bart Hague, Reporter
Don Van Sickle
Bob Deeds
Pam Bissonnette
Tom Mountz
Steve Kay
Joan Lee
Eric Livingston
David Peterson
David Zeno

Discussion centered around recommended research in the institutional issues area and activities that would promote better understanding of the Urban Stormwater Runoff Issues, **particularly related to local, regional and state governments.** The evenings' discussion can be distilled to five recommendations on activities and two recommendations on research needs.

RECOMMENDED ACTIVITIES

FOCUS: Integrating activity at local, regional, and state levels and private sector.

A) NPDES Permitting of Storm Sewers

In some manner, EPA should encourage and seek out local government and professional participation at the earliest possible time in the rule/ regulation development process.

B) State Non-Point Source Implementation

Workshops for staffs of state and local agencies and affected professionals are needed to strengthen the urban runoff elements of these state implementation programs. We see this as a valid activity of regional EPA offices, actively supported by appropriate professional organizations.

C) Information and Technology Transfer

The group sees the need for a single repository of information on various important aspects of Urban Stormwater Runoff. Examples of information categories include:

a) Local, regional, state criteria and design manuals.
b) Inventory of BMP facilities.
c) Information on BMP facility operation and maintenance.
d) Information on cost and financing for BMP facility.
e) Monitoring program information.
f) Ordinances and enforcement information.
g) Names/addresses/phone numbers of key contacts at various state, regional, local, and federal agencies.

D) Education and Certification

Education and certificate training programs for local government staffs, the engineering community, and the development (construction) community related to BMPs for urban stormwater.

E) Professional Activities

ASCE, APWA and other appropriate organizations should continue sponsoring programs, activities, conferences, on urban stormwater quantity and quality. The group felt that this professional activity should be concurrent and supportive of official federal or state activities in the urban stormwater area.

RESEARCH NEEDS

A) Costs of BMPs

Research is needed into costs for installation and/or constructing, maintenance and operation, monitoring and compliance of urban stormwater BMPs.

B) Integration of Responsibility

Research is needed into institutional frameworks in which state responsibility for water quality and local government responsibility for land use decisions can be integrated. For example, Florida's objective is delegating quality and quantity permitting to the local level. In this type of approach, program criteria need to be established which could allow this delegation of authority.

Workgroup on NPDES Permits and Data Requirements

Michael Sonnen, Chairman
Pam Bissonette
Dennis Athayde
Robbie Comer
Ayoub Talhami
Linda Hinson
Jerry Higgins
Mary Peters
Fay Baird

The Permittee - Who are they?

The September 26, 1984, Federal Register regulations require all 6,000 or so municipalities with a population over 2,500 that are within the 366 urbanized areas of the US to obtain NPDES stormwater permits. Is this feasible? Who, in fact, should be the responsible party? Can municipalities with common receiving waters take common responsibility in a single permit? What legislative mechanisms would be needed to provide these permittees with financing/sampling/decisionmaking/enforcement authority? The 9 states with general permit authority today can currently apply for a general stormwater permit, but is that a beneficial thing to do, given the varying conditions and site specificity within a state?

Objectives of the Permit

The objectives for the entire permit process should be established, and they should be established with certain minimally acceptable scientific and engineering underpinnings -- no matter what the enabling legislation or compelling lawsuits say they are.

For example, the objectives must include these:

1) Protection of beneficial use of the nation's waterways, whether these are precisely and everywhere the exact same ones as in 303e Basin Plans for "normal" flow periods or not.

2) Ground water beneficial users who are or may be impacted by the permitted flow are also to be protected against deleterious impacts therefrom.

3) Variabilities in conditions of weather, geomorphology, land use mixes and positionings, and perceptions of aesthetic values of natural and man-made waterways exist. Given that they exist, one objective of the permitting process and the permits (plural) themselves shall be (should be) to take such variabilities into account.

Criteria for a Permit

Criterion 1 - Variability of rainfall

The stormwater criteria should be able to reflect the variable nature of rainfall and runoff (in duration, frequency, intensity, etc.) at any monitored site. Criteria that work in Bellevue, WA, may not work in Chicago, IL, or Chesapeake, VA. A feasible first step in stormwater permit criteria development should be to prevent degradation of the extant biota in each region. The "extant biota" in every urban area include, among others, homo sapiens. We need research on the state-of-the-receiving waters and the effects which stormwater may or will have on them.

Criterion 2 - Definition of "natural water quality"

In determining just exactly what water quality criteria should be set, it makes sense to determine stormwater runoff's effects on the biota currently residing in each permittee's waterways. But what baseline can be established if we have a "dead-river" situation or for a river that is severely impaired due to activities occurring up-stream? What could be used as a surrogate model for the establishment of standards by which a given degraded "natural" water's or an outlier stormwater's quality can be judged? (Some among the general audience later warned that attempts by local permittees to defend themselves as naturally ugly outliers will and should be looked upon with high suspicion.)

Criterion 3 - Storm Definition

Likewise, what is the storm event with which we should be con-cerned? Bellevue, WA has used the 1-year, 6-hour rainfall volume as the point beyond which the receiving water quality standards cannot be expected to be maintained. Treatment of rainfall volumes up to that level would, according to well-established research, account for 95% of the pollutant loadings. Should similar definitions be adopted by each permittee, or should they be rainfall and runoff and load-accumu-lation and washoff characteristics of each area? Or would other definitions or limitations be more appropriate?

Criterion 4 - Violation Definition

Once we have the standards established for each permit area, what should be considered to be a violation of those standards? If we exceed the standards we have set, by how much and how often do we have to exceed them to be justifiably, actionably considered to be "in violation of the permit"?

Analyses

Nobody yet understands what to do with the data the permittee will surely be asked to submit. No data-requester/demander should ever request or demand until he tells the demandee what he intends to do with the data. So EPA or whoever should know first what analyses are intended.

One supposes the minimum analyses will be done and those will address the basic point, i.e., is this permittee operating in a "nor-mal" background situation or is he abnormal? How abnormal is he? That can be determined by comparing the permittee's sample data against national averages. (Some among the general audience later thought this was a somewhat gross simplification of what ought to be done. That's true, but comparisons against the historical NURP data are to be anticipated!) One expects the NURP data will represent the national average, but the national average should be an ever-improved set of computations based on data from all local cooperators, NURP, USGS, and all other available sources. Some institution should be commissioned to accept the data and continually update the "average." The "average" should be a combination of statistics on rainfall amounts, frequencies, storms per year, flashiness of storms, length of dry periods and similar related weather and climatological data.

Next the analyses should include permittee's quality distributions and how they compare with the national averages. Statistics such as exceedance or frequency relationships of concentrations in a number of samples at a point should be computed and arrayed. For example, there should be a plot of concentration of, say, zinc vs. % of time that concentration is exceeded in samples -- of dry weather flow and of storm flow.

Additionally, the permittee's submitted quality records should be analyzed against the submitted records of other applicants in his own region. For example, if city E in the center of a box configuration of cities A, B, C, and D says his background receiving water lead concentration is 12.4 mg/l and the city A-to-D data show 0.02, 0.004, 0.8, and 0.000358 mg/l; then city A's data should be held suspect.

Data

The basic physical, stream or outfall data requirements to support a requested permit will be the menu of properties and constituent concentrations that describe the baseline condition of the permittee's receiving water or waters. That menu is not knowable at this point as a single list of properties applicable to all permit requesters. There is nothing sacred about NURP's sampling scheme that would preclude testing for different, more relevant stormwater constituents.

The second data need will be the minimum acceptable sampling plan for each permittee. At a minimum this should include the number of sites to be sampled, the number of storms to be sampled at each site or at all sites, and the number of samples to be taken at each site or at all sites. (The "ors" should be negotiable.)

There are also important, very basic definitions required, which are basic "data" too. What is the definition to be of:

1) a "receiving water" (and is there only one definition?);

2) a "sampling site" (in a pipe, in a pond, in a stream, at the edge of a parking lot, in a "watershed" someplace?);

3) what is an "outfall" and when or how is an "outfall" not an outfall?

Lastly, a regulator may never require a permittee to submit information on cost effectiveness or cost justification, but most, if not all permittees will want to have the cost justification data to display at the drop of a hat. Useful, information-containing, visually compelling data formats and data entries should be developed (in tables or graphs -- such as: Monitoring Cost in $ per saved human life (say $100,000,000) or BMP cost in $ per unaffected Anabena cell (say $12.50)).

Workgroup on Control Technology No. 1

Cliff Randall, Chairman
Marty Wanielstia
Sue Burke
Vincent Vignaly
Ron Gardner
Morton Lipschultz
Andrew Boisvert
Steven Seachrist
Karen Thorpe
Bethany Eisenberg

The workgroup based its recommendations on the principle that nonpoint pollution will be decreased by practices that increase

a) infiltration rates
b) absorption, reaction rate and subsequent sediment deposition
c) biological consumption

or that decrease

a) Desorption
b) Erosion
c) Initial concentration of chemicals in rainfall, on surfaces, or in the top layer of soil.

RESEARCH NEEDS:

Several areas were suggested as worthy of further investigation, including:

A) Source Controls

Research is needed into the potential for source control measures such as modification of automobile and highway materials and practices to reduce undesirable pollutants, i.e., Zn, Cd, Cr, and wood treating chemicals such as creosote, etc.

B) Effectiveness of BMP's

a) Infiltration techniques lose effectiveness because of clogging such as in porous pavement.
b) Chemical treatment of stormwater, i.e., alum, activated carbon, reverse osmosis, etc.

C) Structural Control

a) In-line Filters
b) Evaluation of Outlet Control Structures
c) Swirl concentrators
d) Plate separators
e) Pre-settling filtration
g) Backwash of filters and filter cloth

D) Effect of depth on wet pond performance - nutrients, etc.

E) Evaluation of Wetlands

a) Contact times for Removal
b) Yearly mass balances
c) Include shallow marshes

F) Use of trees for pollution reduction

ACTIVITIES:

Several activities were considered worthy of consideration:

A) Public Awareness campaigns to reduce dumping and littering.

B) Clearing House for Information Exchange (Perhaps as an EPA function)

C) Regional Workshops for Technology Transfer.

D) Development of Design Manuals for BMP's

Workgroup on Control Technology

Stuart G. Walesh, Chairman
Rodney H. Kingria, Reporter
Jeff Elledge
Ronald A. Etzel
Patrick Hartigan
Byron N. Lord
Christopher J. Pratt
Larry A. Roesner
Thomas Schueler

Introduction

To confine the scope of our workshop, we defined control technology as
engineered systems used to mitigate non-point source (NPS) pollution.
Control technologies include source control (e.g., mulching, seeding),
vegetative buffer strips (e.g., natural vegetation along stream
channels), infiltration/exfiltration (e.g., perforated pipes discharging
into the ground water system), retention with no discharge to the
surface water system (e.g., as applied in Florida), "wet" detention
(i.e., permanent pool with discharge to the surface water system), "dry"
detention (i.e., discharge to the surface water system), "wet" and "dry"
detention with filtration (followed by discharge to the surface water
system), wetlands and other vegetative systems, and chemical treatment.

Non-structural measures such as land zoning or down-zoning and public
education are excluded from our definition of control technology.
However, such measures are an integral part of NPS pollution control
systems and, therefore, should be considered in planning and design.

There is a large gap between the state-of-the-art (SOA) and the state-
of-the-practice (SOP) in NPS control technology. As a group, water
resource engineers seem to be using only a small portion of what is
known about NPS control technology. Stated differently, only a very
small fraction of practitioners seem to be using SOA technology.

Comments on the State-Of-The-Art

For purposes of discussion, NPS pollutants/contaminants were categorized
as being primarily solids, nutrients, or toxics. Given this scheme, we
believe that engineers can be confident in controlling solids using
source control, retention, and "dry" and "wet" detention. By
"confident", we mean that an engineer with sufficient watershed and site
data and familiarity with the SOA, could design a solids control
facility, "sign off" on a design, and see it go to construction and into
operation. With the exception of special situations, we lack adequate
information to confidently control solids using detention with
filtration and using vegetative buffer strips.

We are confident that nutrients can be controlled with retention.
Natural and artificial or restored wetlands appear promising. We need
to advance the SOA in controlling nutrients with all other technologies.

Finally, toxics can be confidently controlled with two technologies --
retention and infiltration/exfiltration. We need to advance the SOA in
using other technologies to manage toxics in the environment.

In summary, the SOA provides at least one technology to control each of
the three pollution categories. Therefore, we can proceed with
implementation of NPS controls in at least some parts of the United
States as local problems may require. However, cost-effective
solutions are much more likely to be achieved if the SOA is advanced
with respect to all technologies. That is, availability of a range of
technologies will provide the designer with more options and increase
the likelihood of a more cost effective solution. Furthermore,
advancing the SOA for all technologies will make proven controls

available regardless of climatic, soil, topographic, and other conditions.

We observed that almost all SOA control technologies are "gravity driven". That is, there is little or no use of mechanical devices (i.e., moving parts), automatic controls and pumping. Reliance on gravity systems seems prudent for two reasons. First, the introduction of mechanical and electrical devices will exacerbate the already difficult inspection and maintenance function. Second, mechanical and electrical devices are most likely to fail when they are needed most — during storms.

Research Needs

A) We need to know more about the field performance of some control technologies. Of particular interest, because of their potential application to two or more classes of pollutants or contaminants, are source control, vegetative buffer strips, infiltration/exfiltration, "wet" and "dry" detention with filtration, and wetlands.

B) Performance criteria should be developed for commonly used materials such as filter cloth, particularly when used as a silt fence.

C) To the extent feasible, control technology failures should be documented and shared.

D) Although we have sufficient information to estimate construction costs, we need additional research to define inspection, maintenance, and operation requirements or tasks and associated costs. We also need to know the useful life of system components, that is, the various parts of a given control technology. The over-riding concern is that NPS technologies may be operation and maintenance intensive. Therefore, the present value of inspection, maintenance, operation and replacement costs may be of the same order of magnitude as construction cost.

E) It seems possible, if not probable, that SOA NPS control technologies could be satisfactorily applied to an urbanizing watershed and serious channel erosion and sedimentation still develop over a period of years and decades on the trunk channel system. Such erosion and sedimentation would be caused by the change in the hydrologic regime (e.g., higher discharges and velocities) in the channel system. Concern with long term erosion and sedimentation in the trunk channel system is one reason that stormwater management in urbanizing areas must simultaneously address quantity and quality problems. The early emphasis on quantity at the expense of quality must not be replaced by a new emphasis on quality at the expense of quantity. We need case study data to highlight the importance of simultaneously addressing quantity and quality.

Other Recommended Activities

Research such as recommended in the preceeding section of this report
will advance the SOA. However, research will not significantly or
rapidly advance the SOP. Accordingly, various vigorous technology
transfer efforts must continue or be initiated.

A) We recommend the convening, in two years, of an Engineering
    Foundation Conference (EFC) on Design, Construction, and Operation
    Criteria for Urban Stormwater Management Facilities. The thrust of
    this EFC should be the presentation of design, construction, and
    operation criteria based on field data and other actual experience.

    Between now and the conference, we hope that researchers will
    examine their data to identify and quantify design perameters.
    Similarly, design practitioners, contractors, and operating
    personnel should distill their experience as it relates to design,
    construction, and operating criteria. Because of the informal,
    confidential nature of EFC's, the conference could be a forum to
    share failures as well as successes.

    We suggest that co-sponsors or participants in this EFC include,
    but not necessarily be limited to, our international colleagues and
    U.S. organizations such as the American Association of State
    Highway and Transportation Officials, the National Home Builders
    Association, the American Public Works Association, and selected
    scientific groups. Conference proceedings should include presented
    papers plus an annotated bibliography of design, construction, and
    operation manuals and other documents.

B) We recommend that engineering colleges introduce students to urban
    stormwater management by using this field as an example of the
    application of engineering sciences such as hydraulics, hydrology,
    soil mechanics, sanitary engineering, and structures.

C) We recommend that engineers invite representatives from other
    disciplines such as chemistry and biology to participate on
    planning and design teams.

CASE STUDIES OF NEED-BASED
QUALITY-QUANTITY CONTROL PROJECTS
Stuart G. Walesh(a)

INTRODUCTION

Much of the non-point source (NPS) pollution management activity in the
U.S. to date has been driven primarily by government regulatory and
funding programs. Examples of these programs are the federal 208
Program and local (e.g., county, city, village, and special district)
erosion and sedimentation control ordinances. Stated differently, NPS
management activities have been primarily in a "top-down" mode, that is,
government directing individuals and entities to mitigate or prevent NPS
pollution problems. The historic "top-down" approach to NPS management
is characterized by emphasis on research and development, large-scale
studies, broad recommendations, and, in general, absence of specificity
and little implementation.

The "top-down" approach contrasts with a "grass-roots" approach. With
the latter, individuals and entities undertake NPS pollution management
because they have NPS problems that must be solved now. These
situations provide opportunities to apply NPS pollution management
measures on a problem resolution basis completely outside of, but
consistent with the intent of, government programs.

PURPOSE

This paper briefly describes several NPS pollution control projects
motivated largely by local need, not by government regulatory and
funding programs. The case studies are intended to stimulate thinking
concerning the technical approaches used and the value of encouraging a
"grass roots" approach to NPS pollution management. In the absence of,
and perhaps unfettered by, government controls, innovative, cost-
effective NPS pollution control measures have been designed and
implemented. Experience gained on these and similar "grass roots"
projects is used to draw conclusions and make certain recommendations
concerning NPS pollution control.

(a) By Stuart G. Walesh, P.E., Ph.D., Dean, College of Engineering,
Valparaiso University, and consultant, Valparaiso, IN 46383 (219-464-
5121). Update of a paper presented at the Non-Point Pollution
Symposium, Milwaukee, Wisconsin, April 23-25, 1985.

CASE STUDY 1:   SEDIMENTATION BASINS IN SERIES WITH A DETENTION FACILITY

Physical Setting

The setting for this project, as shown in Figure 1, is a 640 acre almost
completely urbanized watershed at the southern limits of the City of
Madison, Wisconsin. The watershed contains parts of three government
entities -- the City of Madison, the Town of Madison, and the Town of
Fitchburg -- plus the University of Wisconsin arboretum. The arboretum
is a sanctuary for native plants and wildlife and is used for research
and teaching.

Problems

Two growing problems were of concern to area residents several years ago
at the beginning of the engineering feasibility phase of this project.
First, flooding of increased frequency and severity was occurring in the
peninsula of single-family residential development which protrudes into
the arboretum from the east, as shown in Figure 1. Watershed runoff
from the entire watershed passing northerly through and over this area
caused surface and basement flooding.   Second, debris and sediment
carried from the urbanizing watershed were being deposited in and
causing damage to meadows, wetlands, and lagoons in the arboretum.

Solution

The three government entities and the Arboretum Committee agreed to a
surface water management system consisting of two sedimentation basins
and a sedimentation facility as shown in Figure 2. The sedimentation
basins are located on the upstream side of the arboretum and trap
objectionable sediment and attached pollutants, floatables, and other
debris before it enters the arboretum. During and immediately after
runoff events, the normally empty detention facility temporarily
impounds stormwater in the arboretum and provides flood protection to
the downstream residential area.

The 2,200 foot long berm required for the detention facility was
designed with a curvilinear alignment and irregular cross-section to
minimize its visual impact on the aesthetically sensitive arboretum.
The sedimentation basin-detention system was constructed in 1982 at a
total of cost of $103,000 and is in operation (Donohue, 1981; Raasch,
1982).

CASE STUDY 2:   SEDIMENTATION BASIN IN SERIES WITH RESTORED WETLAND

Physical Setting

McCarron Lake in Roseville, Minnesota receives runoff from a fully
urbanized 1.6 square mile watershed. The 72 acre lake is heavily used
for fishing, swimming, and boating. It also provides a setting for a
contiguous residential area and a county park.

Problems

A one-year diagnostic study confirmed that McCarron Lake is eutrophic.

FIGURE 1
WATERSHED MAP

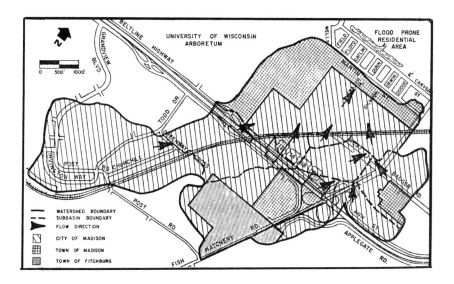

Source: Raasch, 1982

FIGURE 2
SEDIMENTATION BASINS—DETENTION FACILITY SYSTEM

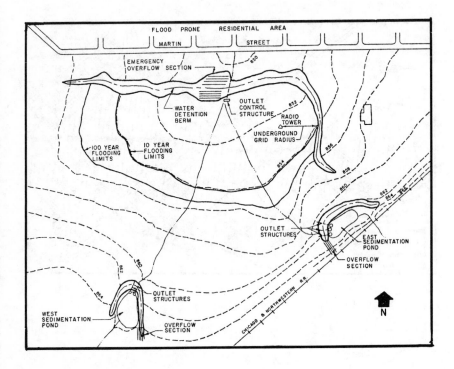

Source: Raasch, 1982

Hypolimnetic oxygen depletion releases nutrients into the water column when the lake is stratified and there are abundant nutrients in the water column throughout the year. Objectionable sediment accumulation is beginning to occur in the lake. Surface water runoff into the lake is the principal contributor of troublesome nutrients and sediment.

The solution to the nutrient and sediment problem has two components. As shown in Figure 3, the first component is a sedimentation basin in series with a restored wetland on a drainageway that controls 80 percent of the runoff into the lake. The sedimentation basin and related detention area trap sediment and control flow into the restored wetland. The wetland was restored to a size of about 8.0 acres by building a series of low berms across the existing channel, as shown in Figures 3 and 4. Native vegetation was planted as part of the wetland restoration. The sedimentation basin-restored wetland is expected to remove about 75 percent of incoming total phosphorus and suspended solids.

Construction on the sedimentation basin-restored wetland-sump system was completed in spring of 1986 at a total cost of about $300,000. Post construction performance monitoring will be carried out over an 18 month period beginning in fall, 1986.

CASE STUDY 3: SURFACE AND SUBSURFACE DETENTION IN AN URBAN AREA

Physical Setting

The 1,200 acre Skokie, Illinois Howard Street Sewer District (HSSD), as shown in Figure 5, is a combined sewer service area. The HSSD is completely and densely developed and over 80 percent of the district is single-family residential with the rest being commercial and industrial. The long, narrow HSSD is very flat having an overall slope of only 0.2 percent.

The combined sewer system serving the HSSD discharges at the east end of the district to an interceptor paralleling the North Shore Channel. The start-up of the Chicago Area Tunnel and Reservoir Plan (TARP) in 1985, primarily a pollution control facility, was expected to mitigate wet weather overflow to the channel.

Problem

Even though TARP is operational, serious basement flooding would have continued to occur in many of the over 5,000 single-family residences and other buildings in the HSSD. TARP improves outlet conditions at the extreme eastern end of the HSSD, but it does not resolve deficient sewer capacities throughout most of the district. Design, construction, and operation of a conveyance or detention system to take full advantage of TARP was necessary to solve the flooding problem and was the complete responsibility of the Village of Skokie. Although a relief sewer system, such as new separate storm sewers, was technically feasible, the cost was prohibitively high.

Solution

FIGURE 3
CONCEPT OF SEDIMENTATION BASIN IN SERIES WITH RESTORED WETLAND

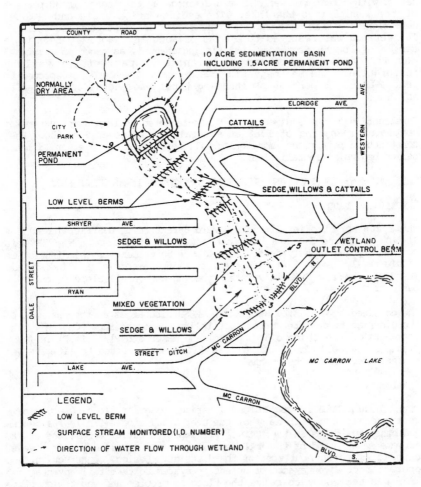

Source: Donohue, 1983

FIGURE 4
LONGITUDINAL SECTION THROUGH SEDIMENTATION BASIN AND RESTORED WETLAND

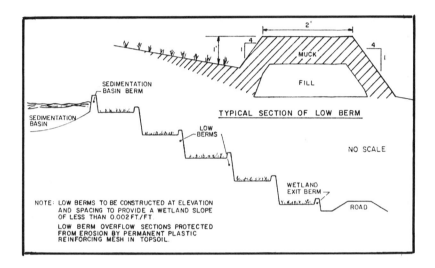

Source: Donohue, 1983

FIGURE 5
STUDY AREA: HOWARD STREET SEWER DISTRICT IN SKOKIE, ILLINOIS

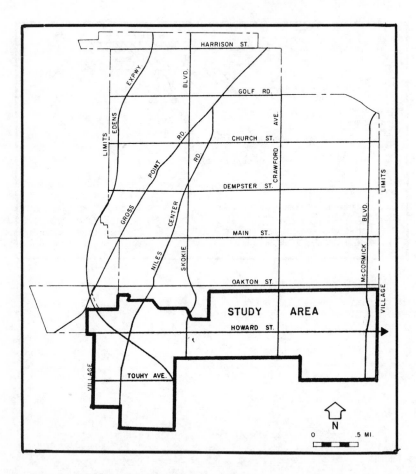

Source: Walesh and Schoeffmann, 1984

After extensive field and office investigations spanning several years, the Village of Skokie began implementation of a runoff control system (RCS) in which stormwater detention was retrofitted into the existing stormwater drainage and combined sewer system (Donohue, 1982, 1984a, 1984b, 1984c; Walesh and Schoeffmann, 1984). The concept is shown in schematic form in Figure 6 for existing and proposed conditions.

Stormwater is intentionally ponded in streets in a controlled fashion and then gradually released to the combined sewer system at a rate that can be conveyed by the combined sewer system without surcharging. On those streets where insufficient surface storage was available, supplemental subsurface storage tanks or surface detention are used. More specifically, the RCS consists of (Raasch, 1986):

* 484 flow regulators functioning in conjunction with 180 street berms.

* Eight subsurface storage tanks and two surface detention facilities.

* 10,000 feet of separate relief sewer for the downstream commercial end of the HSSD.

Most of the temporary street detention was accomplished by construction of low, mildly sloping street berms as shown in Figure 7 and installation of simple flow regulating devices in existing catch basins as shown in Figure 8. Each catch basin contains a sump which traps both settleable and buoyant material. In addition, each subsurface tank will, as illustrated in Figure 9, contain a large sump to trap soluble and buoyant material.

Therefore, essentially all stormwater, while in route to the combined sewer, passes through and is detained in a sump where some settleable and buoyant material, along with adsorbed and absorbed potential pollutants, are removed. These sumps will be regularly cleaned and maintained by Village personnel.

The construction costs for the recommended RCS, excluding engineering, legal, and administration fees, was about $8.0 million or less than 20 percent of the cost of a conventional relief sewer system. Construction was completed in the fall of 1985 with the exception of relief sewers which will be constructed in 1986. Preliminary engineering of a similar system is underway for the remainder of the Village (Raasch, 1986).

Control of suspended solids and other potential NPS pollutant is not a primary objective of the Skokie RCS because TARP provides pollution protection to the receiving streams. However, the RCS or a variation on it has the potential to control NPS pollutants near their source because of the widespread detention and the presence of numerous sumps and traps. An engineered RCS built into a new separately sewered development or retrofitted into an existing separately sewered or combined sewered area could have the following water quality benefits:

* Reduce frequency and volume of combined sewer overflows to the receiving waters.

FIGURE 6
STREET PONDING, REGULATED CATCH BASIN AND UNDERGROUND TANK

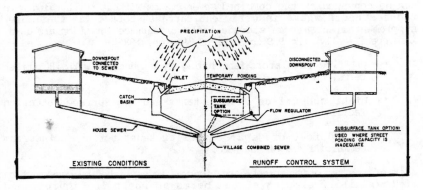

Source: Walesh and Schoeffmann, 1984

FIGURE 7
TYPICAL STREET BERM

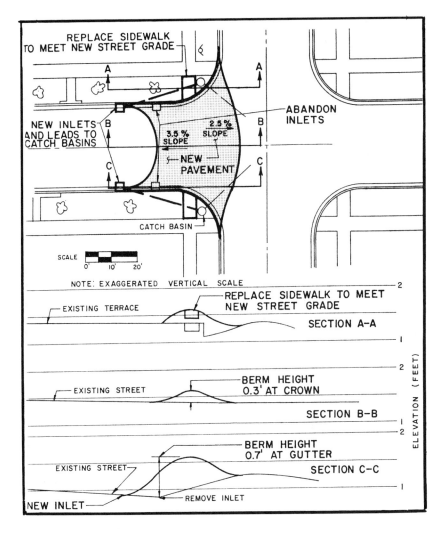

Source: Donohue, 1984c

FIGURE 8
FLOW REGULATOR AND SUMP IN CATCH BASIN

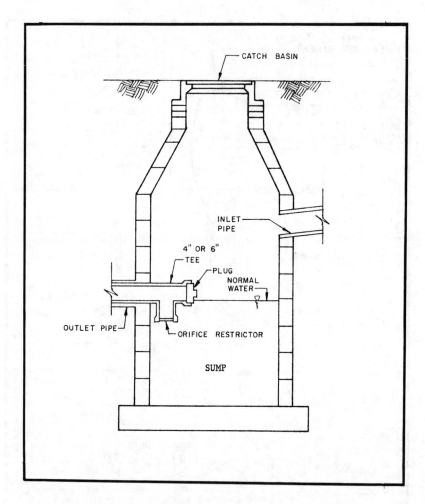

Source: Walesh and Schoeffmann, 1984

FIGURE 9
UNDERGROUND TANK

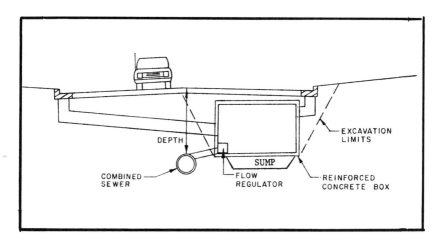

Source: Walesh and Schoeffmann, 1984

*   Control NPS pollution near its source for subsequent removal as
    a part of sump cleaning and maintenance.

*   Decrease peak flows at wastewater treatment plants.

OBSERVATIONS

The following observations are made based on experience, such as the
examples presented in this paper, with engineering of NPS controls at
the "grass roots" level in response to particular environmental
problems:

1. Suspended Sediment is the Primary Target: In addition to being
    a potential pollutant, suspended sediment can be a transporter
    of potential pollutants such as phosphorus, pesticides, heavy
    metals, bacteria, and oxygen-demanding materials. Therefore,
    the successful control of suspended solids should indirectly
    result in substantial control of other non-point source
    pollutants.

2. Small Incremental Expense Concept: In terms of land
    acquisition and construction costs, relatively little
    additional expenditures are likely to be required to add
    effective water quality control components to planned
    stormwater detention/retention facilities. Control of the
    quality of stormwater can often be achieved for a small
    incremental cost above that needed to control the quantity of
    stormwater.

3. Stringent Inspection and Maintenance Requirements: The
    principal purpose of NPS control measures is removal and
    concentration of potential pollutants from stormwater runoff.
    At minimum, sediment and other debris will be collected in NPS
    control facilities. These facilities must be regularly cleaned
    and otherwise maintained if they are to function as intended.
    Designers should clearly indicate the type and frequency of
    inspection and maintenance and provide cost estimates.

4. Resist Mandating Specific NPS Measures: Given the limited, but
    growing, knowledge concerning the design and operation of NPS
    pollution control measures, local, state, and federal
    governmental units should "go slow" in mandating specific means
    of controlling NPS pollutants. Government agencies should
    instead focus on statements of intent and performance.
    Premature rule-making and regulation are likely to result in
    "action" but little progress. More is likely to be
    accomplished in advancing the state-of-the-art of NPS pollutant
    control by (a) funding additional research and development
    projects and pilot studies and (b) by encouraging the control
    of NPS pollutants but not dictating the means.

Acknowlegements

The author gratefully acknowledges the ideas and information provided by
former colleagues and drawn from project experience at Donohue &

Associates, Inc. However, the author is soley responsible for the
paper's content.

CITED REFERENCES

Donohue & Associates, Inc., Lake Forest Storm Water Detention Facility –
Preliminary Engineering, 1981.

Donohue & Associates, Inc., McCarron Lake Diagnostic – Feasibility
Study – Roseville, Minnesota, November, 1983.

Donohue & Associates, Inc., Preliminary Engineering – Runoff Control
Program – Howard Street Sewer District – Skokie, Illinois, July, 1982.

Donohue & Associates, Inc., Monitoring – 1983 – Runoff Control Program –
Howard Street Sewer District – Skokie, Illinois, January, 1984a.

Donohue & Associates, Inc., Flow Regulator Pilot Study – Runoff Control
Program – Howard Street Sewer District – Skokie, Illinois, February,
1984b.

Donohue & Associates, Inc., Preliminary Engineering – Addendum – Runoff
Control Program – Howard Street Sewer District – Skokie, Illinois,
March, 1984c.

Raasch, G.E., "Urban Stormwater Control Project in an Ecologically
Sensitive Area", Proceedings – 1982 International Symposium on Urban
Hydrology, Hydraulics and Sediment Control, University of Kentucky,
Lexington, Kentucky, July 27-29, 1982, pp. 187-192.

Raasch, G.E., Donohue & Associates, Inc., personal communication with,
June 11, 1986.

Walesh, S.G. and M.L. Schoeffmann, Surface and Sub-Surface Detention in
Developed Urban Areas: A Case Study, presented at the American Society
of Civil Engineers Conference "Urban Water – 84", Baltimore, MD, May 28-
31, 1984.

LOGNORMALITY OF POINT AND NON-POINT SOURCE
POLLUTANT CONCENTRATIONS

by : Eugene D. Driscoll
(Woodward Clyde Consultants)
Oakland, New Jersey 07436

ABSTRACT

This paper presents a series of probability plots of water quality data from a variety of discharge sources. It is intended to provide a visual display of the appropriateness of characterizing the variable pollutant concentrations by a log normal distribution.

Representative examples of observed data that have been analyzed and plotted to test whether they can be treated as lognormally distributed random variables, are presented for data sets from the following applications:

Highway stormwater runoff

Combined sewer overflows

Urban runoff

Point Source discharges from POTW's

Agricultural runoff

Such examination suggests that a lognormal distribution either actually defines the underlying population of pollutant concentrations, or is at the least a satisfactory approximation for most environmental analyses.

INTRODUCTION

It has always been recognized that natural processes are variable. The value of **quantifying** this variability in some appropriate way has increased substantially in recent years. This is because many of the issues, problems, situations that the environmental engineering community is now dealing with are more effectively addressed in a probabalistic context.

A number of articles have appeared in the technical literature over the past five years or so, in which the authors report that the particular data they are dealing with has a log normal distribution. Almost invariably, such statements carry a qualifier. Some examples

The log normal distribution was found to fit . . . . most consistently.

(Three distributions). . . were found to be adequate, with log normal preferred because of ease of application.

Visual examination . . . indicated that data were best described by a log normal distribution.

Generally log normal distributions were observed for all but the data extremes.

Overall, the . . . data tend to fit a log normal distribution.

Space constraints will nearly always preclude the inclusion of any significant number of distribution plots in a paper or report, so the reader has no independent basis for deciding how well, or how poorly, the general conclusion on lognormality really applies.

The simple objective of this paper is to present a set of probability plots for water quality data from a number of different applications, to provide the reader with a visual picture of the extent to which the sampled observations fit a log normal distribution.

During the inspection of the probability plots, it will be useful to bear in mind the following considerations. I submit that the important issue is not whether a specific data set can be reliably concluded to have a log normal distribution. The real issue is whether it is appropriate or reasonable to infer that the underlying population of events represented by the sample of observations is lognormally distributed.

Each data set is a small sample of the much larger population of values represented by the sample. The particular sample taken will be representative of the underlying population to an unknown extent, and may be fairly good or rather poor. There is no way to resolve this satisfactorily when it is the only sample available for inspection. However, when similar pollutant data are available for inspection from a large number of comparable sites, or for a variety of other pollutants at the same site, the information to guide the desired inferences is extended.

HIGHWAY STORMWATER RUNOFF

The probability distribution of event mean concentrations (EMC's) of four pollutants are shown for each of four highway sites. Three of the sites, Nashville, Milwaukee and Denver are urban highways. The Harrisburg site is in a rural setting. Figure 1 is for TSS, Figure 2 for Total N, Figure 3 is for Lead and Figure 4 is for Zinc. These data are from a study currently in progress for the Federal Highway Administration.

COMBINED SEWER OVERFLOWS

The probability distribution of event mean concentrations (EMC's) of BOD (Fig 5) and suspended solids (Fig 6) are shown for four CSO sites. Three of the sites, are in Richmond VA, the fourth in Toronto.

Figure 7 shows the distribution of the site median concentrations of BOD and TSS at the six CSO sites that were monitored in Richmond, and at 13 sites from 6 cities. All data is from the University of Florida Data Base.

URBAN RUNOFF

The probability distribution of event mean concentrations (EMC's) of Total P (Fig 8) and COD (Fig 9) are shown for six urban runoff sites. Figure 10 shows the distribution of the site median concentrations of Total P at 69 of the urban runoff sites that were monitored under the Nationwide Urban Runoff Program (NURP)

POINT SOURCE DISCHARGES - POTW's

There have been a number of studies over the past 6 or 8 years that have looked at the variability of daily average effluent concentrations from municipal sewage treatment plants. The authors have, as cited earlier, concluded that distributions of daily average concentrations are at least adequately approximated by a log normal distribution. I haven't had access to such daily values and have no plots to present to illustrate this level of detail. However the papers and reports do present summaries of the mean and coefficient of variation (COV) of daily values for a sample that generally covers one to three years of plant records.

Figure 11 shows the distribution on mean influent concentrations of Cadmium for a large sample of POTW's. Figure 12 shows the distribution of the overall mean effluent BOD concentration, and the COV of daily values for 66 Conventional Activated Sludge plants. The correlation plot shows that there is no relation between the mean effluent that a particular plant produces and the degree of variability of daily concentration values - for all plants in this process category.

AGRICULTURAL RUNOFF

Figure 13 shows the distribution of the EMC's of three pollutants (ammonia, nitrate and TKN) at two study sites in Watkinsville, Georgia.

The ammonia nitrogen EMC's for agricultural runoff from four study sites in the Four Mile Creek watershed in Iowa are presented in Figure 14. Total Phosphorus EMC's at two of these sites are shown by Figure 15. The second of the plots for each site excludes 4 observations during one of the winter periods when manure was applied on frozen ground and not worked into the soil.

Figure 16 displays the distribution of annual average values for the concentration of soluble phosphorus and nitrogen in both surface runoff and subsurface stormwater discharges at the site of a long term study at a different location in Iowa. The final plots describe the variability of the concentration ratio between subsurface and surface discharges.

CONCLUSIONS

1. Whether or not it is rigorously true that the distribution of the underlying population of pollutant concentrations from the indicated sources are log normal (as suggested by the material presented), it appears to be an acceptable approximation that will be adequate for many of the uses to which it may be put.

2. Lognormality can be assumed for the distribution of EMC's at a site, or for the distribution of mean or median concentrations from a number of different sites that are in the same category.

3.   If the underlying distribution of a variable is log normal, then the best estimate of the mean and variance is provided by standard statistical computations performed on the log transforms of the individual observations. The statistics of interest are then computed from the log mean and log standard deviation, using the equations presented in Table I.

TABLE I   LOG NORMAL RELATIONSHIPS

	ARITHMETIC	LOGARITHMIC
MEAN	M	U
STD DEVIATION	S	W
COEF OF VARIATION	CV	
MEDIAN	T	

$T = \exp(U)$ $W = SQR\left(LN(1 + CV^2)\right)$

$M = \exp(U + \frac{1}{2}W^2)$ $U = LN\left(M / \exp(\frac{1}{2}W^2)\right)$

$M = T * SQR(1 + CV^2)$ $U = LN\left(M / SQR(1 + CV^2)\right)$

$V = SQR\left(\exp(W^2) - 1\right)$

$S = M * CV$

$$X_a = \exp(U + Z_a W)$$

$$Z = \frac{LN(X) - U}{W}$$

$$X_a/T = \exp(Z_a W)$$

$$X_a/M = \exp(Z_a W - W^2/2)$$

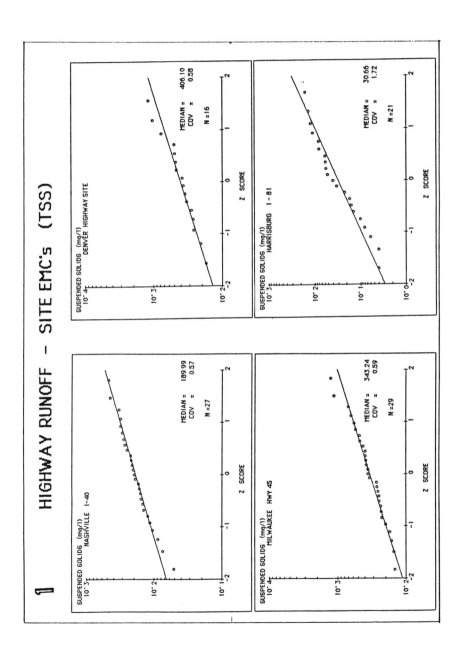

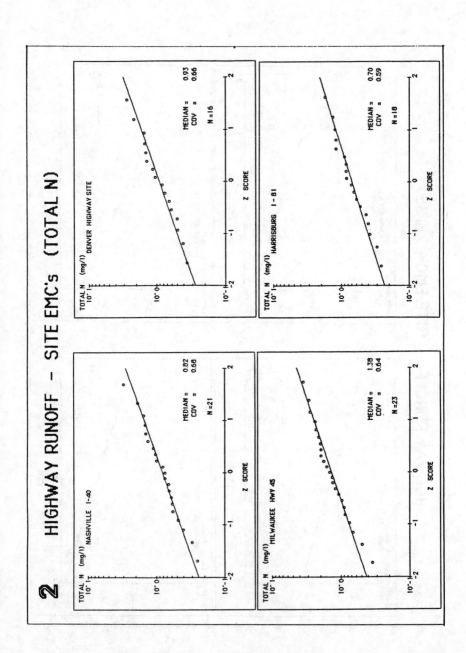

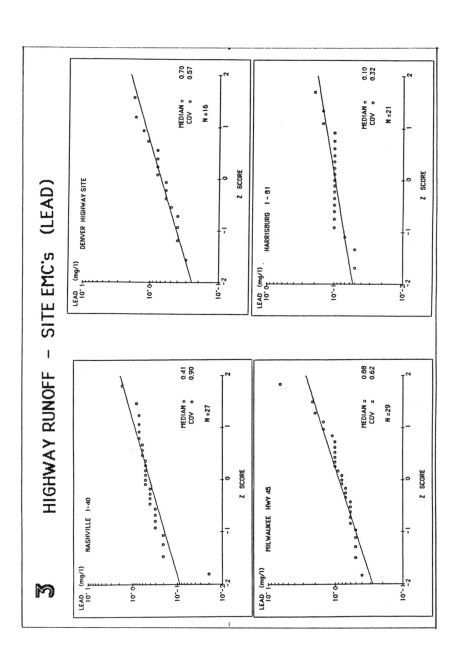

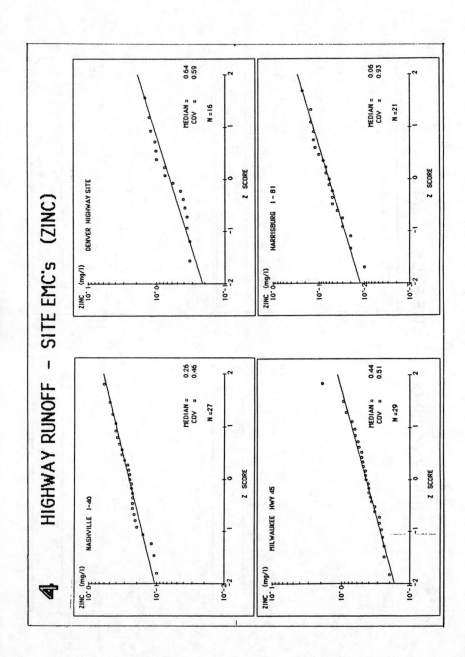

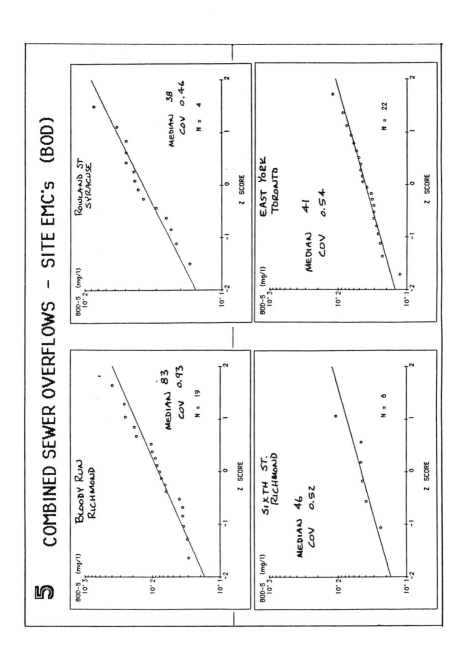

5 COMBINED SEWER OVERFLOWS – SITE EMC's (BOD)

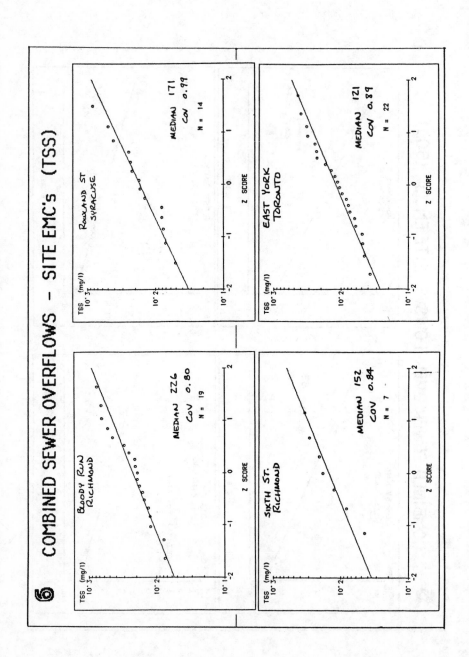

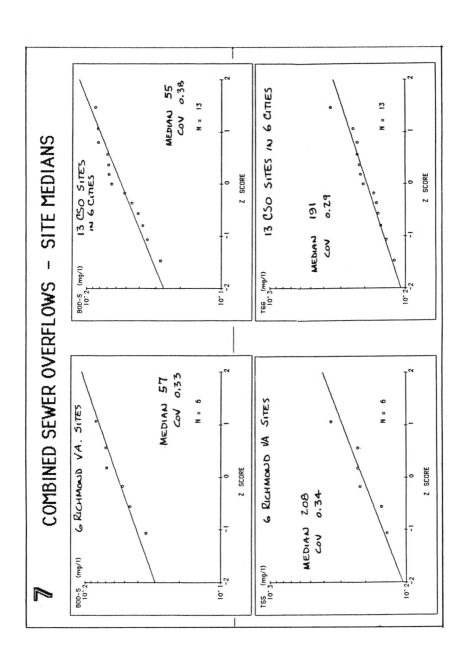

COMBINED SEWER OVERFLOWS – SITE MEDIANS

URBAN RUNOFF

DATA FROM NURP STUDY

EVENT MEAN CONCENTRATIONS OF CHEMICAL OXYGEN DEMAND

AT SIX STUDY SITES

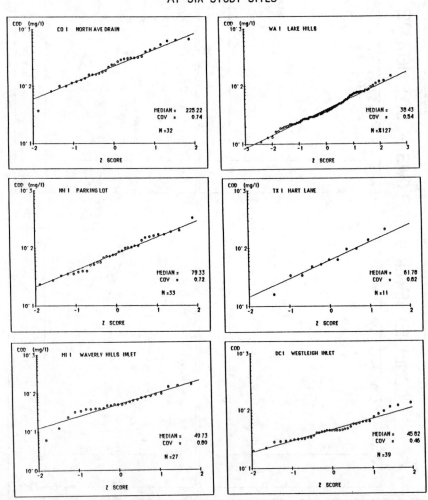

URBAN RUNOFF

DATA FROM NURP STUDY

EVENT MEAN CONCENTRATIONS OF TOTAL P

AT SIX STUDY SITES

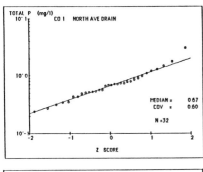

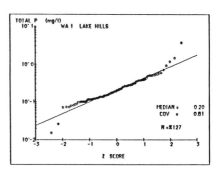

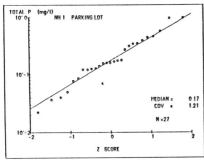

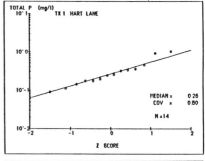

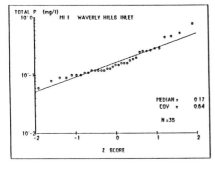

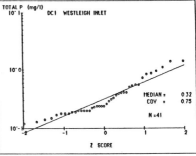

10   URBAN RUNOFF

DATA FROM NURP STUDY

SITE MEDIAN CONCENTRATIONS OF TOTAL P

FOR 69 URBAN RUNOFF STUDY SITES

LOG MEAN	=	5.787
LOG SIGMA	=	0.640
MEAN	=	400.143
SIGMA	=	284.565
MEDIAN	=	326.092
COEF VAR	=	0.711

****

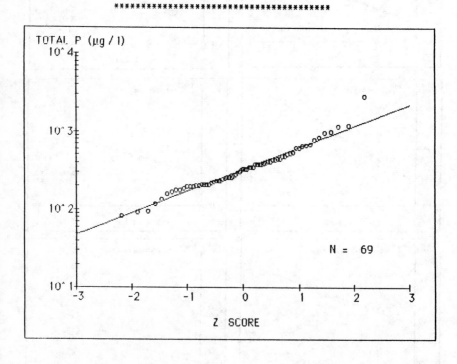

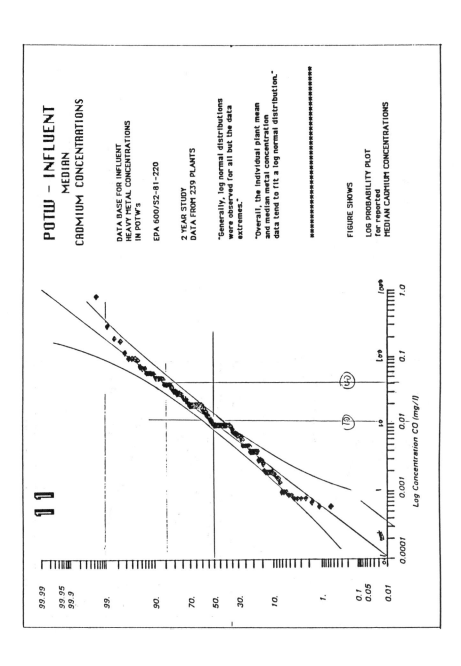

POTW – INFLUENT
MEDIAN
CADMIUM CONCENTRATIONS

DATA BASE FOR INFLUENT
HEAVY METAL CONCENTRATIONS
IN POTW's

EPA 600/S2-81-220

2 YEAR STUDY
DATA FROM 239 PLANTS

"Generally, log normal distributions
were observed for all but the data
extremes."

"Overall, the individual plant mean
and median metal concentration
data tend to fit a log normal distribution."

FIGURE SHOWS

LOG PROBABILITY PLOT
for reported
MEDIAN CADMIUM CONCENTRATIONS

Log Concentration CO (mg/l)

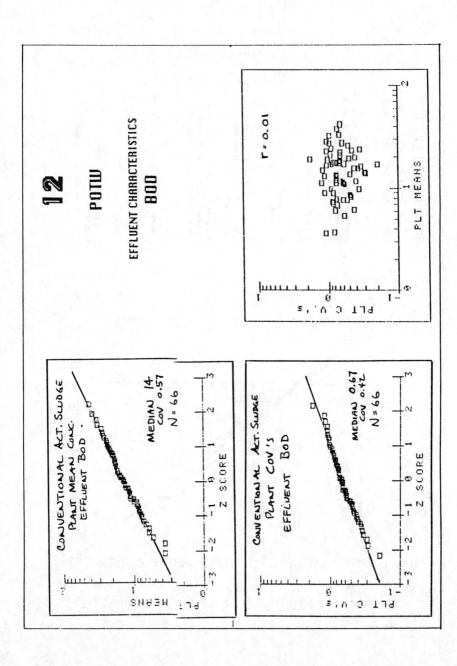

13 AGRICULTURAL NPS RUNOFF

WATKINSVILLE GA STUDY

EVENT MEAN CONCENTRATIONS OF NITROGEN FORMS

$$(NH_4 - N , NO_3 - N , TKN)$$

STATION P2   STATION P4

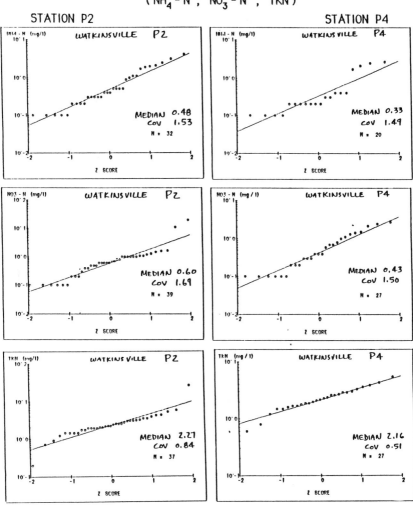

14   AGRICULTURAL NPS RUNOFF
FOUR MILE CREEK IOWA STUDY

EVENT MEAN CONCENTRATIONS OF AMMONIA NITROGEN
AT FOUR MONITORING STATIONS

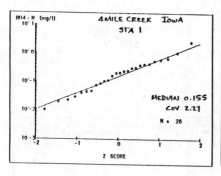

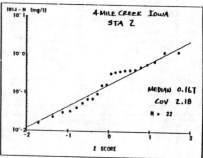

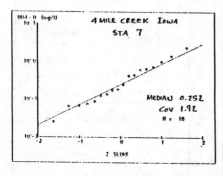

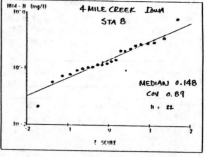

15 AGRICULTURAL NPS RUNOFF
FOUR MILE CREEK IOWA STUDY

EVENT MEAN CONCENTRATIONS OF DISSOLVED PHOSPHORUS
AT TWO MONITORING STATIONS

STATION 1   STATION 2

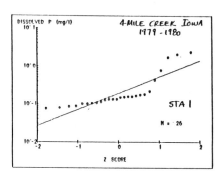

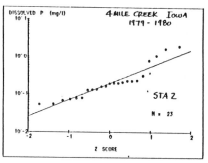

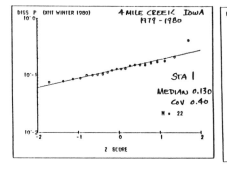

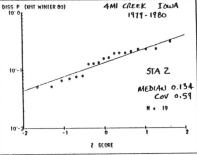

16   SURFACE AND SUBSURFACE RUNOFF CONVENTIONAL TILLAGE

ALBERTS and SPOONER, J SOIL AND WATER CONSERVATION, FEB 1985

ANNUAL AVERAGE CONCENTRATIONS OF SOLUBLE POLLUTANTS

PHOSPHORUS (PO_4)   NITROGEN (NO_3)

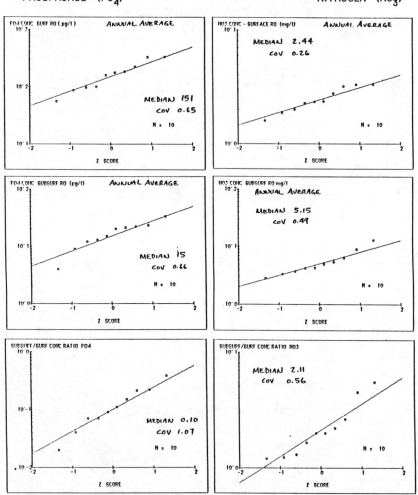

ESTIMATION OF POLLUTION FROM HIGHWAY RUNOFF—INITIAL RESULTS

Philip E. Shelley* and David R. Gaboury**

INTRODUCTION

For over ten years the Federal Highway Administration (FHwA) of the United States Department of Transportation has been engaged in a research program to characterize stormwater runoff from highways, assess its impacts on receiving waters, and determine the effectiveness of various control measures for possible instances where their use to mitigate impairment of designated beneficial uses of receiving waters might be required. As a part of this research program, a contractor team headed by Woodward-Clyde Consultants, and including EG&G Washington Analytical Services Center, Inc. and the University of Florida, has been tasked with developing models that could be used by planners and highway engineers for predicting pollutant runoff loads from highways.

Approaches to predicting pollutant runoff loads from highways can be generally grouped into one of two classes;

- those that are based on regression equations, and

- those that use some form of simulation model.

Approaches that use simulation models can be further characterized mechanistically into three types:

- those employing rating curve methodologies—actually an extension of regression analysis based on a power law relationship between flow and sediment load or concentration;

- those where pollutant build-up and wash-off relationships are used as, for example, in SWMM, STORM, HSPF, and the FHwA Urban Highway Storm Drainage Model; and

- probabilistic based approaches, wherein probability density functions are assigned to runoff flows and concentrations, and the resulting pollutant loads are characterized statistically, as was done, for example, in the Environmental Protection Agency's Nationwide Urban Runoff Program.

* EG&G Washington Analytical Services Center, Inc., Rockville, MD
** Woodward-Clyde Consultants, Walnut Creek, CA

Thus, prediction of highway stormwater runoff quality may be performed using a number of procedures that range from the very simple to detailed deterministic simulation models, and a large body of literature exists describing them. However, all of the approaches have one common aspect—their predictive capabilities tend to be rather poor without suitable site-specific data for calibration. For this reason, one of the first tasks in the present effort was to assemble a data base of highway runoff characteristics. In the following sections of this paper, that data base will be described, the data will be summarized, and best preliminary estimates of highway stormwater runoff will be made.

HIGHWAY RUNOFF DATA BASE CHARACTERISTICS

The data in the highway stormwater data base are taken from monitoring projects supported by the FHwA and several states. At the present time, there is coverage of twelve sites, with several more to be added as the data become available. There are from seven to 139 monitored events at each site. The data base consists of three categories of data;

- rainfall and runoff,

- water quality, and

- fixed site.

Each of these categories will be discussed in turn.

RAINFALL AND RUNOFF DATA

Rainfall data were taken with recording raingages. For each rainfall event there is a start time and date, five-minute raingage readings that describe the hyetograph, and a stop time and date. In a similar fashion, runoff data were taken from flowmeters and consist of a start time and date, (typically) five-minute instantaneous flow readings that describe the hydrograph, and a stop time and date. The lag between the time rainfall starts and the time runoff starts, although highly variable for a given site due to antecedent conditions, provides an indication of basin response time or "flashiness."

Taken together, the rainfall and runoff data describe the water quantity characteristics of the site. The rainfall data can be analyzed to provide information on rainfall frequency (i.e., the time between storms), intensity, duration, and total amount. For example, the total quantity of rainfall for the event is simply the difference between the raingage readings at the beginning and end of the event. The flowmeter data can be analyzed to determine peak flow, time to peak, total quantity discharged, etc. The total quantity of runoff discharged during the event is computed by integrating the flow rate record over the time period of the event. Of particular interest in this preliminary analysis are the total rainfall and runoff quantities.

WATER QUALITY DATA

The highway runoff quality data consist of the results of laboratory analyses of sequential discrete samples that were taken at recorded times throughout the runoff event, plus the results of laboratory analyses of flow-weighted composite samples taken over the entire runoff event.

Although over 24 analytical determinations were made for the different sites contained in the data base so far, there was consistent coverage of up to eighteen pollutants, and these were selected for this preliminary analysis. By category, they are:

• Solids	TS, TSS, VSS
• Physical Parameters	pH, Cl^-
• Oxygen Demanding Substances	BOD, COD, TOC
• Nutrients	TKN, NO_2+NO_3, TPO_4
• Metals (Total)	Cu, Pb, Zn, Fe, Cr, Cd
• Hydrocarbons	Oil and Grease

FIXED SITE DATA

The fixed site data, so called because they tend to be fixed rather than variable on an event to event basis, fall into three general categories. They are:

- Highway Site Data

    — configuration (e.g., elevated, ground level, depressed)

    — pavement composition, quantity, and condition

    — design, geometrics, cross-sections

    — vegetation types on right-of-way

    — drainage features

- Operational Characteristics

    — traffic characteristics (e.g., density, speed, braking)

    — vehicle characteristics (e.g., type, age, maintenance)

    — maintenance practices (e.g., sweeping, mowing, weed control)

    — institutional characteristics (e.g., litter laws, speed limit enforcement, vehicle emission regulations)

- Surrounding Land Use Characteristics

  - land use type (residential, commercial, industrial, agricultural, forest)

  - geologic features (relief, soil types and horizons, groundwater characteristics)

  - agricultural practices (e.g., tillage, irrigation, and cropping practices)

In this preliminary analysis, the chief fixed site data to be used are the size of the drainage area, the average traffic density expressed as vehicles per day, the percentage of the basin area that is impervious, and three roadway features—the surface type, number of lanes, and the presence of curbs.

DATA ANALYSIS METHODOLOGY

Pollutant runoff from highway sites (as well as from other types of non-point source sites) is quite variable, especially as compared to discharges from point sources. Therefore, new methodological frameworks are required for analysis of data from nonpoint sources in general and highway runoff in particular, especially with respect to characterization of pollutant loads and their possible effects upon receiving waters. New approaches to water quality criteria and standards also seem warranted when one is dealing with nonpoint sources, due to the high variability and intermittent nature of the latter.

When one has flow and pollutant concentration data for runoff from a monitored site, there is a need for a sensible way to reduce the data to summary form in a way that will be useful to decision makers. For this task, it was decided to follow the general data analysis approach developed for the Environmental Protection Agency's Nationwide Urban Runoff Program (NURP).

In NURP, flow and concentration data for a site were first analyzed to determine event mean concentrations (EMCs). The EMC is defined as the concentration that would result if the entire storm event discharge were collected in a container, and its concentration determined; i.e., it is the total mass of pollutant discharged during the event divided by the total quantity of water discharged during the event. In practice the EMC is simply taken to be the concentration of a flow-weighted composite sample collected over the duration of the runoff event. If sequential discrete samples are taken over the period of the runoff event, an acceptable approximation to the EMC can be formed by manually compositing aliquots that are sized in proportion to flow (manual flow-weighted composite sample) and performing analytical determinations on the resulting composite sample. If separate analytical determinations have been performed on the individual sequential discrete samples, an acceptable approximation to the EMC often can be computed from the individual concentration values and the corresponding flow values.

The main point is that, in dealing with nonpoint sources, the basic unit of water quality information is the average concentration of each pollutant of interest in the total volume of runoff produced by each individual storm event. Thus, within-storm fluctuations in pollutant concentration are completely ignored. Hence, for a particular pollutant and a particular site, there will be one EMC value for each storm event monitored, and the EMC is considered to be the random variable.

Given a set of nonpoint source monitoring data for a site, the first step is to determine the EMC values for the pollutants of interest. This set of EMC values is then analyzed to compute the statistics of runoff quality for the site. However, in order to properly interpret the site statistics, it is usually convenient to know something about the nature of the underlying distribution function (or, equivalently, the underlying probability density function). From physical considerations, it can be shown that a normal distribution cannot be exactly correct for EMCs (e.g., pollutant concentrations can never be negative, they are always skewed, etc.). It can also be shown, by appeal to the central limit theorem, that when a series of multiplicative processes are involved (as is the case with nonpoint sources), the resulting distribution function will be asymptotically lognormal. The adequacy of this lognormality assumption has been checked with data from urban runoff, highway stormwater runoff, combined sewer overflows, and limited sets of agricultural runoff data. In no case has the lognormal distribution been clearly inappropriate, and in most cases it seems to fit the data better than other possible distributions.

Under the asumption that the lognormal distribution would be an adequate representation for the highway runoff data sets in question, it remained to compute the EMC values for each event at a site, transform these values into the logarithmic domain, compute the mean and variance in log-space, and then properly transform these values into the appropriate statistics in arithmetic space (typically the median, mean, and coefficient of variation). For surface runoff data, the two-parameter lognormal distribution is adequate. It is completely specified by a central tendency parameter (say, the median) and a dispersion parameter (say, the coefficient of variation).

Having determined the two EMC statistics for a pollutant at a site (say, the median and coefficient of variation), they completely describe the variable runoff characteristics for that site. They can then be compared with similar data from other sites to evaluate similarities and differences in the context of physical site characteristics. This amounts to comparing the underlying probability distributions for the sites in question. The main point is that the foregoing methodology recognizes that the natural processes that lead to highway runoff are highly variable and provides an appropriate way of quantifying this variability.

Each data set is a small sample of the much larger population of values represented by the sample. The particular sample taken will be representative of the unknown population to an unknown extent, and may be fairly good or rather poor. There is no way to resolve this satisfactorily when one has only one sample available for inspection. However, when similar pollutant data sets are available for inspection from a large number of comparable sites, or for a variety of pollutants at the same site, the information to guide the desired inferences is extended. One way to shed further light on the representativeness of a nonpoint source data set is to compare the rainfall statistics for the monitored events with similar statistics computed from long-term rainfall records for the site. If the average rainfall volume for monitored storms is, for example, 0.80" while the long-term average for all storms is only 0.40", one can be reasonably certain that the monitored storms are not representative of the total population of storms at that site.

For reasons just alluded to, as well as the fact that an integral part of the assessment of the impact of storm loads on receiving water quality is the statistical evaluation of rainfall records, a program to summarize the important rainfall variables was set up on FHwA's computer as a part of this effort. The purpose of the Synoptic Rainfall Data Analysis Program (SYNOP) is to provide the user with a tool that can be used to summarize and statistically characterize a rainfall record in terms of its important variables (volume, intensity, duration, and time between storms). Since hourly rainfall records of many years duration are cumbersome and difficult to analyze, SYNOP provides an easy to use tool to facilitate the determination of, for example, seasonal trends important to the assesment of impacts and selection of control alternatives for storm-related loads.

SYNOP summarizes the hourly rainfall data by storm events, each with an associated volume (inches), duration (hours), average intensity (inches/hour), time since the previous storm (hours) as measured from the end of the previous storm, the antecedent rainfall (inches) for the last 24, 48, 72, and 168 hours, the hours of missing data, and the hours that the gage did not read. A storm definition, or interevent time, must be established to determine when, in the hourly record, a storm begins and ends. SYNOP delineates storm events as rainfall periods separated by a minimum number of consecutive hours without rainfall, a user supplied number. After the entire record has been read, SYNOP computes the statistics of relevant storm parameters by month and year and for the entire period of record.

INITIAL RESULTS

RAINFALL AND RUNOFF DATA

Let us first consider the relationship of runoff to rainfall. Figure 1 is a scatter plot of the rainfall and runoff expressed in inches for a site on Highway Number 45 in Milwaukee, Wisconsin. There it can be seen that, although there is some scatter, there does tend to be a rather strong linear correlation, supporting the notion that a runoff coefficient might adequately characterize the site and allow runoff quantity to be predicted from rainfall data with a known degree of uncertainty. To examine this notion further, a scatter plot of runoff coefficient (Rv = runoff/rainfall) versus rainfall is presented in Figure 2. The lack of any correlation further supports the notion of a single runoff coefficient.

Although the claim for a single runoff coefficient is indicated in the foregoing, it is less than totally compelling. One of the reasons for the scatter might lie in the limited sample size for that site. We now turn to a site on Highway 94 in Milwaukee for which there are 137 monitored events. The corresponding scatter plots are presented as Figures 3 and 4. As can be seen, the argument becomes much more compelling.

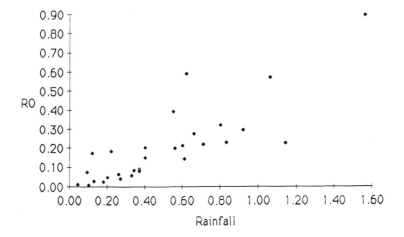

Figure 1. Runoff (RO) versus rainfall for Milwaukee Highway 45

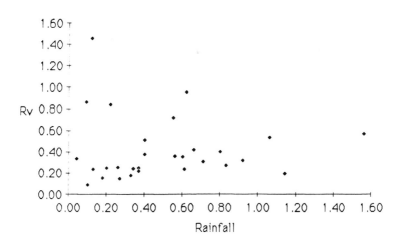

Figure 2. Runoff coefficient (Rv) versus rainfall for Milwaukee Highway 45

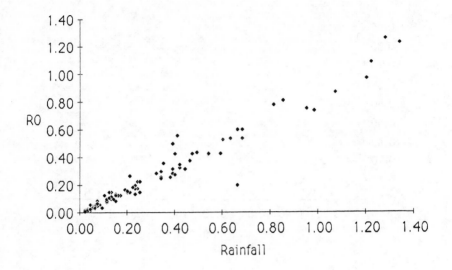

Figure 3. Runoff (RO) versus rainfall for Milwaukee Highway 94

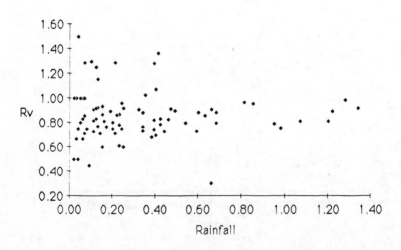

Figure 4. Runoff coefficient (Rv) versus rainfall for Milwaukee Highway 94

A summary of the highway site rainfall and runoff data is presented in Table 1. The computed statistics (mean, median, coefficient of variation—the standard deviation divided by the mean and abbreviated as COV, and the number of samples N) are indicated for rainfall quantity, storm duration, runoff quantity, and runoff coefficient—the runoff divided by rainfall and abbreviated as Rv. The results of regression analyses of the form

$$Runoff = A \times Rain + B \qquad and \qquad Rv = A \times Rain + B$$

are presented in Table 2. In the first case, the value of A is the desired run-off coefficient, and one wants the residual term (B) to be small. In the second case, the value of B is the runoff coefficient, and one wants the value of A to be small. As can be seen from Table 2, the foregoing tends to be the case for all but the last two sites. The mean, median, and coefficient of variation for the runoff coefficient for each site are presented for comparison purposes in Table 2.

Since one would expect that the percent impervious area will affect the runoff coefficient for a site, this is examined in Figures 4 and 5. Taken together, these figures suggest that, lacking any other information, it is not unreasonable to assign a runoff coefficient equal to the percent imperviousness for a site, with an upper bound of around 0.9 or so to account for initial abstraction.

RUNOFF QUALITY DATA

To compare the runoff data from the highway sites in the data base, data for six of the eighteen water quality parameters are presented in Table 3. Since data from NURP and other nonpoint source studies have indicated that data from individual sites tend to be lognormally distributed, the summary statistics given in Table 3 were computed in the same way as the summary statistics for an individual site. In order to provide a basis for comparison, the median values computed from the NURP data base are also presented in Table 3, along with the ratio of the highway median values to them. Thus, it can be seen that the concentrations of suspended solids and phosphorus in highway runoff are virtually the same as those in urban runoff, concentrations of COD and zinc are slightly higher in highway runoff, and concentrations of lead and TKN are significantly higher in highway run-off. In reviewing these numbers, it is important to remember that we are talking about concentrations and not loads. On a load basis, highways would be much smaller contributers, because they account for only a small percen-tage of the land in an urban area.

Ratio techniques are frequently used to facilitate comparison among similar data sets, since they provide a simplistic form of normalization. In the present case we have divided the median value for a pollutant at a site by the median value for all of the sites to form the ratio. A value greater than unity indicates that that particular site is "dirtier" than average, while a value less than unity indicates that the site is "cleaner" than average. The results are presented in Table 4. The last column in Table 4 (labeled mean) is a sort of site cleanliness index, formed by simply averaging the ratio

TABLE 1. SUMMARY HIGHWAY SITE RAINFALL/RUNOFF DATA

		Denver I-25	Milwaukee I-94	Nashville I-40	Sacramento Hwy. 50	Milwaukee Hwy. 45	Milwaukee I-795	Harrisburg I-81 (Ph. II)	Efland I-85	Harrisburg I-81 (Ph.I)
RAIN (in.)	Mean	0.42	0.27	0.83	0.52	0.54	0.63	0.71	0.86	0.76
	Median	0.27	0.14	0.44	0.32	0.37	0.39	0.49	0.66	0.61
	COV	1.14	1.64	1.58	1.31	1.05	1.26	1.07	0.84	0.74
	N	16	137	31	34	29	35	21	36	23
DURATION (hr)	Mean	5.23		5.34		7.29	5.56			8.14
	Median	1.93		2.76		3.34	3.28			4.35
	COV	2.51		1.66		1.94	1.36			1.58
	N	16		31		29	35			23
RUNOFF (in.)	Mean	0.194	0.24	0.34	0.45	0.23	0.53	0.18	0.84	0.40
	Median	0.086	0.11	0.16	0.26	0.13	0.32	0.02	0.33	0.18
	COV	2.01	1.89	1.97	1.43	1.53	1.30	8.63	2.33	2.03
	N	16	139	31	34	29	34	21	38	23
Rv	Mean	0.36	0.84	0.41	0.82	0.42	0.86	0.11	0.67	0.44
	Median	0.31	0.81	0.35	0.81	0.35	0.85	0.04	0.47	0.31
	COV	0.54	0.28	0.58	0.18	0.68	0.14	2.32	1.03	1.72
	N	16	137	31	34	29	35	21	36	23

TABLE 2. RUNOFF/RAINFALL REGRESSIONS

			Mean	Median	COV
Milwaukee, I-94	Runoff= 0.86 RAIN - 0.00	Rv= 0.04 RAIN + 0.83	0.84	0.81	0.28
Milwaukee, I-795	Runoff= 0.84 RAIN + 0.01	Rv= 0.06 RAIN + 0.80	0.86	0.85	0.14
Sacramento, Hwy 50	Runoff= 0.88 RAIN - 0.02	Rv= 0.06 RAIN + 0.79	0.82	0.81	0.18
Milwaukee, Hwy 45	Runoff= 0.45 RAIN - 0.02	Rv= -0.02 RAIN + 0.43	0.42	0.35	0.68
Nashville, I-40	Runoff= 0.33 RAIN - 0.04	Rv= -0.02 RAIN + 0.41	0.42	0.35	0.58
Denver, I-25	Runoff= 0.60 RAIN - 0.06	Rv= 0.37 RAIN + 0.21	0.36	0.31	0.54
Harrisburg Ph II, I-81	Runoff= 0.29 RAIN - 0.08	Rv= 0.15 RAIN - 0.01	0.11	0.04	2.32
Efland, I-85	Runoff= 0.94 RAIN - 0.20	Rv= 0.20 RAIN + 0.41	0.67	0.47	1.03
Harrisburg Ph I, I-81	Runoff= 0.84 RAIN - 0.25	Rv= 0.39 RAIN + 0.12	0.44	0.31	1.72

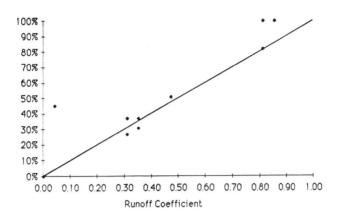

Figure 4. Percent imperviousness versus median runoff coefficient

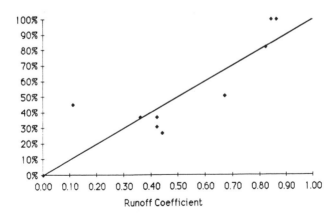

Figure 5. Percent imperviousness versus mean runoff coefficient

TABLE 3. SITE MEDIAN DATA SUMMARY AND COMPARISON

SITE	SS (mg/l)	COD (mg/l)	TKN (mg/l)	TP04 (mg/l)	Pb (mg/l)	Zn (mg/l)
DENVER	410	289	3.38	0.82	0.68	0.62
MILWAUKEE HWY 795	183	130	2.52	0.38	2.03	0.46
LOS ANGELES	172	196	4.22	0.45	0.99	0.55
MILWAUKEE HWY 45	343	134	2.76	0.45	0.88	0.44
NASHVILLE	190	113	1.90	1.69	0.41	0.26
MILWAUKEE HWY 94	161	122	3.20	0.30	0.90	0.52
WALNUT CREEK	224	120	2.24	0.41	0.75	0.30
HARRISBURG (Ph. II)	184	34	2.20	1.08	0.03	0.17
SACRAMENTO	90	51	1.90	0.12	0.28	0.27
HARRISBURG (Ph. I)	31	31	1.20	0.29	0.10	0.06
EFLAND	19	49	2.50	0.13	0.01	0.06
BROWARD COUNTY	9	38	0.68	0.06	0.23	0.07
Mean	221	113	2.46	0.55	1.03	0.35
Median	108	86	2.18	0.35	0.31	0.24
COV	1.78	0.85	0.52	1.21	3.21	1.09
NURP MEDIAN	100	65	0.68	0.33	0.14	0.16
HIGHWAY/NURP	1.08	1.32	3.21	1.07	2.18	1.48

TABLE 4. SITE MEDIAN RATIO SUMMARY AND COMPARISON

SITE	SS	COD	TKN	TP04	Pb	Zn	MEAN
DENVER	3.78	3.36	1.55	2.32	2.23	2.62	2.64
MILWAUKEE HWY 795	1.69	1.51	1.16	1.08	6.65	1.94	2.34
LOS ANGELES	1.59	2.28	1.94	1.27	3.24	2.32	2.11
MILWAUKEE HWY 45	3.17	1.55	1.27	1.26	2.87	1.86	2.00
NASHVILLE	1.75	1.31	0.87	4.77	1.34	1.10	1.86
MILWAUKEE HWY 94	1.49	1.42	1.47	0.85	2.95	2.20	1.73
WALNUT CREEK	2.07	1.40	1.03	1.16	2.46	1.27	1.56
HARRISBURG (Ph. II)	1.70	0.40	1.01	3.06	0.09	0.71	1.16
SACRAMENTO	0.83	0.59	0.87	0.34	0.92	1.14	0.78
HARRISBURG (Ph. I)	0.28	0.36	0.55	0.82	0.32	0.26	0.43
EFLAND	0.18	0.57	1.15	0.37	0.04	0.25	0.42
BROWARD COUNTY	0.08	0.44	0.31	0.17	0.75	0.30	0.34

values for each of the six pollutants at the site.

Based upon data in the fixed site data base, we have chosen to simplisti-
cally group the highway sites into one of two categories, urban and rural,
and repeat the ratio analysis just described. The results are presented in
Tables 5 and 6. From these data, it appears that median pollutant
concentrations in runoff from urban highway sites are from two to four
times greater than those found in urban runoff, while those from rural
highway sites tend to be around one quarter to a little over one half of that
found in urban runoff. TKN is an exception to this last observation, and the
data will be examined more carefully to attempt to find an explanation.

Thus far we have only been dealing with pollutant concentration median
values. The same types of analyses could be performed on the site coefficients of variation, and an example for the urban highway sites is given in
Table 7. Here again, the lead values for the Harrisburg Phase II site seem
suspect and warrant further examination. Otherwise, the results seem quite
reasonable and fairly consistent.

The "bottom line" of this preliminary data analysis is presented in Table
11. If a planner has to estimate the pollutant load coming from an ungaged
highway site, the values for concentration and coefficient of variation for
each pollutant that are given there represent the best initial estimates for
screening purposes.

As our work continues, we plan to refine the foregoing analyses and to
add the remaining twelve pollutants as well as other highway sites. We also
plan a rather extensive data quality assurance and quality control effort
(unscreened raw data have been used up to this point). Hopefully, this will
reduce the number of seeming anomalies pointed out earlier.

TABLE 5. URBAN SITE MEDIAN DATA SUMMARY AND COMPARISON

SITE	SS (mg/l)	COD (mg/l)	TKN (mg/l)	TP04 (mg/l)	Pb (mg/l)	Zn (mg/l)
DENVER	410	289	3.38	0.82	0.68	0.62
MILWAUKEE HWY 795	183	130	2.52	0.38	2.03	0.46
LOS ANGELES	172	196	4.22	0.45	0.99	0.55
MILWAUKEE HWY 45	343	134	2.76	0.45	0.88	0.44
NASHVILLE	190	113	1.90	1.69	0.41	0.26
MILWAUKEE HWY 94	161	122	3.20	0.30	0.90	0.52
WALNUT CREEK	224	120	2.24	0.41	0.75	0.30
HARRISBURG (Ph. II)	184	34	2.20	1.08	0.03	0.17
Mean	234	149	2.81	0.70	1.31	0.42
Median	220	124	2.72	0.59	0.55	0.38
COV	0.36	0.67	0.27	0.66	2.14	0.47
NURP MEDIAN	100	65	0.68	0.33	0.14	0.16
HIGHWAY/NURP	2.20	1.91	4.00	1.78	3.94	2.40

TABLE 6. RURAL SITE MEDIAN SUMMARY AND COMPARISON

SITE	SS (mg/l)	COD (mg/l)	TKN (mg/l)	TP04 (mg/l)	Pb (mg/l)	Zn (mg/l)
SACRAMENTO	90	51	1.90	0.12	0.28	0.27
HARRISBURG (Ph. I)	31	31	1.20	0.29	0.10	0.06
EFLAND	19	49	2.50	0.13	0.01	0.06
BROWARD COUNTY	9	38	0.68	0.06	0.23	0.07
Mean	42	43	1.65	0.16	0.26	0.12
Median	26	41	1.40	0.13	0.09	0.09
COV	1.24	0.23	0.62	0.71	2.64	0.85
NURP MEDIAN	100	65	0.68	0.33	0.14	0.16
HIGHWAY/NURP	0.26	0.64	2.06	0.39	0.67	0.56

TABLE 7. URBAN SITE COEFFICIENT OF VARIATION RESULTS

SITE	SS	COD	TKN	TP04	Pb	Zn
DENVER	0.60	0.71	0.76	0.51	0.56	0.59
MILWAUKEE HWY 795	1.13	1.55	0.87	0.77	0.87	0.94
MILWAUKEE HWY 45	0.59	0.58	0.64	0.60	0.62	0.51
NASHVILLE	0.57	0.60	1.02	0.56	0.90	0.46
MILWAUKEE HWY 94	1.04	0.74	0.50	0.63	1.30	0.84
HARRISBURG (Ph. II)	1.16	0.40	0.51	0.52	3.93	0.51
Mean	0.86	0.77	0.72	0.60	1.36	0.65
Median	0.81	0.70	0.69	0.59	1.06	0.62
COV	0.36	0.47	0.29	0.15	0.81	0.30

TABLE 8. HIGHWAY RUNOFF CHARACTERISTICS

		URBAN SITES	RURAL SITES	ALL SITES	COEFFICIENT OF VARIATION
SS	(mg/l)	220	26	108	0.8 – 1.0
COD	(mg/l)	124	41	86	0.5 – 0.8
TKN	(mg/l)	2.72	1.4	2.18	0.7 – 0.9
TPO4	(mg/l)	0.59	0.13	0.35	0.6 – 0.9
Pb	(mg/l)	0.55	0.09	0.31	0.7 – 1.4
Zn	(mg/l)	0.38	0.09	0.24	0.6 – 0.7

SUBJECT INDEX
Page number refers to first page of paper.

AUTHOR INDEX
Page number refers to first page of paper.